UNCERTAIN TIMES:

KENNETH ARROW

AND THE

CHANGING

ECONOMICS OF

HEALTH CARE

Edited by

Peter J. Hammer,

Deborah Haas-Wilson,

Mark A. Peterson,

and William M. Sage

DUKE UNIVERSITY PRESS

Durham and London 2003

Printed in the United States of

America on acid-free paper ∞

Designed by Amy Ruth Buchanan

Typeset in Minion by Tseng Information

Systems, Inc. Library of Congress

Cataloging-in-Publication Data appear

on the last printed page of this book.

Portions of this book originally appeared in the

Journal of Health Politics, Policy and Law.

CONTENTS

MARK V. PAULY

■ *Foreword*

Kenneth Arrow's article made research in health economics respectable, but it did more than that. It also made it interesting. His essay was the gracious response of an already distinguished economic theorist to an invitation to write something for the Ford Foundation on the economic properties of the medical services industry. Before this article appeared in 1963, economists, even those interested in industry applications, had either steered clear of trying to understand (much less analyze) a product and an industry that appeared to depart so greatly from the competitive model, or they had written policy papers alternately justifying or condemning the differences from that model. Either perspective was largely irrelevant because medical care was "special" or because economics could be applied only to show that the guild and regulatory features of this industry were the result of a long-term conspiracy by medical providers to gain monopoly rents at the expense of efficiency and consumer welfare.

Arrow's article was and still is exciting, I believe, for two reasons:

1. It showed how some behaviors in medical markets could be brought within the purview of standard economic models of competing, maximizing agents. The primary examples of this type are those having to do with insurance.

2. It offered an explanation that atypical institutional arrangements in medical care markets are a reaction to special features of this market. The primary source of the problem here is imperfect or asymmetric consumer information, and the hypothesized solution was nonmarket organizations, public or private. In doing so, it discussed concepts that made (and make)

economists attentive but uncomfortable, like *trust* and *morals*. (These concepts do not tend to disquiet lawyers or policy makers.)

The essays in this remarkable collection reflect on these two different sets of ideas. They analyze and dissect them, they contrast their implications for what medical markets were like then and now, and how they have changed, and they offer suggestions about where to go from here. I will not summarize the individual essays, but in what follows I will offer my views on the reactions to the two sets by these scholars, by researchers in general, by the market, and by the policy arena.

From the viewpoint of applied microeconomic theory, a major contribution of Arrow's article was the development of some typically elegant and provocative models of optimal insurance. There was a policy question here, of course. In 1963, why was it that many medical care services were not covered by insurance and that many people had no health insurance coverage at all? (The proportion of uninsured then was about twice what it is now.) Arrow began the discussion that actually generated the most-published commentary on his article by restating the well-known proposition that if insurance is available at actuarially fair premiums, all risky events should be insured. But he then pointed out in the text, and developed further in an often-quoted appendix, that in real markets with insurer administrative costs, the optimal pattern of insurance is full coverage above a deductible. He also hinted at (though not forthrightly enough for my tastes) the idea that *moral hazard*—any effect of insurance coverage on expected losses—could also explain incomplete coverage and that one remedy here would be proportional co-insurance.

The introduction to health economics of the topic of moral hazard ignited a firestorm of interest in the impact of insurance on the process of care, with both theoretical and empirical dimensions. The major empirical topic was the measurement of the extent of moral hazard, and the major theoretical question was how that magnitude would affect the ideal design of an insurance policy that relied on patient cost-sharing to limit medical spending. The Rand Health Insurance Experiment defined the measurement of moral hazard as a key empirical question and provided bulletproof evidence on the question, but both the theoretical and empirical investigations of this topic continue the extension of Arrow's initial modest hints.

The main theme of Arrow's article, as a number of essays in this collection note, was that nonmarket institutions tend to arise to deal with the special features of markets in medical services or medical insurance that cannot be handled efficiently in conventional markets. What Arrow was arguing for here is what might be called *positive Pareto optimality*: if markets fail to achieve the efficient outcomes (as economists define them), that observation is more than a stimulus to hand wringing. *Inefficiency* in economics means more than waste or sloth; it means that mutual gains that could be achieved have not been achieved; there is money (or welfare) left lying on the table, and one would expect institutional arrangements to emerge in order to permit people to claim it. Nonprofit organization of health care and health insurance providers proceed from, or are explained by, this model, as is the role of trust in patient relationships with medical providers. Arrow's insights here are very imaginative and appealing to noneconomists (who have trouble, for example, with moral hazard, especially the moral part).

What is surprising (and more than a little disappointing) is that these insights have been much less aggressively pursued in health economics. There has been some modeling and analysis of nonprofit firms, especially hospitals. And there have been some attempts to model patient behavior in searching for doctors or in reacting to physician advice. But I think it is fair to say that there have been no definitive breakthroughs on either front. We still have few definitive formal models of market equilibrium with physicians and patients having different sets of information and few empirical tests of the economics of trust or of the effect of patient information on market equilibrium. (There has been a voluminous but aggressively inconclusive literature on demand inducement, which is largely atheoretical and in any case does not refer to Arrow's article.)

Why has this happened? One obvious answer is that, in contrast to a theory of insurance, developing a theory of trust or even of nonprofit firms puts economists in much less well charted territory, with few familiar or reassuring signposts and few guarantees that they will be able to refer any new work to existing theory to generate face validity. Some of these things are just too weird, from the viewpoint of conventional economics, and there are no quick rule-of-thumb tests of professional respectability. You could get tenure for developing an economic theory of trust, but you could also be viewed as a kook. In this sense, the special features of medical care that Arrow tried to tame still lie in wait for the cautious researcher.

But I believe there is another and even more remarkable reason that Arrow's insights about health economics are still being regarded with various amounts of speculation. The special nonmarket features that existed in 1963 either no longer exist or have been substantially transformed, and we don't understand why, either from Arrow's or any other theory. The missing link here is a theory of what might be called *institutional transformation*.

To be more specific: Arrow's analysis provided a rich and perceptive treatment of what might be called the "Marcus Welby medical economy." That respected but fictional physician worked in a world of benign nonprofit institutions, self-sacrificing health professionals with well-developed (and good) reputations in their communities, and generally permissive financing of care. Lawyers and MBAS appeared only as patients, and consumer advocates and maltreated minorities were nowhere to be seen.

It is beyond obvious that, if that world ever existed in more than the golden glow of memory, it does so no longer. In the United States the medical economy has been substantially transformed to one in which nonmarket institutions play a much less central role. Nonprofit firms have virtually disappeared from health insurance and specialized medical services markets; while hospitals remain predominantly nonprofit in organizational form, both research and casual observation suggests that they have much the same financial concerns as their for-profit counterparts and engage in highly similar behavior. The trusted physician now faces patients concerned about giving or withholding informed consent; health insurers, themselves under fire, who question or deny physician choices; and a medical profession engaged in a process of self-criticism for its suddenly discovered errors in treatment.

What happened? (Many health professionals are asking the same thing.) The logic of Arrow's argument would be that, for some reason, the previous market failures began to evaporate—perhaps because of new technologies allowing markets to operate better for previously untradeable commodities—and so the newly more efficient market sector was able to conquer more territory. There is a little (but only a little) evidence consistent with the theory. The development of electronic techniques for processing small insurance claims probably facilitated insurance coverage of prescription drugs, and some combination of the removal of bans on advertising and the consumer movement has led to the provision of some information, which some of the commentators think will be useful.

But there were, I would hypothesize, two main and related causes of this change that need to be fitted into Arrow's theory. One is rising health care spending. When services became ever more expensive, trust was a casualty of pocketbook protection. The other was the breakneck development of beneficial but costly technology that both fueled spending growth and disquieted consumers, politicians, and even physicians about the possible overuse of now highly costly (as well as dangerous) medical services. There was a third noneconomic cause, the passage of legislation permitting selective contracting (over the objections of organized medicine), which allowed one physician to be played off against another in the search for discounts and discipline. Arrow indeed notes that the benign collective force of medical professionalism that produced trust also was being used to suppress what he called "closed-panel prepayment."

If these are the causes of the new health economics, it is much less plausible that we should regard the framework in which they have played out as benign positive Pareto optimality as mentioned earlier. As several of the essays point out, we have no reason to conclude that there is an invisible hand choosing institutional arrangements (and Arrow did not really make that claim), especially when job number one is choosing the rate and form of innovation.

Despite the current fashion for insurer bashing, I think there is no doubt that those private and public markets now deal better with uncertainty than was true in 1963. Insurance coverage is now more widespread, and private insurance covers a much larger fraction of total spending. The improvement is not perfect; compared to indemnity insurance, managed care insurance has greatly reduced the risk of unexpected financial payment but also (as I and Scott Ramsey have pointed out) [1999] increased the risk that the patient may not get the care best suited to a complex medical situation. Managed care plans at least permit the generation of more informative prices and quality measures than existed in the Marcus Welby world, where the only way to obtain quality information was to ask a nurse. (That is still a good way.) The Wennberg-documented variations in treatment patterns or the prevalence of medical errors that recently has upset the Institute of Medicine are surely no worse now than they were then and probably are much better — even if far from understood or accepted. Arrow's theory can explain these developments, but it could not have predicted them.

The most important missing element in a theory of institutional change is the absence of a definitive model of the most important nonmarket institution of all, the government. Arrow's article gives government the traditional normative welfare economics role of assuring allocative efficiency when the market fails (after appropriate redistribution of income). Of course, Arrow's own impossibility theorem strongly suggests that a government motivated to take the role economists give it is unlikely to exist. Some of the essays in this collection do yearn for government to take hold and control the process of institutional change, but others raise appropriate skepticism about the likelihood of that happening in the face of vested interests and erstwhile ignorant consumers as voters. And yet, on a whole range of issues, from the uninsured to optimal Medicare drug coverage (catastrophic, not first dollar) to quality assurance, it is clear that the problem is not so much market failure as it is government failure. Perhaps the problem is even worse the more democratic the collective choice institutions; misinformed consumers tend to make misinformed voters.

Arrow himself, in his 1963 article and elsewhere, remains an optimist that real governments can be instructed in welfare economics and be persuaded to do what is right (or at least efficient). I tend to agree with this view, based on some evidence of progress (free trade) but even more on the recognition that, for economists (as economists) wishing to influence policy, welfare economics is the only real game in town. A possible model of government is one in which analysts try to discover and explain solutions that come reasonably close to the mutually beneficial change that must be possible if there is inefficiency and hope that the democratic process will be able (at least sometimes, when it is really important) to seize the gains from trade. But, more generally, I would argue that the next frontier in health economics should be one in which public and private institutional choices are themselves explained. Arrow's work has both made this question respectable and cleared away much of the underbrush and debris so that we all know what the questions are. The essays in this collection make a start. There will never be another essay as definitive and provocative as Arrow's; it provides the inspiration to carry on the work.

REFERENCE

Pauly, M., and S. Ramsey. 1999. Would You Like Suspenders to Go with That Belt? An Analysis of Optimal Combinations of Cost Sharing and Managed Care. *Journal of Health Economics* 18(4):443–458.

VICTOR R. FUCHS

■ *Preface*

This volume celebrates the fortieth anniversary of the publication of Kenneth Arrow's classic article, "Uncertainty and the Welfare Economics of Medical Care." By reprinting the article which launched modern health economics, along with more than a score of stimulating new papers by scholars from a half dozen disciplines, Duke University Press performs a valuable service for teachers, students, and researchers in health economics, health services research, health policy, and related fields.

Because I was involved with the article from the start, have been active in the health field for almost four decades, and have had the good fortune to be a colleague and friend of Kenneth Arrow for more than twenty years, I welcome this opportunity to contribute a brief prefatory note. Arrow's accomplishments need no embellishments from me, but I can provide the background and circumstances surrounding the origins of the article, describe its impact, and say a few words about its author.

In the early 1960s, the Ford Foundation Program in Economic Development and Administration devoted the bulk of its funds to traditional subjects such as economic growth and unemployment. As a Program Associate at the Foundation, it seemed to me there were large areas of the economy such as health, education, and welfare that were relatively neglected. I thought that Ford Foundation sponsorship of a series of monographs and shorter "think pieces" on these subjects would stimulate interest within economics and related fields and prove helpful to those responsible for policy and operating decisions in these areas.

At my request, the foundation trustees approved a $25,000 project to be administered within the foundation. The funds were to be used for publication subsidies, distribution of ten thousand copies of each study, and modest honoraria for the authors. My plan was to commission three monographs by economists who were familiar with the institutional and empirical features of their particular field and to find three outstanding economic theorists, each of whom would bring his or her analytical skills to bear on one of the fields.

For the three applied monographs, I chose Margaret Gordon for welfare, Herbert Klarman for health, and Theodore Schultz for education. Each of them came through splendidly with small books that were published by Columbia University Press. In baseball terms, Gordon delivered a clean hit. She placed U.S. welfare programs in historical context, provided international comparisons, and offered detailed analyses of major U.S. programs such as social security and unemployment compensation. Klarman's book was good for extra bases. It is the definitive description and assessment of the health economics field prior to 1963. In the absence of suitable textbooks in health economics, Klarman's book was assigned to students for many years to provide a grounding for work in this field. With his short essay "The Economic Value of Education," Schultz hit a home run. Its impact on the fields of economics, education, and development was tremendous. Although Columbia University Press was certain that the distribution of ten thousand free copies would preclude any further sales, the book went on to sell many times that number, and was translated into several languages. As recently as 2001, the study was cited in six social science journals.

The results for the economic theory portion of the project were decidedly more mixed. Robert Dorfman, who had the welfare assignment, found that he could not produce the desired kind of article. Carl Kaysen, who was supposed to write on education, departed for Washington midway through the project to join the Kennedy administration. Only Arrow remained to bat, and he delivered what can only be described as a home run with the bases loaded in the ninth inning with his team behind by three runs.

According to the dictionary, a classic is "a work generally considered to be of the highest rank or excellence, especially one of enduring significance." Arrow's article fits that description perfectly. It is the seminal article of modern health economics. As Mark Pauly puts it in his perceptive and provocative foreword to this volume, "Kenneth Arrow's article made research in health economics respectable.... It also made it interesting." In Hollywood, they say that Fred Astaire gave Ginger Rogers class, and she made him sexy. Arrow did both for health economics.

In 1963, there were few courses in health economics offered at any university. Subsequently, the field began to develop, slowly at first, then exponentially. If any of the new courses did not include "Uncertainty" on its reading list, one can only feel sympathy for the students and outrage at the instructor. In the last two decades, health economics courses and Arrow's article have spread beyond the economics curriculum to schools of business, public health, medicine, law, and public policy. Equally important, health economics has become completely international; approximately two thousand health economists from all over the world are expected to attend the Fourth International Congress of Health Economics in San Francisco June 2003. For evidence that Arrow's article has had — and continues to have — a large impact on many fields other than economics, the reader need go no further than this book. It is doubtful that any other social science article published in the last half-century could elicit so many thoughtful commentaries from so many different perspectives

One indicator of the continuing influence of Arrow's article is the frequency with which it is cited in social science and related journals. In 2001 alone, there were twenty-four citations in nineteen journals (excluding the special issue of the *Journal of Health, Politics, Policy and Law*). This almost equals the twenty-eight citations per year pace set in 1991–2000. This is clearly a work of "enduring significance."

What kind of man produced this classic article? There are many who deem this question irrelevant. They believe that the value of a scholarly work is independent of any biographical information regarding its creator. John Meurig Thomas made this point forcefully when he wrote, "Truth is independent of the stimulus that has provoked its discovery, and the conditions that guided its expression."[1] There is something to be said for this view. Consider for example, a proof of a mathematical theorem. The validity of this proof can be judged quite independently of whether the person providing the proof was Mother Teresa or a serial rapist.

There are, however, reasons to think that sometimes biographical background can be helpful. For example, in economic discussions less formal than a mathematical proof, values are nearly always present, either explicitly or implicitly. As Gunnar Myrdal wrote in an earlier volume celebrating Arrow's many theoretical contributions to economic policy, "Prior to answers, there must be questions . . . In the questions raised and the viewpoints chosen, valuations are implied."[2] For that reason alone, some readers may wish to know more about the author. A related point is that no article can be complete. There are always things that are left out. Biographical information about the author can in some instances help to fill in these unavoidable gaps. Finally, in this particular instance readers should find it inspiring to learn what an extraordinary person Arrow is.

Non-economists may not realize that "Uncertainty" is not Arrow's only "classic," or even his first. Beginning with his Ph.D. dissertation on social choice and on through other classic contributions to theories of general equilibrium, welfare, uncertainty, information, and much more, Arrow is considered by many to be the premier economic theorist of the last sixty years. When weighed against the totality of the Arrow oeuvre, the article we celebrate in this volume would be judged by most economists as simply another small addition, albeit the most frequently cited of any of his single-author papers.

Intellectually, Arrow is as broad as he is deep. He commands an encyclopedic knowledge of many fields from mathematics to literature. He is interested in and appreciative of music and the arts. He is a prime example of Friedrich Hayek's observation that "nobody can be a great economist who is only an economist."

Politically, Arrow is quite liberal. He has a deep understanding of the efficiency advantages of a market-price system, but distributive issues are also very important to him, and he is willing to accept trade-offs between efficiency and equity. To understand Arrow's values, we need only look at the dedication in his Collected Papers, where he praises his Columbia mentor Harold Hotelling for setting "the example of human concern combined with analytical rigor that I have always attempted to follow."

Perhaps the most unusual aspect of Arrow is the purely personal side. He is devoted to his family and is a warm and caring friend to many at Stanford and around the world. He cheerfully takes on much more than his fair share of community and professional responsibilities. He is modest, thoughtful, attentive to others. Compared with most who rise to the peak of a difficult field, he is less personally ambitious, less eager to prosclytize, less driven by ego.

In short, Arrow is living proof that being a genius does not rule out being an exceptionally nice person. At a luncheon celebrating Arrow's eightieth birthday, he was toasted as "supermensch." "Super" because of his extraordinary intellectual powers, and "mensch" because he is an exemplar of the decency and dependability denoted by that Yiddish term. This volume celebrates a great article and a great man.

NOTES

1 "Rumford's Remarkable Creation," *Proceedings of the American Philosophical Society*, 142, no. 4 (December 1998): 597–613.

2 "Utilitarianism and Modern Economics," in George I. Feiwell, ed., *Arrow and the Foundations of the Theory of Economic Policy* (London: Macmillan, 1987), 273–78.

PETER J. HAMMER

DEBORAH HAAS-WILSON

WILLIAM M. SAGE

■ *Kenneth Arrow and the Changing Economics of Health Care:*

"Why Arrow? Why Now?"

Brand New '64 Dodge
Money comes out of Dad's billfold. Hankies come out of Mom's purse.
The engine hardly makes a sound, even when you put it in reverse.
Its got a push-button transmission, hardtop convertible, 4-door.
Its November of '63 and the brand new Dodge is a '64.
— *The Poet Game*, Greg Brown (1994)

Why Arrow? Why now? Kenneth Arrow is a Nobel laureate and one of the most important economists of our time. "Uncertainty and the Welfare Economics of Medical Care" (Arrow 1963) is a landmark contribution to health economics that is required reading in health economics, health policy, and health law courses. While most of Arrow's economic insights transcend time and can fit comfortably within modern economic theory, his institutional analysis of medical markets is layered in amber. This turns out to be a blessing. By offering a point of reference that only time and distance can provide, Arrow's interpretation of medical markets circa 1960 affords an extraordinarily useful framework for understanding the health care economy and health care policy of today.

The year 1963 evokes an era as well as being a specific date. It was a time of perceived innocence and Camelot. People had faith in their government, in the functioning of private markets, and in the family doctor. The Dodgers beat the Yankees in the World Series, *Cleopatra* played in the movie theaters, and television audiences tuned in to *My Favorite Martian* and *The Fugitive*. At the same time, rumblings of unrest could be heard, the start of revolutionary social change. Martin Luther King, Jr. led his historic civil rights march on Washington in 1963.

President Diem was assassinated in South Vietnam, marking deepening U.S. involvement in a quagmire war. America's own President Kennedy had just brought the world back from the brink of nuclear war but would not himself survive the year.

For medicine, 1963 was a time of hope and optimism, though most of the profession's accomplishments still lay in the future. Most physicians were in solo practice, and many still made house calls. Medical science had made tremendous strides with antiseptic surgery, antibiotics for the treatment of infections, and vaccines for the prevention of diseases such as polio, but few specific therapies for important diseases yet existed. The delivery of professional services was undoubtedly a market transaction, but medical charity was also common, by necessity if not by design. Private health coverage was not yet widespread, and although national health insurance came periodically into political debate, the government still played little direct role in the purchase of medical services. Aggregate national spending on health care amounted to roughly 6 percent of the gross domestic product—a substantial but hardly a daunting sum.

Some forty years later, health care occupies a far more central role in the national economy. Today, it is common to speak of a "medical-care industry" comprising large physician organizations and hospital networks and of using "competitive forces" to discipline health care spending. But even as economics and competition have gained ascendance, we are wrestling with many of the same questions that Arrow attempted to address: What is the proper role of markets in delivering health care services? Can we base our health care system exclusively on private competition? What place should be reserved for government or for social mechanisms such as professionalism, nonprofit status, or trust? Do these "nonmarket institutions" help markets overcome uncertainty, or do they replace markets that have failed because of informational asymmetry? How does one define the proper boundary between market and nonmarket institutions?

It is also fitting that both Arrow's original contribution in 1963 and this retrospective collection today are the products of public policy initiatives by major philanthropic foundations. The Robert Wood Johnson Foundation's Investigator Awards in Health Policy Research program exists to encourage broad, interdisciplinary thinking about the design and operation of the American health care system. Because of the foundation's interest in promoting the exchange of ideas among Investigator Award recipients, a "cluster group" was formed to consider the proper role of competition in health care. Discussion at an introductory meeting in 1999 identified Arrow's 1963 article as a useful lens through which to view current health care markets and attendant public policy concerns. Drawing on this discussion, we developed an intellectual agenda for the cluster group's work, redefining our project as a published volume that would transform general interest in Arrow's article into a specific scholarly contribution. We then recruited leading members of the health economics and health policy community, from both inside and outside the ranks of the Investigator Awards in Health Policy Research program, to address a series of questions that emerged from Arrow's analysis. A first working meeting of the group was held in June 2000; subsequent meetings for discussion of draft essays took place in October 2000 and March 2001.

We have all been inspired and assisted in these efforts by Kenneth Arrow himself, whose involvement in the process and contribution to this volume have made the project complete. In July 2000, Professor Arrow hosted a memorable lunch and afternoon meeting at Stanford University with us as editors of this volume, where we discussed the 1963 article and post-1963 changes in health care markets. He was also an active discussant at the October 2000 meeting where many of the essays were presented. This introduction draws liberally from notes of those meetings.

In preparing these essays, we employed an innovative form of peer review. In addition to being reviewed by the volume's editors, each essay was assigned to at least two other project participants to act as commentators. Most essays were discussed as well at formal meetings of the group. Further feedback was facilitated by a project Web site where drafts, comments, and revisions were posted and easily shared. In making this collective journey we gained a deep respect for the text of Arrow's article, for the article's role in the evolution of the still-young disciplines of health economics and health policy research, and for the degree to which Professor Arrow's encounter with the medical industry influenced his own intellectual development and subsequent thinking about economics. Before outlining more fully the themes which these essays address, however, it is useful to put the discussion in perspective by telling the story of how and why the original article was written and briefly exploring the article's impact.

HISTORY OF THE 1963 ARTICLE

Arrow's Commission from the Ford Foundation

Kenneth Arrow's intellectual engagement with health care was largely serendipitous. Arrow had not written about medical markets before 1963 and seldom returned to health economics in later years (1972a, 1972b, 1974). Why the initial foray? Arrow was invited by the Ford Foundation to examine medical markets as part of a larger initiative addressing policy arenas with substantial public-private overlap, such as: health, education, and welfare. Marshall A. Robinson (1965), director of the Ford Foundation Program in Economic Development and Administration, explained: "The Ford Foundation was influenced by the fact that expenditures in these three fields are in excess of $100 billian annually, that they are among the most important and sensitive areas of the entire economy, and that communication between economists and those making policy and operating decisions in these areas has been infrequent and irregular." Robinson went on to note that "of the three areas, health economics is perhaps the most neglected by economists."

The Ford Foundation's plan was to combine the work of a practitioner in the field with that of a theoretician not necessarily working in the area. Victor Fuchs reports that Arrow's invitation to participate as the theoretical economist resulted from Fuch's own involvement at the time with the Ford Foundation. Arrow was paired with Herbert Klarman at Johns Hopkins University.

Given that Arrow was selected, in part, because he had not previously written about health care, he had to expend significant energy simply learning the industry. Arrow views his article as being part "survey," describing the existing literature, and part "insight," particularly regarding the role of information. He read the existing literature and talked to various people. In the article, he acknowledges comments from Francis Bator, Robert Dorfman, Victor Fuchs, Saul Gilson, Ruben Kessel, Selma Mushkin, and C. Rufus Rorem. Arrow recalls finding the existing health care and insurance literatures incomplete. There was standard risk theory along with loose concepts which posited that people will take advantage of insurance, although he does not remember seeing the catchphrases "moral hazard" and "adverse selection" in use at that time. According to Arrow, existing work did not adequately explain the complicated array of nonmarket relationships in health care, such as between physicians and patients, or the role that professionalism played more broadly. Arrow sought some unifying theory to encompass the existence of specialized professional knowledge and the underlying issues of insurance.

Arrow's Own Experience with Insurance and Medical Markets
In addition to the literature, Professor Arrow drew upon his own life experience. He recalls purchasing a private health insurance policy in the mid-1950s. A high school friend who had become a physician told him about the policy. Arrow asked his general insurance agent, but the agent was unaware that health insurance policies existed. He ended up purchasing a plan with coverage up to $15,000. He laughs at the policy today, saying, "That should have been the deductible, not the coverage. Insurance should cover only rare events." Arrow was also familiar with the role of certain private employers in providing health insurance for their workers, although they did so largely as a result of successful union efforts. Arrow was intrigued by the contrast in General Motors' two-pronged approach to health insurance, which he describes as a capped plan for blue-collar workers that was negotiated by the union and an uncapped plan for salaried workers.

Arrow's acquaintance with insurance markets was more than casual. He had

acquired practical knowledge of the industry while working one summer between college and graduate school calculating life insurance premiums. By his
own account, he narrowly escaped life as an actuary, a prospect that horrified his
graduate school professors. Arrow is still conversant in the "loads" that insurance
companies place upon actuarial risk, and he remains sensitive to the role that
transaction costs can play in the development and marketing of policies. One
lesson he derived from this knowledge is that the evolution of insurance markets
is likely to be path dependent in subtle ways. For example, Professor Arrow observed in our conversations how insurance companies do not like to cover areas
where they do not have much experience-based data, but that they only collect
statistics in the first place if they write policies in an area. This chicken-and-egg
problem helps to explain both the limited nature of private medical coverage
and the dearth of reliable actuarial information in the early 1960s. Indeed, the
empirical understanding of health insurance that emerged in the late 1960s and
1970s was largely the result of government reporting requirements accompanying
receipt of payments under Medicare and Medicaid.

Professor Arrow's personal contacts with the health care delivery system were
more limited. In addition to conversations with his doctor friend, he recalls talking with his personal physician while preparing the article. Despite his affiliation
with a major university, Arrow had little opportunity to examine large hospitals
or academic medicine because the Stanford Medical School was then located in
San Francisco. At one point, he reports, he was a member of the Palo Alto Clinic
and had a bad personal experience at the facility. Overall, Arrow claims to be
skeptical about medicine, as about most things, and states that he never had any
impression that doctors were infallible.

Arrow's Knowledge of the Health Policy Questions of the Time
We also inquired into Professor Arrow's awareness of health policy concerns at
the time of the 1963 article. Arrow recalls being struck by organized medicine's
long-standing antagonism to prepaid medical practice, the precursor of today's
HMOs. The AMA's fight against closed panels and forms of contract medicine were
well known at the time, and the issue figures prominently in Ruben Kessel's 1958
work, which Arrow cited and discussed. Arrow recalls as well that discussions of
physician shortages were part of the policy agenda in the early 1960s, as was the
use of limited-license practitioners to supplement physician practice. Arrow also
remembers that the Flexner Report on medical education was still controversial
in the late 1940s when he was completing his own academic studies, and that it
had been criticized by Chicago School economists such as Kessel as pure scarcity
control. Arrow, however, was and remains unenthusiastic about strict Chicago
School "physician conspiracy" theories of professional practice restrictions, find-

ing those stories incomplete because they do not explain how restrictions arise in the first place or why they perpetuate themselves politically.

The potential role of government as a direct purchaser of health care is absent from Arrow's 1963 article. Obviously, Medicare and Medicaid did not yet exist, but similar proposals had been around for decades. Arrow says that he was aware of the political debates that preceded the enactment of Medicare. He was also aware of the earlier Truman Commission work. However, he did not view his article as a policy piece, and therefore chose not to comment on or evaluate specific legislation. Instead, he confined himself "to scholarship, not public advocacy." This was made easier, he recollects, by the fact that 1963 was a "trough" in the Medicare debate. Discussions of government insurance figure more prominently in Arrow's replies (1965, 1968) to comments on the original article by Dennis Lees and Robert Rice (1965) and Mark Pauly (1968).

The Role of Economic Theory and Information
While the survey elements of the 1963 article are important, Arrow's lasting contribution was his theoretical insights regarding the economics of uncertainty. His use of the term "uncertainty" is itself a complicated matter, embracing not only insurance and underlying issues of risk but also differential or asymmetric information. The challenge undertaken in his article was to make economic sense of behavior in medical markets that had to confront and work its way through multiple layers of uncertainty. The common thread for unraveling this puzzle was information — Arrow describes his approach as "a study of rational behavior in the presence of differential information."

Significantly, theorizing about medical markets led Arrow to appreciate the full importance of asymmetric information in economic relationships as a general matter. Arrow recalls a flash of insight that came to him while working on the economics of medical care as he traveled cross-country by train (his wife did not like for him to fly). Previously, Arrow had thought about information mainly as the "cost of sampling" in statistical analysis. There was little in the economics of information to draw upon in 1963. Arrow remembers that there had been some work on the economics of innovation, including work by Arrow himself, Richard Nelson (a contributor to this volume), and RAND (in a study of military information). Bell Labs had examined the economics of efficient sampling, specifically the trade-off between accuracy and cost in testing telephone circuit relays. Jacob Marschak had worked in the 1950s on a general theory of information that viewed information as an economic good and proposed a "team theory" of cooperative decision making. However, there was little understanding of market failure resulting from informational problems, and not until Arrow's study of health care had anyone connected the precursors of such a theory in a coherent fashion.

Kenneth Arrow has made many valuable contributions to economics, including his mathematical proofs of the existence of a general competitive equilibrium and his "impossibility theorem" governing problems of social choice. His work on information and uncertainty, while different in nature, is of equally lasting importance. In his autobiographical essay for *Lives of the Laureates*, Arrow contrasts his work on information with his other accomplishments. The significance of his insights on information, he observes, was not the production of a single well-defined theorem, but rather the introduction of "a point of view that has served to reorient economic theory" (Arrow 1995: 55).

IMPACT, CRITICS, AND CONTEMPORARY RELEVANCE OF THE ARTICLE

Impact of Arrow's Article

Although (because?) written by an outsider, it would be hard to identify a more seminal contribution to the health policy field—both inside and outside health economics—than Arrow's 1963 article. We have not done the comparative statistics, but with at least 675 citations to it from 1963 to 2000 by authors in a multitude of disciplines, our guess is that no other single article has entered the scholarly domain of health policy as deeply, pervasively, and persistently. Young entrants into the fields of health services research and health policy probably recognize Arrow's article more than any other published four decades, three decades, two decades, or perhaps even one decade ago — even if they have not seen it with their own eyes.

The citations to Arrow's 1963 article show both the reach it has achieved in scholarship and the significance of revisiting his analysis with a multidisciplinary perspective. Table 1 presents a disciplinary-based analysis of these citations. It compares the types of journals in which the referencing articles appeared for two different time periods: the first ten years following publication of Arrow's essay and the most recent ten years. Although inferences must be made cautiously given the substantial changes over forty years in the number and type of journals themselves, several features of these data are worth noting. First, to say that Arrow's contribution has endured in the literature is to be guilty of almost criminal understatement. Based on this compendium of articles, Arrow's essay was cited in 51 articles between 1963 and 1972, but in a whopping 282 articles between 1991 and 2000, a ratio of 5.53. Second, Arrow's work originally had greater significance for economics in the first decade (51 percent of the citations were in economics journals of various types) but became a focal point for the non-economics world in the most recent decade (only 34 percent of the citing articles were in economics journals). As the number of citations grew in both economics and noneconomics settings, the major sources of change in the distribution of journals were the phenomenal escalation of citations reported in health policy

Table 1   Article Citations to Kenneth Arrow's "Uncertainty and the Welfare Economics of Medical Care" by Type of Journal

| | PERIOD OF PUBLICATION | | | | |
| | FIRST TEN YEARS (1963–1972) | | MOST RECENT TEN YEARS (1991–2000) | | Ratio— Last Ten Years to First Ten |
Type of Journal	Number	Column (%)	Number	Column (%)	
Economics[a]	26	51	95	34	3.65
Noneconomics	25	49	187	66	7.48
Total	51	100	282	100	5.53
BREAKDOWN OF NONECONOMICS JOURNALS					
Insurance	3	6	11	4	3.67
Human resources/ industrial relations	3	6	3	1	1.00
Law[b]	6	12	26	9	4.33
Medical	3	6	48	17	16.00
Health policy[c]	2	4	52	18	26.00
Political science	1	2	0	0	—
Sociology	0	0	6	2	All
Other	7	14	41	14	5.85

Source: Tabulations based on information provided in Memo, Reference Department, University of Michigan Law Library, 7 July 2000.

[a]Includes health economics and law and economics journals.

[b]Does not include law and economics journals.

[c]Does not include health economics journals.

publications (twenty-six-fold) and medical publications (sixteen-fold). One may fairly suggest that in the 1960s and early 1970s, Arrow's analysis resonated most in one way or another in the combined domain of economics, insurance, and human resources and industrial relations (a total of 63 percent of the citations). In the 1990s, the shift was to the combination of economics, health policy, and medicine (69 percent of the citations).

We cannot assess from this simple numerical overview, however, how well understood, evaluated, or critiqued has been Arrow's investigation of health care, health care markets, and the health care system as a whole. Indeed, when we shared the results of the bibliographic search with Arrow, it was clear from his reaction that he himself had no idea just how much his article permeated not only the literature, but so many literatures. All we know from this numerical summary of the past nearly forty years is that there have been many individual uses made of Arrow's article, or at least passing references.

Two substantive strands of the article's impact deserve special mention because of their continued relevance to health policy and their more general importance to the economics of information and insurance. As discussed above, Arrow's article identified problems of asymmetric information in markets for both medical services and health insurance. With respect to the first set of informational problems, George Akerlof (1970) and Hayne Leland (1979) extended Arrow's analysis to explore the implications for product and service markets when sellers have information concerning product quality that buyers are incapable of verifying. For example, "lemons" can cause markets for used cars to collapse. With respect to the second set of informational problems, Arrow (1963: 964) had observed that if insurance markets are genuinely competitive, "insurance plans could arise which charged lower premiums to preferred risks and draw them off, leaving the plan which does not discriminate among risks with only an adverse selection of them." Michael Rothschild and Joseph Stiglitz (1976) used Arrow's work to explore the possible unraveling of competitive insurance markets when, as is often the case, buyers of insurance have better information concerning their own risk than insurers do.

Critics of the Article

Arrow has had his share of prominent critics. Perhaps the most controversial aspect of the 1963 article is the economic role that Arrow postulates for social institutions, including professional norms and ethics: "I propose here the view that, when the market fails to achieve an optimal state, society will, to some extent at least, recognize the gap, and nonmarket social institutions will arise attempting to bridge it" (947). Arrow reasons further that "the special structural characteristics of the medical-care market are largely attempts to overcome the lack of optimality due to the nonmarketability of the bearing of suitable risks and the imperfect marketability of information" (ibid.).

Arrow's contention is somewhat surprising, considering that a Nobel Prize–winning economist ultimately embraces nonmarket mechanisms as the antidote for market failure. Mark Pauly (1978: 29) was the first to question the "optimality-gap-filling" role of social institutions, because "we have no assurance that these characteristics really are attempts by politicians and medical trade associations to do what the welfare economists would suggest." Paul Starr (1982: 227) was also critical of Arrow's analysis: "The result is not so much to explain as to explain away the particular institutional structure medical care has assumed in the United States."

Professor Arrow was refreshingly open-minded when discussing these criticisms. He acknowledges that his discussion of professional norms as an optimality-gap-filling mechanism was probably too functional and too formalistic. He also appreciates the need to incorporate interest group theory into the analysis of nonmarket institutions. Nevertheless, he still believes that the existence of market failures helps predict where nonmarket institutions are likely to take root and that such failures give these institutions political legitimacy in the first instance. He defends this proposition as an important conjecture, not as a proof in itself. Obviously, he admits, there should be fuller explanations for why particular norms emerge, what they do, and why they persist. This echoes the reasons he provided in 1963 for rejecting the special interest, rent-seeking explanations for professional licensing in favor of his own more nuanced story about information and uncertainty. "I think this explanation, which is perhaps the naive one, is much more tenable than any idea of monopoly seeking to increase incomes. No doubt restriction on entry is desirable from the point of view of the existing physicians, but the public pressure needed to achieve the restriction must come from deeper causes" (966).

Contemporary Relevance of the 1963 Article
Much has changed since the early 1960s. Despite the popular belief that the U.S. health care system is predominantly private and market based, health care markets operate in the shadow of substantial government regulation and sizable public investment. Some of the legislative and quasi-legislative developments that reshaped the health care system were in the wind when Arrow penned his article. In 1962 Congress passed substantial amendments to the Food, Drug and Cosmetic Act, requiring proof of drug efficacy and enacting stricter standards for drug approval. The World Health Organization issued the Helsinki Declaration in 1964, establishing international standards for medical experiments involving human subjects and furthering the causes of informed consent and patient autonomy. Perhaps most significantly, Medicare and Medicaid were passed in 1965, setting the stage not only for rapid increases in public financing of medical care, but also for extensive government regulation and the intense politicization of health care markets. Finally, on the journey from the preindustrial medicine of 1963 to today's managed care marketplace, one should not forget initiatives such as the National Health Resource Planning and Development Act of 1974, which relied on government planning instead of market competition as the preferred means of allocating health care resources.

Fundamental changes have also taken place in medical markets themselves. The evolution of health care markets provides clear evidence of the Coasian contestability of boundaries between markets, firms, and contracts. The study of health care is the study of a system undergoing continual change. Even the "managed care revolution" of the 1990s failed to produce a dominant Coasian unit for assessing interrelated health care markets, contracting processes, or the extent of integration within health care firms. In Arrow's parlance, no stable equilibrium has yet been achieved.

This changing context again demonstrates the analytical value of Arrow's 1963 reference point. When one reads Arrow's article, one is struck by the "physician-centricity" of his analysis. Arrow may have overstated this point even in 1963, but it is clearly not an accurate description of contemporary health care markets. One of the most important developments in the past forty years has been the transition from a physician-based unit of production for medical services to an institution- or system-based unit of production. This is often, although not necessarily, associated with the rise of prepaid managed care. The ability to contrast contemporary markets with markets and institutions from a substantially different era helps to place many current problems into economic as well as historical perspective.

CONTENTS AND ORGANIZATION OF THE PRESENT VOLUME

Background, Theory, and Terminology

The essays in this volume actively engage Arrow's article from a modern perspective. In the process of discussing and commenting upon as well as writing the various contributions, the text of Arrow's article attained an almost talmudic significance for the contributors herein. Accordingly, the presentation begins with a reproduction of Arrow's masterpiece in its original form, with marginal annotations to pertinent essays in this book. For those who have never read Arrow's article, this provides a wonderful opportunity to become acquainted with a classic of health economics. To those who have encountered the article at various points in their professional careers, it offers a chance to reexplore both the text itself and one's original reactions to it. During our deliberations, we discovered that each contributor entered the process with distinctly different memories of the article's principal claims. Discussion revealed that mistaken recollections were often held as strongly as accurate ones. Moreover, participants were uniformly struck by how much more was in the article than they had remembered and how well the text stands up not only to time, but also to repeated examination.

Methodologically, Arrow approaches health care markets through the lens of welfare economics and general equilibrium theory, employing a set of economic tools that seeks to understand the simultaneous interaction of markets and the role that prices play in allocating resources among them. The enduring contributions of the article flow primarily out of Arrow's attempt to reconcile the institutional idiosyncrasies of health care markets with the theoretical predictions of welfare economics. Approaching the problem in any other manner would have failed to produce the same insights. For noneconomists, Arrow's condensed summary of these topics may make for difficult reading, but the payoff is well worth the effort. Some assistance is available from Uwe Reinhardt's and Michael Chernew's essays in this volume, the latter of which also looks at health care markets from a general equilibrium perspective and provides a useful introduction to these theories.

Terminology also presents a challenge. As suggested earlier, Arrow uses the term "uncertainty" in holistic fashion, grouping under a common label notions of risk, insurance, and imperfect information. Other economists, both before and after 1963, segment Arrow's notion of uncertainty into component parts (Knight 1921: 233). Some theorists try to distinguish a notion of "risk," where the probability distributions associated with particular outcomes are known, from a notion of "uncertainty," where such probability distributions are unknown. This can lead, for example, to an analysis of why particular events are or are not insurable. Other theorists focus on the informational dimensions of uncertainty. Analyses of asymmetric information can lead either to discussions of quality deterioration or to discussions of agency, delegation, trust, and monitoring. Alternatively, one can view information as a commodity in itself. This can lead to discussions of the conditions that determine whether information will be privately produced or should be treated as a public good and of interventions such as credentialing and accreditation as means of supplying information to the market. Finally, medical uncertainty can have a technological or scientific component. If uncertainty is understood as the absence of knowledge, the prevailing level of uncertainty depends in part on the potential for innovation. In our discussions, Professor Arrow resisted efforts to overcompartmentalize the notion of uncertainty, often seeing more interconnections than differences in these distinctions. In the end, contributors to this volume were simply asked to use the terms *uncertainty*, *risk*, *insurance*, and *asymmetric information* in as self-conscious and consistent a manner as possible.

THEMES AND ISSUES EXAMINED IN THE ESSAYS

Contributors to this book struggle with a wide range of contemporary health care concerns. Professor Arrow's article provides a common backdrop to each essay, but each author uses the article differently in his or her attempt to explain the changes that have taken place in medical markets since 1963. Contributors come from diverse backgrounds—economists, health care providers, political scientists, journalists, and lawyers. In fact, the diffuse nature of current health policy studies is reflected in the departmental affiliations of the authors: medical schools, schools of public health, schools of public policy, law schools, business schools, and special programs designed for the study of health policy as well as traditional economics departments.

Some essays examine matters of perennial concern, such as the role of the consumer, the composition of the health care workforce, the nature of insurance markets, the importance of nonprofit institutions, and the impact of medical technology. In addition, there are thoughtful discussions of shifting attitudes toward government regulation and a succinct explanation of how antitrust enforcement helped facilitate the rise of modem health care markets. While systems of prepayment constituted an interesting subnarrative for Arrow's article, the rise of managed care and the backlash against it are the dominant stories of today. Essays discuss the evolution of provider compensation arrangements, assess the extent and character of informational asymmetry, and examine the awkward role that financial intermediaries play as multiple agents in markets with divided loyalties. There are also essays addressing issues often overlooked in literature, such as the role that capital markets have played in restructuring the health care system and the "lawyerization" of medicine since 1963. Importantly, critical voices are also heard, openly questioning claims in the 1963 article, pointing out omissions, and challenging the ways in which the article has been used and interpreted since its publication. Finally, there are a number of essays discussing Arrow's treatment of professional norms and social institutions, evaluating their efficiency attributes, examining the continued role of trust in the provision of medical services, and exploring the loss of faith in professional institutions as a source of political authority and legitimacy.

Kenneth Arrow is given the first and last word. He is given the first word by including here the full text of his 1963 article. He is given the last word, and an opportunity to explore the health care markets of a new millennium, in his own concluding essay. As readers will attest, time has not dimmed Professor Arrow's intellect. Nor has it diminished his good nature and generosity. We are deeply grateful for his interest in this project and for his contribution to this collection.

Arrow's article and this collection of essays should be of interest to anyone concerned about health care and health policy. We have designed this collection to be useful and provocative for the most seasoned health policy professional as well as for those just beginning to understand the puzzles presented by health care markets. In doing so, we have adopted an interdisciplinary approach that seeks to transcend unhelpful distinctions between economists and noneconomists or between those who generally trust and those who generally mistrust markets. Because it pays attention to both the functioning of medical markets and the role of social institutions, norms, and ethics, Arrow's article is a potential source of information and inspiration for partisans of all stripes and for noncombatants as well.

Our privileged opportunity to produce this volume did not happen by accident. A confluence of resources, intellectual infrastructure, spirited determination, and goodwill among many people has made this book possible, as well as the special issue of the *Journal of Health Politics, Policy and Law* on which it is based. First came, as noted earlier, the fertilization of the ground by the Robert Wood Johnson Foundation's Investigator Awards in Health Policy Research program. The Investigator Awards program office, represented initially by Alvin Tarlov and Barbara Krimgold (who nurtured us all with special care) and now by David Mechanic and Lynn Rogut as the program's director and deputy director, afforded the opportunity, with no limit of encouragement, for the emerging group.

The Robert Wood Johnson Foundation provided additional direct assistance for the project. A grant from the foundation to the *Journal of Health Politics, Policy and Law* made it possible for a significant number of the authors to meet repeatedly to discuss outlines of proposed articles and early drafts. It also facilitated the luncheon meeting and afternoon session that we held with Kenneth Arrow at Stanford University to discuss the origins of the project, learn the history of his 1963 article, and make arrangements for his participation. We are all enormously grateful that Professor Arrow not only shared the historical background on the article, but so generously gave of his time, actively participated in the project, and contributed the closing essay.

Others warrant special mention as well. We are delighted that Mark Pauly, who more than thirty years ago as an assistant professor of economics at Northwestern University was one of the first scholars to engage formally the arguments made by Arrow, wrote the foreword. We are especially pleased, too, that Victor Fuchs — long-time friend and Stanford colleague of Kenneth Arrow, former president of the American Economic Association, and a leading health economist — contributed the preface to this book. At Peter Hammer's request, Nancy Vettorello, reference librarian at the University of Michigan Law Library, compiled the bibliography of citations to Arrow's article that gave concrete indication of its wide impact, permitted us to convey that evidence to Arrow, and made possible our calculations in table 1. As always, the production staff at Duke University Press recognized a good opportunity for the health policy field and energetically did everything possible to move what became a monster-sized project through the pipeline, without complaint. The same needs to be said of Byerly Woodward, then managing editor of *JHPPL*, who with enthusiasm for the project put in decidedly extra-long hours to take us from the disparate final drafts of the twenty-five essays — some on schedule, some not — to a whole, copyedited issue, and now to this edited book. The special issue became this edited volume thanks to the tremendous enthusiasm and support, as well as felicitous action, of Raphael Allen, editor in the books division of Duke University Press. We are also grateful that the *American Economic Review* so swiftly and graciously granted permission for us to reprint Arrow's original article. Thanks are owed, too, to Jennifer Colamonico, who with her usual professional skill made all the air travel arrangements for our March 2001 meeting in North Carolina, and to Tami Cole, who so efficiently handled the other arrangements for the session. We are also grateful to Miryam Frieder for the hard work of compiling a comprehensive national mailing list of instructors in health economics and health policy courses, which helped to disseminate the original special journal issue.

Some forty years ago the Ford Foundation commissioned a creative and thoughtful theoretical economist to examine the economics of health. Today, with the assistance of myriad institutions and colleagues, the journey continues.

REFERENCES

Akerlof, G. A. 1970. The Market for "Lemons": Quality Uncertainty and the Market Mechanism. *Quarterly Journal of Economics* 84(3): 488–500.

Arrow, K. J. 1963. Uncertainty and the Welfare Economics of Medical Care. *American Economic Review* 53(3): 941–73.

———. 1964. The Role of Securities in the Optimal Allocation of Risk-Bearing. *Review of Economic Studies* 31(2): 91–96.

———. 1965. Uncertainty and the Welfare Economics of Medical Care: Reply (The Implications of Transaction Costs and Adjustment Lags). *American Economic Review* 55(1–2): 154–58.

———. 1968. The Economics of Moral Hazard: Further Comment. *American Economic Review* 58(3): 537–38.

———. 1972a. Gifts and Exchanges. *Philosophy & Public Affairs* 1(4): 343–62.

———. 1972b. Social Responsibility and Economic Efficiency. *Public Policy* 21: 303–17.

———. 1974. Government Decision Making and the Preciousness of Life. In *Ethics of Health Care: Papers of the Conference on Health Care and Changing Values*, ed. L. R. Tancredi. Washington: Institute of Medicine.

———. 1995. Kenneth J. Arrow. In *Lives of the Laureates: Thirteen Nobel Economists*, ed. W. B. Breit and R. W. Spencer. Cambridge: MIT Press.

Brown, G. 1994. "Brand New '64 Dodge." *The Poet Game*. St. Paul: Red House Records.

Kessel, R. A. 1958. Price Discrimination in Medicine. *Journal of Law & Economics* 2(1): 20–53.

Klarman, H. E. 1965. *The Economics of Health*. New York: Columbia University Press.

Knight, F. H. 1921. *Risk, Uncertainty and Profit*. Chicago: University of Chicago Press.

Lees, D. S., and R. G. Rice. 1965. Uncertainty and the Welfare Economics of Medical Care: Comment. *American Economic Review* 55(1–2): 140–54.

Leland, H. E. 1979. Quacks, Lemons, and Licensing: A Theory of Minimum Quality Standards. *Journal of Political Economy* 87(6): 1328–46.

National Health Care Expenditures Projections Tables. 1998. Office of the Actuary, Health Care Financing Administration, Washington, September.

Pauly, M. V. 1968. The Economics of Moral Hazard: Comment. *American Economic Review* 58(3): 531–37.

———. 1978. Is Medical Care Different? In *Competition in the Health Care Sector: Past,*

Present, and Future: Proceedings of a Conference Sponsored by the Bureau of Economics, Federal Trade Commission, March 1978, ed. W. Greenberg. Germantown, Md.: Aspen Systems.

Peterson, Mark A., ed. 1998. *Healthy Markets? The New Competition in Medical Care*. Durham: Duke University Press.

Robinson, M. A. 1965. Foreword to *The Economics of Health*, by H. E. Klarman. New York: Columbia University Press.

Rothschild, M., and J. Stiglitz. 1976. Equilibrium in Competitive Insurance Markets: An Essay on the Economics of Imperfect Information. *Quarterly Journal of Economics* 90(4): 629–49.

Starr, P. 1982. *The Social Transformation of American Medicine*. New York: Basic Books.

THE AMERICAN
ECONOMIC REVIEW

VOLUME LIII   DECEMBER 1963   NUMBER 5

UNCERTAINTY AND THE WELFARE
ECONOMICS OF MEDICAL CARE

By KENNETH J. ARROW*

I. *Introduction: Scope and Method*

This paper is an exploratory and tentative study of the specific differentia of medical care as the object of normative economics. It is contended here, on the basis of comparison of obvious characteristics of the medical-care industry with the norms of welfare economics, that the special economic problems of medical care can be explained as adaptations to the existence of uncertainty in the incidence of disease and in the efficacy of treatment.

It should be noted that the subject is the *medical-care industry,* not *health.* The causal factors in health are many, and the provision of medical care is only one. Particularly at low levels of income, other commodities such as nutrition, shelter, clothing, and sanitation may be much more significant. It is the complex of services that center about the physician, private and group practice, hospitals, and public health, which I propose to discuss.

The focus of discussion will be on the way the operation of the medical-care industry and the efficacy with which it satisfies the needs of society differ from a norm, if at all. The "norm" that the economist usually uses for the purposes of such comparisons is the operation of a competitive model, that is, the flows of services that would be

* The author is professor of economics at Stanford University. He wishes to express his thanks for useful comments to F. Bator, R. Dorfman, V. Fuchs, Dr. S. Gilson, R. Kessel, S. Mushkin, and C. R. Rorem. This paper was prepared under the sponsorship of the Ford Foundation as part of a series of papers on the economics of health, education, and welfare.

Reinhardt,
Chernew
(general
equilibrium)

offered and purchased and the prices that would be paid for them if each individual in the market offered or purchased services at the going prices as if his decisions had no influence over them, and the going prices were such that the amounts of services which were available equalled the total amounts which other individuals were willing to purchase, with no imposed restrictions on supply or demand.

The interest in the competitive model stems partly from its presumed descriptive power and partly from its implications for economic efficiency. In particular, we can state the following well-known proposition (First Optimality Theorem). If a competitive equilibrium exists at all, and if all commodities relevant to costs or utilities are in fact priced in the market, then the equilibrium is necessarily *optimal* in the following precise sense (due to V. Pareto): There is no other allocation of resources to services which will make all participants in the market better off.

Both the conditions of this optimality theorem and the definition of optimality call for comment. A definition is just a definition, but when the *definiendum* is a word already in common use with highly favorable connotations, it is clear that we are really trying to be persuasive; we are implicitly recommending the achievement of optimal states.[1] It is reasonable enough to assert that a change in allocation which makes all participants better off is one that certainly should be made; this is a value judgment, not a descriptive proposition, but it is a very weak one. From this it follows that it is not desirable to put up with a nonoptimal allocation. But it does not follow that if we are at an allocation which is optimal in the Pareto sense, we should not change to any other. We cannot indeed make a change that does not hurt someone; but we can still desire to change to another allocation if the change makes enough participants better off and by so much that we feel that the injury to others is not enough to offset the benefits. Such interpersonal comparisons are, of course, value judgments. The change, however, by the previous argument ought to be an optimal state; of course there are many possible states, each of which is optimal in the sense here used.

However, a value judgment on the desirability of each possible new distribution of benefits and costs corresponding to each possible reallocation of resources is not, in general, necessary. Judgments about the distribution can be made separately, in one sense, from those about allocation if certain conditions are fulfilled. Before stating the relevant proposition, it is necessary to remark that the competitive equilibrium achieved depends in good measure on the initial distribution of purchasing power, which consists of ownership of assets and skills that

[1] This point has been stressed by I. M. D. Little [19, pp. 71-74]. For the concept of a "persuasive definition," see C. L. Stevenson [27, pp. 210-17].

ARROW: UNCERTAINTY AND MEDICAL CARE   943

command a price on the market. A transfer of assets among individuals will, in general, change the final supplies of goods and services and the prices paid for them. Thus, a transfer of purchasing power from the well to the ill will increase the demand for medical services. This will manifest itself in the short run in an increase in the price of medical services and in the long run in an increase in the amount supplied.

With this in mind, the following statement can be made (Second Optimality Theorem): If there are no increasing returns in production, and if certain other minor conditions are satisfied, then every optimal state is a competitive equilibrium corresponding to some initial distribution of purchasing power. Operationally, the significance of this proposition is that if the conditions of the two optimality theorems are satisfied, and if the allocation mechanism in the real world satisfies the conditions for a competitive model, then social policy can confine itself to steps taken to alter the distribution of purchasing power. For any given distribution of purchasing power, the market will, under the assumptions made, achieve a competitive equilibrium which is necessarily optimal; and any optimal state is a competitive equilibrium corresponding to some distribution of purchasing power, so that any desired optimal state can be achieved.

The redistribution of purchasing power among individuals most simply takes the form of money: taxes and subsidies. The implications of such a transfer for individual satisfactions are, in general, not known in advance. But we can assume that society can *ex post* judge the distribution of satisfactions and, if deemed unsatisfactory, take steps to correct it by subsequent transfers. Thus, by successive approximations, a most preferred social state can be achieved, with resource allocation being handled by the market and public policy confined to the redistribution of money income.[2]

If, on the contrary, the actual market differs significantly from the competitive model, or if the assumptions of the two optimality theorems are not fulfilled, the separation of allocative and distributional procedures becomes, in most cases, impossible.[3]

The first step then in the analysis of the medical-care market is the

[2] The separation between allocation and distribution even under the above assumptions has glossed over problems in the execution of any desired redistribution policy; in practice, it is virtually impossible to find a set of taxes and subsidies that will not have an adverse effect on the achievement of an optimal state. But this discussion would take us even further afield than we have already gone.

[3] The basic theorems of welfare economics alluded to so briefly above have been the subject of voluminous literature, but no thoroughly satisfactory statement covering both the theorems themselves and the significance of exceptions to them exists. The positive assertions of welfare economics and their relation to the theory of competitive equilibrium are admirably covered in Koopmans [18]. The best summary of the various ways in which the theorems can fail to hold is probably Bator's [6].

comparison between the actual market and the competitive model. The methodology of this comparison has been a recurrent subject of controversy in economics for over a century. Recently, M. Friedman [15] has vigorously argued that the competitive or any other model should be tested solely by its ability to predict. In the context of competition, he comes close to arguing that prices and quantities are the only relevant data. This point of view is valuable in stressing that a certain amount of lack of realism in the assumptions of a model is no argument against its value. But the price-quantity implications of the competitive model for pricing are not easy to derive without major—and, in many cases, impossible—econometric efforts.

Hammer (institutions as economic data)

In this paper, the institutional organization and the observable mores of the medical profession are included among the data to be used in assessing the competitiveness of the medical-care market. I shall also examine the presence or absence of the preconditions for the equivalence of competitive equilibria and optimal states. The major competitive preconditions, in the sense used here, are three: the *existence* of competitive equilibrium, the *marketability* of all goods and services relevant to costs and utilities, and *nonincreasing returns*. The first two, as we have seen, insure that competitive equilibrium is necessarily optimal; the third insures that every optimal state is the competitive equilibrium corresponding to some distribution of income.[4] The first and third conditions are interrelated; indeed, nonincreasing returns plus some additional conditions not restrictive in a modern economy imply the existence of a competitive equilibrium, i.e., imply that there will be some set of prices which will clear all markets.[5]

The concept of marketability is somewhat broader than the traditional divergence between private and social costs and benefits. The latter concept refers to cases in which the organization of the market does not require an individual to pay for costs that he imposes on others as the result of his actions or does not permit him to receive compensation for benefits he confers. In the medical field, the obvious example is the spread of communicable diseases. An individual who fails to be immunized not only risks his own health, a disutility which presumably he has weighed against the utility of avoiding the procedure, but also that of others. In an ideal price system, there would be a price which he would have to pay to anyone whose health is endangered, a price sufficiently high so that the others would feel compensated; or, alternatively, there would be a price which would be paid to him by others to induce him to undergo the immunization procedure.

[4] There are further minor conditions, for which see Koopmans [18, pp. 50-55].

[5] For a more precise statement of the existence conditions, see Koopmans [18, pp. 56-60] or Debreu [12, Ch. 5].

Either system would lead to an optimal state, though the distributional implications would be different. It is, of course, not hard to see that such price systems could not, in fact, be practical; to approximate an optimal state it would be necessary to have collective intervention in the form of subsidy or tax or compulsion.

By the absence of marketability for an action which is identifiable, technologically possible, and capable of influencing some individual's welfare, for better or for worse, is meant here the failure of the existing market to provide a means whereby the services can be both offered and demanded upon payment of a price. Nonmarketability may be due to intrinsic technological characteristics of the product which prevent a suitable price from being enforced, as in the case of communicable diseases, or it may be due to social or historical controls, such as those prohibiting an individual from selling himself into slavery. This distinction is, in fact, difficult to make precise, though it is obviously of importance for policy; for the present purposes, it will be sufficient to identify nonmarketability with the observed absence of markets.

The instance of nonmarketability with which we shall be most concerned is that of risk-bearing. The relevance of risk-bearing to medical care seems obvious; illness is to a considerable extent an unpredictable phenomenon. The ability to shift the risks of illness to others is worth a price which many are willing to pay. Because of pooling and of superior willingness and ability, others are willing to bear the risks. Nevertheless, as we shall see in greater detail, a great many risks are not covered, and indeed the markets for the services of risk-coverage are poorly developed or nonexistent. Why this should be so is explained in more detail in Section IV.C below; briefly, it is impossible to draw up insurance policies which will sufficiently distinguish among risks, particularly since observation of the results will be incapable of distinguishing between avoidable and unavoidable risks, so that incentives to avoid losses are diluted.

The optimality theorems discussed above are usually presented in the literature as referring only to conditions of certainty, but there is no difficulty in extending them to the case of risks, provided the additional services of risk-bearing are included with other commodities.[6]

However, the variety of possible risks in the world is really staggering. The relevant commodities include, in effect, bets on all possible occurrences in the world which impinge upon utilities. In fact, many of these "commodities," i.e., desired protection against many risks, are

Chernew
(marketability)

Glied
(insurance and
risk bearing)

---

[6] The theory, in variant forms, seems to have been first worked out by Allais [2], Arrow [5], and Baudier [7]. For further generalization, see Debreu [11] and [12, Ch. 7].

simply not available. Thus, a wide class of commodities is nonmarketable, and a basic competitive precondition is not satisfied.[7]

Haas-
Wilson,
Robinson
(information
as a com-
modity)

There is a still more subtle consequence of the introduction of risk-bearing considerations. When there is uncertainty, information or knowledge becomes a commodity. Like other commodities, it has a cost of production and a cost of transmission, and so it is naturally not spread out over the entire population but concentrated among those who can profit most from it. (These costs may be measured in time or disutility as well as money.) But the demand for information is difficult to discuss in the rational terms usually employed. The value of information is frequently not known in any meaningful sense to the buyer; if, indeed, he knew enough to measure the value of information, he would know the information itself. But information, in the form of skilled care, is precisely what is being bought from most physicians, and, indeed, from most professionals. The elusive character of information as a commodity suggests that it departs considerably from the usual marketability assumptions about commodities.[8]

That risk and uncertainty are, in fact, significant elements in medical care hardly needs argument. I will hold that virtually all the special features of this industry, in fact, stem from the prevalence of uncertainty.

The nonexistence of markets for the bearing of some risks in the first instance reduces welfare for those who wish to transfer those risks to others for a certain price, as well as for those who would find it profitable to take on the risk at such prices. But it also reduces the desire to render or consume services which have risky consequences; in technical language, these commodities are complementary to risk-bearing. Conversely, the production and consumption of commodities and services with little risk attached act as substitutes for risk-bearing and are encouraged by market failure there with respect to risk-bearing. Thus the observed commodity pattern will be affected by the nonexistence of other markets.

[7] It should also be remarked that in the presence of uncertainty, indivisibilities that are sufficiently small to create little difficulty for the existence and viability of competitive equilibrium may nevertheless give rise to a considerable range of increasing returns because of the operation of the law of large numbers. Since most objects of insurance (lives, fire hazards, etc.) have some element of indivisibility, insurance companies have to be above a certain size. But it is not clear that this effect is sufficiently great to create serious obstacles to the existence and viability of competitive equilibrium in practice.

Gelijns et al.
(R & D and
technology)

[8] One form of production of information is research. Not only does the product have unconventional aspects as a commodity, but it is also subject to increasing returns in use, since new ideas, once developed, can be used over and over without being consumed, and to difficulties of market control, since the cost of reproduction is usually much less than that of production. Hence, it is not surprising that a free enterprise economy will tend to underinvest in research; see Nelson [21] and Arrow [4].

ARROW: UNCERTAINTY AND MEDICAL CARE   947

The failure of one or more of the competitive preconditions has as its most immediate and obvious consequence a reduction in welfare below that obtainable from existing resources and technology, in the sense of a failure to reach an optimal state in the sense of Pareto. But more can be said. I propose here the view that, when the market fails to achieve an optimal state, society will, to some extent at least, recognize the gap, and nonmarket social institutions will arise attempting to bridge it.[9] Certainly this process is not necessarily conscious; nor is it uniformly successful in approaching more closely to optimality when the entire range of consequences is considered. It has always been a favorite activity of economists to point out that actions which on their face achieve a desirable goal may have less obvious consequences, particularly over time, which more than offset the original gains.

Bloche,
Chernew,
Glied,
Hammer
(nonmarket
institutions)

But it is contended here that the special structural characteristics of the medical-care market are largely attempts to overcome the lack of optimality due to the nonmarketability of the bearing of suitable risks and the imperfect marketability of information. These compensatory institutional changes, with some reinforcement from usual profit motives, largely explain the observed noncompetitive behavior of the medical-care market, behavior which, in itself, interferes with optimality. The social adjustment towards optimality thus puts obstacles in its own path.

The doctrine that society will seek to achieve optimality by nonmarket means if it cannot achieve them in the market is not novel. Certainly, the government, at least in its economic activities, is usually implicitly or explicitly held to function as the agency which substitutes for the market's failure.[10] I am arguing here that in some circumstances other social institutions will step into the optimality gap, and that the medical-care industry, with its variety of special institutions, some ancient, some modern, exemplifies this tendency.

Jacobson
(government
and self-
regulation)

It may be useful to remark here that a good part of the preference for redistribution expressed in government taxation and expenditure policies and private charity can be reinterpreted as desire for insurance. It is noteworthy that virtually nowhere is there a system of subsidies that has as its aim simply an equalization of income. The subsidies or other governmental help go to those who are disadvantaged in life by events the incidence of which is popularly regarded as unpre-

Reinhardt
(redistribu-
tion)

[9] An important current situation in which normal market relations have had to be greatly modified in the presence of great risks is the production and procurement of modern weapons; see Peck and Scherer [23, pp. 581-82] (I am indebted for this reference to V. Fuchs) and [1, pp. 71-75].

[10] For an explicit statement of this view, see Baumol [8]. But I believe this position is implicit in most discussions of the functions of government.

dictable: the blind, dependent children, the medically indigent. Thus, optimality, in a context which includes risk-bearing, includes much that appears to be motivated by distributional value judgments when looked at in a narrower context.[11]

This methodological background gives rise to the following plan for this paper. Section II is a catalogue of stylized generalizations about the medical-care market which differentiate it from the usual commodity markets. In Section III the behavior of the market is compared with that of the competitive model which disregards the fact of uncertainty. In Section IV, the medical-care market is compared, both as to behavior and as to preconditions, with the ideal competitive market that takes account of uncertainty; an attempt will be made to demonstrate that the characteristics outlined in Section II can be explained either as the result of deviations from the competitive preconditions or as attempts to compensate by other institutions for these failures. The discussion is not designed to be definitive, but provocative. In particular, I have been chary about drawing policy inferences; to a considerable extent, they depend on further research, for which the present paper is intended to provide a framework.

II. *A Survey of the Special Characteristics of the Medical-Care Market*[12]

This section will list selectively some characteristics of medical care which distinguish it from the usual commodity of economics textbooks. The list is not exhaustive, and it is not claimed that the characteristics listed are individually unique to this market. But, taken together, they do establish a special place for medical care in economic analysis.

A. *The Nature of Demand*

Sloan
(role of the
consumer)

The most obvious distinguishing characteristics of an individual's demand for medical services is that it is not steady in origin as, for example, for food or clothing, but irregular and unpredictable. Medical services, apart from preventive services, afford satisfaction only in the event of illness, a departure from the normal state of affairs. It is hard, indeed, to think of another commodity of significance in the average budget of which this is true. A portion of legal services, devoted to defense in criminal trials or to lawsuits, might fall in this category but the incidence is surely very much lower (and, of course, there

---

[11] Since writing the above, I find that Buchanan and Tullock [10, Ch. 13] have argued that all redistribution can be interpreted as "income insurance."

[12] For an illuminating survey to which I am much indebted, see S. Mushkin [20].

are, in fact, strong institutional similarities between the legal and medical-care markets.)[13]

In addition, the demand for medical services is associated, with a considerable probability, with an assault on personal integrity. There is some risk of death and a more considerable risk of impairment of full functioning. In particular, there is a major potential for loss or reduction of earning ability. The risks are not by themselves unique; food is also a necessity, but avoidance of deprivation of food can be guaranteed with sufficient income, where the same cannot be said of avoidance of illness. Illness is, thus, not only risky but a costly risk in itself, apart from the cost of medical care.

B. *Expected Behavior of the Physician*

It is clear from everyday observation that the behavior expected of sellers of medical care is different from that of business men in general. These expectations are relevant because medical care belongs to the category of commodities for which the product and the activity of production are identical. In all such cases, the customer cannot test the product before consuming it, and there is an element of trust in the relation.[14] But the ethically understood restrictions on the activities of a physician are much more severe than on those of, say, a barber. His behavior is supposed to be governed by a concern for the customer's welfare which would not be expected of a salesman. In Talcott Parsons's terms, there is a "collectivity-orientation," which distinguishes medicine and other professions from business, where self-interest on the part of participants is the accepted norm.[15]

A few illustrations will indicate the degree of difference between the behavior expected of physicians and that expected of the typical businessman.[16] (1) Advertising and overt price competition are virtually eliminated among physicians. (2) Advice given by physicians as to further treatment by himself or others is supposed to be completely

Margin notes:

Sage
(lawyerization
of medicine)

Bloche, Hall,
Millenson,
Peterson
(expected
behavior of
physicians)

Havighurst
(antitrust
restraints of
trade)

---

[13] In governmental demand, military power is an example of a service used only irregularly and unpredictably. Here too, special institutional and professional relations have emerged, though the precise social structure is different for reasons that are not hard to analyze.

[14] Even with material commodities, testing is never so adequate that all elements of implicit trust can be eliminated. Of course, over the long run, experience with the quality of product of a given seller provides a check on the possibility of trust.

[15] See [22, p. 463]. The whole of [22, Ch. 10] is a most illuminating analysis of the social role of medical practice; though Parsons' interest lies in different areas from mine, I must acknowledge here my indebtedness to his work.

[16] I am indebted to Herbert Klarman of Johns Hopkins University for some of the points discussed in this and the following paragraph.

950   THE AMERICAN ECONOMIC REVIEW

Kronick
(charity)

Sage
(lawyerization
of medicine)

Needleman
(nonprofits)

divorced from self-interest. (3) It is at least claimed that treatment is dictated by the objective needs of the case and not limited by financial considerations.[17] While the ethical compulsion is surely not as absolute in fact as it is in theory, we can hardly suppose that it has no influence over resource allocation in this area. Charity treatment in one form or another does exist because of this tradition about human rights to adequate medical care.[18] (4) The physician is relied on as an expert in certifying to the existence of illnesses and injuries for various legal and other purposes. It is socially expected that his concern for the correct conveying of information will, when appropriate, outweigh his desire to please his customers.[19]

Departure from the profit motive is strikingly manifested by the overwhelming predominance of nonprofit over proprietary hospitals.[20] The hospital per se offers services not too different from those of a hotel, and it is certainly not obvious that the profit motive will not lead to a more efficient supply. The explanation may lie either on the supply side or on that of demand. The simplest explanation is that public and private subsidies decrease the cost to the patient in nonprofit hospitals. A second possibility is that the association of profit-making with the supply of medical services arouses suspicion and antagonism on the part of patients and referring physicians, so they do prefer nonprofit institutions. Either explanation implies a preference on the part of some group, whether donors or patients, against the profit motive in the supply of hospital services.[21]

[17] The belief that the ethics of medicine demands treatment independent of the patient's ability to pay is strongly ingrained. Such a perceptive observer as René Dubos has made the remark that the high cost of anticoagulants restricts their use and may contradict classical medical ethics, as though this were an unprecedented phenomenon. See [13, p. 419]. "A time *may come* when medical ethics will have to be considered in the harsh light of economics" (emphasis added). Of course, this expectation amounts to ignoring the scarcity of medical resources; one has only to have been poor to realize the error. We may confidently assume that price and income do have some consequences for medical expenditures.

[18] A needed piece of research is a study of the exact nature of the variations of medical care received and medical care paid for as income rises. (The relevant income concept also needs study.) For this purpose, some disaggregation is needed; differences in hospital care which are essentially matters of comfort should, in the above view, be much more responsive to income than, e.g., drugs.

[19] This role is enhanced in a socialist society, where the state itself is actively concerned with illness in relation to work; see Field [14, Ch. 9].

[20] About 3 per cent of beds were in proprietary hospitals in 1958, against 30 per cent in voluntary nonprofit, and the remainder in federal, state, and local hospitals; see [26, Chart 4-2, p. 60].

[21] C. R. Rorem has pointed out to me some further factors in this analysis. (1) Given the social intention of helping all patients without regard to immediate ability to pay, economies of scale would dictate a predominance of community-sponsored hospitals. (2)

ARROW: UNCERTAINTY AND MEDICAL CARE   951

Conformity to collectivity-oriented behavior is especially important since it is a commonplace that the physician-patient relation affects the quality of the medical care product. A pure cash nexus would be inadequate; if nothing else, the patient expects that the same physician will normally treat him on successive occasions. This expectation is strong enough to persist even in the Soviet Union, where medical care is nominally removed from the market place [14, pp. 194-96]. That purely psychic interactions between physician and patient have effects which are objectively indistinguishable in kind from the effects of medication is evidenced by the use of the placebo as a control in medical experimentation; see Shapiro [25].

Bloche, Hall (physician-patient relationships)

C. *Product Uncertainty*

Uncertainty as to the quality of the product is perhaps more intense here than in any other important commodity. Recovery from disease is as unpredictable as is its incidence. In most commodities, the possibility of learning from one's own experience or that of others is strong because there is an adequate number of trials. In the case of severe illness, that is, in general, not true; the uncertainty due to inexperience is added to the intrinsic difficulty of prediction. Further, the amount of uncertainty, measured in terms of utility variability, is certainly much greater for medical care in severe cases than for, say, houses or automobiles, even though these are also expenditures sufficiently infrequent so that there may be considerable residual uncertainty.

Sloan (consumer decision-making)

Further, there is a special quality to the uncertainty; it is very different on the two sides of the transaction. Because medical knowledge is so complicated, the information possessed by the physician as to the consequences and possibilities of treatment is necessarily very much greater than that of the patient, or at least so it is believed by both parties.[22] Further, both parties are aware of this informational inequality, and their relation is colored by this knowledge.

Haas-Wilson, Robinson (information)

To avoid misunderstanding, observe that the difference in information relevant here is a difference in information as to the consequence of a purchase of medical care. There is always an inequality of information as to production methods between the producer and the purchaser of any commodity, but in most cases the customer may well

Some proprietary hospitals will tend to control total costs to the patient more closely, including the fees of physicians, who will therefore tend to prefer community-sponsored hospitals.

[22] Without trying to assess the present situation, it is clear in retrospect that at some point in the past the actual differential knowledge possessed by physicians may not have been much. But from the economic point of view, it is the subjective belief of both parties, as manifested in their market behavior, that is relevant.

Millenson (physicians' actual knowledge)

have as good or nearly as good an understanding of the utility of the product as the producer.

D. *Supply Conditions*

Cooper and Aiken (licensing and medical education)

In competitive theory, the supply of a commodity is governed by the net return from its production compared with the return derivable from the use of the same resources elsewhere. There are several significant departures from this theory in the case of medical care.

Most obviously, entry to the profession is restricted by licensing. Licensing, of course, restricts supply and therefore increases the cost of medical care. It is defended as guaranteeing a minimum of quality. Restriction of entry by licensing occurs in most professions, including barbering and undertaking.

A second feature is perhaps even more remarkable. The cost of medical education today is high and, according to the usual figures, is borne only to a minor extent by the student. Thus, the private benefits to the entering student considerably exceed the costs. (It is, however, possible that research costs, not properly chargeable to education, swell the apparent difference.) This subsidy should, in principle, cause a fall in the price of medical services, which, however, is offset by rationing through limited entry to schools and through elimination of students during the medical-school career. These restrictions basically render superfluous the licensing, except in regard to graduates of foreign schools.

The special role of educational institutions in simultaneously subsidizing and rationing entry is common to all professions requiring advanced training.[23] It is a striking and insufficiently remarked phenomenon that such an important part of resource allocation should be performed by nonprofit-oriented agencies.

Since this last phenomenon goes well beyond the purely medical aspect, we will not dwell on it longer here except to note that the anomaly is most striking in the medical field. Educational costs tend to be far higher there than in any other branch of professional training. While tuition is the same, or only slightly higher, so that the subsidy is much greater, at the same time the earnings of physicians rank highest among professional groups, so there would not at first blush seem to be any necessity for special inducements to enter the profession. Even if we grant that, for reasons unexamined here, there is a social interest in subsidized professional education, it is not clear why the rate of subsidization should differ among professions. One might ex-

---

[23] The degree of subsidy in different branches of professional education is worthy of a major research effort.

pect that the tuition of medical students would be higher than that of other students.

The high cost of medical education in the United States is itself a reflection of the quality standards imposed by the American Medical Association since the Flexner Report, and it is, I believe, only since then that the subsidy element in medical education has become significant. Previously, many medical schools paid their way or even yielded a profit.

Gelijns et al. (R & D and medical technology)

Another interesting feature of limitation on entry to subsidized education is the extent of individual preferences concerning the social welfare, as manifested by contributions to private universities. But whether support is public or private, the important point is that both the quality and the quantity of the supply of medical care are being strongly influenced by social nonmarket forces.[24,25]

One striking consequence of the control of quality is the restriction on the range offered. If many qualities of a commodity are possible, it would usually happen in a competitive market that many qualities will be offered on the market, at suitably varying prices, to appeal to different tastes and incomes. Both the licensing laws and the standards of medical-school training have limited the possibilities of alternative qualities of medical care. The declining ratio of physicians to total employees in the medical-care industry shows that substitution of less trained personnel, technicians, and the like, is not prevented completely, but the central role of the highly trained physician is not affected at all.[26]

E. *Pricing Practices*

The unusual pricing practices and attitudes of the medical profession are well known: extensive price discrimination by income (with an extreme of zero prices for sufficiently indigent patients) and, formerly, a strong insistence on fee for services as against such alternatives as prepayment.

Kronick (charity)

---

[24] Strictly speaking, there are four variables in the market for physicians: price, quality of entering students, quality of education, and quantity. The basic market forces, demand for medical services and supply of entering students, determine two relations among the four variables. Hence, if the nonmarket forces determine the last two, market forces will determine price and quality of entrants.

[25] The supply of Ph.D.'s is similarly governed, but there are other conditions in the market which are much different, especially on the demand side.

[26] Today only the Soviet Union offers an alternative lower level of medical personnel, the feldshers, who practice primarily in the rural districts (the institution dates back to the 18th century). According to Field [14, pp. 98-100, 132-33], there is clear evidence of strain in the relations between physicians and feldshers, but it is not certain that the feldshers will gradually disappear as physicians grow in numbers.

954   THE AMERICAN ECONOMIC REVIEW

Bazzoli
(provider
compensa-
tion)

The opposition to prepayment is closely related to an even stronger opposition to closed-panel practice (contractual arrangements which bind the patient to a particular group of physicians). Again these attitudes seem to differentiate professions from business. Prepayment and closed-panel plans are virtually nonexistent in the legal profession. In ordinary business, on the other hand, there exists a wide variety of exclusive service contracts involving sharing of risks; it is assumed that competition will select those which satisfy needs best.[27]

Havighurst
(antitrust
enforcement)

The problems of implicit and explicit price-fixing should also be mentioned. Price competition is frowned on. Arrangements of this type are not uncommon in service industries, and they have not been subjected to antitrust action. How important this is is hard to assess. It has been pointed out many times that the apparent rigidity of so-called administered prices considerably understates the actual flexibility. Here, too, if physicians find themselves with unoccupied time, rates are likely to go down, openly or covertly; if there is insufficient time for the demand, rates will surely rise. The "ethics" of price competition may decrease the flexibility of price responses, but probably that is all.

III. *Comparisons with the Competitive Model under Certainty*

A. *Nonmarketable Commodities*

As already noted, the diffusion of communicable diseases provides an obvious example of nonmarket interactions. But from a theoretical viewpoint, the issues are well understood, and there is little point in expanding on this theme. (This should not be interpreted as minimizing the contribution of public health to welfare; there is every reason to suppose that it is considerably more important than all other aspects of medical care.)

Reinhardt
(redistribu-
tion)

Beyond this special area there is a more general interdependence, the concern of individuals for the health of others. The economic manifestations of this taste are to be found in individual donations to hospitals and to medical education, as well as in the widely accepted responsibilities of government in this area. The taste for improving the health of others appears to be stronger than for improving other aspects of their welfare.[28]

In interdependencies generated by concern for the welfare of others there is always a theoretical case for collective action if each participant derives satisfaction from the contributions of all.

---

[27] The law does impose some limits on risk-shifting in contracts, for example, its general refusal to honor exculpatory clauses.

[28] There may be an identification problem in this observation. If the failure of the market system is, or appears to be, greater in medical care than in, say, food an individual otherwise equally concerned about the two aspects of others' welfare may prefer to help in the first.

B. *Increasing Returns*

Problems associated with increasing returns play some role in allocation of resources in the medical field, particularly in areas of low density or low income. Hospitals show increasing returns up to a point; specialists and some medical equipment constitute significant indivisibilities. In many parts of the world the individual physician may be a large unit relative to demand. In such cases it can be socially desirable to subsidize the appropriate medical-care unit. The appropriate mode of analysis is much the same as for water-resource projects. Increasing returns are hardly apt to be a significant problem in general practice in large cities in the United States, and improved transportation to some extent reduces their importance elsewhere.

C. *Entry*

The most striking departure from competitive behavior is restriction on entry to the field, as discussed in II.D above. Friedman and Kuznets, in a detailed examination of the pre-World War II data, have argued that the higher income of physicians could be attributed to this restriction.[29]

There is some evidence that the demand for admission to medical school has dropped (as indicated by the number of applicants per place and the quality of those admitted), so that the number of medical-school places is not as significant a barrier to entry as in the early 1950's [28, pp. 14-15]. But it certainly has operated over the past and it is still operating to a considerable extent today. It has, of course, constituted a direct and unsubtle restriction on the supply of medical care.

Cooper and Aiken (supply of physicians)

There are several considerations that must be added to help evaluate the importance of entry restrictions: (1) Additional entrants would be, in general, of lower quality; hence, the addition to the supply of medical care, properly adjusted for quality, is less than purely quantitative calculations would show.[30] (2) To achieve genuinely competitive conditions, it would be necessary not only to remove numerical restrictions on entry but also to remove the subsidy in medical education. Like any other producer, the physician should bear all the costs of production,

Cooper and Aiken, Hammer (medical education)

[29] See [16, pp. 118-37]. The calculations involve many assumptions and must be regarded as tenuous; see the comments by C. Reinold Noyes in [16, pp. 407-10].

[30] It might be argued that the existence of racial discrimination in entrance has meant that some of the rejected applicants are superior to some accepted. However, there is no necessary connection between an increase in the number of entrants and a reduction in racial discrimination; so long as there is excess demand for entry, discrimination can continue unabated and new entrants will be inferior to those previously accepted.

including, in this case, education.[31] It is not so clear that this change would not keep even unrestricted entry down below the present level. (3) To some extent, the effect of making tuition carry the full cost of education will be to create too few entrants, rather than too many. Given the imperfections of the capital market, loans for this purpose to those who do not have the cash are difficult to obtain. The lender really has no security. The obvious answer is some form of insured loans, as has frequently been argued; not too much ingenuity would be needed to create a credit system for medical (and other branches of higher) education. Under these conditions the cost would still constitute a deterrent, but one to be compared with the high future incomes to be obtained.

Silvers (capital markets)

If entry were governed by ideal competitive conditions, it may be that the quantity on balance would be increased, though this conclusion is not obvious. The average quality would probably fall, even under an ideal credit system, since subsidy plus selected entry draw some highly qualified individuals who would otherwise get into other fields. The decline in quality is not an over-all social loss, since it is accompanied by increase in quality in other fields of endeavor; indeed, if demands accurately reflected utilities, there would be a net social gain through a switch to competitive entry.[32]

Cooper and Aiken, Hammer (licensing and nonphysician clinicians)

There is a second aspect of entry in which the contrast with competitive behavior is, in many respects, even sharper. It is the exclusion of many imperfect substitutes for physicians. The licensing laws, though they do not effectively limit the number of physicians, do exclude all others from engaging in any one of the activities known as medical practice. As a result, costly physician time may be employed at specific tasks for which only a small fraction of their training is needed, and which could be performed by others less well trained and therefore less expensive. One might expect immunization centers, privately operated, but not necessarily requiring the services of doctors.

In the competitive model without uncertainty, consumers are presumed to be able to distinguish qualities of the commodities they buy. Under this hypothesis, licensing would be, at best, superfluous and exclude those from whom consumers would not buy anyway; but it might exclude too many.

D. *Pricing*

The pricing practices of the medical industry (see II.E above) de-

---

[31] One problem here is that the tax laws do not permit depreciation of professional education, so that there is a discrimination against this form of investment.

[32] To anticipate later discussion, this condition is not necessarily fulfilled. When it comes to quality choices, the market may be inaccurate.

part sharply from the competitive norm. As Kessel [17] has pointed out with great vigor, not only is price discrimination incompatible with the competitive model, but its preservation in the face of the large number of physicians is equivalent to a collective monopoly. In the past, the opposition to prepayment plans has taken distinctly coercive forms, certainly transcending market pressures, to say the least.

Kessel has argued that price discrimination is designed to maximize profits along the classic lines of discriminating monopoly and that organized medical opposition to prepayment was motivated by the desire to protect these profits. In principle, prepayment schemes are compatible with discrimination, but in practice they do not usually discriminate. I do not believe the evidence that the actual scale of discrimination is profit-maximizing is convincing. In particular, note that for any monopoly, discriminating or otherwise, the elasticity of demand in each market at the point of maximum profits is greater than one. But it is almost surely true for medical care that the price elasticity of demand for all income levels is less than one. That price discrimination by income is not completely profit-maximizing is obvious in the extreme case of charity; Kessel argues that this represents an appeasement of public opinion. But this already shows the incompleteness of the model and suggests the relevance and importance of social and ethical factors.

Certainly one important part of the opposition to prepayment was its close relation to closed-panel plans. Prepayment is a form of insurance, and naturally the individual physician did not wish to assume the risks. Pooling was intrinsically involved, and this strongly motivates, as we shall discuss further in Section IV below, control over prices and benefits. The simplest administrative form is the closed panel; physicians involved are, in effect, the insuring agent. From this point of view, Blue Cross solved the prepayment problem by universalizing the closed panel.

The case that price discrimination by income is a form of profit maximization which was zealously defended by opposition to fees for service seems far from proven. But it remains true that this price discrimination, for whatever cause, is a source of nonoptimality. Hypothetically, it means everyone would be better off if prices were made equal for all, and the rich compensated the poor for the changes in the relative positions. The importance of this welfare loss depends on the actual amount of discrimination and on the elasticities of demand for medical services by the different income groups. If the discussion is simplified by considering only two income levels, rich and poor, and if the elasticity of demand by either one is zero, then no reallocation of medical services will take place and the initial situation is optimal. The

---

Havighurst (anticompetitive physician conduct)

Kronick (charity)

Bazzoli (systems of provider compensation)

Casalino (financial intermediaries)

only effect of a change in price will be the redistribution of income as between the medical profession and the group with the zero elasticity of demand. With low elasticities of demand, the gain will be small. To illustrate, suppose the price of medical care to the rich is double that to the poor, the medical expenditures by the rich are 20 per cent of those by the poor, and the elasticity of demand for both classes is .5; then the net social gain due to the abolition of discrimination is slightly over 1 per cent of previous medical expenditures.[33]

The issues involved in the opposition to prepayment, the other major anomaly in medical pricing, are not meaningful in the world of certainty and will be discussed below.

IV. *Comparison with the Ideal Competitive Model under Uncertainty*

A. *Introduction*

In this section we will compare the operations of the actual medical-care market with those of an ideal system in which not only the usual commodities and services but also insurance policies against all conceivable risks are available.[34] Departures consist for the most part of

---

[33] It is assumed that there are two classes, rich and poor; the price of medical services to the rich is twice that to the poor, medical expenditures by the rich are 20 per cent of those by the poor, and the elasticity of demand for medical services is .5 for both classes. Let us choose our quantity and monetary units so that the quantity of medical services consumed by the poor and the price they pay are both 1. Then the rich purchase .1 units of medical services at a price of 2. Given the assumption about the elasticities of demand, the demand function of the rich is $D_R(p) = .14 \ p^{-.5}$ and that of the poor is $D_P(p) = p^{-.5}$. The supply of medical services is assumed fixed and therefore must equal 1.1. If price discrimination were abolished, the equilibrium price, $\bar{p}$, must satisfy the relation,

$$D_R(\bar{p}) + D_P(\bar{p}) = 1.1,$$

and therefore $\bar{p} = 1.07$. The quantities of medical care purchased by the rich and poor, respectively, would be $D_R(\bar{p}) = .135$ and $D_P(\bar{p}) = .965$.

The inverse demand functions, the price to be paid corresponding to any given quantity are $d_R(q) = .02/q^2$, and $d_P(q) = 1/q^2$. Therefore, the consumers' surplus to the rich generated by the change is:

$$(1) \qquad \qquad \int_{.1}^{.135} (.02/q^2)dq - \bar{p}(.135 - .1),$$

and similarly the loss in consumers' surplus by the poor is:

$$(2) \qquad \qquad \int_{.965}^{1} (1/q^2)dq - \bar{p}(1 - .965)$$

If (2) is subtracted from (1), the second terms cancel, and the aggregate increase in consumers' surplus is .0156, or a little over 1 per cent of the initial expenditures.

[34] A striking illustration of the desire for security in medical care is provided by the expressed preferences of *émigrés* from the Soviet Union as between Soviet medical practice and German or American practice; see Field [14, Ch. 12]. Those in Germany preferred the German system to the Soviet, but those in the United States preferred (in a ratio of 3 to 1) the Soviet system. The reasons given boil down to the certainty of medical care, independent of income or health fluctuations.

ARROW: UNCERTAINTY AND MEDICAL CARE   959

insurance policies that might conceivably be written, but are in fact not. Whether these potential commodities are nonmarketable, or, merely because of some imperfection in the market, are not actually marketed, is a somewhat fine point.

To recall what has already been said in Section I, there are two kinds of risks involved in medical care: the risk of becoming ill, and the risk of total or incomplete or delayed recovery. The loss due to illness is only partially the cost of medical care. It also consists of discomfort and loss of productive time during illness, and, in more serious cases, death or prolonged deprivation of normal function. From the point of view of the welfare economics of uncertainty, both losses are risks against which individuals would like to insure. The nonexistence of suitable insurance policies for either risk implies a loss of welfare.

B. *The Theory of Ideal Insurance*

In this section, the basic principles of an optimal regime for risk-bearing will be presented. For illustration, reference will usually be made to the case of insurance against cost in medical care. The principles are equally applicable to any of the risks. There is no single source to which the reader can be easily referred, though I think the principles are at least reasonably well understood.

As a basis for the analysis, the assumption is made that each individual acts so as to maximize the expected value of a utility function. If we think of utility as attached to income, then the costs of medical care act as a random deduction from this income, and it is the expected value of the utility of income after medical costs that we are concerned with. (Income after medical costs is the ability to spend money on other objects which give satisfaction. We presuppose that illness is not a source of satisfaction in itself; to the extent that it is a source of dissatisfaction, the illness should enter into the utility function as a separate variable.) The expected-utility hypothesis, due originally to Daniel Bernoulli (1738), is plausible and is the most analytically manageable of all hypotheses that have been proposed to explain behavior under uncertainty. In any case, the results to follow probably would not be significantly affected by moving to another mode of analysis.

It is further assumed that individuals are normally risk-averters. In utility terms, this means that they have a diminishing marginal utility of income. This assumption may reasonably be taken to hold for most of the significant affairs of life for a majority of people, but the presence of gambling provides some difficulty in the full application of this view. It follows from the assumption of risk aversion that if an individual is given a choice between a probability distribution of income, with a given mean m, and the certainty of the income m, he would prefer

Chernew
(nonmarketability)

Glied
(insurance)

the latter. Suppose, therefore, an agency, a large insurance company plan, or the government, stands ready to offer insurance against medical costs on an actuarially fair basis; that is, if the costs of medical care are a random variable with mean m, the company will charge a premium m, and agree to indemnify the individual for all medical costs. Under these circumstances, the individual will certainly prefer to take out a policy and will have a welfare gain thereby.

Will this be a social gain? Obviously yes, if the insurance agent is suffering no social loss. Under the assumption that medical risks on different individuals are basically independent, the pooling of them reduces the risk involved to the insurer to relatively small proportions. In the limit, the welfare loss, even assuming risk aversion on the part of the insurer, would vanish and there is a net social gain which may be of quite substantial magnitude. In fact, of course, the pooling of risks does not go to the limit; there is only a finite number of them and there may be some interdependence among the risks due to epidemics and the like. But then a premium, perhaps slightly above the actuarial level, would be sufficient to offset this welfare loss. From the point of view of the individual, since he has a strict preference for the actuarially fair policy over assuming the risks himself, he will still have a preference for an actuarially unfair policy, provided, of course, that it is not too unfair.

In addition to a residual degree of risk aversion by insurers, there are other reasons for the loading of the premium (i.e., an excess of premium over the actuarial value). Insurance involves administrative costs. Also, because of the irregularity of payments there is likely to be a cost of capital tied up. Suppose, to take a simple case, the insurance company is not willing to sell any insurance policy that a consumer wants but will charge a fixed-percentage loading above the actuarial value for its premium. Then it can be shown that the most preferred policy from the point of view of an individual is a coverage with a deductible amount; that is, the insurance policy provides 100 per cent coverage for all medical costs in excess of some fixed-dollar limit. If, however, the insurance company has some degree of risk aversion, its loading may also depend on the degree of uncertainty of the risk. In that case, the Pareto optimal policy will involve some element of co-insurance, i.e., the coverage for costs over the minimum limit will be some fraction less than 100 per cent (for proofs of these statements, see Appendix).

These results can also be applied to the hypothetical concept of insurance against failure to recover from illness. For simplicity, let us assume that the cost of failure to recover is regarded purely as a money cost, either simply productive opportunities foregone or, more gener-

Silvers
(capital
markets)

ally, the money equivalent of all dissatisfactions. Suppose further that, given that a person is ill, the expected value of medical care is greater than its cost; that is, the expected money value attributable to recovery with medical help is greater than resources devoted to medical help. However, the recovery, though on the average beneficial, is uncertain; in the absence of insurance a risk-averter may well prefer not to take a chance on further impoverishment by buying medical care. A suitable insurance policy would, however, mean that he paid nothing if he doesn't benefit; since the expected value is greater than the cost, there would be a net social gain.[35]

C. *Problems of Insurance*

1. *The moral hazard.* The welfare case for insurance policies of all sorts is overwhelming. It follows that the government should undertake insurance in those cases where this market, for whatever reason, has failed to emerge. Nevertheless, there are a number of significant practical limitations on the use of insurance. It is important to understand them, though I do not believe that they alter the case for the creation of a much wider class of insurance policies than now exists.

One of the limits which has been much stressed in insurance literature is the effect of insurance on incentives. What is desired in the case of insurance is that the event against which insurance is taken be out of the control of the individual. Unfortunately, in real life this separation can never be made perfectly. The outbreak of fire in one's house or business may be largely uncontrollable by the individual, but the probability of fire is somewhat influenced by carelessness, and of course arson is a possibility, if an extreme one. Similarly, in medical policies the cost of medical care is not completely determined by the illness suffered by the individual but depends on the choice of a doctor and his willingness to use medical services. It is frequently observed that widespread medical insurance increases the demand for medical care. Coinsurance provisions have been introduced into many major medical policies to meet this contingency as well as the risk aversion of the insurance companies.

To some extent the professional relationship between physician and patient limits the normal hazard in various forms of medical insurance. By certifying to the necessity of given treatment or the lack thereof, the physician acts as a controlling agent on behalf of the insurance companies. Needless to say, it is a far from perfect check; the physicians themselves are not under any control and it may be convenient for them or pleasing to their patients to prescribe more expensive medi-

Reinhardt
(universal
coverage)

Bazzoli
(controllable
and
uncontrollable
forms of risk)

Millenson
(physicians as
a check on
moral hazard)

[35] It is a popular belief that the Chinese, at one time, paid their physicians when well but not when sick.

cation, private nurses, more frequent treatments, and other marginal variations of care. It is probably true that hospitalization and surgery are more under the casual inspection of others than is general practice and therefore less subject to moral hazard; this may be one reason why insurance policies in those fields have been more widespread.

2. *Alternative methods of insurance payment.* It is interesting that no less than three different methods of coverage of the costs of medical care have arisen: prepayment, indemnities according to a fixed schedule, and insurance against costs, whatever they may be. In prepayment plans, insurance in effect is paid in kind—that is, directly in medical services. The other two forms both involve cash payments to the beneficiary, but in the one case the amounts to be paid involving a medical contingency are fixed in advance, while in the other the insurance carrier pays all the costs, whatever they may be, subject, of course, to provisions like deductibles and coinsurance.

In hypothetically perfect markets these three forms of insurance would be equivalent. The indemnities stipulated would, in fact, equal the market price of the services, so that value to the insured would be the same if he were to be paid the fixed sum or the market price or were given the services free. In fact, of course, insurance against full costs and prepayment plans both offer insurance against uncertainty as to the price of medical services, in addition to uncertainty about their needs. Further, by their mode of compensation to the physician, prepayment plans are inevitably bound up with closed panels so that the freedom of choice of the physician by the patient is less than it would be under a scheme more strictly confined to the provision of insurance. These remarks are tentative, and the question of coexistence of the different schemes should be a fruitful subject for investigation.

3. *Third-party control over payments.* The moral hazard in physicians' control noted in paragraph 1 above shows itself in those insurance schemes where the physician has the greatest control, namely, major medical insurance. Here there has been a marked rise in expenditures over time. In prepayment plans, where the insurance and medical service are supplied by the same group, the incentive to keep medical costs to a minimum is strongest. In plans of the Blue Cross group, there has developed a conflict of interest between the insurance carrier and the medical-service supplier, in this case particularly the hospital.

The need for third-party control is reinforced by another aspect of the moral hazard. Insurance removes the incentive on the part of individuals, patients, and physicians to shop around for better prices for hospitalization and surgical care. The market forces, therefore, tend to be replaced by direct institutional control.

Bazzoli (provider compensation)

Casalino (financial intermediaries)

Chernew, Gelijns et al., Glied (moral hazard, insurance, technology)

4. *Administrative costs.* The pure theory of insurance sketched in Section B above omits one very important consideration: the costs of operating an insurance company. There are several types of operating costs, but one of the most important categories includes commissions and acquisition costs, selling costs in usual economic terminology. Not only does this mean that insurance policies must be sold for considerably more than their actuarial value, but it also means there is a great differential among different types of insurance. It is very striking to observe that among health insurance policies of insurance companies in 1958, expenses of one sort or another constitute 51.6 per cent of total premium income for individual policies, and only 9.5 per cent for group policies [26, Table 14-1, p. 272]. This striking differential would seem to imply enormous economies of scale in the provision of insurance, quite apart from the coverage of the risks themselves. Obviously, this provides a very strong argument for widespread plans, including, in particular, compulsory ones.

5. *Predictability and insurance.* Clearly, from the risk-aversion point of view, insurance is more valuable, the greater the uncertainty in the risk being insured against. This is usually used as an argument for putting greater emphasis on insurance against hospitalization and surgery than other forms of medical care. The empirical assumption has been challenged by O. W. Anderson and others [3, pp. 53-54], who asserted that out-of-hospital expenses were equally as unpredictable as in-hospital costs. What was in fact shown was that the probability of costs exceeding $200 is about the same for the two categories, but this is not, of course, a correct measure of predictability, and a quick glance at the supporting evidence shows that in relation to the average cost the variability is much lower for ordinary medical expenses. Thus, for the city of Birmingham, the mean expenditure on surgery was $7, as opposed to $20 for other medical expenses, but of those who paid something for surgery the average bill was $99, as against $36 for those with some ordinary medical cost. Eighty-two per cent of those interviewed had no surgery, and only 20 per cent had no ordinary medical expenses [3, Tables A-13, A-18, and A-19 on pp. 72, 77, and 79, respectively].

The issue of predictability also has bearing on the merits of insurance against chronic illness or maternity. On a lifetime insurance basis, insurance against chronic illness makes sense, since this is both highly unpredictable and highly significant in costs. Among people who already have chronic illness, or symptoms which reliably indicate it, insurance in the strict sense is probably pointless.

6. *Pooling of unequal risks.* Hypothetically, insurance requires for its full social benefit a maximum possible discrimination of risks. Those

Glied
(insurance)

in groups of higher incidences of illness should pay higher premiums.

Reinhardt (redistribution)

In fact, however, there is a tendency to equalize, rather than to differentiate, premiums, especially in the Blue Cross and similar widespread schemes. This constitutes, in effect, a redistribution of income from those with a low propensity to illness to those with a high propensity. The equalization, of course, could not in fact be carried through if the market were genuinely competitive. Under those circumsances, insurance plans could arise which charged lower premiums to preferred risks and draw them off, leaving the plan which does not discriminate among risks with only an adverse selection of them.

As we have already seen in the case of income redistribution, some of this may be thought of as insurance with a longer time perspective. If a plan guarantees to everybody a premium that corresponds to total experience but not to experience as it might be segregated by smaller subgroups, everybody is, in effect, insured against a change in his basic state of health which would lead to a reclassification. This corresponds precisely to the use of a level premium in life insurance instead of a premium varying by age, as would be the case for term insurance.

Reinhardt (universal coverage)

7. *Gaps and coverage.* We may briefly note that, at any rate to date, insurances against the cost of medical care are far from universal. Certain groups—the unemployed, the institutionalized, and the aged—are almost completely uncovered. Of total expenditures, between one-fifth and one-fourth are covered by insurance. It should be noted, however, that over half of all hospital expenses and about 35 per cent of the medical payments of those with bills of $1,000 a year and over, are included [26, p. 376]. Thus, the coverage on the more variable parts of medical expenditure is somewhat better than the over-all figures would indicate, but it must be assumed that the insurance mechanism is still very far from achieving the full coverage of which it is capable.

D. *Uncertainty of Effects of Treatment*

1. There are really two major aspects of uncertainty for an individual already suffering from an illness. He is uncertain about the effectiveness of medical treatment, and his uncertainty may be quite different from that of his physician, based on the presumably quite different medical knowledges.

Bazzoli (payment for benefits)

2. *Ideal insurance.* This will necessarily involve insurance against a failure to benefit from medical care, whether through recovery, relief of pain, or arrest of further deterioration. One form would be a system in which the payment to the physician is made in accordance with the degree of benefit. Since this would involve transferring the risks from the patient to the physician, who might certainly have an aversion to bearing them, there is room for insurance carriers to pool the risks,

either by contract with physicians or by contract with the potential patients. Under ideal insurance, medical care will always be undertaken in any case in which the expected utility, taking account of the probabilities, exceeds the expected medical cost. This prescription would lead to an economic optimum. If we think of the failure to recover mainly in terms of lost working time, then this policy would, in fact, maximize economic welfare as ordinarily measured.

3. *The concepts of trust and delegation.* In the absence of ideal insurance, there arise institutions which offer some sort of substitute guarantees. Under ideal insurance the patient would actually have no concern with the informational inequality between himself and the physician, since he would only be paying by results anyway, and his utility position would in fact be thoroughly guaranteed. In its absence he wants to have some guarantee that at least the physician is using his knowledge to the best advantage. This leads to the setting up of a relationship of trust and confidence, one which the physician has a social obligation to live up to. Since the patient does not, at least in his belief, know as much as the physician, he cannot completely enforce standards of care. In part, he replaces direct observation by generalized belief in the ability of the physician.[36] To put it another way, the social obligation for best practice is part of the commodity the physician sells, even though it is a part that is not subject to thorough inspection by the buyer.

Hall, Peterson (trust)

Haas-Wilson, Robinson (information)

One consequence of such trust relations is that the physician cannot act, or at least appear to act, as if he is maximizing his income at every moment of time. As a signal to the buyer of his intentions to act as thoroughly in the buyer's behalf as possible, the physician avoids the obvious stigmata of profit-maximizing. Purely arms-length bargaining behavior would be incompatible, not logically, but surely psychologically, with the trust relations. From these special relations come the various forms of ethical behavior discussed above, and so also, I suggest, the relative unimportance of profit-making in hospitals. The very word, "profit," is a signal that denies the trust relations.

Needleman (nonprofits)

Bloche, Millenson (physician behavior)

Price discrimination and its extreme, free treatment for the indigent, also follow. If the obligation of the physician is understood to be first of all to the welfare of the patient, then in particular it takes precedence over financial difficulties.

Kronick (charity)

As a second consequence of informational inequality between physician and patient and the lack of insurance of a suitable type, the patient must delegate to the physician much of his freedom of choice.

---

[36] Francis Bator points out to me that some protection can be achieved, at a price, by securing additional opinions.

966   THE AMERICAN ECONOMIC REVIEW

Casalino
(agency)

He does not have the knowledge to make decisions on treatment, referral, or hospitalization. To justify this delegation, the physician finds
himself somewhat limited, just as any agent would in similar circumstances. The safest course to take to avoid not being a true agent is to
give the socially prescribed "best" treatment of the day. Compromise
in quality, even for the purpose of saving the patient money, is to risk
an imputation of failure to live up to the social bond.

Peterson
(sources of
political and
cultural
legitimacy)

The special trust relation of physicians (and allied occuptions, such
as priests) extends to third parties so that the certifications of physicians as to illness and injury are accepted as especially reliable (see
Section II.B above). The social value to all concerned of such pre-
sumptively reliable sources of information is obvious.

Notice the general principle here. Because there are barriers to the
information flow and because there is no market in which the risks
involved can be insured, coordination of purchase and sales must take
place through convergent expectations, but these are greatly assisted
by having clear and prominent signals, and these, in turn, force patterns of behavior which are not in themselves logical necessities for
optimality.[37]

4. *Licensing and educational standards.* Delegation and trust are the
social institutions designed to obviate the problem of informational in-

Cooper and
Aiken,
Hammer
(licensing and
entry
restrictions)

equality. The general uncertainty about the prospects of medical treatment is socially handled by rigid entry requirements. These are designed to reduce the uncertainty in the mind of the consumer as to
the quality of product insofar as this is possible.[38] I think this explanation, which is perhaps the naive one, is much more tenable than any
idea of a monopoly seeking to increase incomes. No doubt restriction
on entry is desirable from the point of view of the existing physicians,
but the public pressure needed to achieve the restriction must come
from deeper causes.

The social demand for guaranteed quality can be met in more than
one way, however. At least three attitudes can be taken by the state or
other social institutions toward entry into an occupation or toward
the production of commodities in general; examples of all three types
exist. (1) The occupation can be licensed, nonqualified entrants being
simply excluded. The licensing may be more complex than it is in
medicine; individuals could be licensed for some, but not all, medical
activities, for example. Indeed, the present all-or-none approach could

[37] The situation is very reminiscent of the crucial role of the focal point in Schelling's
theory of tacit games, in which two parties have to find a common course of action
without being able to communicate; see [24, esp. pp. 225 ff.].

[38] How well they achieve this end is another matter. R. Kessel points out to me that
they merely guarantee training, not continued good performance as medical technology
changes.

be criticized as being insufficient with regard to complicated specialist treatment, as well as excessive with regard to minor medical skills. Graded licensing may, however, be much harder to enforce. Controls could be exercised analogous to those for foods; they can be excluded as being dangerous, or they can be permitted for animals but not for humans. (2) The state or other agency can certify or label, without compulsory exclusion. The category of Certified Psychologist is now under active discussion; canned goods are graded. Certification can be done by nongovernmental agencies, as in the medical-board examinations for specialists. (3) Nothing at all may be done; consumers make their own choices.

Jacobson (self-regulation)

The choice among these alternatives in any given case depends on the degree of difficulty consumers have in making the choice unaided, and on the consequences of errors of judgment. It is the general social consensus, clearly, that the *laissez-faire* solution for medicine is intolerable. The certification proposal never seems to have been discussed seriously. It is beyond the scope of this paper to discuss these proposals in detail. I wish simply to point out that they should be judged in terms of the ability to relieve the uncertainty of the patient in regard to the quality of the commodity he is purchasing, and that entry restrictions are the consequences of an apparent inability to devise a system in which the risks of gaps in medical knowledge and skill are borne primarily by the patient, not the physician.

Haas-Wilson, Robinson (information)

Postscript

I wish to repeat here what has been suggested above in several places: that the failure of the market to insure against uncertainties has created many social institutions in which the usual assumptions of the market are to some extent contradicted. The medical profession is only one example, though in many respects an extreme one. All professions share some of the same properties. The economic importance of personal and especially family relationships, though declining, is by no means trivial in the most advanced economies; it is based on non-market relations that create guarantees of behavior which would otherwise be afflicted with excessive uncertainty. Many other examples can be given. The logic and limitations of ideal competitive behavior under uncertainty force us to recognize the incomplete description of reality supplied by the impersonal price system.

Bloche, Chernew, Glied, Hammer (nonmarket institutions)

REFERENCES

1. A. A. ALCHIAN, K. J. ARROW, AND W. M. CAPRON, *An Economic Analysis of the Market for Scientists and Engineers*, RAND RM-2190-RC. Santa Monica 1958.

2. M. ALLAIS, "Géneralisation des théories de l'équilibre économique général et du rendement social au cas du risque," in Centre National de la Recherche Scientifique, *Econometrie,* Paris 1953, pp. 1-20.

3. O. W. ANDERSON AND STAFF OF THE NATIONAL OPINION RESEARCH CENTER, *Voluntary Health Insurance in Two Cities.* Cambridge, Mass. 1957.

4. K. J. ARROW, "Economic Welfare and the Allocation of Resources for Invention," in Nat. Bur. Econ. Research, *The Role and Direction of Inventive Activity: Economic and Social Factors,* Princeton 1962, pp. 609-25.

5. ———, "Les rôle des valeurs boursières pour la répartition la meilleure des risques," in Centre National de la Recherche Scientifique, *Econometrie,* Paris 1953, pp. 41-46.

6. F. M. BATOR, "The Anatomy of Market Failure," *Quart. Jour. Econ.* Aug. 1958, *72,* 351-79.

7. E. BAUDIER, "L'introduction du temps dans la théorie de l'équilibre général," *Les Cahiers Economiques,* Dec. 1959, 9-16.

8. W. J. BAUMOL, *Welfare Economics and the Theory of the State.* Cambridge, Mass. 1952.

9. K. BORCH, "The Safety Loading of Reinsurance Premiums," *Skandinavisk Aktuariehdskrift,* 1960, pp. 163-84.

10. J. M. BUCHANAN AND G. TULLOCK, *The Calculus of Consent.* Ann Arbor 1962.

11. G. DEBREU, "Une économique de l'incertain," *Economie Appliquée,* 1960, *13,* 111-16.

12. ———, *Theory of Values.* New York 1959.

13. R. DUBOS, "Medical Utopias," *Daedalus,* 1959, *88,* 410-24.

14. M. G. FIELD, *Doctor and Patient in Soviet Russia.* Cambridge, Mass. 1957.

15. MILTON FRIEDMAN, "The Methodology of Positive Economics," in *Essays in Positive Economics,* Chicago 1953, pp. 3-43.

16. ——— AND S. S. KUZNETS, *Income from Independent Professional Practice.* Nat. Bur. Econ. Research, New York 1945.

17. R. A. KESSEL, "Price Discrimination in Medicine," *Jour. Law and Econ.,* 1958, *1,* 20-53.

18. T. C. KOOPMANS, "Allocation of Resources and the Price System," in *Three Essays on the State of Economic Science,* New York 1957, pp. 1-120.

19. I. M. D. LITTLE, *A Critique of Welfare Economics.* Oxford 1950.

20. SELMA MUSHKIN, "Towards a Definition of Health Economics," *Public Health Reports,* 1958, *73,* 785-93.

21. R. R. NELSON, "The Simple Economics of Basic Scientific Research," *Jour. Pol. Econ.,* June 1959, *67,* 297-306.

22. T. PARSONS, *The Social System.* Glencoe 1951.

23. M. J. PECK AND F. M. SCHERER, *The Weapons Acquisition Process: An Economic Analysis.* Div. of Research, Graduate School of Business, Harvard University, Boston 1962.

24. T. C. Schelling, *The Strategy of Conflict*. Cambridge, Mass. 1960.
25. A. K. Shapiro, "A Contribution to a History of the Placebo Effect," *Behavioral Science*, 1960, *5*, 109-35.
26. H. M. Somers and A. R. Somers, *Doctors, Patients, and Health Insurance*. The Brookings Institution, Washington 1961.
27. C. L. Stevenson, *Ethics and Language*. New Haven 1945.
28. U. S. Department of Health, Education and Welfare, *Physicians for a Growing America*, Public Health Service Publication No. 709, Oct. 1959.

Appendix

On Optimal Insurance Policies

The two propositions about the nature of optimal insurance policies asserted in Section IV.B above will be proved here.

Proposition 1. If an insurance company is willing to offer any insurance policy against loss desired by the buyer at a premium which depends only on the policy's actuarial value, then the policy chosen by a risk-averting buyer will take the form of 100 per cent coverage above a deductible minimum.

Note: The premium will, in general, exceed the actuarial value; it is only required that two policies with the same actuarial value will be offered by the company for the same premium.

Proof: Let W be the initial wealth of the individual, X his loss, a random variable, $I(X)$ the amount of insurance paid if loss X occurs, P the premium, and $Y(X)$ the wealth of the individual after paying the premium, incurring the loss, and receiving the insurance benefit.

$$(1) \qquad Y(X) = W - P - X + I(X).$$

The individual values alternative policies by the expected utility of his final wealth position, $Y(X)$. Let $U(y)$ be the utility of final wealth, y; then his aim is to maximize,

$$(2) \qquad E\{U[Y(X)]\},$$

where the symbol, E, denotes mathematical expectation.

An insurance payment is necessarily nonnegative, so the insurance policy must satisfy the condition,

$$(3) \qquad I(X) \geq 0 \quad \text{for all} \quad X.$$

If a policy is optimal, it must in particular be better in the sense of the criterion (2), than any other policy with the same actuarial expectation, $E[I(X)]$. Consider a policy that pays some positive amount of insurance at one level of loss, say X_1, but which permits the final wealth at some other loss level, say X_2, to be lower than that corresponding to X_1. Then, it is intuitively obvious that a risk-averter would prefer an alternative policy with the same actuarial value which would offer slightly less protection for losses in the neighborhood of X_1 and slightly higher protection for those in the neighborhood of X_2, since risk aversion implies that the marginal utility of $Y(X)$ is greater when $Y(X)$ is smaller: hence, the original policy cannot be optimal.

To prove this formally, let $I_1(X)$ be the original policy, with $I_1(X) > 0$ and $Y_1(X_1) > Y_2(X_2)$, where $Y_1(X)$ is defined in terms of $I_1(X)$ by (I). Choose δ sufficiently small so that,

(4) $I_1(X) > 0$ for $X_1 \leq X \leq X_1 + \delta$,

(5) $Y_1(X') < Y_1(X)$ for $X_2 \leq X' \leq X_2 + \delta$, $X_1 \leq X \leq X_1 + \delta$.

(This choice of δ is possible if the functions $I_1(X)$, $Y_1(X)$ are continuous; this can be proved to be true for the optimal policy, and therefore we need only consider this case.)

Let π_1 be the probability that the loss, X, lies in the interval $\langle X_1, X_1+\delta \rangle$, π_2 the probability that X lies in the interval $\langle X_2, X_2+\delta \rangle$. From (4) and (5) we can choose $\epsilon > 0$ and sufficiently small so that,

(6) $I_1(X) - \pi_2\epsilon \geq 0$ for $X_1 \leq X \leq X_1 + \delta$,

(7) $Y_1(X') + \pi_1\epsilon < Y_1(X) - \pi_2\epsilon$

$$\text{for}   X_2 \leq X' \leq X_2 + \delta,   X_1 \leq X \leq X_1 + \delta.$$

Now define a new insurance policy, $I_2(X)$, which is the same as $I_1(X)$ except that it is smaller by $\pi_2\epsilon$ in the interval from X_1 to $X_1+\delta$ and larger by $\pi_1\epsilon$ in the interval from X_2 to $X_2+\delta$. From (6), $I_2(X) \geq 0$ everywhere, so that (3) is satisfied. We will show that $E[I_1(X)] = E[I_2(X)]$ and that $I_2(X)$ yields the higher expected utility, so that $I_1(X)$ is not optimal.

Note that $I_2(X) - I_1(X)$ equals $-\pi_2\epsilon$ for $X_1 \leq X \leq X_1+\delta$, $\pi_1\epsilon$ for $X_2 \leq X \leq X_2+\delta$, and 0 elsewhere. Let $\phi(X)$ be the density of the random variable X. Then,

$$E[I_2(X) - I_1(X)] = \int_{X_1}^{X_1+\delta} [I_2(X) - I_1(X)]\phi(X)dX$$

$$+ \int_{X_2}^{X_2+\delta} [I_2(X) - I_1(X)]dX$$

$$= (-\pi_2\epsilon) \int_{X_1}^{X_1+\delta} \phi(X)dX + (\pi_1\epsilon) \int_{X_2}^{X_2+\delta} \phi(X)dX$$

$$= -(\pi_2\epsilon)\pi_1 + (\pi_1\epsilon)\pi_2 = 0,$$

so that the two policies have the same actuarial value and, by assumption, the same premium.

Define $Y_2(X)$ in terms of $I_2(X)$ by (1). Then $Y_2(X) - Y_1(X) = I_2(X) - I_1(X)$. From (7),

(8) $Y_1(X') < Y_2(X') < Y_2(X) < Y_1(X)$

$$\text{for}   X_2 \leq X' \leq X_2 + \delta,   X_1 \leq X \leq X_1 + \delta.$$

Since $Y_1(X) - Y_2(X) = 0$ outside the intervals $\langle X_1, X_1+\delta \rangle$, $\langle X_2, X_2+\delta \rangle$, we can write,

$$(9) \quad E\{U[Y_2(X)] - U[Y_1(X)]\} = \int_{X_1}^{X_1+\delta} \{U[Y_2(X)] - U[Y_1(X)]\}\phi(X)dX$$

$$+ \int_{X_2}^{X_2+\delta} \{U[Y_2(X)] - U[Y_1(X)]\}\phi(X)dX.$$

By the Mean Value Theorem, for any given value of X,

$$(10) \quad U[Y_2(X)] - U[Y_1(X)] = U'[Y(X)][Y_2(X) - Y_1(X)]$$

$$= U'[Y(X)][I_2(X) - I_1(X)],$$

where $Y(X)$ lies between $Y_1(X)$ and $Y_2(X)$. From (8),

$$Y(X') < Y(X) \quad \text{for} \quad X_2 \leq X' \leq X_2 + \delta, \quad X_1 \leq X \leq X_1 + \delta,$$

and, since $U'(y)$ is a diminishing function of y for a risk-averter,

$$U'[Y(X')] > U'[Y(X)]$$

or, equivalently, for some number u,

$$(11) \qquad U'[Y(X')] > u \quad \text{for} \quad X_2 \leq X' \leq X_2 + \delta,$$

$$U'[Y(X)] < u \quad \text{for} \quad X_1 \leq X \leq X_1 + \delta.$$

Now substitute (10) into (9),

$$E\{U[Y_2(X)] - U[Y_1(X)]\} = -\pi_2\epsilon \int_{X_1}^{X_1+\delta} U'[Y(X)]\phi(X)dX$$

$$+ \pi_1\epsilon \int_{X_2}^{X_2+\delta} U'[Y(X)]\phi(X)dX.$$

From (11), it follows that,

$$E\{U[Y_2(X)] - U[Y_1(X)]\} > -\pi_2\epsilon u\pi_1 + \pi_1\epsilon u\pi_2 = 0,$$

so that the second policy is preferred.

It has thus been shown that a policy cannot be optimal if, for some X_1 and X_2, $I(X_1) > 0$, $Y(X_1) > Y(X_2)$. This may be put in a different form: Let Y_{min} be the minimum value taken on by $Y(X)$ under the optimal policy; then we must have $I(X) = 0$ if $Y(X) > Y_{min}$. In other words, a minimum final wealth level is set; if the loss would not bring wealth below this level, no benefit is paid, but if it would, then the benefit is sufficient to bring up the final wealth position to the stipulated minimum. This is, of course, precisely a description of 100 per cent coverage for loss above a deductible.

We turn to the second proposition. It is now supposed that the insurance company, as well as the insured, is a risk-averter; however, there are no administrative or other costs to be covered beyond protection against loss.

Proposition 2. If the insured and the insurer are both risk-averters and there are no costs other than coverage of losses, then any nontrivial Pareto-optimal policy, $I(X)$, as a function of the loss, X, must have the property, $0 < dI/dX < 1$.

That is, any increment in loss will be partly but not wholly compensated by the insurance company; this type of provision is known as coinsurance. Proposition 2 is due to Borch [9, Sec. 2]; we give here a somewhat simpler proof.

Proof: Let $U(y)$ be the utility function of the insured, $V(z)$ that of the insurer. Let W_0 and W_1 be the initial wealths of the two, respectively. In this case, we let $I(X)$ be the insurance benefits less the premium; for the present purpose, this is the only significant magnitude (since the premium is independent of X, this definition does not change the value of dI/dX). The final wealth positions of the insured and insurer are:

$$
\begin{aligned}
Y(X) &= W_0 - X + I(X), \\
Z(X) &= W_1 - I(X),
\end{aligned}
\tag{12}
$$

respectively. Any given insurance policy then defines expected utilities, $u = E\{U[Y(X)]\}$ and $v = E\{V[Z(X)]\}$, for the insured and insurer, respectively. If we plot all points (u, v) obtained by considering all possible insurance policies, the resulting expected-utility-possibility set has a boundary that is convex to the northeast. To see this, let $I_1(X)$ and $I_2(X)$ be any two policies, and let (u_1, v_1) and (u_2, v_2) be the corresponding points in the two-dimensional expected-utility-possibility set. Let a third insurance policy, $I(X)$, be defined as the average of the two given ones,

$$
I(X) = (\tfrac{1}{2})I_1(X) + (\tfrac{1}{2})I_2(X),
$$

for each X. Then, if $Y(X)$, $Y_1(X)$, and $Y_2(X)$ are the final wealth positions of the insured, and $Z(X)$, $Z_1(X)$, and $Z_2(X)$ those of the insurer for each of the three policies, $I(X)$, $I_1(X)$, and $I_2(X)$, respectively,

$$
\begin{aligned}
Y(X) &= (\tfrac{1}{2})Y_1(X) + (\tfrac{1}{2})Y_2(X), \\
Z(X) &= (\tfrac{1}{2})Z_1(X) + (\tfrac{1}{2})Z_2(X),
\end{aligned}
$$

and, because both parties have diminishing marginal utility,

$$
\begin{aligned}
U[Y(X)] &\geq (\tfrac{1}{2})U[Y_1(X)] + (\tfrac{1}{2})U[Y_2(X)], \\
V[Z(X)] &\geq (\tfrac{1}{2})V[Z_1(X)] + (\tfrac{1}{2})V[Z_2(X)].
\end{aligned}
$$

Since these statements hold for all X, they also hold when expectations are taken. Hence, there is a point (u, v) in the expected-utility-possibility set for which $u \geq (\tfrac{1}{2})u_1 + (\tfrac{1}{2})u_2$, $v \geq (\tfrac{1}{2})v_1 + (\tfrac{1}{2})v_2$. Since this statement holds for every pair of points (u_1, y_1) and (u_2, v_2) in the expected-utility-possibility set, and in particular for pairs of points on the northeast boundary, it follows that the boundary must be convex to the northeast.

From this, in turn, it follows that any given Pareto-optimal point (i.e., any point on the northeast boundary) can be obtained by maximizing a linear function, $\alpha u + \beta v$, with suitably chosen α and β nonnegative and at least one positive, over the expected-utility-possibility set. In other words, a Pareto-optimal insurance policy, $I(X)$, is one which maximizes,

$$
\alpha E\{U[Y(X)]\} + \beta E\{V[Z(X)]\} = E\{\alpha U[Y(X)] + \beta V[Z(X)]\},
$$

ARROW: UNCERTAINTY AND MEDICAL CARE 973

for some $\alpha \geq 0$, $\beta \geq 0$, $\alpha > 0$ or $\beta > 0$. To maximize this expectation, it is obviously sufficient to maximize:

$$(13) \qquad\qquad \alpha U[Y(X)] + \beta V[Z(X)],$$

with respect to $I(X)$, for each X. Since, for given X, it follows from (12) that,

$$dY(X)/dI(X) = 1, \qquad dZ(X)/dI(X) = -1,$$

it follows by differentiation of (13) that $I(X)$ is the solution of the equation,

$$(14) \qquad\qquad \alpha U'[Y(X)] - \beta V'[Z(X)] = 0.$$

The cases $\alpha = 0$ or $\beta = 0$ lead to obvious trivialities (one party simply hands over all his wealth to the other), so we assume $\alpha > 0$, $\beta > 0$. Now differentiate (14) with respect to X and use the relations, derived from (12),

$$dY/dX = (dI/dX) - 1, \qquad dZ/dX = -(dI/dX).$$

$$\alpha U''[Y(X)][(dI/dX) - 1] + \beta V''[Z(X)](dI/dX) = 0,$$

or

$$dI/dX = \alpha U''[Y(X)]/\{\alpha U''[Y(X)] + \beta V''[Z(X)]\}.$$

Since $U''[Y(X)] < 0$, $V''[Z(X)] < 0$ by the hypothesis that both parties are risk-averters, Proposition 2 follows.

PART I

Supply, Demand,

and Health Care

Competition

MICHAEL CHERNEW

■ *General Equilibrium and Marketability*

in the Health Care Industry

Kenneth Arrow's 1963 article, "Uncertainty and the Welfare Economics of Medical Care," has become a seminal essay in the field of health economics. Its fundamental contribution is a detailed and thoughtful comparison of the deviations between the workings of markets for medical care and the competitive ideal. As Arrow demonstrates, a variety of factors prevents the medical care market from yielding an optimal allocation of resources. Prime among those factors is the "lack of marketability" for many products. Essentially, certain products that would improve the allocation of resources if they existed are not available for purchase (nonmarketable).

Arrow provides a complementary analysis of how "nonmarket social institutions" may arise to fill the gaps left by the lack of markets for certain products and thereby improve resource allocation. By *nonmarket social institutions*, he largely means norms of behavior that deviate from those typically observed in a competitive model.

This essay examines nonmarketability in the health care sector. The first section outlines Arrow's notion of general equilibrium in the health care sector and the problem of nonmarketability. The second section examines the markets (and market failures) in the early 1960s and how those market failures can be traced to a lack of markets for several types of products. It concludes with a discussion of how nonmarket institutions could be viewed as filling the gaps for those missing markets. The final two sections discuss how, since 1963, there has been an expansion in markets and an associated change in the role of nonmarket institutions. The central thesis of this essay is that market and nonmarket institutions have a symbiotic relationship, with nonmarket institutions serving to improve resource allocation in areas where markets fail or do not exist. As the role of the market has expanded, the role of social institutions has changed to fill new gaps that have arisen in the increasingly market-oriented environment.

ARROW'S GENERAL EQUILIBRIUM ORIENTATION AND
THE PROBLEM OF NONMARKETABILITY

Much of Arrow's acclaim reflects his exposition of the theory of general equilibrium. In economics, *general equilibrium* refers to the situation in which all markets (consumer and producer markets as well as markets for inputs such as labor and capital) are in equilibrium (namely, supply meets demand). It is largely a theory in which prices adjust to achieve this balance, and the theory recognizes the interconnection between markets.

The theory of general equilibrium is founded on decentralized action by consumers and firms, with consumers maximizing their well-being (utility) and firms maximizing profits. In standard models, individuals are assumed to be perfectly informed. Perfect information does not mean that everyone knows what the future will hold, only that they know the probabilities with which different events may occur. Outcomes are uncertain, but individuals are not uninformed (or misinformed). General equilibrium models also assume that, when faced with a set of prices, individuals (and firms) are cognitively capable of maximizing their well-being through their behavior. A variety of other assumptions, such as those that relate to market power (or lack thereof), complete the general equilibrium model but are less salient for this discussion.

As Arrow notes in his essay, much of the appeal of the general equilibrium model relates to its implications for economic efficiency. Specifically, in general equilibrium settings two theorems of welfare economics link optimal resource allocation and competition. First, if a competitive equilibrium exists, it will be optimal; second, if we do not like the particular competitive equilibrium that arises from the market, we could reallocate incomes to achieve, through competition, any other optimal allocation we desired.

Such an analysis relies heavily on one's definition of optimal resource allocation, and Arrow is careful to introduce early in his essay the standards he uses and their precise meaning. Specifically, he adopts the economic concept of *Pareto optimality*, which defines an *optimal allocation* of resources as one in which no one person can be made better off without making at least one person worse off. He is careful to note that this is a weak definition of optimality. Many such allocations may exist, and though some value judgments would be required, society may not view each of them as equally desirable.

Arrow recognized several prerequisites for competitive equilibrium. Among the key requirements is that markets exist for all of the relevant goods and services (all relevant goods and services are marketable). Arrow views nonmarketability essentially as synonymous with a lack of markets. Marketability is necessary if individuals are to be able to match their purchases to their preferences, a fundamental feature of optimality. Without markets, there are commodities that would enhance welfare if produced, but they are not produced.

Arrow recognized that in the competitive ideal, general equilibrium would be characterized by a very rich set of markets. In the absence of this rich set of markets, Arrow contended that nonmarket institutions would develop so that resource allocation would come closer to the competitive ideal than would otherwise occur if only the incomplete set of markets were relied upon.

MARKETS, MARKETABILITY, AND THE ROLE OF NONMARKET
INSTITUTIONS IN THE EARLY 1960S

The medical care market, as outlined by Arrow, really comprises two distinct, but interrelated, markets — the market for health care services and the market for health insurance. Arrow recognized that risk-averse individuals desire insurance against the financial and nonfinancial consequences of illness. Individuals purchasing health insurance products in the early 1960s typically purchased policies that reimbursed them for some portion of their expenditures. In this dominant insurance model of the time, the insurer did not interfere with the patients' choice of physician or the recommended treatment. Payment from insurer to physician was on a fee-for-service (FFS) basis.

This system could mitigate the financial risks associated with illness, at least for those with some insurance coverage. Yet several market failures were apparent. First, many individuals lacked coverage, a suboptimal outcome in a general equilibrium model if one assumes individuals are risk averse. Second, even insured individuals were not insured against the nonfinancial consequences of illness or treatment. Third, the system of insurance encouraged medical care prices and utilization to rise above their optimal levels (i.e., prices rising above marginal costs and utilization rising above that where the marginal benefit equals marginal cost). The phenomenon of consumption rising above optimal levels is commonly referred to as *moral hazard* (Pauly 1968; Manning et al. 1987; Newhouse 1992).

Each of these market failures could be traced to a gap in markets (a lack of marketability). Before discussing missing markets, it is important to recognize that the number of potential markets is enormous. The ramifications associated with the lack of any particular market depend on both the number of consumers who would benefit from the existence of that market and the ability of other markets to approximate outcomes that would arise had markets been complete. For example, the lack of a market for an insurance product with an 18 percent coinsurance rate for office visits might not be a big deal if not many people would have wanted such a policy or if policies with, say, 20 percent coinsurance rate existed.

In his analysis of the health care sector, Arrow identified several important market gaps. First, because the health care environment is particularly complex, characterized by considerable uncertainty, complete markets would imply that markets must exist for *contingent contracts*. These contracts would allow the consumer to purchase prespecified products, at prespecified prices, from prespecified vendors in different states of the world.

One type of contingent contract would involve the commitment to purchase health care goods and services only in certain states of the world. For example, a contract to provide open-heart surgery (or the financial equivalent), if, at some later date, one has a heart attack, would be one such contingent contract. If there were meaningful differences in open-heart surgery facilities, the contract would specify which facility would provide the service. In theory, widespread use of contingent contracts would reduce the price of services because individuals could shop for providers at a point in time when they were price sensitive as opposed to once they were ill and aware that insurance would share the cost. The contract would also limit excessive utilization because individuals could commit to the amount of care they desired when purchasing insurance, thereby avoiding insurance-induced excess consumption.

Another type of contingent contract would involve purchasing a warrant to compensate the patient for nonfinancial consequences of illness. This includes health status changes that cannot be remedied by medical care as well as failures of treatment to achieve intended outcomes. Warrants to insure against bad treatment outcomes are analogous to contingent contracts to mitigate the financial cost of illness. Ideally, a portion of the cost of treatment failure would be transferred to physicians and thereby improve incentives. Of course, given the importance of health, it is difficult to see how markets for such warrants could exist to transfer all of the risk from consumers to other parties. In the absence of markets for warrants, risk-averse individuals are forced to bear the risk associated with poor health and treatment outcomes.

In general, markets for contingent contracts do not exist, at least not at the level of detail envisioned by Arrow in a general equilibrium setting. The lack of marketability reflects the vast number of possible contingent contracts that would be required and the tremendous informational burden that writing, verifying, and enforcing those contracts would entail. Moreover, the transactions costs associated with individuals purchasing such insurance contracts, prior to illness, for care in the eventuality of any possible disease would be prohibitive.

A second type of market gap, which, along with excessive prices and moral hazard, deters insurance purchase, involves the absence from the market of certain insurance policies that would ideally be available. Considerable research, largely in the mid-1970s, examined the consequences of the asymmetric information regarding consumer risk and built on the basic outline contained in Arrow's article (see Rothschild and Stiglitz 1976; Wilson 1977; Cave 1985). The work in this area emphasizes that free entry into a market with asymmetric information limits the set of policies available. Certain standard products will not be sold, at least not at attractive prices.

This gap in markets arises because individuals can sort themselves in insurance markets so that relatively low-risk individuals separate from high-risk individuals in the insurance pool through their actions or through those of insurers. The process of sorting is referred to as *adverse selection* and arises because of the inability of insurers to assess enrollee risk. Specifically, individuals may have a better sense than the insurer if they are relatively high risk or relatively low risk. Low-risk individuals will try to avoid plans that attract high-risk individuals. In markets where the process of adverse selection is important, under certain conditions, equilibrium may not exist. Under other conditions it may exist, but certain groups of individuals may receive no coverage or incomplete coverage. In either case, Arrow notes the outcome is suboptimal. A recent summary of the empirical literature suggests that the quantitative impact of adverse selection is large (Cutler and Zeckhauser 2000).

A third important market gap arises because many types of information are not marketable. Lack of information is central to many of Arrow's arguments. In ideal conditions, information would be treated as a commodity in general equilibrium models. Imperfect information exists at all levels of the market, but Arrow emphasizes imperfect information among consumers. Prior to becoming ill, individuals may be unaware of the probabilities that they will contract various ailments and their associated consequences. After falling ill, patients may be unaware of the various treatment options and associated probabilities of various outcomes. They may be unaware of the natural course of the disease (which may be stochastic), and they may be unaware of the quality of their physician. In an ideal competitive environment, information would be marketable so that individuals could purchase the desired information.

Yet Arrow recognizes, for a variety of reasons, markets for information violate standard assumptions regarding products. For example, information has some of the properties of public goods. Even conceptualizing these markets (and associated demand curves) is often challenging, because of, as Arrow notes, "the elusive character of information as a commodity" (946). This lack of markets for information is a marketability problem. It contributes to the inability of other markets, such as those for contingent contracts, to exist and contributes to the adverse selection problem.

Given the marketability problems in the health care sector, Arrow contends that nonmarket norms and institutions arise to fill the gaps. Perhaps the most important of the nonmarket responses is the physician code of behavior. Because warrants are not marketable, patients must place extraordinary trust in their physician, both because the physician may not have the ideal incentives and because the patient is not insured against treatment failure. Arrow sees the code of physician ethics as an outgrowth of the need for trust in the physician-patient relationship, though others, such as Paul Starr (1982) and Charles D. Weller (1984), have questioned Arrow's interpretation of the reasons for the development of these ethics. This code of ethics results in unique expectations of physician behavior. These nonmarket standards of behavior and their extraordinary importance in this sector represent the most fundamental deviation of health care markets from other markets and, in part, fill gaps arising due to the absence of a market for the insurance against poor treatment outcomes.

The code of physician ethics, in theory, could mitigate problems associated with a lack of markets for contingent contracts for health care services, specifically over utilization and excessive prices. If physicians acted as perfect agents for their patients, utilization would be optimal, with physicians prescribing care based on what the patients would have desired at the time of insurance purchase, and pricing would be based on marginal cost.

Interestingly, the principles of physician conduct shaped the norms of behavior in the insurance industry, which tended to prevent marketing of products that could minimize the market gaps associated with the lack of contingent contract markets for health care services. Specifically, insurers did not interfere with the physician practice patterns and did not steer patients to particular providers. Any other set of norms for the insurance industry would have conflicted with the preeminent role played by physicians and perhaps threatened the central role of trust in the physician-patient relationship. In essence, the nonmarket norms that addressed, in part, the lack of markets for warrants resulted in norms of behavior in the insurance market that limited the ability of markets to address the nonmarketability of contingent contracts for medical care.

Arrow notes that other nonmarket norms existed as well, which could be interpreted as filling market gaps. For example, he indicates that for the purposes of price setting, market forces tend to be replaced by direct institutional control, but he does not elaborate. Additionally, nonphysician participants in health care markets, most importantly hospitals and insurers, tended to be organized as nonprofit institutions. Nonprofit status in these areas of the health care industry addressed many of the same issues that relate to the absence of markets for contingent contracts, such as trust, excessive use, and excessive pricing. For example, in theory nonprofit status reduced incentives for hospitals to take advantage of consumers for a profit.

In other cases, government intervention may be the most relevant response to a lack of markets. For example, government action may be the most effective nonmarket response to adverse selection because, as Michael Rothschild and Joseph Stiglitz point out, decentralized insurance markets are inherently subject to adverse selection in the face of asymmetric information. The ability to avoid adverse selection would require cooperation of all insurance carriers, and there is no market mechanism to prevent entry of insurers to provide products desired by low-risk consumers.

In fact, in the period following publication of Arrow's article, several government programs were implemented in the United States to address the lack of insurance coverage among selected subpopulations. These programs, Medicare and Medicaid, form the foundation of publicly provided health insurance to this day and remain among the most important government interventions in health care markets.

THE PRIVATE SECTOR RESPONDS—EXPANDING MARKETABILITY AND THE PRODUCT SPACE

Despite Arrow's analysis regarding how nonmarket norms compensate for the lack of markets, the shortcomings of these norms were becoming ever more apparent even when Arrow's piece was published. Specifically, concern about health care cost growth was substantial, even at what now seems like relatively low levels of spending when compared to GDP. Health services research since the 1960s has demonstrated widespread heterogeneity in practice patterns (Wennberg, Barnes, and Zubkoff 1982; Wennberg and Gittelsohn 1982) and substantial inappropriate use of health care services (Brook et al. 1990; Chassin et al. 1987).

Although Arrow emphasized the importance of nonmarket norms in the health care sector, it would be misleading to imply that he felt that these norms alone would achieve optimal outcomes. The tension is apparent in his discussion of prices, which recognizes that it is unlikely that medical prices were set at profit maximizing levels, but does not go so far as to contend they are set at optimal levels. Despite nonprofit norms, Arrow notes that a conflict of interest frequently arose because Blue Cross plans, which represented about 40 percent of policies, were controlled by physicians. Blue Shield plans were controlled by hospitals.

Similarly, Arrow discusses the professional relationship between patient and physician as a check on moral hazard, yet he notes that this is an imperfect check and that there are many reasons why physicians might prescribe more than is economically ideal. In fact, the ethos described by Arrow, that financial considerations should not matter in care delivery decisions, sets a threshold such that all care that provides any value should be delivered. This threshold differs from the economically optimal one.

In the face of these market shortcomings, the health care system experienced almost continual reform and evolution throughout the period following Arrow's article. Many countries, faced with the same shortcomings, adopted, at various times, nationalized systems to address these issues. Yet, for the most part in the United States, a broader, national system has been politically infeasible.

It is from this environment that managed care emerged. Although several HMOs had existed for years (referred to by Arrow as prepaid or closed panel plans), their enrollment and presence grew rapidly following the relaxation of entry barriers. Largely, these plans were viewed as cost containment devices, although many plans would argue that, through the integration of care, they could improve quality. The system of managed care plans competing against one another, often with various ground rules specified, was labeled *managed competition*.

The idea behind managed competition was essentially that competition in insurance markets could generate competitive outcomes in the market for medical services by forcing health care providers to compete for contracts with the managed care plans. The managed care plans would incorporate various strategies to control moral hazard or secure reduced prices, and then these savings would be passed along through competition in the insurance market. Had nonmarket institutions and norms constrained costs, perhaps managed competition would not have grown so rapidly.

In the context of Arrow's model of incomplete markets, the managed care market could be viewed as a market for moral hazard control (and price shopping). In many ways the system of competing managed care plans could be viewed as an approximation to the missing markets for contingent contracts for medical care. Managed care plans allow individuals to commit at the time of insurance purchase, albeit crudely, to the set of services that they will consume if they become ill, and their prices. Consumers do not make the commitment for each illness and severity level separately as they would with a complete set of contingent contract markets, but instead make a commitment to a *process of care delivery and rationing* that will relate to broad illness and service categories. The development of new managed care products designed to address moral hazard and prices could impact the extent of adverse selection as well. However, theoretical work is equivocal regarding the effects of managed care on adverse selection (Chernew and Frick 1999).

Numerous submarkets arose (or expanded) to support these plans. Several of these new markets represent *unbundling of services* that previously had been largely conceptualized as integrated into the insurance or provider function. For example, markets now exist for building provider networks, providing administrative services such as claims processing, and bearing risk. In some cases markets exist for insurance coverage that are disease specific, such as mental health carve outs, and in other cases markets exist to manage use of only selected types of services, for example, the market for pharmacy benefits management services. Markets for support services such as profiling physician practices, developing and disseminating care guidelines, and conducting utilization review also exist to support managed care efforts to reduce moral hazard. These products contribute to a diverse set of managed care plans, distinguished by how they manage utilization, share risk, and otherwise serve consumers. The diversity could be interpreted as reflecting variation among individuals in preferences for the exact type of contingent contracts that they would have purchased had those contracts been marketable.

To support the new set of markets, new demands for information have arisen, and these demands have generated markets for information that previously were relatively undeveloped. For example, markets for risk-adjustment software that can be used to mitigate adverse selection now exist. There are also markets for creating measures of health plan performance and markets for how these measures might be conveyed to consumers. There are markets to signal plan quality through accreditation of health plans and provider networks. Other markets exist for products that directly convey to consumers information about diseases and individual health care providers. Finally, there are markets for helping health plans and provider organizations generate the data to successfully provide the information demanded in the new markets.

MEDIATING EQUILIBRIUM—INTERACTION BETWEEN
MARKET AND NONMARKET FORCES

The norms that govern the markets in this new competitive environment are still developing. For example, physicians are often working for the insurer as well as the patient, generating a dual agency problem. Certainly in many cases profit maximizing norms exist, but nonmarket norms are also common. There is no hard and fast rule regarding when market or nonmarket institutions evolve. In general, markets fill voids where profit opportunities exist, provided that barriers to market activity can be overcome. Nonmarket institutions and norms evolve in response to needs not satisfied by the market, provided that actors exist to create these institutions and norms of behavior become accepted and can be sustained.

In some situations market and nonmarket norms and institutions can coexist in the same market and even compete against each other. For example, Richard A. Hirth (1999) outlines a model of the nursing home industry in which equilibrium includes both for-profit and nonprofit providers. Nonprofit nursing homes provide high-quality care and, in equilibrium, may limit the ability of for-profits to provide lower quality care. For-profit nursing homes may perform a similar function, disciplining nonprofits to keep costs down. In other cases, one type of behavior may drive out the other. For example, for-profits might drive out non-profits if consumers do not sufficiently value the nonprofit organizational form as a signal of quality. As Arrow's essay might foreshadow, the exact nature of equilibrium would depend on the extent of information and tastes in the market. Empirical evidence suggests that, at least in the hospital market, nonprofit facilities behave in a manner similar to for-profit facilities, perhaps because of competition between the sectors (Sloan 2000).

Despite the new market environment, many of the market gaps discussed by Arrow remain, and, as Arrow would suggest, nonmarket norms and institutions can be viewed as, in part, filling those gaps. Specifically, the new markets can be viewed as approximating markets for contingent contracts for care delivery, thereby addressing issues of moral hazard and excessive prices. Yet markets have not addressed the lack of markets for transferring the nonfinancial risk associated with poor health or treatment outcomes (warrants). Thus, the basic issue of trust outlined by Arrow has remained.

Physicians might not be perfect, but the public has hardly been willing to accept insurers, and the fragmented market system, as the socially responsible guardians of quality care. Most consumers have still been more willing to trust their physician than their insurer. As a result the nonprofit organizational form is heavily represented in many of the new markets, particularly those markets for information where trust is crucial.

In certain cases existing organizations have taken on new roles in which the norms of behavior are unclear. For example, large employers were among the major groups to develop a set of health plan quality indicators and have been central to the development of health plan report cards. Many large employers distribute measures of health plan performance to their employees during open enrollment, and many also evaluate the performance of health care providers such as hospitals. One might interpret the actions of these employers as reflecting a new norm of behavior that transcends the normally pure profit maximizing activities of their firm. Yet an alternative interpretation is that labor market concerns demand that employers take such actions and, in the long run, these activities are profit maximizing.

The federal government and nonprofit research foundations have also played an important role in bridging market gaps. For example, both have supported considerable efforts to learn, in a systematic way, which treatments are effective and how effective care can be encouraged. They have supported development of risk adjustment tools and supported development of mechanisms to measure and convey health plan quality to consumers. Both have also supported efforts to understand how policy variables affect outcomes and how markets function so that various market gaps can be filled and appropriate policy developed.

CONCLUSIONS

Arrow's 1963 essay rigorously outlined the shortcomings in the medical marketplace, including its lack of many important markets. Arrow posited that because of these market gaps, nonmarket institutions arose to compensate. In general these nonmarket institutions were a set of professional norms designed to assure, to some extent, that patients received adequate quality of care.

These institutions, however, were not able to prevent, and in fact have likely encouraged, the continual development of medical technology and associated rapid escalation in health care costs. The response to this, in the United States, has largely been an expansion of markets, particularly to address issues of excessive utilization and pricing.

Many observers have bemoaned this expansion of markets and the associated changes in institutions and behavioral norms. The fundamental issues of trust and information outlined by Arrow remain despite the much greater reliance on markets to allocate resources. Given the importance of health care to individuals and the fundamental issues raised by Arrow, the struggle to achieve a suitable resource allocation through a balance of market and nonmarket institutions seems likely to continue well into the future.

REFERENCES

Brook, Robert H., Rollo Park, Mark R. Chassin, David Solomon, Joan Keesey, and Jacqueline Kosecoff. 1990. Predicting the Appropriate Use of Carotid Endarterectomy, Upper Gastrointestinal Endoscopy, and Coronary Angiography. *New England Journal of Medicine* 323(17): 1173–1177.

Cave, Jonathan A. K. 1985. Subsidy Equilibrium and Multiple-Option Insurance Markets. Advances in Health Economics and Health Services Research 6: 27–45.

Chassin, Mark R., Jacqueline Kosecoff, R. E. Park, Constance M. Winslow, Katherine M. Constance, Katherine L. Kahn, Nancy J. Merrick, Joan J. Keesey, Arline Fink, David H. Solomon, and Robert H. Brook. 1987. Does Inappropriate Use Explain Geographic Variations in the Use of Health Care Services? A Study of Three Procedures. N-2748-CWF/HF/HCFA/PMT/RWJ. Santa Monica, CA: Rand Corporation.

Chernew, Michael E., and Kevin D. Frick. 1999. The Impact of Managed Care on the Equilibrium in Health Insurance Markets. *Journal of Health Economics* 18: 573–592.

Cutler, David M., and Richard J. Zeckhauser. 2000. The Anatomy of Health Insurance. In *Handbook of Health Economics*, vol. 1A, ed. Anthony J. Culyer and Joseph P. Newhouse, 564–643. Amsterdam: Elsevier.

Hirth, Richard A. 1999. Consumer Information and Competition between Nonprofit and For-profit Nursing Homes. *Journal of Health Economics* 18: 219–240.

Manning, Willard G., Joseph P. Newhouse, Naihua Duan, Emmett B. Keeler, Arleen Leibowitz, and M. Susan Marquis, M. Susan. 1987. Health Insurance and the Demand for

Medical Care: Evidence from a Randomized Experiment. *American Economic Review* 77(3): 251–277.

Newhouse, Joseph P. 1992. Medical Care Costs: How Much Welfare Loss? *Journal of Economic Perspectives* 6(3): 3–21.

Pauly, Mark V. 1968. The Economics of Moral Hazard. *American Economic Review* 58(3): 231–237.

Rothschild, Michael, and Joseph Stiglitz. 1976. Equilibrium in Competitive Insurance Markets: An Essay on the Economics of Imperfect Information. *Quarterly Journal of Economics* 80: 629–649.

Sloan, Frank A. 2000. Not-for-profit Ownership and Hospital Behavior. In *Handbook of Health Economics*, vol. 1B, ed. Anthony J. Culyer and Joseph P. Newhouse. Amsterdam: Elsevier.

Starr, Paul. 1982. Transformation of Defeat: The Changing Objectives of National Health Insurance, 1915–1980. *American Journal of Public Health* 72(1): 78–88.

Weller, Charles D. 1984. "Free Choice" as a Restraint of Trade in American Health Care Delivery and Insurance. *Iowa Law Review* 69(5): 1351–1378.

Wennberg, John E., Benjamin A. Barnes, and Michael A. Zubkoff. 1982. Professional Uncertainty and the Problem of Supplier-Induced Demand. *Social Science and Medicine* 16: 811–824.

Wennberg, John E., and Alan Gittelsohn. 1982. Variations in Medical Care among Small Areas. *Scientific American* 246(4): 120–133.

Wilson, Charles. 1977. A Model of Insurance Markets with Incomplete Information. *Journal of Economic Theory* 16: 167–207.

FRANK A. SLOAN

■ Arrow's Concept of the Health Care Consumer:

A Forty-Year Retrospective

ARROW'S CONCEPT OF THE CONSUMER OF MEDICAL CARE

The consumer of medical care is in a unique situation for several reasons. First, in general, the consumer is not well informed about health and medical care, certainly much less well informed than are physicians. Many, if not most, medical encounters are initiated, at least in part, for the explicit purpose of obtaining health information. In contrast to their roles in markets for most goods and services, given their lack of information, it appears that people in their roles as medical care consumers have no well-formed preferences. If people had the necessary amount of information to make themselves fully informed, patients would have "as good or nearly as good understanding of the utility of the product as the producer" (Arrow 1963: 951).

Second, demand for care is probabilistic depending on the person's health state, which is also probabilistic. Thus, although some consumption, such as physical exams, can be planned, demand for care following health shocks, such as heart attacks, cannot be planned before the shocks occur. Prior to treatment, consumers may be faced with choices that have important consequences for either life or death or good quality of life versus a life of disability without having sufficient time or emotional stamina for making adequate decisions. When health shocks occur, the consumer is likely not to be well positioned to search for quality and price among sellers. This set of problems would occur even if consumers were generally well informed about health and medical care but lacked specific information for dealing with a particular health crisis.

Third, many consumption decisions, such as purchase of food and even housing, are repeated events. Therefore, consumers can learn from experience, even if their initial purchase decisions of the commodity are not based on good information. These, in terminology developed much more recently, are *experience goods*.

By contrast, there is a class of goods and services of which only a one-time purchase is made. These are *credence goods*.[1] Consumption decisions about these goods cannot be made on the basis of experience. Rather, one needs to rely on experience of others (reputation) or trust in the seller (professional norms). For example, each of us has only one gallbladder. Once the gallbladder has been removed surgically, there is no possibility for repeating the consumption decision. By contrast, physicians and, to continue the example, general surgeons perform their tasks repeatedly, giving them an absolute informational advantage vis-à-vis the consumer.

Through experience, physicians learn what does or does not work and under what conditions an intervention is successful. Consumers, especially given physical constraints on repetition of consumption, are not exposed to repeated trials and so cannot learn in this way. Therefore, although they too face uncertainty, physicians have an informational advantage not only in terms of having had professional education in medicine, but also because of extensive learning-by-doing.

Fourth, there are externalities in consumption. People are altruistic in the sense that they care not only about their own consumption of medical care, but also about consumption by others. These externalities transcend public health externalities from consumption of such services as immunizations. Fifth, the risk facing consumers is, at most, partially insurable. One can purchase insurance against loss of life and disability, but such insurance is not complete. In particular, for various reasons, there is no insurance for nonpecuniary loss from medical injuries such as loss from pain and suffering and or loss of consortium.

The special characteristics of health care markets have elicited various policy remedies. Asymmetric information between buyers and sellers, though not unique to this market, is sufficiently important here to have led to various institutional arrangements, including professional norms, licensure, and nonprofit institutions, in particular nonprofit hospitals. Externalities in consumption call for various cross subsidies, which may be public or private. The latter includes various forms of price discrimination, which may occur in this market because of externalities, and for other reasons.

Almost four decades have elapsed since publication of the Arrow article, and in that time, two types of changes have occurred. First, views about consumers in general and health care consumers in particular have evolved, and there is much more empirical evidence on this subject than was available in 1963. Second, the institutional context in which the health care consumer operates has changed.

I consider each in turn. To discuss the first, I devise a thought experiment in which institutional arrangements are frozen in time—as of 1963. In the latter, the institutional context, such arrangements are allowed to vary.

Throughout, I maintain the assumption that the individual consumer remains the relevant focus. An alternative to the individual consumer is a group, such as members of an employee group or union members. In many ways, the consumer group is better positioned in the health care marketplace than is the individual since it can take advantage of economies in group purchasing and in collecting information. Search costs on a per member basis are clearly lower, and knowledge about performance of particular hospitals and physicians can be acquired collectively and disseminated to individual group members. Yet, in the end, patients are heterogeneous in their likes and dislikes as well as biologically. Group action can serve to aid decision making, but ultimately, medical decisions are not made in groups. In fact, part of the rebellion against managed care is an assertion of patient and physician heterogeneity.[2]

RECONCEPTUALIZING THE HEALTH CARE CONSUMER OF 1963

Several assumptions about consumers, consumer behavior, and health care underlie Arrow's analysis. First, consumers appear to be quite limited cognitively and hence innately incapable of acquiring knowledge to make informed judgments in medical care markets. The economist's perspective (and Arrow's), however, generally begins from the premise that people know what is best for them. This presumption relies on each individual knowing the consequences of his or her actions so that an *informed choice* is made.

Second, there is little room for patient preferences in medical decision making. Patients clearly initiate contact with physicians, but otherwise, they are passive. Third, medical care is a homogeneous commodity. Fourth, no role is specified for personal health behaviors that may affect health.

Learning and Cognitive Limits
At least explicitly, there is no consumer learning in Arrow's model. During the course of the last four decades, the common but unrealistic assumption that economic agents make decisions in environments of full and complete information has been discarded. Some amount of learning is an integral part of the decision-making process. Further, the class of problems in which the principal, in this context, the patient, does not have as much information as the agent, the physician, is characteristic of a much larger range of economic problems and is not uniquely a characteristic of problems involving choices about health and medical care.

People make decisions every day that involve risk. Health risks underlying the use of medical care and those risks associated with receipt of medical care represent only one subset of risks. Driving to work, flying to a distant city, or engaging in dangerous recreational activities, such as scuba diving or rock climbing, are all choices that imply that people recognize they must accept risks to realize other outcomes contributing to their well-being.[3] People receive information about such risks from various sources — schooling, friends and relatives, experiences with their own health and others, various media, and from physicians and other health professionals. In a Bayesian-updating framework, people start with prior beliefs about a particular risk. As they obtain additional information, such beliefs are updated with a certain weight ("credibility") being applied to the new information for purposes of adjusting prior beliefs.

One may take a pessimistic view toward such updating — that is, decision making will not improve over time as the patient gains experience. For one, there is undoubtedly heterogeneity in individuals' ability to process new information. An empirical question in this context is whether or not people are so cognitively limited on average that they are basically incapable of processing information relevant to their health. If so, this conclusion has rather dire implications. Most people spend more time making choices relevant to their health without doctors than with them. As parents, adults make numerous decisions affecting the well-being of their children. Societies charge parents with this responsibility. Also, updating of beliefs or learning takes time. Again, there is an empirical question about how health information is processed and over what time span. With some exceptions (see studies summarized in Kenkel 2000), we have little empirical evidence about how consumers learn about health risks.

As a conceptual matter, it seems difficult to have faith in consumer sovereignty in general, but to single out health care as an area for which consumer sovereignty does not apply. So many personal decisions have important implications for personal health. These include the signs and symptoms leading people to consume care and to carry out the doctor's recommendations (compliance), watching for adverse drug interactions and reactions, as well as decisions about health risks. The fact that more educated people tend to be healthier must reflect a better capacity to assimilate relevant information in part.

Search-Information Cost
From an alternative perspective, people are reasonably smart, but obtaining relevant health information is costly. It may be quite difficult for individual consumers to know, for example, which hospital in the local market area is best in caring for patients with heart attacks. Of course, this raises the question of how much the patient's agent, the physician, knows about these matters. In 1963, with few computers and virtually no health outcomes data available in machine-readable form, the physician mainly had to rely on personal experience and opin-

ions of peers, which are not likely to be an accurate source of information, especially for rare adverse events. Search costs have probably declined since 1963 for several reasons discussed below.

Product Heterogeneity

In a 1978 article, Mark V. Pauly addressed the question, "Is Medical Care Different?" His short answer was "yes, no, and maybe" (11). He made an important distinction between three types of medical care: (1) services that are purchased relatively frequently by most households, such as pediatric care, normal deliveries, prescription drugs for common conditions, and routine care for persons with chronic conditions; (2) services a typical provider produces relatively frequently but that a typical consumer can consume relatively infrequently, perhaps once a lifetime, such as gallbladder surgery; and (3) services that a typical producer produces and a typical consumer consumes relatively infrequently, which include experimental and unusual procedures, including most care undertaken in medical emergencies. The type of medical care considered by Arrow is some combination of the second and third categories. These are clearly credence goods. Yet much medical care falls into the first category, certainly much care that young and elderly persons receive.

Patient Preferences

In some aspects of health production, the physician knows more, and, in others, the patient knows more.[4] To be a perfect agent for the patient, the physician has to rely on (1) accurate information being supplied by the patient and (2) patient preferences for alternative diagnostic and treatment modalities. With the former, even with a comparative and absolute advantage in textbook knowledge and on-the-job training, for successful diagnosis and treatment the physician relies on the patient to describe relevant signs and symptoms, truthfully and fully, other therapies that patient is receiving, and so on. In this sense, asymmetric information favors the patient. But also, if there is anything that knowledge of markets tells us, it is that people are heterogeneous in their tastes. For example, women with breast cancer plausibly have different tastes, including different discount rates, different risk tolerances, and different disutility from pain and disfigurement. While all would agree that consumer welfare would be improved if diagnostic and treatment decisions reflected patient preferences, it seems difficult to see how the institutional responses described by Arrow's article could be adequate, even in the context of 1963. Admittedly, heterogeneity comes at a cost. Societies may properly decide in favor of some uniformity, given the cost of trying to discern and design the most appropriate diagnostic and treatment strategies for each member of a large group.[5]

If licensure were an effective tool for eliminating a few "bad apples," can one be assured that physicians would be sufficiently sensitive to variations in patient preferences — for example, breast cancer patients' preferences leading to choices between mastectomy versus lumpectomy with radiation (setting aside the technologies for breast cancer treatment extant at the time)? Arrow attributed licensure to a public response to the asymmetric information problem (966). He said that licensure was demanded as a method for protecting consumers, although he did not rule out self-interest on the part of existing physicians. Forty years later, we still lack any sound empirical evidence that licensure laws have adequately served consumers. Advocates for entry restrictions remain primarily physicians and their paid representatives.[6] The same goes for nonprofit hospitals. Differences in hospital behavior by ownership type are far too small for nonprofit hospitals to be a bulwark of consumer protection (Sloan 2000).

In sum, it seems difficult for the physician to be a good agent without a substantial amount of help from the consumer. If the patient's values are not taken into account in a treatment decision, patient compliance with the physician's recommendations becomes highly problematic.

Interestingly, much of the conceptual machinery for physician decision making under uncertainty was available by 1963. In 1959, Robert S. Ledley and Lee B. Lusted published an article in *Science* entitled "Reasoning Foundations of Medical Diagnosis." Citing earlier studies by John Von Neumann and Oskar Morgenstern (1944) and R. D. Luce and Howard Raifa (1957), and a study on punched-card diagnosis of ophthalmological diseases, the article discusses probabilities of diagnosis, conditional on patients' reported signs and symptoms. It admits, "At present it may generally be said that specific probabilities are rarely known; medical diagnostic textbooks rarely give numerical values, although they may use words such as 'frequently,' 'very often,' and 'almost always'" (Ledley and Lusted 1959: 13). The authors recognized that medical judgments are subject to considerable uncertainty.

The authors further noted that, "After the diagnosis has been established, the physician must further decide upon the treatment. Often this is a relatively simple, straightforward application of the currently accepted available therapeutic measures relating to the particular diagnosis. On the other hand, and perhaps just as often, the choice of treatment involves an evaluation and estimation of a complicated situation that not only depends on the established diagnosis but also on therapeutic, moral, ethical, social, and economic considerations concerning the individual patient, his family and the society in which he lives" (ibid.: 15). They used the concept of expected value.

Interestingly, no technique for eliciting patient preferences was proposed. In fact, the game described was between nature and the physician, probably in part because no good method existed — a situation that unfortunately still exists, even given limited progress. The article concluded with a statement reassuring physician readers that "This method in no way implies that a computer can take over the physician's duties" (ibid.: 21).

THE CHANGING ROLE OF THE CONSUMER: 1963-2001

There have also been some important changes in health care affecting the role of consumers in the almost four decades since 1963. The potential list is long. Parenthetically, as a sign of the times, and perhaps reflecting the thrust of his arguments as well, Arrow often referred to "patients" when he described the health care context. However, his more general conceptual points referred to "consumers" or "customers." These are among the more important changes.

Doctrine of Informed Consent
According to the doctrine of informed consent, physicians have a legal obligation to explain care options to patients in advance of care in terms that the patient or the individual to whom the patient has granted a power of attorney to act on his or her behalf can understand. This doctrine was first accepted on a widespread basis in the 1970s, even though it first appeared in a recognizable form in 1957 (Schuck 1994). Patients or their representatives are generally given an explicit right to make the final decision about the procedure that they are to receive. Informed consent reflects a fundamental economic concept that a transaction increases private and social welfare when it results from an informed and voluntary choice by parties to the transaction.[7]

There may be situations in which patients would prefer to be kept in the dark. Or they may not trust their own judgment and prefer that someone with more specialized knowledge or one who is less emotionally involved make the decision. In many such cases, responsibility for decision making devolves to a close relative or friend. Situations in which even such persons are optimally to be denied access to relevant information for decision making would seem to be quite rare. Although the rationale is typically couched in altruistic terms, secrecy often protects interests of providers of care rather than the recipients of such care.

Although medical care is often complex and sometimes involves life-and-death decisions, the notion that sellers have an obligation to properly inform buyers about their options prior to the sale is not unique to medical care. Other complex decisions, including purchase of cellular telephone plans, purchasing energy (electricity and natural gas) in a deregulated environment, retirement planning, and the purchase of other forms of insurance all require considerable knowledge for an informed choice to be made, even though counterpart doctrines of informed consent are lacking.

Medical Malpractice

In 1963, medical malpractice suits based on failure to provide informed consent, an error in diagnosis and treatment, or some other factor were very rare. The first medical malpractice crisis occurred in the mid-1970s (Sloan and Bovbjerg 1991). The threat of tort liability creates an ex post incentive for the physician to exercise care. The legal process provides a method for disclosing detailed aspects of the care process as well as consequences of failure to take care, thus reducing the information asymmetry problem discussed by Arrow. Although the consumer cannot test the product before using it, the physician knows that the patient has some recourse in the event of an error and therefore exercises precaution to prevent occurrence of such errors.

Information Technology

If consumers (or anyone else) are to make meaningful choices in any market, they must have information. At best, impressions based on the experience of an individual practitioner are crude indicators of what they supposedly measure. It seems improbable that anyone could have made very informed choices about effects of treatment or choice of provider (e.g., hospital) with the information technology available in 1963. Joseph Schenthal et al. (1963) described the computer used in research for the article based on a computer with 40,000 characters of core memory, a medium-sized computer for the time. Certainly, the state of technology precluded health outcomes–based comparisons, which are technically possible today.

Growth of Managed Care

Managed care plans, especially those that use restricted provider panels, may act as effective agents for patients, offering another mechanism for assessing quality of care. To perform in this role, such plans must have the capacity to collect and assess data within a market. When the plans disseminate such information, consumers have a basis for comparing relative performance of competing managed care plans. Under managed care, the plan becomes the agent, substituting for the individual physician in the traditional model. How well such plans function in this role is a matter for public debate. The question underlies current discussion about the benefits versus costs of a patient's bill of rights. Part of the controversy involves the extent to which individual consumers should be allowed to exercise their own discretion over such matters as choice of provider. While managed care now dominates the health care marketplace in the United States, it was virtually unknown in 1963 (see, e.g., Glied 2000).

Direct-to-Consumer Advertising

During the 1990s, there was a substantial increase in direct-to-consumer adver-tising by health plans, including HMOs, hospitals, physicians (e.g., for plastic and eye surgery), and by pharmaceutical manufacturers. The major impetus in the United States occurred in 1997 when the rules on direct-to-consumer advertis-ing were relaxed to allow advertising on television and radio (*Lancet* 2000). Such investments were apparently viewed as profitable and represent an acknowledg-ment that consumers initiate much demand. The companies have asserted that by advertising directly, they are trying to increase the number of persons who seek care for underdiagnosed conditions. But such advertising also promotes brand-name recognition and hence consumer resistance to switching to generic products after patent expiration.

Safeguards do exist. False and misleading claims are prohibited and regulated by the Federal Trade Commission. The Food and Drug Administration monitors promotion of therapeutic qualities of drugs. And an advertisement that identi-fies a prescription drug by name must provide information about the drug's uses and side effects, although these effects are cast in very general terms rather than as probabilities.

The advantages and disadvantages of direct-to-consumer advertising are still unknown. Specifically, not much is known about how well consumers under-stand the warnings. Nor is the potential effect on physician-to-patient commu-nication understood (Whyte 1993). But clearly such advertising reflects a major shift in thinking about the role of the consumer in health care. There is a govern-ment role in monitoring the accuracy of claims and their information content (see, e.g., Wilkes, Bell, and Kravitz 2000) but not in suppressing such informa-tion flows.

IMPLICATIONS AND RESEARCH AGENDA

By any standard, Arrow's 1963 article has had an enormous influence on the field of health economics. The article is remarkable in having a place on reading lists in courses on graduate-level health economics four decades after it was pub-lished—a lengthy shelf life by any standard. That the concept of the health care consumer has evolved, as have institutional arrangements in this market, is not at all surprising.

Having said this, however, one may be critical of where notions of consumer ignorance and asymmetric information have taken the field. The idea that con-sumers lack knowledge, especially in relation to their physicians, has spawned much writing and hand-wringing among the experts. There has been much de-bate among specialists in health economics about the importance of supplier-induced demand, which has led to policy concerns about physician surpluses and to proposals for interventions on the supply side of the market. (I do not mean to imply that Arrow's article is a cause of the hand-wringing.)

An alternative approach—in my view, a much more fruitful one—is to recognize the market imperfections and devise various interventions to empower consumers. Rather than complain that consumers lack knowledge, why not study what consumers know and how they learn with the ultimate objective of designing policies and institutional structures that improve performance of consumers in the medical care marketplace? In sum, consumer ignorance should not be taken as a given. We need to learn more about how people process health information and about effective methods for communicating the information about the consequences of personal choices. We need to learn how best to elicit information on personal preferences, including preferences about outcomes that are not priced by markets (nonpecuniary losses). In the final analysis, it seems highly improbable that society will be able to devise foolproof mechanisms for patient protection that do not involve patients.

NOTES

1 For a discussion of experience goods versus credence goods, see, e.g., Emons 1997.

2 My thanks to Peter Hammer for several suggestions reflected in this paragraph.

3 This point was emphasized in Arrow 1974. In that book chapter Arrow wrote, "The starting point in assessing the role of government decision making with regard to life and death, or for that matter any other social end, is the recognition that the government's role is merely part, and not necessarily the major part, of the decisions that jointly determine the final outcome. The individual members of the society make many decisions—their use of medical care, their highway driving habits, their food consumption, their concern for each other in risky situations—all of which powerfully affect the mortality statistics" (34).

4 This is double-sided asymmetric information. In some cases, this type of asymmetry may temper the physician moral hazard problem. For example, the physician may prescribe a drug after the company paid for his family trip to Las Vegas. But the patient may not comply with the physician's recommendation. I thank Joshua Zivin for this point.

5 Arrow (1963: 953) said that licensing laws and the standards of medical school training have limited the possibilities of alternative qualities of care. If this were ever true, it is no longer true. Licensure laws are sufficiently general and medical school curricula are sufficiently varied to permit appreciable variation in styles of care.

6 Citing the Arrow article, Havighurst (2001: 9) noted that, "There would also undoubtedly be, in most cases, politically influential industry or professional groups that also prefer, and can fight effectively for, high standards as a way of increasing demand for their services and eliminating low-cost competitors."

7 See Schuck 1994 for a detailed discussion of this issue and other issues related to the doctrine of informed consent.

REFERENCES

Arrow, Kenneth J. 1963. Uncertainty and the Welfare Economics of Medical Care. *American Economic Review* 53(5): 941–973.

———. 1974. Government Decision Making and the Preciousness of Life. In *Ethics of Health Care*. Institute of Medicine. Washington, DC: National Academy of Sciences.

———. 1994. Government Decision Making and the Preciousness of Life. In *Conference on Health Care and Changing Values*. Institute of Medicine. Washington, DC: National Academy Press.

Emons, Winand. 1997. Credence, Goods and Fraudulent Experts. *Rand Journal of Economics* 28(1): 107–119.

Glied, Sherry. 2000. Managed Care. In *Handbook of Health Economics*, ed. Anthony J. Culyer and Joseph P. Newhouse. Amsterdam: Elsevier.

Havighurst, Clark C. 2001. The Backlash against Managed Health Care: Hard Politics Make Bad Policy. *Indiana Law Review* 34(1): 1–23.

Kenkel, Donald S. 2000. Prevention. In *Handbook of Health Economics*, vol. 1B, ed. Anthony J. Culyer and Joseph P. Newhouse. Amsterdam: Elsevier.

Lancet. 2000. Experimenting with Direct-to-Consumer Advertising. *Lancet* 356(9230): 607–608.

Ledley, Robert S., and Lee B. Lusted. 1959. Reasoning Foundations of Medical Diagnosis. *Science* 130(3366): 9–21.

Luce, R. D., and Howard Raifa. 1957. *Games and Decisions*. New York: Wiley.

Pauly, Mark V. 1978. Is Medical Care Different? In *Competition in the Health Care Sector: Past, Present, and Future: Proceedings of a Conference Sponsored by the Bureau of Economics, Federal Trade Commission, March 1978*, ed. Warren Greenberg. Germantown, MD: Aspen Systems.

Schenthal, Joseph E., James W. Sweeney, Wilson J. Nettleton Jr., and Richard D. Yoder. 1963. Clinical Application of Electronic Data Processing Apparatus. *Journal of the American Medical Association* 186(2): 101–105.

Schuck, Peter H. 1994. Rethinking Informed Consent. *Yale Law Journal* 103(4): 899–959.

Sloan, Frank A. 2000. Not-for-Profit Ownership and Hospital Behavior. In *Handbook of Health Economics*, vol. 1B, ed. Anthony J. Culyer and Joseph P. Newhouse. Amsterdam: Elsevier.

Sloan, Frank A., and Randall Bovbjerg. 1991. *Insuring Medical Malpractice*. New York: Oxford University Press.

Von Newmann, John, and Oskar Morgenstern. 1944. *Theory of Games and Economic Behavior*. Princeton, NJ: Princeton University Press.

Whyte, John. 1993. Direct Consumer Advertising of Prescription Drugs. *Journal of the American Medical Association* 468(25): 146–150.

Wilkes, Michael S., Robert A. Bell, and Richard Kravitz. 2000. Direct-to-Consumer Prescription Drug Advertising: Trends, Impact, and Implications. *Health Affairs* 19(2): 110–128.

ANNETINE C. GELIJNS

JOSHUA GRAFF ZIVIN

RICHARD R. NELSON

■ Uncertainty and Technological Change in Medicine

At the heart of Kenneth Arrow's landmark article on the economics of medical care is the pervasive influence of uncertainty, both in regard to the occurrence of disease and to the efficacy of treatment. These uncertainties, as Arrow contends, have led to the following distortions in the operation of health care: (1) health insurance schemes that have insulated patients and physicians from the financial implications of their medical decisions (i.e., the moral hazard argument), and (2) delegation of medical care decisions from patients to physicians because of the extreme information asymmetry between the two parties (the principal agent theory). These arguments are made with little reference to technology or technological change, issues that Arrow explores in numerous other works (1962, 1969). Yet these issues of moral hazard and agency provide a significant thrust behind technological development in medicine. In the past forty years, physicians have faced strong clinical, economic, and social incentives to adopt and use new technologies in management of disease. The insulation of patients from true medical costs through insurance has compounded these effects. The growth of insurance has led to strong, positive feedback to the R&D sector, which fueled such rapid technological change that both the quality and costs of U.S. health care bear little resemblance to those prevailing at the time of Arrow's writing.

This essay explores the dynamics of technological change in medicine and is divided into three parts.[1] First, we briefly sketch the complex institutional interplay through which medical innovation emerges. Second, we propose that innovation must be understood as a process of "cultural" learning or evolution. That cultural evolutionary process, in turn, involves the coevolution of technique and knowledge. Third, we discuss several special features of the nature and process of technological change in medicine that set it apart from other sectors of the economy. In this respect, we highlight the persistence of uncertainty and expand on Arrow's (1963: 951) observations that "uncertainty as to the quality of the product is perhaps more intense here than in any other important commodity. Recovery from disease is as unpredictable as its incidence." We then draw some concluding observations.

INSTITUTIONAL INTERPLAY IN MEDICAL INNOVATION

Since the 1960s, the technological contours of clinical practice have undergone considerable change. One useful index of the high degree of technological change is the plethora of new drugs and devices that have been introduced: Burton Weisbrod (1991), for example, reported that approximately 35 percent of the 200 largest-selling prescription drugs are new each year. Furthermore, in 1999, the Food and Drug Administration (FDA) approved some 5,000 new and modified devices. Over the same time period, physician-innovators were pioneering new clinical procedures, whose development did not necessarily center on a particular health care product. These procedures ranged from high-tech coronary artery bypass grafting to preventive measures for changing lifestyles of high-risk population groups.

This virtual explosion in medical technology raises a central question: How did all this innovation come about? Since World War II, powerful demand- and supply-side forces have encouraged medical innovation in most industrialized nations. On the demand side, we have witnessed an ongoing expansion of health insurance, and the existence of generous insurance schemes. Recall that the creation of large federal insurance plans, that is, Medicare and Medicaid, occurred after the writing of Arrow's seminal work on medical care. On the supply side, government funds for medical research and education increased significantly during these years. This expansion, in part, arose out of the wartime successes of government-sponsored research and development efforts and the resulting report entitled, "Science the Endless Frontier," which called for federal investment in basic biomedical research. In the United States, expenditures for medical research increased fortyfold in real terms between 1940 and 1987; the budget of the National Institutes of Health (NIH) in 2001 is now over $20 billion. Moreover, currently over 50 percent of the overall federal research budget is spent in the life sciences. These trends vastly strengthened the position of two major actors in the production of medical technology: academic health centers (AHCs) and the pharmaceutical, medical device, and biotechnology industries.

Universities and their academic health centers are among the more complex institutions in modern societies. AHCs are multifunctional organizations that have a three-pronged mission: (1) they provide primary care as well as advanced specialty and tertiary care and are early adopters of the "latest" in technology;

(2) they train biomedical researchers and clinicians, and, thereby, shape the distribution of skills and specialties; and (3) they conduct a wide range of biomedical research activities, ranging from laboratory-based fundamental research to population-based clinical studies. There is an inherent tension among the various missions of AHCs, but, at the same time, their high degree of research productivity may well be related to the fact that they house these three missions within one organization. In the language of economists, there may be "complementarities" between missions, where engaging in one mission makes the organization more effective in pursuing the other missions. For example, the experience derived from delivering specialty care may inspire new research directions as well as enhance physician training. These complementarities are likely to arise as a result of the AHC structure that allows for the close proximity of scientists and clinicians, which promotes mutual learning and collaborative efforts.

New medical technologies are manufactured by several industries with distinct and complex organizational characteristics. The oldest is the pharmaceutical industry, emerging in nineteenth-century Europe as an offspring of the dye and chemical industry. The pharmaceutical industry is multinational in scope and is undergoing significant consolidation. In the past few years, there have been more than a dozen major acquisitions or mergers involving world-class, research-based pharmaceutical firms, including Novartis, GlaxoSmithKline Wellcome, and Pfizer-Warner-Lambert. The pharmaceutical industry is highly competitive (not one of the companies holds more than an 8 percent share of the market) and extremely research intensive (investing 18 percent of annual sales in R&D). The modern medical device industry is essentially a post–World War II phenomenon. In the United States, it comprises some 16,000 firms. The majority of firms are small (80 percent have less than 50 employees), but the medical device sector also contains some large multinational firms, such as Philips, Siemens, and General Electric. The device industry is also highly research intensive (investing over 12 percent of annual sales in R&D, with the most innovative firms investing up to 18 percent) (Lewin Group 2000). The biotechnology industry is the youngest addition, emerging in the past quarter century as a result of the revolution in genetics and molecular biology that began nearly half a century ago. Through continued innovation in the tools and techniques of genetic engineering, this sector has assumed an increasingly prominent role. In the United States alone, it involves numerous start-up firms, although most of the more than 2,000 firms are not currently producing products, but rather are investor-funded R&D ventures. It too is highly research intensive (investing $8 billion in R&D in 1999) and has strong university ties as well as many collaborative arrangements with pharmaceutical firms.

The common image of the university-industry interface assigns to universities the role of generating fundamental (basic) knowledge and to industry the conduct of applied research and the development of medical technology. A closer look at the ways in which medical innovation arises and spreads, however, suggests that both parties play much more complex, subtle, and wide-ranging roles than conventional wisdom maintains (Gelijns and Thier in review). If one were to be led, blindfolded, into one of the many R&D labs of the biotech industry, it would be hard to discern, upon removing the blindfold, whether one was in industry or academia. Industry performs basic research in part because the ability to learn about new scientific opportunities requires that industrial scientists be part of scientific networks and interact as peers with their academic colleagues. Moreover, universities play very important roles in the development, modification, and sometimes even in the manufacturing of technology, roles which have become more visible as a result of the Bayh-Dole Act in 1980, that gave universities strong incentives to patent federally funded research findings. Medical innovation thus thrives on extensive interactions between universities and industry, with knowledge and technology transfer occurring in both directions. In today's knowledge-based economy, where the lines between science and technology are blurring, innovations are thus generated within complex organizational networks of both public and private sector institutions.

TECHNOLOGICAL CHANGE AS AN EVOLUTIONARY PROCESS

Scholars of technology from a wide variety of disciplines have argued that technological change proceeds through an evolutionary process (Nelson and Winter 1982). This process is evolutionary in the sense that the large advances that occur over time are not the result of a conscious process of planning and design. The uncertainty that is the focus of our discussion precludes this. Rather, it is the result of a process in which at any time a wide range of technological possibilities are being pursued to address a particular need or demand. In addition to competing with prevailing practice, these innovations are often in competition with one another as well. The technologies that ultimately prevail are determined by ex post evaluation and selection, rather than ex ante planning.

This characterization does not deny purpose and direction to the technological enterprise or the existence of sophisticated bodies of scientific knowledge that guide efforts at advancing technology. Rather, it is to highlight that inevitably there remains a fundamental uncertainty regarding what will work and what will work best. Walter Vincenti 1990, for example, expands on this notion in an illuminating study of technological innovation in aviation. He shows how various bodies of complex knowledge help guide modern aeronautical engineers in discovering the optimal design characteristics of aircraft. However, he argues that these efforts at technological problem solving almost always reach beyond the range of options that are perfectly understood and therefore are to a considerable extent "blind." Thus, technological change in aviation, as well as other high-tech industries, often involves a combination of sophisticated science and learning through trial-and-error processes. Indeed, Arrow 1962 explored this phenomenon in one of his other seminal works, "The Economic Implications of Learning by Doing." The presence of sophisticated scientific knowledge and learning through experience is also very strong in medicine, as we elaborate later.

This evolutionary characterization is true for the work of the individual inventor, research groups, or at the level of firms. It is also true for the collection of individuals and organizations that is working on a particular problem. In every area where rapid technological advance has been sustained, progress has been the fruit of the work of many parties, competing with one another and also building from one another's work. Of course, some portions of new technologies are proprietary, and portions of what is learned are kept secret, at least for a while. However, over the long run progress is dependent on the ability of researchers and inventors to freely use and further develop one another's work.

In the modern era, every field of technology that has experienced rapid, sustained technological advance has been closely connected to a field or collection of fields of science that is dedicated to illuminating solutions to shared problems. This is strikingly the case in medicine as well as in other high-tech sectors, such as aviation, electronics, and chemical products. Increasingly, advances in scientific understanding have stimulated technological change, enabling inventive efforts to be more focused and productive. In other cases, however, technological knowledge has come about initially with very little understanding, and the "science" has then been marshaled to try to understand what is going on (Rosenberg 1982). The development and introduction of the steam engine, for instance, which has been referred to as the technological innovation on which industrial society was founded, sparked interest in the mechanical effect of heat and helped spawn the science of thermodynamics. Similarly, the invention of the transistor resulted in a tremendous expansion of solid-state research in physics. When such understanding has been gained, it has generally facilitated rapid improvement and refinement of technological products or processes. Thus in a basic sense, understanding and technique coevolve. This is very much the case in medicine.

MEDICAL INNOVATION AS AN EVOLUTIONARY PROCESS

Remarkable advances have recently occurred in the understanding of the molecular and genetic bases of disease. In fact, many of the significant medical advances introduced in recent years have resulted from these insights. Indeed, some have argued that this knowledge will allow us to develop drugs tailored to the specific needs of population subgroups and perhaps even individuals sometime in the near future. Yet, despite the enormous increase in our understanding of disease pathways and the physiological models that belay them, tremendous uncertainty remains. The pervasiveness of these informational shortcomings in the face of huge technological advances is a result of several special characteristics that uniquely define medical innovation. These characteristics include: (1) a high degree of uncertainty that persists long after the introduction of a new medical technology, (2) complex interplay between practice and understanding, and (3) an increasingly complex selection environment. Given this reality, it seems especially appropriate to view medical innovation as an evolutionary process.[2]

Uncertainty

Nathan Rosenberg (1996), a scholar of technical change, has argued that innovation is a learning process that takes place over time and that a fundamental meaning of learning is the reduction of uncertainty. Economists have long understood that a central and unavoidable feature of all research activities is that they are conducted under varying conditions of uncertainty. In considering the spectrum of activities incorporated in R&D—basic research, applied research, and development—it has become common practice to emphasize the high degree of uncertainty attached to the basic research end of the spectrum in contrast with much lower levels of uncertainty in the realms of applied research and development. Indeed, the development process in medicine typically involves a lengthy process of clinical testing, which is principally geared toward the reduction of uncertainty. However, in medicine, even after new technologies have been introduced, uncertainty over their eventual uses often remains extremely high.

Elsewhere we have argued that the sources of this uncertainty are twofold: (1) the complexity of the human body and (2) the heterogeneity of the human population (Gelijns, Rosenberg, and Moskowitz 1998). For example, alpha-blockers were first tested for hypertension. At the time of their introduction, it was not known that alpha-receptors existed in the urological tract as well as in the arterial system and that, therefore, their blockade could constitute a symptomatic treatment for benign prostate disease. Initial trials, which focused on hemodynamics, did not notice its urological value. In fact, it took another twenty years to establish this. Generally speaking, the full range of information on a technology's effectiveness cannot be expected to emerge in clinical trials that are designed to test a narrowly defined set of clinical benefits. Further, much of the additional focus in these trials is placed on identifying and eliminating complications. While the considerable testing conducted during the development process provides invaluable information, there are inherent limits to how much can be known about a technology prior to its widespread use. It is often the case that the detection of delayed or rare adverse events requires exposure of hundreds of thousands of people and/or prolonged observation periods.

A second factor generating high uncertainty in medical innovation is the heterogeneity of the human population, which may be due to genetic, environmental, or behavioral differences. Because of it, the same technology may have wide-ranging eventual effects in treating different individuals with observationally equivalent medical conditions. Randomized controlled trials do little to minimize this uncertainty because the selection criteria often exclude, by design, many patients who might benefit from and eventually receive the intervention. A case in point is bypass surgery — only 4 to 13 percent of patients who now undergo this surgery would have qualified for the initial randomized controlled trials that established its efficacy.

The history of medical innovation, therefore, is replete with instances in which new indications have been discovered only after drugs and devices have been introduced into clinical practice. Recently, we examined the top twenty blockbuster drugs from 1993 and discovered that by 1995, 40 percent of revenues came from secondary indications (ibid.). A similar pattern exists for medical devices. Identification of these new uses is often possible only after these new technologies have spent numerous years in the hands of physicians and patients. Medical innovation involves great uncertainties that require especially heavy reliance upon information that can only be generated by extensive clinical experience.

Interplay between Practice and Understanding

The resolution or reduction of uncertainty through "applied" learning in clinical practice occurs by means of trial, error, and seeming serendipity. As such, learning-by-using experiences generate different types of knowledge. At one end of the spectrum, these experiences may generate information about shortcomings or potential new applications of a technology that require significant modifications. The evolution of technology, in this case, requires lines of communication that allow information to freely flow from practitioners back to the research enterprise. For example, the laparoscope, which was commonly used in gynecological procedures, could only be extended to orthopedic procedures after the equipment was appropriately modified with a connection to a television camera. Complex knee surgery requires the participation of several physicians who must all be able to view the intricacies of the operation simultaneously. Only through feedback about the special needs of the orthopedic community could this technological advance take place. In other cases, information generated through clinical practice may influence future directions for basic science research.

At the other end of the spectrum, the knowledge generated in clinical practice leads to alterations in technological use that require no modifications in design. In this case, the change is simply one of indications, and the feedback between practitioners and researchers plays a less central role. A case in point is the treatment of peptic ulcer disease. The clinical observation in 1983 that some peptic ulcers were caused by a bacterium, *H. Pylori*, led to the use of antibiotics in the treatment of this disease. Similarly, buproprion, which was introduced as an anti-depressant drug, was found to be quite successful as an aid in smoking-cessation programs. In general, the unexpected and anomalous findings of clinical experience often pose new questions and applications for both translational and basic biomedical research. This feedback, in turn, promotes future technological development, thus enriching the eventual payoff from the initial research.

Selection Environment

The number of potential technological innovations is very large in comparison with the number of those that actually "survive" the development process. These figures are even more dramatic in comparison to those that survive in the health care system. The central question of interest here is, Why do some survive while others fail? The answer is complex because various user groups have different views about what aspects of a technology are problematic or successful. These views are often derived from unique experiences and preferences and are articulated according to differential abilities to marshal power and expertise to influence the process.

Traditionally, physicians acting as agents for their patients have been considered the principal users by the developers of new technology. The experience and preferences of physicians heavily determined which technologies would be selected and accepted into practice. Judgments by the relevant medical specialty about a technology's clinical performance also predominated in determining the direction in which improvements were sought. Over time, however, other actors—such as regulatory agencies (e.g., the FDA), payers, and patients—have begun to exert an important influence as well.

■ FOOD AND DRUG ADMINISTRATION Since the thalidomide tragedy of the early 1960s and the subsequent amendments to the Food, Drug and Cosmetic Act in 1962, the role of regulatory agencies—to approve a drug before it can be marketed—has been strengthened. Regulatory schemes generally allow considerable latitude for subjective interpretation of the terms *safety* and *effectiveness* in determining the acceptable risk-benefit ratio for approval. Under social and political pressures to reduce pharmaceutical risks and owing to growing sophistication in animal toxicology and clinical research techniques, premarketing requirements for drugs have become increasingly detailed over time. In the 1970s, the U.S. government extended the mandate of the FDA to incorporate certain classes of medical devices.

■ PAYERS There has been a rapid growth in managed care organizations and, in turn, in the use of cost containment mechanisms designed to limit the utilization of certain costly medical services. In addition, insurers are taking a more critical stance regarding the technologies that they will cover as part of a standard benefit package. Either explicitly or implicitly, cost-effectiveness criteria are taking on an increasingly important role in the technological selection process.

■ PATIENTS   Patients are making a stronger independent contribution to the choice of particular technologies. Direct-to-consumer advertising and the explosion of medical information on the Internet has led to dramatic changes in the knowledge base of the general public. Further, the rapid pace of technological change has, in many cases, led to multiple treatment options for a single condition. In this context where patients are better informed and face genuine choices, patient preferences about treatment risks, costs, and benefits associated with each technology have taken on an increasingly important role in the selection process.

The interaction of these actors and their subsequent influence on technological change is itself an evolutionary process. Very little is known about the precise manner in which these feedback signals are incorporated in the activities of the research enterprise. Of course, each actor wants effective, quality-enhancing, safe, and affordable technology, but in practice these are not all achievable. The design of technology requires trade-offs across these characteristics, and agents differ in their attitudes regarding these trade-offs. If the preferences of payers become more prominent, an emphasis will be placed on the search for cost-reducing innovations. If, on the other hand, patient preferences become more influential, considerations regarding quality of life may become more important. Irrespective of these differences in focus across actors, concerns about uncertainty unite them. The recent renewed emphasis on clinical evaluative research can be thought of as a means to address these unified concerns.

CONCLUDING OBSERVATIONS

At the time of Arrow's writing it would have been impossible to predict the incredible growth of the technology sector in health care. Yet his astute focus on the interplay of uncertainty with insurance, patients, and caregivers lies at the heart of this technological evolution. Arrow writes of two major players in health care, the patient and the physician, attributing a relatively minor role to a third player, insurance. Today, we note that insurance has become a more prominent player, and a major fourth player has emerged: the medical research enterprise. These four players interact and coevolve with each other in complex ways, but uncertainty remains at the centerpiece of them all.

This essay highlights a neglected source of uncertainty, whose reduction is heavily dependent on the interplay between practice and the research enterprise. From this interplay, wide ranges of new and unexpected indications of use for existing technologies arise. However, the dynamics of clinical practice have undergone significant changes; new players have emerged that help shape utilization patterns for medical technology. In particular, payers have taken on a more prominent role in response to the spiraling costs of health care and seemingly unexplainable variations in treatment practices. Payers obviously have an important role in ensuring that health care resources are used effectively and efficiently. Yet, we must be careful not to allow payers to supplant the physician in medical decision making, and current payer policy trends, such as highly detailed coverage decisions and utilization reviews, appear to be moving in that direction. Some clinical variation is desirable when patients are heterogeneous in their preferences. Moreover, this variation, as we have argued, leads to important downstream benefits in research. In the important quest to reduce unnecessary health care costs, we should beware of inadvertently eliminating an exploratory and evaluative process that often leads to important medical advances. Of course, practice diversity should not proceed unchecked and will require a stronger emphasis on medical professionalism. Again, we find ourselves returning to the insights developed some forty years ago by Ken Arrow.

NOTES

1 Note that in this article we explicitly focus on technologies for the diagnosis and treatment of disease. A discussion of information technologies and its unique characteristics is beyond the scope of this article.

2 This section draws heavily on insights developed in Gelijns, Rosenberg, and Moskowitz 1998.

REFERENCES

Arrow, K. J. 1962. The Economic Implications of Learning by Doing. *Review of Economic Studies* 29: 155–173.

———. 1963. Uncertainty and the Welfare Economics of Medical Care. *American Economic Review* 53(5): 941–973.

———. 1969. Classificatory Notes on the Production and Transmission of Technological Knowledge. *American Economic Review* 59: 29–35.

Gelijns, A. C., N. Rosenberg, and A. J. Moskowitz. 1998. Capturing the Unexpected Benefits of Medical Research. *New England Journal of Medicine* 339: 693–698.

Gelijns, A. C., and S. O. Thier. Under review. Medical Innovation and Institutional Interdependence: Rethinking University-Industry Connections. *Journal of the American Medical Association.*

Lewin Group. 2000. *The State of the Industry, a Report for AdvaMed.* Unpublished report. Washington, DC.

Nelson R., and S. Winter. 1982. *An Evolutionary Theory of Economic Change.* Cambridge: Belknap Press of Harvard University Press

Rosenberg, N. 1982. *Inside the Black Box: Technology and Economics*. Cambridge, U.K.: Cambridge University Press.

———. 1996. Uncertainty and Technological Change. In *The Mosaic of Economic Growth*, ed. R. Landau, T. Taylor, and G. Wright. Palo Alto, CA: Stanford University Press.

Vincenti, W. 1990. *What Engineers Know and How They Know It*. Baltimore, MD: Johns Hopkins University Press.

Weisbrod, B. 1991. The Health Care Quadrilemma: An Essay on Technological Change, Insurance, Quality of Care, and Cost Containment. *Journal of Economic Literature* 29: 523–552.

RICHARD A. COOPER

LINDA H. AIKEN

■ Human Inputs: The Health Care Workforce

and Medical Markets

In commenting on the health care workforce, Kenneth Arrow (1963) indentified three elements that are imposed on the natural market for medical care to enhance quality but that also decrease price competition. These are licensure, the rationing of entry into medical schools, and the financial subsidization of medical education. Arrow argues that, to achieve genuinely competitive conditions, all three would have to be eliminated. While he acknowledges that doing so could result in some practitioners of lower quality, in a competitive market without uncertainty consumers would have the opportunity to choose from among practitioners of varying quality at suitably varying prices. Entry barriers simply exclude practitioners whom consumers would not choose anyway.

But Arrow worries. He worries about eliminating licensure. Although high educational standards have made licensure "superfluous" for U.S.-trained physicians, licensure does maintain minimal levels of quality for both international medical graduates (IMGs) and nonphysician clinicians (NPCs), and, therefore, it does has value in alleviating uncertainty. Arrow also worries about eliminating entry rationing. Without it students might be of lower quality, and, although entry rationing may also lead to higher physician incomes, the maintenance of quality is more important. Finally, he worries about eliminating medical education subsidies, fearing that doing so could cause a shortage of qualified medical school applicants, and he suggests that, if subsidies were to be eliminated, insured loans might be used to lessen the financial burden.

Arrow's worries are well founded. A truly competitive market might not supply the quantity or quality of practitioners that are now being sustained through social nonmarket forces. Moreover, a market in which a spectrum of quality is offered at corresponding prices could only work if it were free of uncertainty, but health care is richly laced with uncertainty. Indeed, Americans look to government and social institutions to assure them that practitioner quality will be maintained within a narrow range. Even if the purchase of quality through a competitive market did work, a democracy that allowed health care to be doled out to its citizens at levels of quality that were proportional to their financial capacity would pay a large political price. Arrow reaches the same conclusion. He declares that the laissez-faire solution for medicine is intolerable and explains that licensure, entry rationing, and educational subsidies exist specifically because there are few alternative ways to minimize the risks associated with information asymmetry.

However, despite Arrow's recognition of their merits, the roles played by licensure, entry rationing, and educational subsidies have changed substantially over the past forty years.

— Licensure has shifted from restricting entry to empowering a diverse array of NPCs whose scope of practice overlaps that of physicians. This has less to do with enhancing quality than with the potential to reduce price and increase access. Indeed, the licensing of a broad range of disciplines adds uncertainty about the uniformity of quality that is being offered.

— Entry rationing has shifted from medical school education to graduate medical education (GME), which is also the route of entry of IMGs. However, GME rationing has been seized upon less as a means of sustaining quality than as a way to limit the supply of physicians in order to decrease health care spending.

— Subsidies for medical students have largely vanished because of the belief that there are ample, if not excessive, numbers of physicians. As a result, students are now accumulating increasing debt burdens, which is one factor contributing to the current decline in size of the applicant pool. At the same time, subsidies for GME through Medicare, a process that began after Arrow's article was published, have decreased and now seem further threatened. But there is little enthusiasm for reversing these trends in the face of perceived surpluses of providers.

Thus, while in 1960, licensure, entry rationing, and the subsidization of medical education contributed to assuring quality against a background of information asymmetry, forty years later they function principally to influence the size and composition of the health care workforce against a background of belief that health care spending is increasing too rapidly, that physician supply is excessive, and that other practitioners can provide care less expensively. Arrow offered cogent arguments for their use as tools for sustaining quality. The question is whether equally cogent arguments exist for their use in effecting changes in the characteristics of the workforce. And how can quality be assured without the use of these tools?

LICENSURE

Licensing Nonphysician Clinicians

Arrow concluded that the value of licensure in assuring physician quality outweighed its impediment as a barrier to practice. In his formulation, the two were linked, and a choice could be made. But, by 1960, licensure laws served principally as barriers to NPCs, such as chiropractors, optometrists, psychologists, nurse anesthetists, and nurse midwives, and, following Arrow's publication, to newer disciplines, including nurse practitioners (NPS), physician assistants (PAS), and acupuncturists (Cooper, Henderson, and Dietrich 1998a). Perhaps anticipating the future, Arrow argued that the "present all-or-none" approach to licensing physicians is both insufficient for complex specialty treatment and excessive for minor medical skills, and he suggested that better quality might be achieved by offering graded licensing to other health professionals, although he noted that such licensure might be more difficult to enforce. Over the past four decades, the NPC disciplines have been successful in obtaining such graded licensure and in progressively expanding the breadth of their privileges. In addition, they have achieved increasing degrees of autonomy from physician supervision and oversight (Sage and Aiken 1997; Cooper, Henderson, and Dietrich 1998a).

In achieving their status, each of the NPC disciplines has incurred opposition from the AMA and other elements of organized medicine, a process that continues. While such opposition has overtones that are anticompetitive, it also raises legitimate issues. The separate licensure and regulation of a multiplicity of disciplines, coupled with differences among them in entry requirements and education, pose concerns about the uniformity of quality that practitioners will provide. The AMA would attempt to eliminate this uncertainty through regulation that assures physician control. The individual disciplines have sought to assure quality through the establishment of separate accreditation and certification standards and through higher educational requirements, although, paradoxically, Medicare's educational subsidies remain tied to hospital training programs rather than to programs in colleges and universities (Aiken and Gwyther 1995).

The result of these efforts is a panorama of cooperation and competition between physicians and NPCs. The licensing responsibilities of state legislators often thrust them into the middle of interprofessional conflicts, such as those between ophthalmologists and optometrists over eye care, between anesthesiologists and nurse anesthetists over supervision, and between family physicians and nurse practitioners over prescriptive privileges. It is just this kind of competitive interaction that Arrow was concerned about; and, while Americans look to government to decrease the uncertainty that it engenders, the relaxation of state and federal restrictions has, if anything, exacerbated the problem and strained the institutions that bear oversight responsibility.

Market Incentives and the Licensure of NPS and PAS

While issues of quality and access underlie many of the efforts to expand the NPC disciplines, their growth has principally been a response to the market. During the 1950s and 1960s, increasing health expenditures created pressures to move more services outside of hospitals, thus diluting physicians' authority over other health care providers (Abbott 1988). Concurrently, the burden of illness shifted from acute to chronic conditions, and the social definition of medical care expanded to incorporate a wide range of everyday problems for which physicians had received little training and often had little interest. NPCs with a more holistic view of health exploited these changing boundaries and forged larger roles. However, the most powerful stimulus to their expansion was the perceived shortage of primary care physicians and the ability of NPCs not only to provide the needed services, but also to enhance the productivity of clinical teams. This led to public subsidies for the advanced training of nurses and former military medics, thus legitimizing NPCs as physician substitutes and allowing them to test new roles (Ford 1982). Similar pressures for more primary care providers emerged in the early 1990s (Aiken and Sage 1992) and led not only to additional laws granting licensure and prescriptive privileges for NPS and PAS but also to large increases in the numbers trained annually (Cooper, Laud, and Dietrich 1998b). Parallel growth occurred within the alternative disciplines, such as chiropractic and acupuncture. These dynamics have brought into question the appropriate roles of primary care physicians. Should they work "down market," undertaking tasks for which NPCs are qualified, or "up market," using the advanced technologies associated with specialists (Christensen, Bohmer, and Kenagy 2000)? Given the evolving shortage of physicians (Cooper et al. 2002), the latter seems more desirable. Indeed, it is beginning to occur already, as more generalist physicians gravitate to positions as hospitalists or emergency physicians or undertake other roles associated with increased acuity and complexity.

Assuring Quality

The declining utility of licensure as a means of guaranteeing any more than minimum physician quality, coupled with its availability to a wide range of NPC disciplines, has created an additional problem for physicians. In the late nineteenth and early twentieth centuries, licensure aided the profession in communicating its legitimacy and in gaining popular support for its activities (Starr 1982). But if licensure no longer functions to assure quality, how can the medical profession provide that assurance? In addition, while licensure might be expected to distinguish physicians from NPCs, whose scope of practice is limited, and from healers who, lacking licensure, are barred altogether from the practice of medicine, it is useless in distinguishing among physicians, who, by the 1960s, were increasingly distinguishing themselves into specialties and subspecialties (Donini-Lenhoff and Hedrick 2000).

The counterpart of licensure for specialists is board certification, which, although not mandatory, is generally believed to confer stature and is widely sought. Certification gives the imprimatur of knowledge and competence, much as licensure had earlier, and therefore functions to decrease uncertainty. But is it enough? A robust quality movement has developed in the United States. Physicians find themselves facing criticism about medical errors (Kohn, Corrigan, and Donaldson 2000), and pressure mounts for governmental regulation to protect patients (Brennan and Berwick 1996). On the other side are hospital systems and managed care organizations that would gladly take responsibility for judging the quality of physicians and limit their access to facilities or to reimbursement based on these judgments (Iglehart 1996). In either case, the stature and, therefore, the economic power of the profession could be diminished.

Specialty boards and societies have responded by proposing to carry out ongoing assessments of physicians' outcomes and competencies, a labor-intensive activity that, if it were onerous or intrusive, could actually impair quality (Casalino 1999). But the alternatives are unacceptable, both professionally and economically. And what will this mean for the other professions? Will certification, which is common among the NPC disciplines now, be elevated to a higher plane, such as that contemplated for medicine? And how can separate processes administered by each discipline help to alleviate the uncertainty that multiple disciplines create? Thus, licensure has become an instrument of the market, directed toward expanding the array of providers, thereby leaving a vacuum in quality assurance that has been difficult to fill.

EDUCATIONAL RATIONING AND SUBSIDIES

Entry rationing, too, has taken on a different role. Arrow's paper was published in the waning days of the thirty-year effort by organized medicine to limit physician supply in order to maximize incomes. It was believed that controlling the number of medical students would produce that result, but control also was rationalized as a way to sustain a high level of quality by admitting only the best. Arrow believed that the value of the latter outweighed the negative market effects of the former. However, the pressure to expand medical education was growing, and in 1963, the Health Professions Education Assistance Act was passed, unleashing a process that ultimately led to a doubling of medical school places. Student quality was maintained at these higher levels because the applicant pool increased proportionately. Two years later, Congress added further support for medical education by reimbursing hospitals for the costs of GME. At the same time it liberalized the immigration laws, permitting more IMGs to enter the United States. With that, the number of residency positions grew to exceed the number of U.S. medical graduates (USMGs) by an amount that peaked at approximately 25 percent in the early 1990s and that has held steady since then (Brotherton, Simon, and Tomany 2000). Thus, there are now two avenues of entry into the medical profession, and, as a result, policy has shifted from a singular focus on medical schools to a dual focus that also includes residency programs. Moreover, the focus of policy has shifted from Arrow's formulation, in which additional physicians were seen as a means of price competition, to one in which additional physicians are seen as the stimulus for additional health care spending.

Medical School
Medical school rationing clearly occurs. However, data from the Association of American Medical Colleges (AAMC) indicate that applicant numbers are declining (AAMC 2000). One reason appears to be the rising debt burden of students, a manifestation of the substantial increases in tuition that have occurred, principally in schools without state support. While the low tuition of the 1950s was viewed as a subsidy (albeit one that Arrow saw as socially useful), few medical students today perceive that their education is being subsidized, despite the fact that the true costs significantly exceed even the current lofty levels of tuition (Jones and Korn 1997). And while the loan guarantees that Arrow spoke of are widely available, they do little to alleviate the increasing levels of student debt.

Other reasons for the decline in applicants may include the falling prestige of physicians and the availability of other career opportunities. This repeats the experience of the late 1980s, which was ended not by a reversal of any of these underlying problems but by the growing interest of women in medical careers. That interest has peaked, and the numbers of both men and women applying to medical school is declining (AAMC 2000). Indeed, the ratio of first-time applicants to places has fallen from 1.8:1.0 only five years ago to less than 1.5:1.0, raising concerns that it may drift lower and reach the "magic number" of 1.2:1.0 last reached in 1989 when, to preserve entry rationing as a means of maintaining quality, some medical schools chose not to fill their classes.

Residency Programs
The total number of first-year residents has been quite constant at approximately 23,000 for almost ten years (Brotherton, Simon, and Tomany 2000). Because most medical educators and regulators believe that this number is too great, proposals have been advanced to reduce it to approximately 20,000, equivalent to 110 percent of the number of U.S. medical graduates (COGME 1994). The lever to

affect such a change is Medicare, which is the major federal subsidy for medical education. Direct medical education support (DME), including both the salaries of residents and funds for faculty supervision, was part of the original Medicare legislation in 1965. This revenue stream has been used before in attempts to implement policy. For example, during the late 1970s there was concern about excessive subspecialization (Petersdorf 1978), and in the mid-1980s, DME support was halved for those residents who had completed training in their parent specialty. Coincidentally, fearing an overall physician surplus, federal support for medical schools was abruptly terminated.

As originally enacted, Medicare's cost reimbursement system compensated teaching hospitals for certain activities resulting from their broad mission, such as emergency services, advanced technologies, and care for the poor. When, in 1984, cost reimbursement was replaced by prospective payment, these costs were reimbursed as indirect medical education (IME) payments, so termed because the number of residents was used as a proxy for the magnitude of payment. These payments are large, double those for DME, and both represent the public investment in education that Arrow endorsed.

In the late 1980s and early 1990s, the total number of residency positions increased sharply, raising further concern about physician surpluses. The lever of Medicare GME was used again to influence policy, this time through provisions of the Balanced Budget Act (BBA) of 1997, which included caps on the numbers of residents and inducements to cut specialty training positions. Leaders in academic medicine have called for additional restrictions, focused specifically on reducing the number of IMGs (Whitcomb 1995), and the federal budget recently submitted by President Bush calls for deep cuts in the small amount of federal support that exists for medical education outside of Medicare, an action that also was justified in terms of a physician surplus. It is unclear what the long-term effects of such cuts will be. Prior restrictions on support for subspecialty trainees in the 1980s had no apparent effect. Indeed, the number of trainees grew substantially. The loss of Medicare funding simply put added financial burdens on medical schools, hospitals, and subspecialty fellowship programs. It seems likely that attempts will be made once again to fill the void. But it will be harder this time. The 1980s was a period of ballooning faculty practice revenues and hospital surpluses, some of which were diverted to this purpose. Neither source is readily available today.

These downward pressures on medical education subsidies come at a time when the fundamental rationale for GME financing through Medicare has been challenged by the Medicare Payment Advisory Commission (MedPAC). MedPAC has proposed that DME and IME should be merged into a single fund, removed from the Medicare entitlement program, and considered in the annual congressional appropriation process. At the heart of this is whether DME is for education or for service, and the whole matter is clouded by ambiguity concerning the exact purposes of IME. MedPAC argues that residents bear the cost of their own education by accepting compensation at a rate that is less than the market value of their services. Therefore "there are no education costs for Medicare to reimburse," and, since both IME and DME are for service, they should be merged (Newhouse and Wilensky 2001). However, others have argued that both are for education. In fact, history argues that one (DME) is for the admixture of service and education that is inherent in apprenticeship training and that the other (IME) is for the unusual services provided by teaching hospitals. Moreover, because residencies span multiple years, exposing Medicare GME payments to the vagaries of annual congressional appropriations has the potential to destabilize the educational process.

Concern about Physicians and Health Care Expenditures
These various efforts to constrain both undergraduate and graduate medical education through the manipulation of federal subsidies are products of a broadly held concern that the nation will soon experience a physician surplus, if it does not have one already. This perspective is derived from a series of studies over the past twenty years predicting that vast physician surpluses would exist by the year 2000, with estimates as high as 165,000 physicians (equal to 30 percent of the all physicians) (GMENAC 1981; Weiner 1994; COGME 1994). Although their methodology and conclusions were challenged (Schwartz, Sloan, and Mendelson 1988; Reinhardt 1991; Cooper 1995), these studies have been widely accepted by professional organizations, foundations, and agencies (AAMC 1997). The year 2000 has come and gone with no evidence of a physician surplus, and there are indications that shortages are developing in some of the specialties (Cooper 2002). Nonetheless, the perception of surplus continues.

Concern about the impact of such surpluses is rooted in the knowledge that physicians are increasingly becoming specialists and in the belief that physicians generally, and specialists in particular, drive health care spending through a process of supplier-induced demand (Shain and Roemer 1959; Rice and Labelle 1989; Schroeder and Sandy 1993). In his classic article, Victor Fuchs (1978) invoked supplier-induced demand to explain the observation that the number of surgeons correlates with the number of operations, but so too does the number of obstetricians correlate with the number of births (Dranove and Wehner 1994). Moreover, while supplier-induced demand implies the provision of excessive or inappropriate care, increasing attention is now being given to the large amounts of appropriate care that physicians are not providing (Hemingway et al. 2001), and even when it appears that additional services are being rendered, their utility is rarely addressed (Labelle, Stoddart, and Rice 1994). Viewing the entire literature, many analysts have concluded that, to the extent that it occurs at all, physician-induced demand is of small magnitude, and it is impossible to distinguish from the demands of patients themselves (Ernst and Yett 1985; Feldman and Sloan 1988; Newhouse 1992).

Thus, the relationship between health care spending and physician supply becomes one of cart-and-horse. Is it physicians whose avarice pulls health care spending along, or is it patients whose demands offer opportunities for physicians to provide care? Or is there a third reality? Studies of long-term trends indicate that health care spending levels are determined principally by the state of economic development (Getzen 1990) and that physician supply grows to fill the needs that are created in this manner (Cooper, Getzen and Laud 2003). Viewed from this perspective, the horse is the economy and the cart is health care spending. Physicians and patients are simply passengers, and the financial leverage that either has is small in proportion to the pace of the ride.

This debate becomes mute when limiting physician supply is viewed, instead, as a means of decreasing utilization in the context of unfettered access (Barer and Stoddart 1992; Grumbach and Lee 1991). Under these circumstances, supply must be constrained, whether demand is induced by physicians or by patients or, as is more likely the case, whether it is governed by the resources of the economy. Limiting physician supply becomes the instrument for rationing health care. This logic, which developed in Canada in the 1980s (Barer and Stoddart 1992), migrated south in the early 1990s and became embedded in U.S. policy (Schroeder and Sandy 1993; Grumbach and Lee 1991; COGME 1994). As a result, educational subsidies were increased for primary care trainees and decreased for specialists, but physician supply overall did not suffer, as it did in Canada. However, the long-term consequences of these policies are now beginning to be felt in the United States, as waiting times for specialists lengthen and as an overabundance of primary care providers becomes apparent, trends that are projected to worsen over the coming years (Cooper et al. 2002). Thus, the redeployment of entry rationing and educational subsidies for purposes of modifying the size and composition of the health care workforce appears to have achieved its goals, but those goals no longer appear to be consonant with the needs of the public.

SUMMARY AND CONCLUSIONS

Arrow wrote his classic article in simpler times, as those who chance upon this article forty years hence will say of today. It was a new era in science and medicine, soon to be fueled by new resources from Medicare and the National Institutes of Health. Fiscal constraint was a stranger, physicians were in short supply, and information asymmetry was pervasive.

In the intervening years, Americans have become more comfortable with health care issues. Fatal illness, which was rarely discussed with patients in 1960, is now researched by them on the Internet, and greater attention is paid to patient rights. Nonetheless, concerns about quality have, if anything, increased. Indeed, it is public concern about quality that has invited governmental regulation and induced a defensive posture among medical organizations, which are rushing to establish their own instruments of quality, and it is these same public concerns that have facilitated the ability of managed care to offer itself as the guarantor of quality. However, center stage is now held by another issue: health care costs. As a result, the focus has shifted from resolving information asymmetry by enhancing quality to controlling national health expenditures by changing the size and composition of the health care workforce.

Licensure, which was restrictive in 1960, is more relaxed today, thereby reducing the entry barriers for the NPC disciplines, several of which were just beginning when Arrow wrote his article. The entry of NPCs into the realm of physician's services partially counterbalances the constraints that have been placed on physician supply, although the major contributions of NPCs are skewed to the primary care end of the spectrum while the major constraints on physician supply affect specialists. The growing presence of NPCs creates a dynamic market in which practitioners in various disciplines both compete and collaborate. It is, in fact, the perfect market that Arrow reluctantly longed for, in which providers who have different levels of skill offer their services at varying prices. But consumers have little upon which to base their choices. And while many of the services offered by NPCs replace physician services at a lower price, others represent additional services, which add to aggregate spending.

Arrow sought to explain how a market replete with uncertainty could function. He saw that licensure, entry rationing, and educational subsidies could work to enhance quality, but they did so at the expense of the market. The market has seen it differently and has usurped these tools for its own purposes, leaving quality to look for other sponsors. Has it done so wisely? We have yet to see how well a multidisciplinary workforce of autonomous providers will function, but both successes and failures abound. What is more apparent is how entry rationing and restrictions on educational subsidies have capped the supply of physicians and limited the production of specialists at a time when there is increasing demand for their services. Arrow identified potent tools for affecting the characteristics of the health care workforce. They now must be redirected to the needs of the future.

REFERENCES

Abbott, A. 1988. *The System of Professions.* Chicago: University of Chicago Press.
Aiken, L. H., and M. E. Gwyther. 1995. Medicare Funding of Nurse Education: The Case for Policy Change. *Journal of the American Medical Association* 273: 1528–1532.

Aiken, L. H., and W. M. Sage. 1992. Staffing National Health Care Reform: A Role for Advanced Practice Nurses. *Akron Law Review* 26(2): 187–211.

Arrow, K. J. 1963. Uncertainty and the Welfare Economics of Medical Care. American *Economic Review* 53(5): 941–973.

Association of American Medical Colleges (AAMC). 1997. American Medical Association, American Osteopathic Association, Association of American Medical Colleges, American Association of Colleges of Osteopathic Medicine, Association of Academic Medical Centers, National Medical Association Consensus Statement on Physician Workforce. *Advisory* no. 97-9, 28 February.

———. 2000. *AAMC Data Book: Statistical Information Related to Medical Schools and Teaching Hospitals*. Washington, DC: Association of American Medical Colleges.

Barer, M. L., and G. L. Stoddart. 1992. Toward Integrated Medical Resource Policies for Canada: 7. Undergraduate Medical Training. *Canadian Medical Association Journal* 147: 305–312.

Brennan, T. A., and D. M. Berwick. 1996. *New Rules: Regulation, Markets, and the Quality of American Medicine*. San Francisco: Jossey-Bass.

Brotherton, S. E., F. A. Simon, and S. C. Tomany. 2000. U.S. Graduate Medical Education, 1999–2000. *Journal of the American Medical Association* 284: 1121–1126.

Casalino, L. P. 1999. The Unintended Consequences of Measuring Quality on the Quality of Medical Care. *New England Journal of Medicine* 341: 1147–1150.

Christensen, C. M., R. Bohmer, and J. Kenagy. 2000. Will Disruptive Innovations Cure Health Care? *Harvard Business Review* September–October: 102–112.

Cooper, R. A. 1995. Perspectives on the Physician Workforce to the Year 2020. *Journal of the American Medical Association* 274: 1534–1543.

———. 2002. There's a Shortage of Specialists. Is Anyone Listening? *Academic Medicine* 77: 761–766.

Cooper, R.A., T. E. Getzen, H. J. McKee, and P. Laud. 2002. Economic and Demographic Trends Affecting Physician Supply and Utilization Signal an Impending Physician Shortage. *Health Affairs (Millwood)* 21(1): 140–154.

Cooper, R. A., T. E. Getzen, and P. Laud. 02003. Economic Expansion Is a Major Determinant of Physician Supply and Utilization. *Health Services Research* 38 (in press).

Cooper, R. A., T. Henderson, and C. L. Dietrich. 1998a. Roles of Nonphysician Clinicians as Autonomous Providers of Patient Care. *Journal of the American Medical Association* 280: 795–802.

Cooper, R. A., P. Laud, and C. L. Dietrich. 1998b. Current and Projected Workforce of Nonphysician Clinicians. *Journal of the American Medical Association* 280: 788–794.

Council on Graduate Medical Education (COGME). 1994. *Fourth Report. Recommendations to Improve Access to Health Care through Physician Workforce Reform*. Washington, DC: U.S. Department of Health and Human Services.

Donini-Lenhoff, F. G., and H. L. Hedrick. 2000. Growth of Specialization in Graduate Medical Education. *Journal of the American Medical Association* 284: 1284–1289.

Dranove, D., and P. Wehner. 1994. Physician-Induced Demand for Childbirths. *Journal of Health Economics* 13: 61–73.

Ernst, R. L., and D. E. Yett. 1985. *Physician Location and Specialty Choice.* Ann Arbor, MI: Health Administration Press.

Feldman, R., and F. Sloan. 1988. Competition among Physicians, Revisited. *Journal of Health Politics, Policy and Law* 13: 239–261.

Ford, L. C. 1982. Nurse Practitioners: History of a New Idea and Predictions for the Future. In *Nursing in the 1980s: Crises, Opportunities, Challenges,* ed. L. H. Aiken. Philadelphia: Lippincott.

Fuchs, V. 1978. The Supply of Surgeons and the Demand for Operations. *Journal of Human Resources* 13(suppl.): 35–56.

Getzen, T. 1990. Macroeconomic Forecasting of National Health Expenditures. *Advances in Health Economics and Health Services Research* 11: 27–48.

Graduate Medical Education National Advisory Committee (GMENAC). 1981. *Report of the Graduate Medical Education National Advisory Committee to the Secretary, Department of Health and Human Services.* DHHS Publication No. HRA 81-652. Washington DC: U.S. Department of Health and Human Services.

Grumbach, K., and P. R. Lee. 1991. How Many Physicians Can We Afford? *Journal of the American Medical Association* 265: 2369–2372.

Hemingway, H., A. M. Crook, G. Feder, S. Banerjee, J. R. Dawson, P. Magee, S. Philpott, J. Sanders, A. Wood, and A. D. Timmis. 2001. Underuse of Coronary Revascularization Procedures in Patients Considered Appropriate Candidates for Revascularization. *New England Journal of Medicine* 344: 645–654.

Iglehart, J. K. 1996. The National Commission for Quality Assurance. *New England Journal of Medicine* 335(13): 995–999.

Jones, R. F., and D. Korn. 1997. On the Cost of Educating a Medical Student. *Academic Medicine* 72(3): 200–210.

Kohn, L.T., J. M. Corrigan, and M. S. Donaldson, eds. 2000. *To Err Is Human: Building a Safer System.* Washington, DC: National Academy Press.

Labelle, R., G. Stoddart, and T. Rice. 1994. A Re-Examination of the Meaning and Importance of Supplier-Induced Demand. *Journal of Health Economics* 13(3): 347–368.

Mullan, F. 2000. The Case for More U.S. Medical Students. *New England Journal of Medicine* 343: 213–217.

Newhouse, J. P. 1992. Medical Care Costs: How Much Welfare Loss? *Journal of Economic Perspectives* 6(3): 3–21.

Newhouse, J. P., and G. R. Wilensky. 2001. Paying for Graduate Medical Education: The Debate Goes On. *Health Affairs (Milwood)* 20(2): 136–147.

Petersdorf, R. G. 1978. The Doctor's Dilemma. *New England Journal of Medicine* 299: 628–643.

Reinhardt, U. E. 1991. Health Manpower Forecasting: The Case of Physician Supply. In *Health Services Research: Key to Health Policy,* ed. E. Ginzberg. Cambridge: Harvard University Press.

Rice, T. H., and R. J. Labelle. 1989. Do Physicians Induce Demand for Medical Services? *Journal of Health Politics, Policy and Law* 14: 587–599.

Safriet, B. J. 1992. Health Care Dollars and Regulatory Sense: The Role of Advanced Practice Nursing. *Yale Journal on Regulation* 9: 417–488.

Sage, W. M., and L. H. Aiken. 1997. Regulating Interdisciplinary Practice. In *Regulation of the Health Professions*, ed. T. Jost. Ann Arbor, MI: Health Administration Press.

Schroeder, S. A., and L. G. Sandy. 1993. Specialty Distribution of U.S. Physicians: The Invisible Drivers of Health Care Spending. *New England Journal of Medicine* 328: 961–963.

Schwartz, W. B., F. A. Sloan, and D. N. Mendelson. 1988. Why There Will Be Little or No Physician Surplus between Now and the Year 2000. *New England Journal of Medicine* 318: 892–897.

Shain, M., and M. I. Roemer. 1959. Hospital Costs Relate to the Supply of Beds. *Modern Hospital* 92: 71–73.

Starr, P. 1982. The *Social Transformation of American Medicine*. New York: Basic Books.

Weiner, J. P. 1994. Forecasting the Effects of Health Reform on U.S. Physician Workforce Requirement: Evidence from HMO Staffing Patterns. *Journal of the American Medical Association* 272: 222–230.

Whitcomb, M. E. 1995. Correcting the Oversupply of Specialists by Limiting Residencies for Graduates of Foreign Medical Schools. *New England Journal of Medicine* 333: 454–456.

CLARK C. HAVIGHURST

■ *Health Care as a (Big) Business: The Antitrust Response*

When Kenneth Arrow wrote about American health care in 1963, its age of arguable innocence was about to end. Two years later, the federal government undertook, in the Medicare and Medicaid programs, to pour virtually unlimited public resources into financing a broad entitlement to private health care for the elderly and the poor. This infusion started a process that soon transformed the substantially charitable, ostensibly noncommercial enterprise that Arrow observed into a controversial growth industry.

By putting third-party financing behind a multitude of patients who had previously been, if not charity cases, at least highly cost-conscious consumers of health services, Medicare and Medicaid made the professional practice of medicine lucrative in ways it had never been before. Public financing also made health care attractive to private capital and entrepreneurs — including many physicians who suddenly saw new business as well as professional opportunities for profit. Although Congress certainly did not intend its largesse to change the culture of American medicine, the entitlements it created made it increasingly difficult to maintain that (as Arrow had at least implied) health care is a noncommercial activity carried on above the morals of the marketplace and appropriately sheltered both from its temptations and from the competition that induces producers in other markets to serve consumers' interests. Whatever the soundness of Arrow's overall assessment of the health care sector circa 1963,[1] U.S. health care is today a huge and dynamic industry, driven for better or for worse by competitive forces that were largely inoperative in the system when Arrow observed it. This article observes how antitrust law, America's unique response to the problem of "big business," was eventually brought to bear on health care, in large part as a consequence of its rapid growth and commercialization after government entered the field as a major purchaser.

LAUNCHING THE ANTITRUST CHALLENGE TO PROFESSIONALISM

Once health care became a big business in the United States, could antitrust law be far behind? Just ten years after the enactment of Medicare and Medicaid, the Supreme Court, in *Goldfarb v. Virginia State Bar* (421 U.S. 773 [1975]), laid to rest the idea that the so-called "learned professions" were somehow exempt from the federal antitrust laws. Even though the Sherman Act was enacted in 1890, it was not settled until the Supreme Court spoke in 1975 that sellers of professional services are engaged in "trade or commerce," restraint of which is the target of the statute's principal prohibition. The possibility that professionals might be in a different legal category than competitors of other kinds had long been entertained, however. Though supported by no definitive legal precedent, this notion rested comfortably on the widespread belief that certain callings are higher than others and on the perception, which Arrow's thinking served to reinforce, that competition does not work well when consumers cannot accurately appraise the quality of services they receive. Even so, the Sherman Act's language sweeps broadly, providing little basis for ignoring whole sectors of the economy. Moreover, the offense alleged in *Goldfarb* was price-fixing (by a state bar association), a hard-core antitrust offense not easily excused. The Supreme Court ruled squarely that professional groups, like other trade associations, are subject to the Sherman Act.

Although *Goldfarb*'s rejection of the putative "learned professions" exemption was symbolically important in opening the professions to new scrutiny, the Supreme Court's decision also addressed a more mundane legal issue that was arguably of greater practical significance for the antitrust campaign in the health care sector. The Court had also to consider when professional services have enough impact on interstate commerce to come within the jurisdictional reach of federal antitrust law. On this issue, it took an expansive view. Although the holding in *Goldfarb* dealt only with legal services and not medical care, the Court amplified it in subsequent cases. In any event, it was soon obvious that the health care industry had become a big business rarely involving only localized conduct. The two prongs of the *Goldfarb* holding together put medicine and health care under antitrust spotlights they had previously managed for the most part to avoid.

Although the professional defendants in *Goldfarb* were lawyers rather than physicians, the decision marked the beginning of an era of active antitrust enforcement throughout the health care sector. While the 1980s were seeing an overall decline in antitrust litigation (as a result of new economic learning, new judicial skepticism, and the laissez-faire policies of the Reagan administration), the trend in health care was in the opposite direction. Other factors besides the decision in *Goldfarb* contributed to this trend. Not only were there many potential targets for antitrust litigation in the questionable practices that had arisen when the health professions enjoyed some immunity from antitrust suits, but there was also less reluctance in the larger culture to challenge elite groups — public respect for which had declined during the period of the Vietnam War and the Watergate scandal. In addition, many competitors who suffered setbacks in the newly competitive health care marketplace attributed their problems to their suppliers' or customers' unlawful market power or to their competitors' wrongful acts, and accordingly brought lawsuits, usually unsuccessfully, to redress these presumed wrongs. In any event, a certain amount of litigation was necessary to clarify how the law applied in the unusual circumstances encountered in the health care field. Unfortunately, courts often added to the legal confusion rather than dispelling it, triggering new lawsuits.

Surprisingly, *Goldfarb* also marked a crucial watershed in American health policy.[2] Before the Court's ruling, nearly everyone believed, along with Arrow, that ordinary market competition was probably inappropriate and certainly unachievable in medical care. The medical profession was universally accepted as a self-regulating profession appropriately invested with substantial power over large segments of the health care industry. The effect of *Goldfarb*, however, was to make competition the legal norm in health care as it is in other parts of the economy. Thus, after the Court spoke, professional competitors were no longer free to regulate either themselves or others in trade-restraining ways but instead were actively prohibited from taking collective action to restrict competition. Few things could have had as revolutionary an effect on the health care sector as the abrupt overturning of the deep-seated policy of trusting medical interests to make and enforce industry rules and set standards for the health care field. The antitrust regime now curbs overt exercises of professional power and allows unprecedented economic competition to govern the price of medical and other health services.

The revolutionary change *Goldfarb* worked in the legal regime governing professional services also dramatically increased the relevance of what had been, pre-*Goldfarb*, a very modest and largely theoretical debate over whether market competition might rectify some of the problems of the health care sector, especially the problem of rising costs.[3] By providing a way to liberate buyers and sellers from the medical profession's previously incontestable control, the *Goldfarb* decision made a market-oriented health policy arguably feasible and thus more thinkable than it had been before — and certainly when Arrow wrote. And Congress quickly became attracted to such policies. In 1979, it finally defeated a Carter administration scheme for regulating hospital revenues, initiating an era in which the federal government largely eschewed direct intervention and expected private purchasers, especially employers, to deal with their own cost problems by "prudent purchasing" in a competitive market. Before *Goldfarb*, government struggled with the medical profession for direct control over U.S. health care. After it, policy makers could and did begin to look to competition to break the medical profession's grip on the health care industry and to expect market forces to allocate resources and guide the industry's development.

SOFTER ANTITRUST RULES FOR PROFESSIONALS AND NONPROFITS?

Both before and after *Goldfarb*, uncertainty about how the law would be applied to professionals and nonprofit enterprises—that is, firms not obviously organized for commercial purposes—was a substantial obstacle to bringing antitrust actions in the health care industry. It seemed likely, for example, that at least physicians would be allowed to plead higher motives in defense of collective actions that would constitute unlawful restraints of trade if undertaken by collaborating competitors of other kinds. For many years, the clearest signal that physicians would be held to softer antitrust standards than other competitors was a 1952 dictum by the Supreme Court in *United States v. Oregon State Medical Society* (343 U.S. 326 [1952]). Federal prosecutors had charged the defendant society with organizing an illegal group boycott of certain health insurers that had the temerity to question physicians' clinical decisions and prices in an effort to control costs (Goldberg and Greenberg 1977). Although the Supreme Court thought the government had not proved such a boycott, it went on to suggest that, even if it had, the boycott might not have been unlawful:

> We might observe in passing, however, that there are ethical considerations where the historic relationship between patient and physician is involved which are quite different than the usual considerations prevailing in ordinary commercial matters. This Court has recognized that forms of competition usual in the business world may be demoralizing to the ethical standards of a profession. (343 U.S. at 336)

This dictum somewhat weakened the precedential effect of an earlier case in which medical organizations were successfully prosecuted under the Sherman Act for coercive boycotts aimed at an early health maintenance organization in the District of Columbia (where the interstate commerce requirement was not a barrier) (AMA v. United States, 130 F.2d 223 [D.C. Cir. 1942], *aff'd*, 317 U.S. 519 [1943]). It also resonated with the common perception that medical care is somehow different from ordinary commercial activity—a view that later found support in Arrow's article.

In the flood of antitrust litigation involving health care providers that followed *Goldfarb*, judges struggled to reconcile their own generally favorable, Arrow-like views of professionals and professional self-regulation with the dictates of antitrust doctrine. The opinion in *Goldfarb* gave them little guidance in this endeavor because the Court, though unwilling to bend the usual per se rule against price-fixing just because professionals were involved, did not want to intimate a "view on any other situation than the one with which we are confronted today." Thus, Chief Justice Burger added much-noted footnote 17 to his opinion:

> The fact that a restraint operates upon a profession as distinguished from a business is, of course, relevant in determining whether that particular restraint violates the Sherman Act. It would be unrealistic to view the practice of professions as interchangeable with other business activities, and automatically to apply to the professions antitrust concepts which originated in other areas. The public service aspect, and other features of the professions, may require that a particular practice, which could properly be viewed as a violation of the Sherman Act in another context, be treated differently. . . . (421 U.S. at 788 n.17)

This language was read by many as a sign that antitrust law should not be applied too strictly against professionals. The Supreme Court, however, increasingly implied in a series of later cases that courts should not relax their vigilance in protecting competition in markets for professional services. To be sure, the Court conceded that careful factual analysis would frequently be necessary to assess the competitive effects of particular practices in the unusual market circumstances in which professionals operate; it also indicated a reluctance to apply so-called per se rules when professionals were involved. On the other hand, the Court was regularly able to satisfy itself that a professional restraint had harmed competition by taking only a so-called "quick look."[4] Once the post-*Goldfarb* dust settled, lawyers could no longer safely advise professional clients that antitrust courts would take a favorable view of their anticompetitive collective actions just because they were taken in defense of professional values.

Thinking like Arrow's also gave other actors on the health care stage besides physicians reason to believe that they might also be allowed to bend the usual antitrust rules. Nonprofit hospitals, like physician organizations, could often assert with some plausibility—at least to unskeptical observers like Arrow—that their trade-restraining activities reflected a primary concern for patient welfare, not commercial advantage, and should therefore be immune from legal standards designed for ordinary firms in ordinary markets. Thus, in the late 1970s, hospital interests maintained that a nonprofit hospital engaged with its competitors in "community health planning" should not be challenged for harming competition by allocating markets—a per se antitrust violation. As it turned out, even though health planning was a popular nonmarket innovation of precisely the kind Arrow admired, antitrust law dealt it a significant blow.[5] On the other hand, a few courts have looked favorably on anticompetitive mergers of nonprofit hospitals, deeming such institutions to be less inclined to exploit consumers (FTC v. Butterworth Health Corp., 946 F. Supp. 1285 [W.D. Mich. 1996]; United States v. Carilion Health Sys., 707 F. Supp. 840 [W.D. Va.], *aff'd*, 892 F.2d 1042 [4th Cir. 1989]). Such exceptionalism is the exception rather than the rule, however, and nonprofits cannot be confident that antitrust standards will be relaxed on their behalf.

Even after the Supreme Court signaled that courts should not bend the law to accommodate professional or nonprofit restraints, the legal standards that would actually be applied to health care providers still remained uncertain. As in the case of hospital mergers, some individual judges, unwilling to demand unbridled competition in the health care field, resisted the implications of antitrust law when applied to professionals and nonprofits. Many of them, moreover, unversed in antitrust analysis, misapprehended those implications and therefore felt called upon to improvise legal exceptions to the usual requirement of competition— even when with more insight they could have reached a satisfying result without compromising the competitive paradigm. For example, many judges, unable to discern a procompetitive rationale for hospital medical staffs' collective action in withholding staff privileges from other doctors, invented unwarranted rationalizations for peer review, which they erroneously assumed the law would otherwise condemn.[6] Indeed, the Health Care Quality Improvement Act of 1986 (which fortunately stopped short of restoring full hegemony to professional interests) was necessitated in large measure by courts' failed attempts to formulate antitrust rules for peer review that were both soft and coherent. Nevertheless, despite continuing uncertainty about how judges will react in individual cases, antitrust law today leaves little leeway for professional competitors to agree not to compete or for organized provider groups to restrict the competitive freedom of their members or other market participants. On the other hand, it not only does not bar, but also is receptive to, collective actions by competing providers who organize themselves in smaller groups for procompetitive purposes—as long as they remain accountable to consumers in a generally competitive market.

A MARKET-FAILURE DEFENSE?

Conceptually, the most difficult cases in the post-*Goldfarb* era were those involving codes of professional ethics. Ethical canons were, after all, paradigmatic instances of the "collectivity oriented behavior" that so impressed Arrow in medicine. To be sure, some ethical canons were easy to condemn under antitrust law because they amounted to little more than agreements not to compete on price

(National Soc'y Prof'l Eng'rs v. United States, 435 U.S. 679 [1978]; American Med. Ass'n v. FTC, 638 F.2d 443 [1980], *aff'd*, 455 U.S. 676 [1982]). Others, however, were plausible responses to the circumstance (prominently noted by Arrow) that consumers often cannot accurately judge the quality of professional services even after receiving them and are thus vulnerable to exploitation by unscrupulous providers. To the extent that professional ethics, maintained and enforced by professional organizations, do indeed serve to prevent individual professionals from taking advantage of their clients' vulnerability, they presented a difficult challenge to antitrust law, which generally presumes that consumers are served best if competitor independence is preserved. Because opportunistic behavior by physicians might harm patients' trust in their physicians and thus generate anxieties harmful to the therapeutic enterprise, there was good reason to consider whether there might be found in antitrust law a principled basis for deeming some ethical canons compatible with a competitive regime.

Many courts saw no need to grapple with this conceptual challenge and simply declared either that an ethical canon would be lawful if it was "reasonable" or that a restraint serving a "noncommercial purpose" was outside the ken of antitrust scrutiny. Yet antitrust law's so-called Rule of Reason is an invitation to judge only a restraint's *competitive* effects not its reasonableness as a matter of public policy. And benign motives are too easily alleged and too often mixed with less admirable impulses to justify not scrutinizing any agreement that limits the scope or nature of competition to determine its actual effects. Moreover, it is difficult to see an ethical canon as anything but a "naked" restraint of trade — that is, one aimed at reducing either the overall vigor of competition or the freedom of each competitor to compete as he or she sees fit. And it is far from obvious how a restraint having no purpose other than the curbing of all-out competition could survive scrutiny under a statute condemning "*every* . . . restraint of trade."

A classic problem of antitrust law has been how to deal with a claim that a particular naked restraint — even though it harms competition — should nevertheless be evaluated to see if it is worthy as a matter of public policy. In general, courts have rejected worthy-purpose defenses on the grounds that it would require courts "to set sail on a sea of doubt" and to rely upon "the vague and varying opinion of judges as to how much, on principles of political economy, men ought to be allowed to restrain competition" (United States v. Addyston Pipe & Steel Co., 85 Fed. 271 [6th Cir. 1898], *aff'd*, 175 U.S. 211 [1899]).[7] On the other hand, courts have never said that all naked restraints are illegal per se — that is, condemnable without any additional proof of their harmfulness (Carstenson 2000). Instead, they have reserved that classification for only certain types of restraint, leaving unclear the rationale or conditions under which a naked restraint of another type might be upheld.[8] Canons of professional ethics aimed at improving the overall performance of the health care marketplace in the interest of consumers would be among the best candidates to slip through whatever loophole exists.

A principled basis for occasionally regarding a naked restraint in a favorable way can be found in the possibility that such a restraint could produce results closer to the results that an efficient market would yield—that would occur, that is, if consumers had good information and if the other assumptions underlying economists' textbook models were also satisfied. Arguably, leaving room for an affirmative "market-failure" defense would not violate the concern about "set[ting] sail on a sea of doubt" since it would turn on rigorous economic analysis, not on judges' policy preferences. Although a market-failure defense, like any other defense for naked restraints, is not easily reconciled with the language of the Sherman Act, it would not be out of keeping with the competitive paradigm underlying antitrust law. Moreover, recognizing a theoretical defense of this kind would protect the law and its enforcers against the charge of being driven by a blind faith in competition and market forces when everyone knows, partly from reading Arrow, that these mechanisms are sometimes seriously imperfect. To be sure, a willingness to entertain collaborating competitors' claims that they merely wanted to make the market serve consumers better would invite some confusion in the law and occasional mistakes enabling powerful groups to control competition in their own interest. But the availability of a market-failure defense might advance the law's larger procompetitive purpose by reducing the force of appeals to Congress for statutory antitrust exemptions. It would not be necessary for enforcers or courts to accept the defense very often, since usually the collaborators' conflicts of interest would be clear enough to make the threat to consumer welfare easily outweigh any arguable benefits. In any event, recognition of a limited market-failure defense for certain professional activities would accommodate the concern of Arrow and others that markets for health care are prone to failure and may require special rules to ensure that professionals are true to their ethical responsibilities.

Another possible defense for professional canons of ethics may lie in their informational value. An ethical canon may limit the competitive independence of a professional organization's members but leave competing nonmembers free to act according to their competitive self-interest. If there was a sufficient number of nonmembers, consumers could choose to have their services provided under different rules but would also know which providers had subscribed to particular professional ideals. Thus, the canon could be viewed as serving the procompetitive purpose of differentiating practitioners who adhere to the canon from those who may not. If the canon arguably served this informational purpose and was not intended to limit competition in the market as a whole, the strict test for identifying a naked restraint (stated above) would not be satisfied. An analysis somewhat along the lines suggested here was apparently accepted in principle in *Koe-*

foot v. American College of Surgeons (652 F. Supp. 882, 904 [N.D. Ill. 1986]), which allowed an organization representing 60 percent of board-certified surgeons to defend a rule against delegating postsurgical care to nonsurgeons by proving that membership in the prestigious organization had informational value and "provides consumers with a shorthand method of locating . . . post-operative care rendered by a surgeon."

The foregoing discussion suggests that neither quality concerns in the health care field nor the concerns expressed by Arrow about the compatibility of market competition and medical services require any bending of antitrust law's procompetitive policy or any essential departure from traditional antitrust analysis focusing on competitive effects (Kauper 1988; Greaney 1989). Unfortunately, however, the Supreme Court's most recent application of the Sherman Act to professional services, next discussed, has again muddied the policy waters. By raising the burden of proof facing anyone challenging certain professional restraints of trade, the Court has created a new risk that professionals will once again be empowered to control their economic environment in their own interests, potentially reversing much of the progress in antitrust enforcement against professionals in the quarter century since *Goldfarb*.

CALIFORNIA DENTAL: FOOTNOTE 17 REDUX

In *California Dental Association [CDA] v. FTC* (526 U.S. 756 [1999]), a 5-to-4 decision in 1999, the Supreme Court significantly widened the field for antitrust defenses based on professional concerns. In CDA, the FTC had condemned a dentists' organization's extensive ethical restrictions on price advertising that, while they did not bar such advertising outright, required that any price claims be "exact, without omissions," and that any discounts offered be accompanied by detailed information concerning the standard price prior to discount. The commission found that, as a practical matter, the "CDA's restrictions on advertising 'low' or 'reasonable' fees, and its extensive disclosure requirement for discount advertising, effectively preclude its members from making low fee and across-the-board discount claims regardless of their truthfulness." The commission then applied the Rule of Reason, utilizing the so-called quick-look approach (see note 4), and condemned both the restrictions on price advertising and the CDA's comparable restrictions on the making of claims about the quality or superiority of services. The Supreme Court, however, held that more than a "quick look" was necessary because, in view of the professional context in which they operated, the restrictions might have a procompetitive rather than an anticompetitive effect.

It is not easy to reconcile the Court's reasoning in CDA or the higher burden of proof it imposed on the FTC with what had previously appeared to be a strong trend in antitrust law away not only from the seemingly permissive dictum in *Goldfarb*'s footnote 17, but also from Panglossian, Arrow-like acceptance of professional control exercised in the name of ethical values. By referring favorably to the 1978 *National Society of Professional Engineers* case, however, the majority opinion suggested that the justices still appreciate the benefits of truncated analysis even in cases involving professional restraints. Indeed, the Court endorsed a "sliding scale," stating that "what is required is an enquiry meet for the case" (526 U.S. at 781), and did not indicate that it was changing the law in any fundamental way. Nevertheless, future litigants and courts, not knowing just how much proof a reviewing court may require to establish that trade was unlawfully restrained, may opt for more extensive discovery, fact-finding, and analysis than would in fact be necessary, raising the cost and thus the difficulty of bringing successful lawsuits against professional organizations engaged in trade-restraining self-regulatory activities. It is noteworthy that Justices Stephen Breyer and John Paul Stevens, the only justices who specialized in antitrust law before joining the Court, differed with the majority, Justice Breyer authoring the persuasive dissenting opinion.

The Supreme Court majority appeared to attach no significance at all to the nakedness of the restraint inherent in the dentists' agreement to advertise only under agreed-upon rules and implied that such restraints could be analyzed just as ancillary ones are analyzed, balancing their "anticompetitive" effects against their "procompetitive" effects. The Court was unclear just how a naked restraint might promote competition, however, and its suggestion that the CDA's restrictions on advertising might be "procompetitive" prompted one commentator to observe, "This is another example of the poverty of the legal language of antitrust because the conduct is explicitly and confessedly anticompetitive in every logical sense even if it may bring about 'good consequences' " (Carstenson 2000: 433). Justice David Souter further demonstrated his confusion about such matters by suggesting that deceptive advertising, which was all that the CDA ostensibly sought to suppress, has an "anticompetitive, not procompetitive," effect— even though advertising of any kind leaves the market no less competitive than it was before. It seems apparent that the majority used the terms *procompetitive* and *anticompetitive* not with reference to the competitive process — the vigor of which has always been thought to be the touchstone of antitrust analysis — but with reference to consumer welfare itself.

The only thing that saved the majority from falling into the trap of accepting a pure "worthy-purpose" defense was its emphasis on the difficulty consumers have in evaluating professional advertising. Indeed, the CDA opinion is the most explicit one to date that embraces the notion that professional self-regulation may directly restrain competition yet still be open to justification by demonstrating the existence of a theoretical market failure that the restraint in question may help to overcome. Nevertheless, the CDA's regulatory regime did not in fact make professional advertising any more helpful to consumers, thereby arguably making competition a more effective force for enhancing consumer welfare. Although the majority was unimpressed by the court of appeals' observation that "the record provides no evidence that the rule has in fact led to increased disclosure and transparency of dental pricing," a truly procompetitive restraint would not prevent all advertising of prices or quality but would instead foster more credible, informative advertising that will enable consumers to choose among providers of dental services with greater confidence. It is of course highly unlikely that the CDA's members wanted to promote competition in this manner. Moreover, there were many less restrictive alternative methods the CDA might have employed if it were truly interested in overcoming consumers' information deficits.

Justice Souter also found irrelevant the FTC's observation that the restraint on advertising reduced the output of information consumers could use to purchase dental services. Information is a public good that is chronically underproduced in the marketplace, and additional restraints on its production might be seen as exacerbating, not curing, a serious market failure. Although the quality (accuracy) of information is also a legitimate concern (because of consumers' inability to evaluate it, another market failure), reduced output of information should be, despite Justice Souter's puzzlement, as much a concern of antitrust law as the output of dental services. Likewise, competitor collaboration that increased the output of reliable professional advertising would be procompetitive in the true sense. In general, antitrust law has not been effectively applied to efforts by professional organizations to produce, and perhaps even to dominate the production of, information useful to consumers in purchasing professional and other services (Havighurst and Brody 1994).

The Supreme Court, it seems, has opened the door for market-failure defenses much wider than is prudent. Although the Court's justification for rejecting quick-look analysis lies in the objectively greater seriousness of the imperfections found in markets for professional services, the Court, by giving professionals the benefit of a number of doubts, has invited professionals to take their chances with highly restrictive self-regulatory rules. Indeed, the policy behind the original invention of the bright-line per se rules of antitrust law seems to have been sacrificed on the assumption that professional competitors can be trusted to exercise dangerous powers in the public interest. As noted above, any market-failure defense is itself a stretch, given the statute's prohibition of "every . . . restraint of trade." Even though recognizing such a defense for modest naked restraints may nevertheless be prudent in order to protect antitrust law against the charge that it is out of touch with economic reality, a market-failure defense arising out of such considerations would be far narrower than the one the Court seemed to recognize in CDA.

On remand, the court of appeals eventually ordered dismissal of the FTC's case against the CDA, this time having nothing whatever to say about the paucity of dentists' advertising of prices or quality claims (California Dental Ass'n v. FTC, 224 F.3d 942 [9th Cir. 2000]). The court found that the FTC had failed to prove the anticompetitive effects of the restrictions and refused to allow the FTC, which had elected to have the lower court revisit the case on the original record, an opportunity to reopen the record to provide additional evidence. The FTC subsequently elected not to seek another Supreme Court review, even though it had serious doubts about the Ninth Circuit's ruling. Three commissioners declared that their "decision to support bringing an end to this case should not be taken as an indication of any lessening of our keen interest in the activities of trade or professional organizations that harm competition" (FTC 2001). Thus, it is far from clear that Justice Souter's troublesome opinion will significantly slow down or divert the antitrust movement against anticompetitive actions by professional organizations. Indeed, because the CDA decision dealt only with the amount of proof needed to invalidate a professional restraint, it is unlikely to enable professional organizations to reassume de facto regulatory powers of the kind they exercised without appreciable challenge when Arrow observed the market for medical care.

CONCLUSION

The antitrust initiative in the health care sector had to overcome many obstacles originating in the perception that competition is somehow inappropriate in the sale and purchase of health services — a perception that found authoritative support in Kenneth Arrow's famous 1963 essay. To its credit, the legal system eventually resisted, for the most part, the impulse to fashion a special antitrust policy tolerant of trade restraints imposed by medical or other professional interests. The result of adhering to the procompetitive policy of the Sherman Act, even in the face of strong arguments to sacrifice it, was to radically transform the health care system that Arrow had observed, ending one-party rule by professional interests and introducing price competition where it had previously been suppressed. These changes, which no one could have fully envisioned when Arrow wrote, have been in many respects, though not unarguably, in the public interest.[9]

Despite its successes, the antitrust initiative has clearly failed to create a true, consumer-driven market for health services in the United States. The reason is quite simple: while effective antitrust enforcement is a necessary condition for a market-oriented policy, it is far from being a sufficient one. Indeed, if a market-oriented health policy seems unworkable in health care today, it may only be because, for whatever reason, the legal system as a whole (in contrast with its machinery for antitrust enforcement) has not embraced it fully and given it a chance to work as other markets do. A principal source of the problems in today's market for health services, for example, is overregulation, which comes in various forms but which has the effect of greatly restricting freedom of contract and denying consumers opportunities to make economizing choices. Arrow himself recognized how regulation and professional standards artificially restricted consumers' choices even in 1963: "It would usually happen in a competitive market that many qualities will be offered on the market, at suitably varying prices, to appeal to different tastes and incomes. Both the licensing laws and the standards of medical-school training have limited the possibilities of alternative qualities of medical care." (953) To be sure, this passage reveals no particular concern on Arrow's part about the restrictions on consumers' choices circa 1963. But one wonders whether he is as sanguine today, with regulation forcing so many Americans either to bear the very high cost of upper-middle-class health care or to go without any health coverage at all (Havighurst 2001). In any event, preemption of consumer choice by the law and the medical profession's standards of clinical practice is even more deeply embedded in law today than it was when Arrow had his insight.[10]

It is regrettable that Arrow's thoughtful contribution to understanding the difficult economics of health care has been most popular among ideological opponents of markets and supporters of government control and regulation. Indeed, scholars almost always cite Arrow's article only to obviate — not to begin — a careful consideration of the market's possibilities. With the idea of building health policy on a market foundation thus relegated to the scrap heap of history because Arrow suggested the market was a theoretical failure, today's policy makers, together with their aides and their academic abettors, continue to construct a health system on no foundation at all, using materials that are probably even more imperfect, and certainly less democratic, than consumer choice.

NOTES

1 Sociologist Paul Starr (1982: 227), although agreeing with Arrow about the problems confronting consumers in the health care marketplace, has suggested that professionalism, which Arrow viewed as a creative social response to inherent market failure, may in fact be a cause of some of the market's difficulties:

> The structural features Arrow discusses have a history. He writes that when the market fails, "society" will make adjustments. This is too abstract. It is as if some inner dynamic were pushing the world toward Pareto optimality. One has to ask:

For whom did the market fail, and how did "society" make these adjustments? The competitive market was failing no one more than the medical profession, and it was the profession that organized to change it — that barred advertising and price competition, lobbied for licensing laws, engaged in price discrimination, and fought against prepaid health plans.

Starr was certainly right that many of the antimarket arrangements that Arrow had viewed as the work of a nonmarket "invisible hand" bore the fingerprints of organized medicine. Although this is not to say that those arrangements were necessarily on balance harmful to consumers, the antitrust campaign that began in the health care sector in the mid-1970s proceeded on that premise, and the litigation it spawned revealed few, if any, instances in which professional or other restraints of trade yielded a clear net benefit for consumers.

2 At the stage where the Supreme Court was considering whether to hear the plaintiff's appeal in *Goldfarb*, the instant author submitted a brief amicus curiae (pro se) specifically arguing the great importance of the legal issue in the case for the health care sector.

3 See, e.g., Havighurst 1970 (early advocacy of a "market-oriented health care system" and of antitrust enforcement to make it feasible).

4 National Soc'y Prof'l Eng'rs v. United States, 435 U.S. 679 (1978) ("no elaborate industry analysis is required to demonstrate the anticompetitive character of such an agreement"); FTC v. Indiana Fed'n Dentists, 476 U.S. 447 (1986) ("Application of the Rule of Reason to these facts is not a matter of any great difficulty"). In *Arizona v. Maricopa County Medical Society* (457 U.S. 332 [1982]), although the Court professed to apply a per se rule (that is, a conclusive presumption of illegality), it in fact treated the presumption as rebuttable and evaluated the defendants' claims that their maximum-price-fixing agreement was procompetitive, finding that "the limited record in this case is not inconsistent with the presumption that the respondents' agreement will not significantly enhance competition."

5 National Gerimedical Hosp. & Gerontology Ctr v. Blue Cross of Kansas City, 452 U.S. 393 (1981) (federal planning legislation held not to create "a 'pervasive' repeal of the antitrust laws as applied to every action taken in response to the health-care planning process"). See generally Havighurst 1983; Bolze and Pennak 1984. Although health planning was promoted as an answer to moral hazard and other perverse incentives contributing to cost-increasing nonprice competition and excessive "duplication" in hospital and other health care markets, it and its regulatory offshoot, entry control by "certificate of need," were generally more successful in legitimizing rapidly rising costs than in containing them. See Payton and Powsner 1980.

6 Such courts failed to distinguish between cases in which a hospital delegates final responsibility for dispensing privileges to its medical staff (and thus to competitors of the aspirants themselves) and cases in which the medical staff operates not as an independent agent of the medical profession as a whole, but as an accountable agent of the hospital itself. In thrall to the same professional paradigm that Arrow seemingly accepted at face value, these judges were simply unable to view hospitals as having

primary responsibility for determining, with their doctors' help, the quality of care to be rendered under their auspices. See Havighurst 1984, arguing that rigorous antitrust thinking could have prevented antitrust law from becoming, through its unpredictability, a significant inhibitor of desirable peer review in hospitals.

7   For a notable rejection of a "worthy purpose" defense, see *National Society of Professional Engineers v. United States*, 435 U.S. 679 (1978), in which the defendants claimed that their restraint on competitive bidding for engineering work yielded a level of safety more consistent with the public interest than would result under unbridled competition. The Supreme Court refused to permit such a defense, which it declared "a frontal assault on the fundamental policy of the Sherman Act."

8   The Court, in *National Society of Professional Engineers* (see note 7), did not declare the engineers' restraint, though a naked one, to be per se unlawful and (by observing that the restraint "operates as an absolute ban on competitive bidding, applying with equal force to both complicated and simple projects and to both inexperienced and sophisticated customers") implied that a minor naked restraint might be justified if it were well tailored to offset a demonstrable market failure.

9   Without antitrust enforcement, things might have taken a quite different path, including one that many observers would undoubtedly have preferred. See Havighurst 2000 (suggesting the likelihood that "without antitrust enforcement clearing the way for private innovation, government would have assumed the dominant role in American health care, as it has in other countries").

10 "It is conventional in health care law for courts to consult custom and consensus in the medical community, not specifications in private contracts, for the standards they use in defining the duties of providers in tort suits or the payment obligations of health plans in disputes over benefits. . . . It is simply ironic that the same legal system that with one arm launched an antitrust initiative successfully challenging overt efforts by the medical profession to exercise decision-making authority has with its other arms given medical interests a monopoly over the most important economic decisions affecting American health care" (Havighurst 2000: 96–97).

REFERENCES

Arrow, K. J. 1963. Uncertainty and the Welfare Economics of Medical Care. *American Economic Review* 53(5): 941–973.

Bolze, R. S., and M. W. Pennak. 1984. Reconciliation of the Sherman Act with Federal Health-Planning Legislation: Implied Antitrust Immunity in the Health Care Field. *Antitrust Bulletin* 29: 225–252.

Carstenson, P. C. 2000. The Per Se Legality of Some Naked Restraints: A (Re)conceptualization of the Antitrust Analysis of Cartelistic Organizations. *Antitrust Bulletin* 45: 349–435.

Federal Trade Commission (FTC). 2001. Statement of Chair Robert Pitofsky et al. Available on-line at www.ftc.gov/os/2001./02/cdastmt.htm.

Goldberg, L., and W. Greenberg. 1977. The Effect of Physician-Controlled Health Insurance: U.S. Oregon State Medical Society. *Journal of Health Politics, Policy and Law* 2: 48–78.

Greaney, T. L. 1989. Quality of Care and Market Failure Defenses in Antitrust Health Care Litigation. *Connecticut Law Review* 21: 605–665.

Havighurst, C. C. 1970. Health Maintenance Organizations and the Market for Health Services. *Law and Contemporary Problems* 35: 716–795.

———. 1983. Health Planning and Antitrust Law: The Implied Amendment Doctrine of the *Rex Hospital Case. North Carolina Central Law Journal* 14(1): 45–74.

———. 1984. Doctors and Hospitals: An Antitrust Perspective on Traditional Relationships. *Duke Law Journal* 1984(6): 1071–1162.

———. 2000. American Health Care and the Law—We Need to Talk! *Health Affairs* 19(4): 84–106.

———. In press. The Backlash against Managed Health Care: Hard Politics Make Bad Policy. *Indiana Law Review.*

Havighurst, C. C., and P. M. Brody. 1994. Accrediting and the Sherman Act. *Law and Contemporary Problems* 57(4): 199–242.

Kauper, T. E. 1988. The Role of Quality of Health Care Considerations in Antitrust Analysis. *Law and Contemporary Problems* 51(2): 273–340.

Payton, S., and R. M. Powsner. 1980. Regulation through the Looking Glass: Hospitals, Blue Cross and Certificate-of-Need. *Michigan Law Review* 79: 203–277.

Starr, P. 1982. *The Social Transformation of American Medicine.* New York: Basic Books.

PART II

Risk, Insurance,

and Redistribution

SHERRY A. GLIED

Health Insurance and Market Failure since Arrow

Illness is usually unexpected and often costly. Health insurance is a contingent claims contract that moves funds from the usual state of the world, when one is healthy, to the unexpected and costly state, when one is ill. In this sense, it is a market success: an institutional response to a natural feature of the demand for health care. Without such an institution, there would be no market to transfer funds between health states. In its operation, however, health insurance introduces its own set of market failures. The key features of the health insurance institutions we observe now are, in turn, responses to the existence of these market failures. This recursive relationship between institutions and market failure is a core organizing theme of Arrow's article.

Arrow described institutional arrangements in health care as responses to the market failures of his time. Strikingly, to a reader in 2001, Arrow gave health insurance relatively little airplay in his article. Instead, Arrow devoted the bulk of his essay to the training and organization of professionals and the nature of hospitals. Today, most writers would view the topics Arrow stressed as largely secondary in importance to the organization and nature of health insurance in explaining the functioning of the health care system as a whole. Health insurance, a source of market failure on its own, has now become a central force in addressing the other market failures Arrow identified throughout the health care market.

The purpose of this article is to build on Arrow's work in examining the evolution of insurance institutions in response to the market failures that arise in individual insurance contracts and in the market for health insurance. This institutional evolution, in turn, explains why health insurance moved from the periphery to the core of the health care sector. Finally, this evolution also illuminates where private market institutions can, and where they cannot, effectively address insurance market failures.

ARROW ON INSURANCE

Arrow addressed two aspects of health insurance in his 1963 article (and in his 1965 response to comments on it): the form of insurance contracts and the functioning of the insurance market.

With respect to the form of insurance, he noted that the scope of insurance coverage was limited. Insurance arises to cover unexpected events, so health insurance sensibly did not typically cover services that were predictable, such as maternity care. Arrow also pointed out that there was little insurance available for illness-related disabilities. He explained these limitations of insurance contracts as a market response to moral hazard, which leads to expanded utilization in the presence of insurance. Arrow described the coexistence of three types of insurance: cash indemnity policies, cost indemnity policies, and prepayment plans. In his view, none of these existing insurance contracts fully addressed the problem of moral hazard. He suggested that insurance contracts generally lacked much incentive for patients or providers to seek, or provide, low-cost services. Thus, expansions of health insurance drove up expenditures on health care.

Arrow emphasized two features of insurance market functioning. First, he noted the role of large groups in the insurance market. He viewed the existence of these groups as an institutional response to administrative economies in the selling of insurance, pointing out the difference in costs between individual and group coverage. Arrow attributed gaps in coverage largely to the difficulty that certain groups had in taking advantage of administrative economies in the purchase of coverage. Groups that did not have direct access to employer-sponsored insurance lacked individual coverage, he implied, because they faced very high loading costs associated with the difficulty of selling individual policies.

Second, he considered the role of the relatively noncompetitive, Blue Cross–dominated insurance market of his day. That market pooled unequal risks — providing insurance that directly contradicted the economic theory of insurance markets. He argued that Blue Cross was an institutional response to the lack of long-term health insurance. Community-rated insurance offers coverage against the risk of a change in one's basic state of health. Similarly, Arrow viewed the low level of competition in the insurance market as an institutional response to the problem of adverse selection.

THE CHANGING FORM OF COVERAGE AND MARKET FOR INSURANCE

The financial role of insurance in the health care sector has nearly doubled since 1963. In 1963, 46 percent of all medical expenses were paid by insurance. In 1998, 83 percent of all medical expenses were paid by insurance (author's tabulations of the National Health Accounts). This expansion is a consequence of shifts both in the form of insurance contracts and in the insurance market.

The form of insurance contracts has changed significantly since 1963. The scope of coverage has broadened dramatically. Virtually every aspect of health care, from hospital stays to eyeglasses, is now covered by insurance. Disability insurance also is widespread, and about 35 percent of workers own a private disability insurance policy, while almost everyone holds limited and implicit disability income insurance through the Social Security Income and Social Security Disability Insurance programs.

The organizational form of health insurance has changed. The coexistence of three types of insurance in Arrow's day suggested a market without a dominant institutional form. Today, virtually all insurance is a form of prepayment. In about 90 percent of instances, what we call *traditional indemnity* coverage includes an out-of-pocket payment limit beyond which insurance pays all (Bureau of Labor Statistics 1999). This change, too, has expanded the share of insurance payments in total expenditures.

There have been substantial changes in the insurance market as well. There has been some expansion in coverage. In 1963, an estimated 78 percent of the population held some form of health insurance coverage (Lees and Rice 1965). By 1999, 85 percent of the population held medical expense coverage. The small overall change masks a major distributional change. While the elderly were most likely to lack coverage in Arrow's day, today virtually all the aged have insurance coverage through the public Medicare program.

Mechanisms for pooling in the health insurance market have changed as well. Community rating has all but disappeared. In its place, public and private institutions now perform the task of pooling risks more broadly. The costliest segments of the market, the elderly and those with permanent disabilities, are now covered by public programs. In the private market, almost all coverage is now purchased through employers, the continuation of a trend that was already well under way by 1963. Individual insurance is only a residual category today.

EXPLAINING THE GROWTH IN THE INSURED SHARE OF EXPENDITURES

The growing share of expenditures that is paid by insurance is a consequence of both public actions and private market forces. Public coverage expansions, particularly the introduction of Medicare and Medicaid in 1965, mean that many of the most costly previously uninsured now hold coverage. New coverage means that some expenses are now paid by insurance rather than out of pocket. In addition, new coverage has led, through moral hazard, to a net increase in health expenditures. Legislation also expanded the scope of coverage, for example, by mandating that insurers cover pregnancy and other services.

In the private sector, the growing role of health insurance is, in large measure, a consequence of the rise in the cost of health services. In 1963, health expenditures accounted for 5.5 percent of the GDP. By 1998, that share had more than doubled to 13.5 percent. But average statistics are not informative about the demand for health insurance to protect against unanticipated risk. Insurance transfers funds from good states of health to bad states, so a better statistic compares good and bad states. Such a measure is the ratio of average expenses for the top 1 percent of health care spenders to average incomes. In 1963, those who found themselves in the "bad state"—the top 1 percent of spenders—spent an average of $12,960 (1996 dollars), about 1.3 times average personal income ($9,886) in that year (Glied 1997). In 1996, by comparison, the top 1 percent spent an average of $61,500 (1996 dollars), nearly 3 times the average income of $21,385 in that year (author's tabulations of the MEPS). While borrowing and saving could plausibly substitute for formal health insurance contracts in 1963, that was not a realistic option for most people in 1996. Expanding the scope of insurance, in turn, led to further increases in cost through moral hazard effects.

Arrow anticipated neither the legislative actions nor the extraordinary cost growth that occurred in health care markets since 1963. In his 1965 article, he argued that the large economies of scale in insurance purchasing were a good argument for government purchasing. His only comment about cost growth concerns the role of moral hazard in raising the cost of major medical insurance. Looking backward, the missing piece in Arrow's article is the role of technological change, the phenomenon that, according to most subsequent observers, has propelled the growth in the cost of health care since the early 1960s (Newhouse 1992).

TECHNOLOGY, MARKET FAILURE, AND
INSURANCE INSTITUTIONS TODAY

Public coverage expansions and regulations have obviously played an enormous role in our health care system. They have not, however, had a profound impact on either the form of insurance or the functioning of the private insurance market.

Indeed, the one remaining 1963-style insurance contract that, with only a few revisions, exists in today's market is the Medicare indemnity policy. Medicare addresses moral hazard through unlimited cost sharing, leaving beneficiaries vulnerable to the financial costs of long-term illnesses. Moreover, it excludes coverage for relatively predictable costs, such as outpatient prescription drugs.

At the market level, Medicare and Medicaid pulled some of the costliest cases and worst risks out of the private insurance market. The categorical nature of eligibility for these programs (especially Medicare), however, means their introduction did not alter the problems of economies of scale in administration and adverse selection that Arrow identified in the private market of 1963.

Instead, the factor that has had the greatest impact on insurance-related market failure and institutional response has been technological change in health care. Technological improvements in the nature and quality of health care have made access to care more important and have driven increases in the cost of care. Better quality and higher cost care have precipitated the expansion in the extent and scope of private health insurance coverage and thus led to increased moral hazard. Many analysts also argue that expanded health insurance has interacted with the process of technological innovation and diffusion to introduce a new form of market failure, dynamic moral hazard, into the market (Goddeeris 1984; Baumgardner 1991).

This line of research argues that the existence of health insurance encourages the development and dissemination of cost-increasing technologies. In the presence of insurance-induced moral hazard, technology developers and providers compete to attract patients by choosing technologies that improve the quality of care. There is little reason to develop or choose technologies that lower costs.

Technological change has altered the forms of market failure in health insurance that Arrow identified in 1963. But the interplay between market failures, wherever they originate, and institutions that Arrow described in 1963 continues now. Just as Arrow argued in 1963, each of these market failures has generated its own set of institutional responses, and, in turn, these institutional responses have led to further market failures.

Technological Change and the Form of Coverage
Health insurance, Arrow points out, provides financial protection against risk. But the types of contracts that Arrow observed would leave purchasers in today's health insurance vulnerable to substantial risk.

Unlike Medicare, private health insurance contracts have evolved since 1963 in ways that have reduced the financial risks of purchasers. The extent of cost sharing has been limited, and the scope of coverage has been expanded. Consider prescription drugs, an area where technological change has led to an explosion in spending. In 1963, prescription drug expenditures averaged $86 per capita (1998 dollars) and 95 percent of these costs were paid out of pocket; today, drug expenditures average $323 per capita. While Medicare does not cover prescription drugs, 73 percent of all drug costs are covered by health insurance today. This more generous coverage corrects the market failure of too much risk bearing, but at a cost.

Better protection against risk through lower cost sharing means that without other changes, insurance contracts today would generate additional moral hazard with respect to the level of utilization. They would also give consumers even less incentive to search for low-cost providers and may generate dynamic moral hazard. For example, in the presence of insurance without strong controls for moral hazard, hospital competition can degenerate into a medical arms race in which hospitals seek to attract physicians (and, by extension, patients) by acquiring better, but more costly, technology (Luft et al. 1986).

The increase in moral hazard at a point in time and over time, associated with lower cost sharing, in turn, has generated a raft of new institutions that address moral hazard problems in other ways. These include various forms of supply-side cost sharing and direct monitoring of utilization through utilization review, which address the direct moral hazard effect. The development of closed, or preferred, panels of providers has shifted the search function from consumers to insurers, who, because they bear most of the financial risk of utilization, have a strong incentive to search efficiently. Some evidence suggests that these new ways of addressing moral hazard also have an effect on dynamic moral hazard. A growing literature shows some differences in the patterns of diffusion and introduction of technologies between markets where managed care is dominant and those where traditional insurance is dominant (see, for example, Chernew et al. 1998).

These new institutions move health insurance squarely to the middle of some of the central health care system problems related to asymmetries of information between consumers and providers identified by Arrow in 1963. In the presence of asymmetric information between consumers and providers, supply-side cost sharing, a technique insurers use to reduce moral hazard, can lead to underservice and skimping on quality. Consumers have difficulty evaluating the quality of panels of providers, just as they did in selecting an individual physician. These developments move existing market failures under the umbrella of health insurance.

In Arrow's original conception, insurers played no part in addressing the market failure associated with the asymmetry of information between consumers and providers. In the context of these new methods of addressing moral hazard, as well as the growing complexity of decision making in this market, insurers are also beginning to act as information intermediaries. The development of quality reporting, health plan report cards, and brand-name health plans may allow insurers to address moral hazard without tripping over these persistent market failures.

Technological Change and the Insurance Market
Technological change has also directly and indirectly affected the asymmetries of information that exist between the purchaser and the insurer at the moment

of purchase. These asymmetries may lead to adverse selection in the insurance market. Better diagnostic tests (likely to be exacerbated in the future with genetic testing) and better (and more costly) treatment of chronic diseases mean that many consumers now have both more information and more incentive to seek out insurance that offers them the best possible package in response to their idiosyncratic risk profile.

In a free market, insurers generally respond to adverse selection with respect to chronic and predictable conditions by removing them from coverage. This is a market failure, as Arrow noted, in that presumably people would prefer to have insurance against the risk of developing such conditions. This problem is exacerbated when technological improvements make treatment more effective and more costly. In that circumstance, limiting insurance coverage leaves many people without financial access to valuable care.

The market response to this increase in selection has been further degeneration of the individual health insurance market and increased reliance on employer-sponsored coverage. This solution is of limited effectiveness. Employees who lose or leave their jobs may lose health coverage entirely or be unable to buy coverage that protects them against chronic conditions. These problems of incomplete coverage (both at a point in time and over time) have generated legislative responses in the form of insurance coverage mandates that compel insurers to include costly chronic conditions, such as mental health problems, within the scope of coverage, and portability legislation.

Improved technology and its attendant costs have increased the normative importance of all gaps in coverage. As the quality of medical care increases, people want more of it. As technology drives costs up, though, growing numbers of people can no longer afford coverage that would give them access to the latest improvements. The insurance market has not effectively addressed this problem. Instead, public funding plays an increasingly important role in paying for the costs of care for those who could not otherwise afford it. Since Arrow wrote, the public sector of health care financing in the United States has expanded vastly—from 25 to 45 percent. And new initiatives, such as Medicare prescription drug coverage and coverage expansion, suggest that the public share is just going to grow further.

HEALTH INSURANCE: MARKET FAILURE OR MARKET SUCCESS?

Arrow identified two types of market failures associated with health insurance: those related to the insurance contract and those related to the insurance market. Both types of market failure have been challenged by technological change over the intervening four decades. The evidence suggests that insurance has been a market success with respect to the problems associated with individual contracts. There have been many effective innovations that help reduce financial risk while controlling moral hazard. Some even seem to be holding back inefficient technological change.

Insurance has been much less of a success with respect to the insurance market. Technological change has improved the quality of care but also increased its costs. In combination, these two factors make it even more valuable for people to hold coverage today than in Arrow's day. Yet the insurance market has not succeeded in developing effective mechanisms, beyond employer-based coverage, for providing coverage to those who have chronic conditions or are at high risk of developing serious problems. Nor has it developed stand-alone mechanisms for redistribution of insurance to those who cannot afford it. In this area, larger pools and government action, as Arrow foresaw, are the only likely solutions.

REFERENCES

Arrow, Kenneth. 1965. Uncertainty and the Welfare Economics of Medical Care: Reply. *American Economic Review* 55(1): 154–157.

Baumgardner, James. 1991. The Interaction between Forms of Insurance Contract and Types of Technological Change in Medical Care. *RAND Journal of Economics* 22(1): 36–53.

Bureau of Labor Statistics. 1999. *Employee Benefits in Medium and Large Private Establishments, 1997.* Bureau of Labor Statistics Bulletin 2517 (Sept.). Washington, DC: Bureau of Labor Statistics.

Chernew, Michael E., Richard A. Hirth, Seema S. Sonnad, Rachel Ermann, and A. Mark Fendrick. 1998. Managed Care, Medical Technology, and Health Care Cost Growth: A Review of the Evidence. *Medical Care Research and Review* 55(3): 259–288.

Glied, Sherry A. 1997. *Chronic Condition.* Cambridge: Harvard University Press.

Goddeeris, John H. 1984. Medical Insurance, Technological Change, and Welfare. *Economic Inquiry* 22: 56–67.

Lees, Dennis S., and Robert G. Rice. 1965. Uncertainty and the Welfare Economics of Medical Care: Comment. *American Economic Review* 55(1): 140–154.

Luft, Harold S., James C. Robinson, Deborah W. Garnick, Susan C. Maerki, and Stephen J. McPhee. 1986. The Role of Specialized Clinical Services in Competition Among Hospitals. *Inquiry* 23: 83–94.

Newhouse, Joseph P. 1992. Medical Care Costs: How Much Welfare Loss? *Journal of Economic Perspectives* 6(3): 3–21.

UWE E. REINHARDT

■ Can Efficiency in Health Care Be Left to the Market?

Kenneth Arrow's "Uncertainty and the Welfare Economics of Medical Care" (1963) was published at a time when health economists were still a small sect of adventurous scholars. Regular economists wondered why any ambitious young academic would venture into such strange, uncharted territory from which one might never be able to return—to the comfort of academic tenure. The natives of the uncharted territory, on the other hand, greeted the sect as arrogant missionaries bent upon imposing neoclassical economic doctrine on a people who viewed their land as a semireligious place that would forever remain impenetrable to commercial forces. What greater comfort for the adventurous sect than to receive from the hand of one of the world's most renowned regular economists a treatise that not only lent professional respect to the sect's exploits, but also served as an authoritative road map for much bolder incursions into health care.

Arrow's script is dated by the graceful prose then still customary among social scientists. It is, however, so richly laden and so compact that it demands from readers nothing less than the academic analogue of talmudic scholarship. As James Robinson remarks at length in his essay in this volume, casually read, or selectively cited, the article can be made to serve all manner of entrenched economic interests or preferred ideology.

Arrow's objective in his article was to identify the special characteristics of medical care that set it apart from the standard norms of welfare economics. To that end he described in passing the main pillars of these norms: the fundamental concept of Pareto optimality (also known among economists as Pareto efficiency) and the First and Second Theorems of Pareto Optimality. He concluded from this exercise that health care differs from the conditions posited for standard welfare economics mainly because two types of markets were insufficiently developed in health care. The first type was markets for the risk inherent in the uncertainty in the incidence of disease and in the efficacy of treatment. The second type was markets for the information assumed to be accessible for all participants in perfectly competitive markets.

Naturally, Arrow's conclusion kindled the hope among legions of younger economic disciples that, with the aid of better information technology, the missing markets could be developed in the foreseeable future. If that could be accomplished, then the efficient allocation of health care resources could be entrusted to the "invisible hand" of a price-competitive marketplace, which economists are uniquely qualified to understand, and public health policy could be confined to sundry externalities (e.g., halting the spread of contagious diseases) and to the redistribution of purchasing power for the sake of social equity. It is now a deeply held credo that has fueled health economics and U.S. health policy ever since. In fact, a good part of the theoretical and empirical work in health economics since the appearance of Arrow's article reminds one of the medieval scholastics who, under Saint Anselm's motto *fides quaerens intelligentiam* [faith seeking understanding], conducted their research to give rational content to their faith (*Columbia Encyclopedia*, 5th ed., 1993: 2447).

Remarkably, nowhere in his article did Arrow himself ever dream that boldly. If he had thought that the missing markets could be developed one day soon, presumably he would have counseled policy makers to see to the careful development of these markets first before turning the health sector to the mercies of a commercial free-for-all. Sadly, U.S. health policy since Arrow's writing has proceeded in precisely the reverse order, as the so-called procompetitive strategy during the 1980s and of managed competition with managed care during the 1990s so amply demonstrate. If the experience of these past two decades in U.S. health policy is to persuade the general public that a market approach will move health care closer to what the public wants to read into the words *efficient* and *optimal*, then the disciples advocating that approach have work to do.

The present essay will use Arrow's seminal article as a springboard to explain to noneconomists what properly trained economists mean by terms such as *efficient* and *optimal* and how much that usage deviates from what the public associates with these terms. The essay begins with an exposition of the First and Second Theorems of Optimality cited by Arrow at the beginning of his article. That exploration requires a careful look at the meaning of Pareto optimality (alias Pareto efficiency) as these terms are used by economists. Next, this essay elaborates upon a passing remark by Arrow suggesting that economists may err when they deem redistribution of purchasing power by government generally superior to the distribution by government of benefits in kind. The third section recounts very briefly what happened when, during the 1990s, the Second Theorem of Optimality encountered the real world. By way of summary, the essay concludes with

Arrow's gentle warning that economists refrain from using their technical jargon wittingly or unwittingly to play politics in the guise of science.

THE NORMS OF WELFARE ECONOMICS

At the time Arrow's article was penned, graduate students in economics were well familiar with the First and Second Theorems of Optimality, which furnished the benchmark against which Arrow examined medical care. Most probably, at the time, students would have been assigned Francis Bator's classic essays on the subject in "The Simple Economics of Welfare Maximization" (1957) and "The Anatomy of Market Failure" (1958). The first article, in particular, offers a lucid, graphic exposition of modern welfare economics and warns students about its limits. As already noted, fundamental to the two theorems is the concept of Pareto optimality.

The Concept of Pareto Optimality

Citing Vilfredo Pareto (1897), Arrow writes that in a competitive equilibrium characterized by a Pareto optimal allocation of resources, "There is no other allocation of resources to services which will make *all* participants in the market better off" (942, emphasis added). The words *all participants* in this phrasing make it a rather stringent condition of optimality. More commonly, economists define a Pareto optimal or Pareto efficient allocation of resources as one at which "the only way to make one individual [or more] better off is to make another individual [or more] worse off" (Katz and Rosen 1991: 424–425). It is hard to disagree with that definition of optimality; it borders on a tautology. In Arrow's words: "It is reasonable enough to assert that a change in allocation which makes all participants better off is one that certainly should be made; this is a value judgment, not a descriptive proposition, but it is a very weak one. From this it follows that it is not desirable to put up with a non-optimal allocation" (942). Figure 1 serves to illustrate the power and limits of the concept of Pareto optimality. It must be emphasized that the axes in this graph represent not real resources but, presumably, quantifiable degrees of human happiness measured in units economists call *utils*. The solid, downward sloping curve in the graph depicts the maximum happiness that a two-person society, with its available real resources, can bestow upon citizen A at a given level of citizen B's happiness. The curve represents this two-person society's happiness-trade-off-possibility frontier. A moment's thought makes it clear that any point on the frontier must be Pareto optimal (Pareto efficient). Any point in the interior of the set bounded by the frontier evidently is Pareto inefficient.

All economists and, indeed, all laypersons ought to agree that any policy that would move the economy from the interior point C to the Pareto-efficient fron-

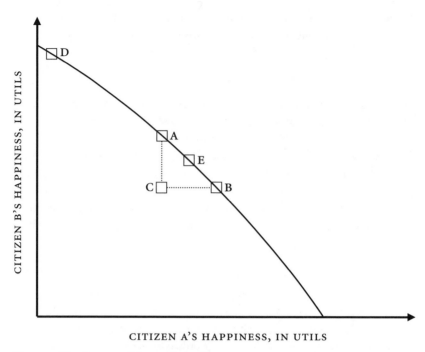

CITIZEN A'S HAPPINESS, IN UTILS

Figure 1   The Concept of Pareto Optimality

tier between (and including) points A and B is to be desired. It would represent not only an increase in efficiency, as economists define that term, but reasonable people generally would view the change as unambiguously an improvement over the previous allocation. To paraphrase Arrow, it would be inexcusable to put up with allocation C if any point on the line segment AB were technically and politically attainable.

As Arrow also is quick to point out, however, there is no reason why society should put up with any one Pareto-efficient allocation. In terms of Figure 1, for example, society might prefer Pareto-efficient allocation E to Pareto-efficient allocation A. In a move from one efficient allocation to another, however, someone necessarily will be made worse off to make someone else better off, which implies that the merit of such a change rests on a pure social value judgment. Unfortunately, the Pareto criterion itself does not offer any way to assess the social desirability of such a change or, for that matter, of any move along the Pareto-efficient frontier, although public policy typically involves precisely just such moves. That is why Pareto's concept of efficiency or optimality by itself typically is useless in the world of practical affairs. As economist William Baumol (1969: 503) has observed on the Paretian construct:

Pareto optimality analysis sidesteps the issue of income distribution. . . . [Optimality rules resting on a Paretian foundation] remain either silent or prejudiced in favor of the status quo on the issue of income distribution and are, therefore, necessarily incomplete or unsatisfactory even on matters for which distribution is not the primary issue. Ultimately, the Paretian criterion can be considered the welfare economists' instrument par excellence for the circumvention of this issue.

In his essay, Arrow argues that under certain highly restrictive conditions, this analytic conundrum can be circumvented with appeal to the First and Second Theorems of Optimality, which imply that the problem can be resolved through reliance on competitive markets. That proposition is so fundamental to modern welfare economics and so momentous in its implications for public policy that it warrants extended review.

The First Theorem of Optimality
Among the more triumphant moments in the life of economics professors is the demonstration, in Arrow's words, that "if a competitive equilibrium exists at all, and if all commodities relevant to costs or utilities are in fact priced in the market, then the equilibrium is necessarily [Pareto] optimal (942, emphasis in original). It is the famous First Theorem of Optimality. Once the professors' students have graduated from college and matured to decision makers in the world of practical affairs, they recite the theorem as the credo that markets always are more efficient than alternative algorithms for resource allocation, with only a distant memory of the stringent conditions underlying the theorem, if any memory at all.

Two observations can be made in connection with this theorem. First, the minimal conditions for the functioning of the competitive markets assumed for the theorem are (1) that both sellers and buyers fully understand and can assess the relevant dimensions of the particular goods and services traded in the market, (2) that both of them are price takers in the sense that as individual participants in the market they are too insignificant to have any influence at all over prices, and (3) that *all* relevant prices are known to *all* participants before transactions are consummated. It is left to the reader to assess how well even now, four decades after Arrow's article was published and almost two decades into the information revolution, the typical transaction in health care meets even these minimal requirements of a competitive market. Further illumination on this issue can be had from Thomas Rice's *The Economics of Health Care Reconsidered* (1998) in which the author examines in great detail how well the health care markets of the late twentieth century own up to the requirements of the First Optimality Theorem. Rice's answer is "Not."

Second, as noted above, Arrow hints in passing (942) at the possibility that a Pareto-efficient allocation of resources might be one in which some members of society are starving while others suffocate in gluttony (e.g., allocation D in Figure 1). Even if an allocation would leave many members of society starving, it would be defined as Pareto efficient by economists as long as even one of the gluttons objected to sharing his or her claim to resources with the starving members of society. Translated into health care, a Pareto-efficient allocation of resources might be one in which many patients suffer unwittingly from the excessive application of medical procedures while others suffer wittingly for want of critically needed care. Although such an allocation of health care resources may be judged abhorrent by many, economists nevertheless would be obliged to certify it as Pareto efficient if any one member of society objected to a redistribution of health-care resources — for example, if any one unwittingly overtreated member of society would object to a tax-and-transfer policy that would bestow critically needed health care to individuals hitherto without access to it.

Unfortunately, textbooks in economics inform students that "when economists use the word efficient, they generally have the notion of Pareto efficiency in mind" (Katz and Rosen 1991: 425). In a debate on public health policy, that usage can easily seduce noneconomists into believing that any particular, efficient allocation of resources is ipso facto superior to any particular, inefficient allocation. In fact, no such statement can legitimately be made by economists. In terms of Figure 1, for example, there is no reason why one should necessarily regard the highly skewed Pareto-efficient distribution of economic privilege represented by allocation D superior to the more egalitarian but Pareto-inefficient allocation C although, as Arrow reminds us (942), it certainly would not be sensible to put up with allocation C if any allocation on line segment AB could be technically and politically attained.

The Second Theorem of Optimality

Figure 1 illustrates that any initial endowment of society with real resources could be allocated among goods and services and subsequently among members of society in many alternative ways to produce many distinct, alternative distributions of economic privilege among members of society, each of them Pareto efficient. The question is how a society is to pick from among the infinite set of alternative, efficient distributions the one that is considered to be truly the best — what laypersons would call the *optimal allocation*. It is here that economists call on the Second Theorem of Optimality. Arrow phrases the theorem as follows (943): "If there are no increasing returns in production,[1] and if certain other minor conditions are satisfied, then every [Pareto] optimal state [distribution of economic privilege among members of society] is a competitive equilibrium corresponding to some initial distribution of purchasing power" among members of society. From this powerful analytic insight follows an equally powerful policy recommendation so far-reaching that it warrants a lengthy quotation from Arrow's essay:

> Operationally, the significance of this proposition is that if the conditions of the two optimality theorems are satisfied, and if the allocation mechanism in the real world satisfies the conditions for a competitive model, then social policy can confine itself to steps taken to alter the distribution of purchasing power. For any given distribution of purchasing power, the market will, under the assumptions made, achieve a competitive equilibrium which is necessarily optimal; and any optimal state is a competitive equilibrium corresponding to some distribution of purchasing power, so that any desired optimal state [distribution of satisfactions among members of society] can be achieved.
>
> The redistribution of purchasing power among individuals most simply takes the form of money: taxes and subsidies. The implications of such a transfer for individual satisfactions are, in general, not known in advance. But we can assume that society can *ex post* judge the distribution of satisfactions and, if deemed unsatisfactory, take steps to correct it by subsequent transfers. Thus, by successive approximations, a most preferred social state can be achieved, with resource allocation being handled by the market and public policy confined to the redistribution of money income. (943)

It is understandable why, on casual reading, this passage may appear as the seal of approval by a world-renowned economist for separating equity from efficiency in the formulation of health policy. If one believes — or acts as if one believes — that health care more or less meets the stringent conditions posited for the norms of welfare economics, then one can feel comfortable in advocating reliance on the market as the best means to attain economic efficiency in the allocation of health care resources, leaving it to the political process to recalibrate the distribution of income so as to render the market's impersonal verdicts ethically acceptable.

In fact, however, Arrow did not offer nearly so soothing an ointment for the problem of distributive justice in health-policy analysis. Even in the main text of his essay he observed that "If, on the contrary, the actual market differs significantly from the competitive model, or if the assumptions of the two optimality theorems are not fulfilled, the separation of allocative and distributional procedures becomes, in most cases, impossible" (943). At the very least, this passage challenges the proponents of a market approach to health care to demonstrate that the modus operandi of the market for health sector more or less satisfies the rather stringent conditions posited for the norms of welfare economics. That obligation remains a major challenge. In fact, it would be stretching things to read that conclusion into Arrow's article. He concluded otherwise.

Quite aside from the behavior of the health care market, however, supply-side economists vehemently question the tacit assumption implicit in the Second

Theorem of Optimality, namely, that purchasing power can easily be transferred among members of society without causing serious economic distortions—distortions causing the so-called "deadweight losses" lamented so much in the welfare economics of public finance. Arrow remarks on this problem in the following footnote:

> The separation between allocation and distribution even under the above assumptions [i.e., even if the conditions of the two optimality theorems are met] has glossed over problems in the execution of any desired redistributive policy; in practice, it is virtually impossible to find a set of taxes and subsidies that will not have an adverse effect on the achievement of an optimal state. (943 n. 2)

The problem identified in this footnote and the damage it does to the Second Theorem of Optimality ought not to be underestimated. In the classroom, economists find it convenient to develop the Second Theorem of Optimality with appeal to head taxes and head income transfers. By their very nature, these taxes and transfers cannot distort economic behavior because they are not linked to any behavioral variable (such as income earned or property owned). Alas, in practice, head taxes, in particular, are very rare because they lack political appeal. The proposal to introduce head taxes, probably with an eye toward economic efficiency, is said to have lost Britain's former prime minister Margaret Thatcher her office.

The adverse effects of redistributing purchasing power to which Arrow alluded in his footnote became a major issue during the U.S. health-reform debate in 1993–1994. Throughout the 1980s, supply-side theorists among U.S. economists had warned policy makers about the adverse economic incentives inherent in health policies that necessarily tax families in the upper half or so of the nation's income distribution to subsidize the health insurance for the families in the lower third. In fact, avoidance of such adverse effects—even at substantial cost of the welfare of the poor—has been a major theme among supply-side economists.[2] Drawing on simulations at the National Bureau of Economic Research made during the health reform debate of the mid-1990s, for example, economist Martin Feldstein (1994) warned policy makers and the public in an editorial entitled "Income-Based Subsidies Won't Work" that, in the end, it would cost $18,000 to insure a currently uninsured family of three (whose policy itself might cost less than a quarter as much).

In short, when the rubber hits the road in the arena of truly applied policy analysis and politics, the fabled Second Theorem of Optimality quickly loses its relevance. If one group of economists specializes in normative rules that advocate a free market for health care, assuming that the political process will put in place an ethically defensible distribution of purchasing power, while another group of economists specializes in alarming the policy makers over the loss of efficiency inherent in such redistributions, thus making sure that the political process does not put in place an ethically defensible distribution of purchasing power, then jointly the economics profession merely demonstrates that, in its own eyes, the conceptual separation of equity and efficiency implied by the Second Theorem of Optimality is just that, an elegant theorem.

Now it may be argued that, in a properly functioning representative democracy, the prevailing distribution of after-tax and after-transfer income at any moment is the most ethically defensible distribution of purchasing power; otherwise the democracy would not tolerate that distribution. On that assumption, it may be argued, one need not worry about social equity in advocating a market approach to health care because the willingness and ability to pay by different members of society interacting in a free market can legitimately be taken as the relevant measure of social value in normative economic analysis. In other words, if one accepts the prevailing after-tax and after-transfer distribution of income as the ethically acceptable platform for the market, then it is also ethical to accept as a working proposition that health care given, say, to the child of a corporate executive has a higher social value than similar health care given to the child of a gas station attendant, because the corporate executive probably would be willing to pay more money for that care than would the gas station attendant.

This argument cannot be dismissed out of hand, but one may point to its weakness. For one, a hard debate can be had over the question whether this nation's democracy does, indeed, function so as to beget the distribution of income that in turn would beget a distribution of health care that a majority of citizens would accept as ethically defensible. One may explore that question by asking the following question: Would the American public, or citizens elsewhere in the world, be content to accept the currently prevailing distribution of general purchasing power among members of society as an ethically adequate platform for the auctioning off of, say, transplantable organs to the highest bidders or of other life-saving and medical interventions that may be in limited supply? The answer is likely to be a resounding "No!" As Arrow observed on this point: "The taste for improving the health of others appears to be stronger than for improving other aspects of their welfare" (954). In other words, Arrow appears to suggest here that there probably is not just one initial distribution of general purchasing power that can satisfy the distributional ethic that society wishes to impose on particular commodities within the entire set of all goods and services. There probably are many different desired initial distributions of purchasing power, each tied to a particular commodity on which society has special attitudes. The desired distributions of purchasing power for health care and for education, for example, might be much more egalitarian than those for food and housing.

This circumstance bears directly on a corollary often extracted by economists from the Second Theorem of Optimality, namely, that the distribution of benefits in kind by government—as, for example, through the Medicare and Medicaid programs—is inherently inferior on economic grounds to a simple distribution of cash in an amount equal to the cost (to taxpayers) of the benefits in kind distributed by government. Because the proclamation of that proposition, too, remains one of the more triumphant moments in first-year courses in economics and, thence, is carried into mature adulthood, it may be well to subject that proposition to closer scrutiny.

The Welfare Economics of Benefits in Kind

Arrow's oblique reference to the distribution of benefits in kind would be obvious to a general public, worldwide, that routinely countenances huge public expenditures on health care for the poor but would be likely to reject quite vehemently a proposal to distribute a like amount of cash instead. It can be asked fairly whether so many people could possibly be so wrong on this issue for so many years, while economists have had it right all along, or whether it may possibly be the other way around.

Economists pretend to be deeply puzzled by the public's tolerance of the patently inefficient distribution of benefits in kind. As noted, every year thousands of economics professors persuade hundreds of thousands of American undergraduates that granting the poor distribution of benefits in kind is less efficient than simply transferring to them cash in an amount equal to the cost of the benefits in kind. In the words of Victor Fuchs (1983: 148–149): "While elementary justice seems to require greater equality in the distribution of medical care, the question is complicated by the fact that the poor suffer deprivation in many directions. Economic theory suggests it might be better to redistribute income and allow the poor to decide which additional goods and services they wish to buy." Similarly, in his exploration of the willingness-to-pay approach for tax-financed benefit-in-kind programs, Mark Pauly (1995: 117) observes:

> If we want to provide benefit to low-income people, a more efficient approach would be to use the money that would have been spent on the program, as opposed to making a direct money transfer to them, since the money will benefit low-income people more than the program would. If the community decides not to make the money income transfer, it must not have attached high value either to low-income persons' health or to their overall welfare.

Ever on to the real world, however, Victor Fuchs (1983: 149) is quick to add to his commentary on benefits in kind: "As a practical matter, however, it may be easier to achieve greater equality through a redistribution of services (such as medical care) than through a redistribution of money income."

By practicality Fuchs may have in mind merely the venal political process that governs the redistribution of benefits in kind by government in a democracy. That distribution inevitably feeds horses to feed the birds, so to speak. Out of pure self-interest, and under almost any form of government, the horses (the producers of benefits in kind) can be counted on to become strong political allies of society's targets of compassion, which is reason enough to make the ideologically committed champions of the poor favor benefits in kind, for purely pragmatic, political reasons. Therein may lie part of the practicality of which Fuchs writes.[3]

But there may be more to the practicality of benefits in kind than merely feeding of the hungry horses that, in turn, provide politicians with campaign financing. Taxpayers themselves may not be impressed by the economist's dictum that cash transfers are inherently superior to the transfer of benefits in kind. In other words, it is possible that, after a century of study, economists still do not understand the utility function of taxpayers in this regard. The economist's dictum is driven by the tacit assumption that taxpayers maximize their own utility when the recipients of tax-financed transfers, the poor, are allowed to maximize any which way they choose their own happiness per dollar of taxes borne by the taxpayers. If the recipients of public transfers are happier spending their transfers on alcohol and visits to Disneyland than on health care for their children, then so be it, as long as the poors' utility is maximized per dollar of taxpayers' money. Is there persuasive empirical evidence that the typical taxpayer's utility function actually does conform to the economist's imagination?

Perhaps a more realistic assumption would be that taxpaying voters typically exhibit a more parental form of altruism toward their poor fellow citizens. Taxpayers would like poor families to use a select few basic commodities (for example, health care and education) in adequate amounts, but specifically *not* use tax-financed subsidies to purchase whatever goods and services the poor fancy (especially gin and Cadillacs). The preference among voters for bestowing on the poor benefits in kind rather than cash transfers — apparently so puzzling to economists who write textbooks — may well rest in good part on that characteristic of the donors' utility function. If that hypothesis is valid, then it would seem hopeless that we would ever find a single, politically acceptable distribution of generalized purchasing power that would distribute through the free market all commodities among members of society in a fashion that the general public will accept as just. Furthermore, if that is so, then economists would actually be misusing the word *efficiency* in this context. They would be misusing it because they would be recommending the maximization of the wrong maximand.

JUDGING THE SOCIAL MERITS OF ALTERNATIVE SOCIAL POLICIES

Alternative public policies in health care, as in other sectors, can be of several distinct types. Occasionally one thinks of policies that represent an actual Pareto improvement in the sense that the policy makes some members of society feel better off without making anyone else feel worse off. Unfortunately, such occasions are rare. More commonly, public policies do make some people feel better off at the expense of others who do feel worse off. It could occur when a resource allocation is changed from one Pareto-inefficient distribution to another or when policy makers seek to move from one Pareto-efficient allocation to another. Finally, it could occur when policy makers, perhaps at the behest of economists, seek to move the allocation of resources from a Pareto-inefficient state to a Pareto-efficient one.

In either case, when a proposed policy makes some members of society better off at the expense of others, policy makers cannot escape the chore of having to make explicit value judgments on the social desirability of the proposed policy. Economists have long debated how such evaluations should be done.

Only a faulty reading of Arrow's article could suggest to the reader that, in health care, this problem could be left to the invisible hand of competitive markets. A careless reader of his article might possibly draw that inference, because in connection with the First Theorem of Optimality, he observed that an explicit "value judgment on the desirability of each possible new [Pareto-efficient] distribution of benefits and costs corresponding to each possible allocation of resources is not, in general, necessary" (942). Evidently he meant that if the conditions of competitive markets are satisfied, these value judgments could be left to the market after social policy has set the ethically preferred distribution of purchasing power.

Even that proposition, however, seems somewhat at variance with Arrow's subsequent observation, offered in connection with the Second Theorem, that the implications of particular distributions of purchasing power among members of society on the ultimate distribution of satisfaction among members of society are, in general, not known in advance, so that the distributions of satisfactions resulting from particular distributions of purchasing power need to be judged by society ex post (943). In other words, according to Arrow, in the end, even perfectly competitive markets do not spare policy makers the chore of making explicit value judgments about the "distributions of satisfactions" that a competitive market will beget with alternative initial distributions of purchasing power among members of society (with alternative social policies). Policy makers certainly are not spared that chore in contexts that do not even meet the conditions for the First and Second Theorems of Optimality, of which health care to this day surely remains one. Thus, the question remains how one is to evaluate the relative social merit of outcomes from alternative social policies that redistribute economic privilege among members of society. Is there really an objective analytic method of accomplishing that seemingly subjective social valuation?

Because this question lies at the core of welfare economics as it is practiced today, and because its pragmatic resolution by many economists has tended to create an intellectual gap between the profession and noneconomists, it merits a wider excursion into the relevant literature, beyond Arrow's article proper.[4] Concretely, then, in terms of the two-member society modeled in Figure 1, the question at issue is how one is to evaluate any reallocation of human happiness that leaves person A feeling better off and person B feeling worse off, or vice versa.

Kaldorian Welfare Analysis

Ever eager to play in the world of practical affairs, economists by now appear to have settled this century-old question pragmatically by relying on a dubious norm originally proposed by the British economist Nicholas Kaldor (1939: 549) and sold to policy makers ever since, to wit:

> A reallocation of resources wrought by a particular policy represents a "social net gain" if the individuals who gain from the reallocation value that gain sufficiently so that they could, in principle, bribe the individuals who are worse off as a result of that policy into accepting that change, *even if that bribe actually is not paid.*

Translated into the realm of standard benefit-cost analysis, for which the Kaldorian criterion has become the gold standard, the postulate can be expressed in a manner that might astound and possibly appall noneconomists:

> If those who stand to gain from a proposed change in the economy would maximally be willing to pay \$B to see that change made, *whoever these people may be, and given their tastes and their particular position in society's income distribution,* and if those who stand to lose from the change would maximally pay \$C to prevent that change, *whoever they may be, and given their tastes and particular position in the nation's income distribution,* then the proposed change represents a "social gain" or "increase in social economic welfare" if the gain \$B exceeds the loss \$C.

For a profession that prides itself on basing its normative dicta on the preferences of individuals, this postulate strikes on a remarkably collectivist approach to social valuations. In essence, it implies that if \$1,000 is taken from person A by a head tax and given to person B by means of a head-transfer, collective social welfare has not changed at all. One can esteem the postulate for its potential practicality but not for its ethical foundation.

Some textbook writers refer to a Kaldorian social gain as a "potential Pareto improvement" and define the latter as ipso facto an "increase in economic efficiency" (Stockman 1996: 305–306). That appears to have become by now the common usage in economics. For example, Steven Landsburg (1995: 258) instructs students in his textbook *Price Theory and Applications*:

According to the efficiency criterion, any change in policy that makes George $2 richer and Martha only $1 poorer *is a good thing*. Any change in policy that makes George $1 richer and Martha $2 poorer *is a bad thing*. More generally, the efficiency criterion pronounces that between two policies, we should always prefer the one that yields the higher social gain. The preferred policy is said to be more efficient than its rival.

One must wonder how many first-year students, struggling with their first brush against the complexity of welfare economics, will stop to ponder just who George and Martha might be. Would the proposition appeal to them if George were Donald Trump and Martha a near-poor waitress?

Critique of the Kaldorian Welfare Criterion

In their professional writings, economists tend to apply the Kaldorian criterion with abandon and with nary a thought or apology for its shaky ethical foundation. How unwise that practice is depends, of course, on the particular context to which the criterion is applied. Within the context of health care, one might judge it reckless. It has not always been so. Earlier economists, writing at about the time at which Arrow's article was penned, were, as Arrow was, far more circumspect on this facet of welfare economics, and they agonized over its validity. In one of the more trenchant reviews of welfare economics in general, for example, William J. Baumol (1977: 530) concluded:

> In my view, the Kaldor test operates on the basis of an implicit and unacceptable value judgement. By using a criterion involving potential money compensation, [it] sets up a concealed interpersonal comparison of utility on a money basis. If [individual] Y's gain is worth $200 to him whereas [individual] X evaluates his loss at $70, we are not entitled to jump to the conclusion that there is a net [social] gain in [the associated change in the economy]. If X is a poor man or a miser, $70 may mean a great deal to him, whereas if Y is a rich man or profligate, $200 may represent a trifle hardly worth his notice. . . . It is no answer to this criterion that these criteria are just designed to measure whether production, and hence potential welfare, are increased by the policy change — that these criteria disentangle the evaluation of a production change from that of the distribution change by which it is accompanied.

Defense of the Kaldorian Welfare Criterion

A defense of the Kaldorian welfare criterion might be that, while its application in particular instances may redistribute economic privilege in undesired ways, its consistent and repeated application to public policy across the entire economy is bound to have a portfolio effect under which individual instances of injustice cancel out one another, so that, in the end, all boats can be made to rise, so to speak, through efficiency-enhancing policies driven by welfare-economic analysis. The most elegant version of this defense is the *expected-utility* or *constitutional* standard originally proposed by James Buchanan and Gordon Tullock (1962).[5] As Pauly (1995: 100–102) has described the constitutional standard it asks:

> given a wide variety of decisions to be made and a wide variety of individual circumstances for any member of a given group, what method would maximize the average or expected well being of a person in that group? In effect, this standard assumes/argues that each person has the group-average probability of being in each of the circumstances that might occur. . . . The constitutional perspective . . . makes the [Kaldorian] potential compensation test more attractive. If society follows the benefit-cost rule [that test implies], on average every person can expect to be better off; the chance that the person will win will more than offset, in expectational terms, the chance that the person will lose.

There clearly is something to that argument, although, as Pauly mentions, the same analytic construct has been employed by John Rawls (1971) to justify policies for a more egalitarian distribution of income. The construct has not carried conviction in that realm any more than it can in health policy. The standard raises two questions.

First, is it in fact the case that each member of society has the group-average probability of being in each circumstance that might occur, or does consistent application of the Kaldorian benefit-cost rule consistently favor one socioeconomic class over the other, or healthy people over chronically sick people?

Second, even if the group-average probability of being in each circumstance were the same for all members of society, over what span of economic activity should policy makers and the affected individuals average (in their minds) the wins and losses from the variety of decisions that are to be adjudicated by the Kaldorian benefit-cost rule? Is it good enough when the disadvantages that the rule may visit on an individual in one economic sector (e.g., health care) are offset, in "expectational terms," through advantages the rule bestows on the same individuals in another sector (e.g., transportation or entertainment)? Or should the assumed portfolio effect take place within sectors (e.g., within health care proper)? For example, if an application of the Kaldorian benefit-cost rule shifts more of the financial burden of ill health onto the shoulders of the chronically ill, is it good enough to tell the chronically ill that, on average, in expectational terms, a consistent application of a normative rule that hurts them in health care will bestow offsetting special benefits on them in other sectors (e.g., in transportation)? Would a consistent application of the Kaldorian benefit-cost rule in health policy not be likely to drive the entire health system inexorably toward systematic income-based rationing and visit the economic cost of ill health more heavily on the sick than is the case even now? If that be the goal, or if it be judged an acceptable outcome, then economists using that line of defense had better articulate their acceptance of that outcome *in health care* very explicitly, at the outset, in any normative analysis they base on the Kaldorian criterion, so that users of the analysis can make their own moral judgment on the matter. As William Baumol (1977) has put it, Kaldor's expedient normative dictum is never an excuse for setting aside moral thought.

THE SECOND OPTIMALITY THEOREM MEETS THE REAL WORLD

Although it is unlikely that Paul Ellwood (1971), Anne and Herman Somers (1972), and later Alain Enthoven (1978) ever consciously followed the road map to the social optimum for health care that many economists perceived in Arrow's article, the shared vision for U.S. health care proposed by these authors at various times — and most fully developed by Enthoven (1978), Enthoven and Kronick (1989), and Ellwood, Enthoven, and Etheredge (1992) — comes closest so far in the attempt to move the health care sector closer to the conditions required by what Arrow calls "the norms of welfare economics." That vision is an attempt to fuse a price-competitive framework for health care with production processes designed to produce medical treatments efficiently and with income transfers designed to achieve a desired degree of social equity. Although the proper description of this construct is "managed care within managed competition," it will be convenient henceforth to refer to it by the conventional shorthand *managed care*.

The Elegant Theory of Managed Care
The fundamental idea underlying the theory of managed care was to achieve social equity through the distribution of vouchers — currently known as defined contributions — that could be used only for the purchase of health insurance offered by a variety of private, competing health insurance plans. Within a formal framework that regulated their conduct, the health plans could be made to compete for enrollees on two distinct bases.

First, they could be forced by government to accept the voucher as payment in full for a defined, basic benefit package. In that case, they would compete strictly on their reputation for quality and, possibly, on the basis of additional services not in the basic benefit package and sold for additional premiums. It would be the closest approach to perfect social equity. Alternatively, the health plans could be allowed to compete on both price and quality. Thus, they would be free to quote for the basic benefit package a premium above or below the amount of the voucher, leaving the insured to pay from their own resources any amount of premium above the voucher amount or to pocket the amount of the premium below the amount of the voucher. The second approach would not be perfectly egalitarian, but it could be calibrated by policy makers to achieve any desired degree of social equity. To make either approach workable, of course, the total money payment ultimately made to the health plans would have to be adjusted somehow for the actuarial risks they attracted in the competitive free-for-all.

For their part, the health plans would have every incentive to produce or pro-cure health care for their enrollees as efficiently as possible. They would do so by bargaining fiercely over the prices of inputs and of monitoring their use with appeal to preestablished practice guidelines—that is, through external micro-management of medical treatments—hence the name managed care.

Crucial to the entire arrangement would be an elaborate information infra-structure that would give all participants in the arrangement—the insured as they select health plans and providers within plans, the managers of the health plans and the providers supplying them—with all relevant information on prices and quality that is fundamental to an efficiently operating economic sector. The existence of this information infrastructure was fundamental to the success of the strategy as, of course, it would be to the validity of the Second Optimality Theorem in any economic context.[6]

The Checkered History of Managed Care

It would strain one's credulity to be told that today's health system in the United States comes anywhere near the ideal set forth in the elegant theory of managed care. As noted in the introduction, economists who would persuade the partici-pants in health care—patients, providers, insurers, and government officials—that the U.S. health system has moved closer to an efficient social optimum dur-ing the past decade or so might be a source of sardonic humor.

A lively debate could be held on the question whether, relative to what needs to be known about today's much more complex health system, patients now are any better informed about their health system and about their health care than they were when Arrow penned his famous essay. To appreciate what is being as-serted here, one need only imagine a patient beset by chest or stomach pain in Anytown, USA, as he or she attempts to "shop around" for a cost-effective reso-lution to those problems. Only rarely, in a few locations, do American patients have access to even a rudimentary version of the information infrastructure on which the theory of competitive market and the theory of managed care rest. The prices of health services are jealously guarded proprietary information.[7] In fact, even the nomenclature of the fee schedules used by the federal Medicare program was made, under contract with the Reagan administration, the private property of the American Medical Association and can be used by others in the private sector only with that trade association's permission. Information on the quality of care is generally unavailable or not trustworthy. Not even the infection or complication rates experienced in hospitals are publicly known. Such information on quality as is made available in the media or on Web sites typically consists of mysteriously weighted aggregate indexes that obscure the detailed information patients would need in a competitive market. Much is made now of the ability of Web-enabled health care consumers to view physicians as full partners or mere ordering clerks. Perhaps the typical American patient will fit that image one day. In the meantime, the image will remain the stuff of futurist tracts and of conference circuit fantasy.

Space does not permit a more careful and detailed analysis of the fate of managed care during the 1990s beyond the brash assertions offered above, nor does space permit an exploration why managed care did not achieve what ought to have been technically feasible. It would be hard to argue, for example, that either the technical know-how or the physical capacity or the availability of funds were effective barriers to a more effective use of modern information technology. Can these factors explain why third-party payers in this country, more so than in most other countries, still rely so heavily on cumbersome paper transactions? More persuasive than appeal to technical factors is J. D. Kleinke's (2000) behavioral theory. In his "Vaporware.com: The Failed Promise of the Health Care Internet" he argues that better transparency and speedier communication in U.S. health care actually has more powerful enemies than friends, that these enemies of transparency have a vested interest in holding genuine competition in health care at bay, and that they tend to triumph in our latitudes, in part, no doubt, because American consumers have never really warmed up to the idea of a price-competitive, commercial health care system.

Although a fuller understanding of this remarkable market failure probably will require the work of many diverse scholars over many years, it would be a worthy enterprise. Economists, in particular, will benefit from pursuing the task, begun by Kenneth Arrow, to understand just why, even forty years later, the health system still deviates so substantially from the norms of welfare economics and whether a convergence on that ideal can ever realistically be expected.

CONCLUDING OBSERVATIONS

In the late 1980s several economists offered a retrospective on the more market-oriented approach that U.S. health policy had taken since 1977, the year of a major national health-policy conference on the potential role of competition in health care. In his introduction to the series of articles, Warren Greenberg, the editor of the volume, remarked:

> It appears that competition has increased substantially among providers and among insurers and health plans since 1977, perhaps more than anyone predicted or thought possible. Economic theory would suggest that this increase

in competition should have resulted in a more *efficient* allocation of health services. . . . But competition may have succeeded only in *improving* the allocation of health resources. In the next ten years, I believe, we will have to combine a *better* allocation of resources with a more equitable distribution of these resources. (Greenberg 1988: 223, 224–225, emphasis added)

Leaving aside the debatable assertion that, in 1988, U.S. health care truly was more efficient than it had been in 1977, the passage suggests that a resource allocation that is more efficient than the one it replaces is ipso facto an improvement and therefore better. This inference reminds me of one of my favorite comments in Arrow's article, by which he gently reminds his peers and his future disciples in passing that: "A definition is just a definition, but when the *definiendum* is a word already in common use with highly favorable connotations, it is clear that we [economists] are really trying to be persuasive; we are implicitly recommending the achievement of optimal states" (942).

The main objective of this essay has been to use Arrow's seminal article as a vehicle for explaining to noneconomists the huge gap between the economist's and the layperson's use of the words *optimal* and *efficient*. In the vernacular, the word *efficiency* has a highly positive connotation. *More efficient* is understood to mean better, and *optimal* is thought to be best. In standard welfare economics, on the other hand, the terms merely imply a state of affairs that satisfies certain conditions but that may or may not be socially desirable and may even be abhorrent in the eyes of modern societies.

Arrow's admonition in this passage puts a burden on economists to be ever mindful of their use of professional jargon in the arena of public policy debates, lest they fall into the trap of proffering particular ideologies under the mantle of science (unless, of course, they actually seek to do so).[8] Among noneconomists, efficiency or optimality always are tied implicitly to a particular goal. In terms of Figure 1, for example, laypersons might not care to enhance efficiency by moving from an interior point, such as C, of the feasible set of allocations to an efficient point, such as D, on the trade-off frontier if they patently do not wish to be at the latter allocation. Indeed, if push came to shove, they might even prefer to remain at the relatively more inefficient point C.

One can explain this point easily to first-year students in economics with a hypothetical road trip (Reinhardt 1998). Suppose a family decided to travel by car from New York City to the West Coast and each of four fairly mature children is charged with the task of finding the most efficient routes to two potential destinations: San Diego and Seattle. The family agrees that the most efficient route is one that leads them to the chosen destination in the least travel time. Youngsters A and B, each and separately, are asked to discover the most efficient route to Seattle. Youngsters C and D similarly are asked to discover the most efficient route to San Diego. Now suppose that A's chosen route will require less travel time than B's and that C's chosen route will require less travel time than D's. Clearly the family would judge C's chosen route to San Diego to be both more "efficient" than D's and also "better" if the family ultimately decided to travel to San Diego. On the other hand, D's inefficient route to San Diego would clearly be preferred by the family to A's efficient route to Seattle if everyone really wished to go to San Diego.

Few people fail to grasp the central point of this homely illustration unless, of course, they are working in health policy rather than on vacation plans. In the context of health policy, one commonly finds alternative policies (or national health systems) ranked in terms of their alleged relative efficiency, even though these policies (or national health systems) may have vastly different distributional consequences. A health policy (or health system) that provides superb health care to, say, 85 to 90 percent of the population but leaves 10 to 15 percent of mainly low-income individuals without critically needed care cannot legitimately be compared in terms of economic efficiency with an alternative policy (or health system) that trims somewhat the benefits enjoyed by the top 85 to 90 percent of the population in order to bestow more health benefits on the lower 10 to 15 percent. The two systems attain different goals. They can be compared on normative grounds only by how well they approximate the goal society actually posits for its health system.

The choices laid out in the example are roughly the choices this country has faced for close to a century and probably will continue to debate deep into the new century. The general public and their political representatives may have distinct preferences concerning these two visions for health care, and their normative judgments must be respected. Economists as professionals, on the other hand, have literally nothing normative to say about these alternative visions besides the purely positive observation that they have different distributional consequences.

Economics will run into the same limitation in the forthcoming debate on the reform of the Medicare program. One set of proposals calls for reforms within the current, defined-benefit structure of Medicare. Those proposals would broaden Medicare's benefit package to include prescription drugs and other items that are now excluded. Furthermore, they would allow Medicare to contract selectively with centers of excellence for certain complex medical procedures and to rely on competitive bidding for many other health services. The rival set of proposals would substantially privatize Medicare along the lines advanced in Senate Bill 357 by Senators John Breaux (D-LA) and Bill Frist (R-TN). That approach would be based on the concept of defined contributions, delegate the task of cost and quality control to private health plans, and force the traditional Medicare program to compete on premium and quality with the private plans. It is unlikely that these conceptually different approaches would have the same distributional consequences. Relative to the Breaux-Frist approach, the enhanced, defined-benefit approach probably would produce less tiering of the health care experience of the elderly by income class, but would shift relatively more of the cost of health care for the elderly onto the working population. It is possible and appropriate to lay out the sundry consequences of these proposals side by side for easy comparison. It would be quite illegitimate, however, to rank them in terms of their alleged, relative "efficiency." It will be fascinating to observe whether or not economists will be able to keep their professional hands clean in the forthcoming debate on Medicare reform.

NOTES

This article draws heavily on previous work by the author, especially Reinhardt 1998.

1 By "increasing returns in production" is meant processes under which a doubling of all inputs would yield more than double the output. That circumstance can create certain analytic problems in general equilibrium analysis.

2 At a congressional retreat during the health reform debate of 1993–1994, James Mongan, M.D., currently president of the Massachusetts General Hospital, asked a prominent economist — who shall remain nameless — why one of the richest nations on earth finds it so difficult to give all of its citizens access to the kind of health care taken for granted by the middle class. To which the economist replied: "Has it occurred to you that that is why we are among the richest nations on earth?" Oral communication from James Mongan.

3 To be sure, in a democracy in which "representative government" contents itself more and more with representing mainly special, monied interests, the hungry horses producing benefits in kind may help stretch their provision beyond the level that could be justified, if one knew the true valuation that donors and recipients jointly attach to some of the benefits taxpayers will be forced to finance.

4 In this connection, see also Rice 1998.

5 Cited in Pauly 1995: 122.

6 If this rendition of the theory of managed care reminds readers of the Clinton health reform plan, they would not err. The core of that plan was very close to the design parameters spelled out above. Unfortunately, that design was hidden behind the additional, often needless, regulatory baggage the Clinton team chose to load on top of that design.

7 With some effort one might be able to obtain a hospital's "charges" for its services, but one would quickly be told that these are meaningless because no one actually pays them.

8 In this connection, see also Reinhardt 1996.

REFERENCES

Arrow, K. J. 1963. Uncertainty and the Welfare Economics of Medical Care. *American Economic Review* 53(5): 941–973.

Bator, F. 1957. The Simple Economics of Welfare Maximization. *American Economic Review* 47: 22–29.

———. 1958. The Anatomy of Market Failure. *Quarterly Journal of Economics* 72: 351–379.

Baumol, W. J. 1969. *Welfare Economics and the Theory of the State.* Cambridge: Harvard University Press.

———. 1977. *Economic Theory and Operations Analysis.* 4th ed. Cambridge: Harvard University Press.

Buchanan, J., and G. Tullock. 1962. *Calculus of Consent.* Ann Arbor: University of Michigan Press.

Ellwood, P. M. 1971. Health Maintenance Strategy. *Medical Care* (May): 250–256.

Ellwood, P. M., A. C. Enthoven, and L. Etheredge. 1992. The Jackson Hole Initiatives for a Twenty-First Century American Health System. *Health Economics* 1(1): 149–168.

Enthoven, A. C. 1978. Consumer-Choice Health Plan 1. Inflation and Inequity in Health-Care Today—Alternative for Cost Control and an Analysis of Proposals for National-Health Insurance. *New England Journal of Medicine* 298(12): 650–658.

———. 1978. Consumer-Choice Health Plan 2. National-Health-Insurance Proposal Based on Regulated Competition in Private Sector. *New England Journal of Medicine* 298(13): 709–720.

Enthoven, A. C., and R. Kronick. 1989. A Consumer-Choice Health Plan for the 1990s—Universal Health-Insurance in a System Designed to Promote Quality and Economy 1. *New England Journal of Medicine* 320(1): 29–37.

———. 1989. A Consumer-Choice Health Plan for the 1990s—Universal Health-Insurance in a System Designed to Promote Quality and Economy 2. *New England Journal of Medicine* 320(2): 94–101.

Feldstein, M. 1994. Income-Based Subsidies Won't Work. *Wall Street Journal*, 17 June, A14.

Fuchs, V. R. 1983. *Who Shall Live? Health, Economics and Social Choice.* New York: Basic Books.

Greenberg, W. 1988. Introduction. *Journal of Health Policy, Politics and Law* 13(2): 223–224.

Kaldor, N. 1939. Welfare Propositions of Economists and Interpersonal Comparison of Utility. *Economic Journal* (September): 549–552.

Katz, M. L., and H. S. Rosen. 1991. *Microeconomics.* Homewood, IL: Richard D. Irwin.

Kleinke, J. D. 2000. Vaporware.com: The Failed Promise of the Health Care Internet. *Health Affairs* 19(6): 57–71.

Landsburg, S. E. 1995. *Price Theory and Applications.* 3d ed. Minneapolis, MN: West.

Pareto, V. 1897. *Cours d'économie politique.* Lausanne, Switzerland: F. Rouge.

Pauly, M. V. 1995. Valuing Health Care in Money Terms. In *Valuing Health Care*, ed. F. A. Sloan. Cambridge: Cambridge University Press.

Rawls, J. 1971. *A Theory of Justice.* Cambridge: Harvard University Press, Belknap Press.

Reinhardt, U. E. 1996. Economics. *Journal of the American Medical Association* 275(23): 1802–1803.

———. 1998. Abstracting from Distributional Effects, This Policy is Efficient. In *Health, Health Care and Health Economics*, ed. M. L. Barer, T. E. Getzen, and G. L. Stoddard. New York: John Wiley.

Rice, T. 1998. *The Economics of Health Reconsidered*. Chicago: Health Administration Press.

Somers, H. M., and A. R. Somers. 1972. Major Issues in Health Insurance. *Milbank Memorial Fund Quarterly* (April): 177–210.

Stockman, A. 1996. *Introduction to Microeconomics*. New York: Dryden.

RICHARD KRONICK

■ *Valuing Charity*

Economist Kenneth Arrow's 1963 article, "Uncertainty and the Welfare Econom-ics of Medical Care," proposed insurance as a solution to many informational problems in the health care system. This insight helped generate a rich literature on the economics of health insurance. At the same time, however, Arrow rec-ognized that residual problems of information might limit the degree to which medical risks are insurable, and therefore the degree to which health care can be successfully governed by market forces. Somewhat surprisingly, Arrow invoked decidedly nonmarket mechanisms such as professional ethics as compensatory solutions to these problems.

Notably, Arrow asserted that the ethical compulsion to treat patients regard-less of their ability to pay was a special feature of medical care. He wrote:

> It is at least claimed that treatment is dictated by the objective needs of the case and not limited by financial considerations. (950)

> The belief that the ethics of medicine demands treatment independent of the patient's ability to pay is strongly ingrained. (950 n. 17)

> Price discrimination and its extreme, free treatment for the indigent, also fol-low. If the obligation of the physician is understood to be first of all to the welfare of the patient, then in particular it takes precedence over financial difficulties." (965)

In Arrow's view, the physician's obligation to provide care without regard to ability to pay contributed to a trusting relationship between patient and physi-cian. In the presence of informational inequalities, the ethical compulsion to treat the patient unconditionally gave the patient confidence that the physician was using his or her knowledge to the best advantage of the patient and not simply to enrich the physician at the patient's expense.

To Arrow, the ethical compulsion for individual physicians to provide care without regard to ability to pay was not a substitute for social insurance. Arrow noted that the elderly and the unemployed were almost completely uncovered by insurance, that "the insurance mechanism is still very far from achieving the full coverage of which it is capable" (964), and that "it follows that the government should undertake insurance in those cases where this market, for whatever reason, has failed to emerge" (961). In practice, moreover, physicians' ethical obligations certainly did not safeguard the financial security or the health of the uninsured elderly or the poor. Charity care in hospitals and physicians' offices provided some protection, but these mechanisms were far from sufficient to provide full protection. The insufficiencies were magnified as commercial insurance eroded the ability of Blue Cross to engage in community rating and insurance became increasingly unaffordable for the elderly (Starr 1982). Arrow was aware of these problems, and his writing presaged (although was apparently not invoked during) the debates over the enactment of Medicare and Medicaid in 1965.

My purpose in this essay is to explore the possibility that Arrow's insurance arguments turned out to be in significant tension with his ethical arguments. Medicare and Medicaid have made tremendous progress by insuring elderly and indigent segments of the population who were not adequately served by physician charity in 1963 and for whom the much more sophisticated and expensive medical technologies of 2001 would be completely inaccessible. Moreover, although Medicare and Medicaid fall well short of universal health coverage, the lion's share of these programs' rapidly rising costs has been borne by nonbeneficiary taxpayers and represents a significant advance from the pre-1963 commitment of the American public to social welfare.

Unfortunately, these programs may also have inadvertently weakened medical ethics, detracting from the ability of professional norms to fill informational gaps in health care markets even as they increased health insurance per se. Specifically, Medicare and Medicaid created the expectation that it was the responsibility of the federal and state governments to assure that patients would be treated without regard to their ability to pay. These programs, which spread the risk of illness across generations and income groups, shifted responsibility for care of the elderly, and at least some of the poor, from the medical profession and the hospital industry to the government.

In addition, Medicare and Medicaid arguably reduced the trust between physicians and patients that Arrow asserted was a special feature of medical care in 1963. This happened in at least three ways. First, by leading to large increases in the net income of physicians, and to increased provision of services that were not highly valued by patients (moral hazard), widespread third-party payment likely led to an increased sense that physicians were not acting solely in the best interests of the patient but were also weighing the effects of treatment on the physicians' net income.

Second, as Arrow predicted, the moral hazard that insurance created could be curbed only through third-party control over payment levels and, eventually, over clinical practice. Even before private managed care became common, federal and state governments fought with physicians and hospitals over reimbursement rules and definitions of medical necessity in the interest of limiting budget growth. While the public's sympathies were often with physicians and hospitals rather than government bureaucrats, continued questioning of the scientific basis of medicine by health service researchers and public payers weakened our collective belief that physicians provide treatment without regard to financial self-interest. The emergence of capitated payment systems in the 1990s further eroded our belief that treatment is provided independent of ability to pay. Physician groups that are paid capitated fees provide fewer services, particularly fewer inpatient services, than physicians paid on a fee-for-service basis (Robinson and Casalino 1995).

Third, and most important for this essay, Medicare and Medicaid adversely affected the ethical norm obligating physicians to provide treatment without regard to ability to pay, reducing both trust and, for certain patients, access to care. In 1963 physicians were expected to donate a half a day per week of their time to provide free care in hospital clinics and commonly charged patients according to their ability to pay (charging upper income patients more and lower income patients less) (Kessel 1958; Starr 1982). It is unclear to what extent these norms were in fact followed: I have seen no data on how many physicians actually did donate a half-day per week to free care and not much data on the extent of price discrimination in physician office practice. But it is almost certainly the case that physicians in 1963 donated much more time to free clinics and provided much more frequent and larger voluntary discounts on charges to low-income patients in their offices than they do today. In 2001, we do not expect physicians to volunteer in free clinics, and low-income, uninsured patients are typically charged, and sometimes pay, more than their insured (and higher income) counterparts (Wielawski 2000).

Why were uninsured patients charged less than insured patients in 1963, with the relationship partially reversed today? Why did many physicians apparently act on a sense of obligation to care for patients without regard to ability to pay in 1963, with many fewer behaving this way today? Part of the explanation is that Medicare and Medicaid reduced the demand for free care as large numbers of uninsured people became insured.[1] Free clinics in hospitals became sources of patient revenue, and house staff were paid for by government and other third-party payers (Ludmerer 1999). These trends reduced the need for medical societies and hospitals to pressure physicians to donate time in the clinics. Similarly, the growth of community health centers, funded initially with money from the Office of Economic Opportunity and nurtured by Medicaid reimbursement, reduced the need for physicians to supply their services without compensation. With pressure reduced, the supply of free care was reduced as well.

While the decline in physician service in hospital charity clinics is clear (if not well documented), it is less clear whether there has been a substantial change in the willingness of physicians to serve low-income, uninsured patients in their offices.[2] Freed of the obligation to donate time in hospital clinics, physicians, one might have imagined, that would donate some of that time (perhaps two hours instead of four) in their offices. While some physicians probably did so, many simply responded to the introduction of Medicare and Medicaid by increasing the time they spent with paying patients and decreasing the time spent with the uninsured. The ubiquitous signs at the front desks of physician offices admonishing patients that "arrangements to settle bills must be made prior to receiving service" are certainly not meant to welcome low-income, uninsured patients into the practice and are a relatively recent development.

To the extent that there has been a decline in the supply of office-based free and reduced fee care, the change may be related to changes in the prevailing forms of physician organization. When most physicians were solo practitioners they could make case-by-case decisions about how much to charge each patient. These decisions might be influenced by the physician's notion of whether the patient was deserving as well as the emotional response many of us have when a person in need comes to our door and asks for help. As physicians moved from solo practice into medium and large groups, charity became no longer the decision of an individual physician treating an identifiable patient but, rather, a collective or corporate decision. The individual physician might still be willing to donate services but might be hamstrung by medical group policy.[3] Furthermore, in a large group practice, a physician is not likely to come face-to-face with a patient who might merit a charitable discount — the patient will not get past the receptionist if he or she does not have insurance and is not able to pay expected charges out of pocket.

Further, technological and organizational changes affected the capacity as well as the willingness of physicians to provide care without regard to ability to pay. The production of health care has changed markedly over the past forty years, becoming much less hospital centered. Pharmaceuticals have become a more important part of the physician's armamentarium, many diagnostic tests are performed in freestanding facilities, and the use of home health and skilled nursing care has increased. With the exception of relatively small donations from pharmaceutical companies, services other than hospital or physician services are rarely delivered as charity care. And the ability to arrange free care for a patient in a hospital is much more limited in 2001 than in 1963 because free clinics have closed and public hospitals have atrophied (Institute of Medicine 2000). This restricts a physician's ability to provide effective treatment and may discourage physicians from establishing a physician-patient relationship with indigent patients.

One must also consider the effects of insurance on the economics of charity care. A potential explanation for a change in the willingness of physicians to provide free or reduced-fee care is that the growth of third-party control over payment rates limited the ability of physicians to cross-subsidize the care of the poor by charging the rich more. However, given the steady and healthy increases in net income per physician following 1965, this would appear to be an unlikely explanation.

A more likely explanation for a decline in charity care is that increased reimbursement opportunities from Medicare and private insurance raised the opportunity costs of providing charity care. Prior to 1965, many physicians were not able to fill their practices with patients who could pay full fees out of pocket; the opportunity costs of charity care were relatively low. Further, as argued by R. A. Kessel (1958), providing care to patients who paid partial fees may have been a profit maximization strategy. Medicare and the growth of private insurance for physician services fundamentally changed this calculus by providing abundant opportunities for additional revenue from well-paying patients and reducing the supply of care to patients who could not pay. This certainly included the uninsured poor, but in many states it also included Medicaid patients for whom reimbursement rates to physicians were much lower than rates from Medicare and even further below the rates that private insurers would pay.

Another potential though partial explanation for the hypothesized decline in the willingness of physicians to offer charity care is related to the larger political environment. One interpretation of Arrow's observation that physicians in 1963 provided services without regard to ability to pay is that the medical profession was attempting to forestall government involvement in health care financing. The AMA was a vociferous opponent of the enactment of Medicare and had similarly opposed almost all the attempts throughout the twentieth century to move toward a greater public role in the financing of health care. Maintaining that treatment should be available without regard to ability to pay arguably helped physicians in their political struggles. Having lost a major battle in 1965, physicians perhaps perceived less value in continuing either the practice or the rhetoric. Further, when lobbying efforts were transformed from opposition to government intrusion into medicine into efforts to increase government payment rates, the logic of arguing that money did not affect treatment choices also changed.[4]

Most of all, Medicare and Medicaid altered public understanding of the locus of responsibility for care for the poor: prior to 1965, physicians were responsible for assuring that the poor received high-quality care. Furthermore, physicians at least partially accepted this as their social role out of a sense of obligation and connection to the community. Medicare and Medicaid challenged that role. Subsequent to 1965, care for the poor was clearly the government's responsibility. Granted, the government did not take responsibility for all of the poor, and the 42 million uninsured who fell between the cracks were left with neither physicians nor the government as the guarantor of their health care.

In addition to changing public perceptions, government entitlement programs sapped physicians' professional resolve to be charitable. Physicians participating in Medicaid were forced to accept discounts from their private fees; physicians serving Medicare patients were strongly pressured to accept such discounts. Thus, when physicians thought about providing charity care to the uninsured, they might have felt that they already "gave at the office." Paradoxically, physicians were receiving much more revenue from Medicare and Medicaid than they would have from wholly uninsured patients. Since the reduced fees (relative to full charges) were a government-imposed discount rather than a result of voluntary physician decisions, however, physicians may have felt less compulsion to provide additional charity care.[5]

SUMMARY

Arrow asserted that a variety of institutional arrangements and observable mores of the medical profession were functional responses to the failure of the market to insure against uncertainties. But one of these norms—the ethic to provide treatment without regard to ability to pay—was also a response to the failure of the political system to assure the elderly and poor would not suffer more than others when they got sick. This ethic is strikingly different from the norm in most other areas of the economy. Automobile dealers and department stores are not expected to give away their products to the poor; neither are grocery stores or farmers. Public education is a closer analogy, reflecting the norm that all children deserve a good education. In education, however, unlike in medicine, we collectively support this norm by providing public funds to accomplish this goal rather than by relying on the private market.

In 1963, physicians argued that a combination of the market and private philanthropy (including the obligations of physicians) would be sufficient to guarantee high-quality care for the elderly and the poor. Government financing, they argued, would lead to socialized medicine, impairing relationships between physicians and patients and between physicians and society. Based on his article,

Arrow would not have agreed. Neither, apparently, did the public. The enactment of Medicare indicated, in part, that many people understood, even in 1965, the extent to which treatment choices and outcomes were affected by ability to pay.

Events since 1965 suggest that there is some tension between insurance and ethical responses to uncertainty despite Arrow's endorsement of both. I have argued here that Medicare and Medicaid further eroded the ethic that treatment should be available without regard to ability to pay by reducing physician willingness to provide charity care and by reducing the resources available to public hospitals and the interest of private teaching hospitals in providing care to the uninsured poor. Largely independent of Medicare and Medicaid, the increasing importance of pharmaceuticals and other services delivered outside of the hospital further strengthened the connection between treatment choices and ability to pay, and the growth of capitated payment systems made this connection salient to many insured patients and their physicians.

In part, then, the AMA was correct: Medicare and Medicaid have contributed to the erosion of trust in physicians as incorruptible agents for patients. Some of this trust undoubtedly was misplaced, even in 1965, and trust alone was not sufficient to guarantee widespread access to medical care or to assure that treatment provided would take true social benefits and costs into account. Medicare and Medicaid, as well as the growth of prepayment insurance plans, represent institutional responses to the failure of the 1963 norms to accomplish societal goals. Still, as we have seen, these responses create their own challenges, and we continue to search for institutions that will allow widespread insurance to coexist with the physician-patient trust that Arrow correctly identified as an important response to uncertainties and information asymmetries in the medical care market.

NOTES

Research for this article was supported by a Robert Wood Johnson Foundation Investigator in Health Policy Research Award. The author is grateful to Burton Weisbrod for helpful comments on an earlier draft.

1 Anderson, Collette, and Feldman (1963) report that 65 percent of the population was insured for hospital services in 1958, coverage rates for physician services were certainly much lower, and coverage rates among the elderly were even lower. In sharp contrast, in 1980, at the high-water mark of insurance coverage, close to 90 percent of the U.S. population had health insurance for both hospital and physician services, including virtually all of the elderly. Further, although the share of the population without health insurance has increased since 1980, the depth of coverage, particularly for physician services, for those with coverage has increased. As a result, the share of physician revenues from out-of-pocket payments has continued to decrease throughout the past forty years — from 62 percent in 1960 to 16 percent in 1998. The share of hospital revenues that comes from out-of-pocket payments also has decreased, but

from a smaller base, from 20 percent in 1960 to 3 percent in 1998 (National Health Accounts, available at www.hcfa.gov/stats).

2 Cunningham et al. (1999) report that physicians, on average, state that 5 percent of their total practice hours are devoted to charity care. I am unaware of comparable data from the 1960s.

3 Cunningham et al. (1999) report that physicians in solo or two-person practices provide substantially more charity care than do physicians in larger groups.

4 However, it is far from clear how any such change in political posture and lobbying strategy at the AMA leadership level would translate into a change in norms at the grassroots level.

5 If this explanation were correct, we might expect charity care to decline as Medicaid participation increases. However, the opposite is true—physicians with more Medicaid involvement provide more charity care, casting some doubt on the explanation, at least at the individual physician level.

REFERENCES

Anderson, O. W., P. Collette, and J. J. Feldman. 1963. *Changes in Family Medical Care Expenditures and Voluntary Health Insurance; A Five-Year Resurvey.* Cambridge: Harvard University Press.

Cunningham, P. J., J. M. Grossman, R. F. St. Peter, and C. S. Lesser. 1999. Managed Care and Physicians' Provision of Charity Care. *Journal of the American Medical Association* 281(12): 1087–1092.

Institute of Medicine. 2000. *America's Health Care Safety Net: Intact but Endangered.* Washington, DC: National Academy Press.

Kessel, R. A. 1958. Price Discrimination in Medicine. *Journal of Law and Economics* 20(1): 20–53.

Ludmerer, K. M. 1999. *Time to Heal: American Medical Education from the Turn of the Century to the Era of Managed Care.* Cambridge: Oxford University Press.

Robinson, J. C., and L. P. Casalino. 1995. The Growth of Medical Groups Paid through Capitation in California. *New England Journal of Medicine* 333(25): 1684–1687.

Starr, P. 1982. *Social Transformation of American Medicine.* New York: Basic Books.

Wielawski, I. 2000. Gouging the Medically Uninsured: A Tale of Two Bills. *Health Affairs* 19(5): 180–185.

GLORIA J. BAZZOLI

■ *Medical Service Risk and the Evolution of*

Provider Compensation Arrangements

Kenneth Arrow (1963: 962) discussed two forms of provider compensation that were in existence during the 1960s: fee-for-service and prepayment. Like many others before him, he recognized a problem with the former that has been the subject of much subsequent discussion in health economics. Under traditional indemnity insurance, consumers face incentives to expand their health services utilization because the effective price for their health services is less than the actual price. Fee-for-service compensation provides no financial incentives for health providers to mitigate consumer moral hazard, but prepayment does. However, Arrow noted that physicians were resistant to prepayment for two reasons: (1) their inherent aversion to accepting financial risk, and (2) the potential impediments to physician autonomy through the use of closed panels for referral (957).

Since Arrow's time, the U.S. health system has experienced rapid growth in HMOs, risk contracting, and a plethora of provider intermediary organizations (e.g., medical groups, Independent Practice Associations [IPAS], Physician Hospital Organizations [PHOS], Management Services Organizations [MSOS], physician practice management companies, organized delivery systems). Taken together, these developments provided a platform for transferring greater amounts and types of medical service risk to health providers through prepayment, or what is now more commonly called *capitation*. Provider intermediary organizations in particular provided the means to address some of the concerns about prepayment raised by Arrow. First, they offered a convenient method to pool and manage financial risks across many affiliated health providers and thus reduce the risks that providers would otherwise individually confront under capitation. Second, the large volume and geographic dispersion of capitated lives encompassed by the contracts of a provider intermediary organization should accommodate a large panel of affiliated providers to whom individual physicians can refer and thus reduce concern about overly restrictive and narrow closed panels.

Despite the development of organizational structures and strategies that should allow expanded transfer and better management of risk, evidence is mounting that retrenchment in broad-based prepayment, especially global capitation, is occurring in several markets across the United States. This essay examines the evolution of provider compensation mechanisms, especially as it relates to the transfer of medical service risk to health providers. Then, it offers explanations for the retrenchment in capitation that is being observed, drawing on themes and arguments raised by Arrow in his seminal article. This essay also examines why there is an incomplete market for insuring health providers against the risks they assume through capitation and how this too adds to the current problems with capitation.

EVOLUTION OF PROVIDER PAYMENT METHODS

Through the 1960s, physicians, hospitals, and other health providers in the United States were largely paid on a fee-for-service basis for the services they delivered. This approach predated the development of health insurance and was likely an artifact of a market-based U.S. economy in which buyers and sellers traded distinct goods and services for mutually accepted prices. Arrow observed that fee-for-service payment could promote inefficient use of services among poorly informed consumers. However, economists subsequently noted certain advantages and other disadvantages with fee-for-service that Arrow did not consider. Joseph P. Newhouse (1996) noted that an advantage of fee-for-service payment was that it minimized provider behavior to select against bad risks because physicians and hospitals are paid more for sicker patients who require more services. James C. Robinson (1999) noted that agency theory supports the use of piece-rate, fee-for-service payment when desirable behaviors can be standardized and easily measured. However, fee-for-service performs poorly when multiple tasks need to be performed and coordinated. Clearly, technological advances in medicine have vastly increased the complexity of care, producing an almost incomprehensible array of potential diagnostic and treatment combinations and blurring the settings of care. In this context, fee-for-service promotes inefficiency because it lacks incentives to coordinate care across providers, to select the lowest cost setting for care, and to avoid costly service duplication.

Fee-for-service payment was further complicated because it was coupled with consumer incentives that encouraged overuse of health care. Consumer copayments in indemnity insurance create a wedge between effective and actual prices of health services and thus increase consumer demand due to moral hazard.

Arrow invoked the idea of physician professional norms as a means to counteract moral hazard, stating that physicians would follow a professional imperative to select only those services based on health needs rather than patient desires (950). However, if physicians seek profit like other economic actors, they will satisfy patient demands under fee-for-service payment because it holds potential for increasing their income. Alternatively, as the agent for a patient, a physician will increase the supply of services as long as his or her marginal reimbursement exceeds marginal costs because the physician's objective function positively weights patient benefit from health services (Ellis and McGuire 1986, 1990). While increasing consumer copayments will reduce moral hazard, this action places consumers at greater financial risk, which conflicts with the principal objectives of risk pooling and spreading underlying insurance.

Capitation of health providers, in which they receive a fixed amount of money per enrolled individual to deliver or arrange a specific set of services, represents a means for reducing moral hazard without increasing patient financial risk. Specifically, as noted by Randall Ellis and Thomas McGuire (1993) and Sherry Glied (2000), capitation is a form of "supply-side cost sharing" in which the provider bears the marginal costs for his or her treatment decisions. Capitation per se actually had existed for quite some time and was especially notable in the 1930s when two large medical groups, Kaiser Permanente Medical Group and Group Health Cooperative of Puget Sound, became major players. These medical groups offered a package of covered medical services to enrollees that would be delivered by the group's physicians in exchange for a fixed, up-front payment. These early efforts blended a traditional insurance function, namely, the payment of a set amount in advance to offset the risk of future expenses, with the promise to deliver specific health services based on patient needs. These early experiments provided a starting point for subsequent HMO development of physician capitation arrangements.

Initial HMO capitation arrangements involved contracting with one or more medical groups in a market on a prepaid basis to provide a specific set of services or involved paying capitation to individual primary care physicians for the primary care services they delivered to HMO enrollees. These early arrangements, which tended to only focus on those services that providers in the medical group personally delivered, were problematic because they did not address issues of coordination of complex care across health providers outside the capitated group. Further, primary care capitation motivated physicians to refer patients to specialists for services they might be able to deliver themselves so as to avoid bearing the marginal costs of these services.

J. C. Robinson and L. P. Casalino (1995) noted that medical groups in California saw opportunity in this environment to manage capitation for large groups of enrollees and a fuller spectrum of professional and institutional health services. As medical groups grew to take advantage of these opportunities, this facilitated further growth of HMOs and thus the number of enrollees covered through global capitation arrangements (Casalino and Robinson 1995). An array of competing organizational arrangements that sought to mimic medical groups in terms of their structure and capitated contracting objectives soon developed. Physicians in small practices came together to form Independent Practice Associations (IPAs) that often had similar physician numbers and specialty mixes as large medical groups but allowed greater physician autonomy through diversified ownership. Hospitals developed PHOs and MSOs as mechanisms to integrate physicians and hospitals and to negotiate and oversee managed care contracts. Finally, physician practice management companies developed quickly across the United States with the purposes of pooling physician practices, either through direct ownership or service agreements, and securing global capitation contracts.

Large medical groups and other provider intermediary organizations all operated under similar principles: capitated lives were pooled across a broad array of affiliated providers to reduce overall risk exposure; a centralized administrative infrastructure was developed to oversee global capitation contracts and to take advantage of administrative economies of scale; and organization-wide approaches were developed to manage patient care and improve efficiency. These intermediary organizations also established payment methods for compensating individual health providers involved with health care delivery. Because the provider intermediary organization held the financial risk of the capitated contract, it had incentives to motivate individual providers to conserve on resources and eliminate minimally beneficial care. Initial payment approaches used by intermediaries to compensate individual physicians focused on simple fee-for-service, salary, and individual provider capitation. As noted above, fee-for-service is problematic and likely promotes overproduction of health services. This certainly conflicts with the objectives of the provider intermediary organization that is attempting to live within a fixed capitated budget. Salary does not encourage overproduction but likely dulls incentives to work hard and to manage a large panel of patients. Finally, individual capitation would align the incentives of the provider intermediary and the physician but could discourage physicians from providing certain patient services, such as preventive care. It may also encourage excessive referral to other providers or may result in selection or avoidance of particular patients based on their health needs.

Through experimentation and experience, provider intermediary organizations developed compensation arrangements that sought to balance a complex set of organizational objectives. These methods often used fee schedules, salary, and individual provider capitation as a base and coupled this base with withholds, performance-based bonuses, and fee-for-service payment for selected services (Conrad et al. 1998; Kralewski et al. 2000; and Robinson 1999). Fee schedules, often patterned after Medicare's Resource-Based Relative Value Scale (RBRVS), were used to reward physician productivity and management of a large patient panel. Such payments also recognized the varying resource costs and intensity of care inherent in particular medical services. Withholds were used in conjunction with individual capitation or fee-for-service payments to create pools of funds from which health providers received bonuses if certain performance standards were met (e.g., a target number of hospital days per thousand, meeting age-specific guidelines for provision of preventive services, compliance with HEDIS guidelines).

Robinson (1999) found that primary care physicians affiliated with large IPAS in California typically were paid a blended system of capitation for primary care services, individual performance bonuses based on quality measures and overall IPA profitability, and fee-for-service for selected preventive and screening procedures. Specialists, on the other hand, were paid either discounted fee-for-service, fee schedules, or blended capitation and bonuses similar to those of primary care physicians. At first blush, these payment systems seem complex and fragmented, but they are designed to motivate a complex set of behaviors by physicians in their treatment decisions. However, some researchers and health executives have expressed concern that these approaches may be attempting to reward too many disparate and potentially conflicting types of physician behavior to be effective (Burns and Wholey 2000). In addition, they may be inherently too complex for many physicians to fully understand, which would defeat the purpose of these payment systems.

In the early to middle 1990s, fierce competition for capitated arrangements occurred between large medical organizations, IPAS, hospital-organized PHOS and MSOS, and physician practice management companies (Bazzoli, Dynan, and Burns 1999/2000; Bazzoli, Miller, and Burns 2000; Kohn 2000; Lesser and Ginsburg 2000). This competition undoubtedly reflected a perception that capitation could be profitable if the right deals were struck with HMOs and a capitation management infrastructure was in place. There was even an anticipation among some who had studied the industry that by the early 2000s, capitation would become the norm systemwide in the United States (cf., Advisory Board 1993; Shortell 1988). This precipitated a frenzy of development of provider intermediary organizational arrangements, often without sufficient investment in the necessary skills and infrastructure for the organizations to achieve their stated objectives (Kohn 2000; Lesser and Ginsburg 2000).

While there are reports in the trade press that certain physician organizations are prospering under global capitation arrangements and thus continue to seek them (Capitation Management Report 2001), there is growing evidence that many health provider organizations and HMOs are backing away from these arrangements (Hurley et al. 2002). Stories abound of financial difficulties and outright bankruptcy of some health organizations due to losses generated from capitated arrangements (Center for Studying Health System Change 2000; Los Angeles Times 2000). Physician practice management companies have largely disintegrated and disappeared, and researchers have suggested that botched management of global capitation is partly to blame (Lesser and Ginsburg 2000; Reinhardt 2000). Between 1995 and 1999, capitation of primary care services by health plans studied by Mathematica Policy Research increased minimally from 56 to 61 percent for primary care services and fell from 20 to 13 percent for specialist services in this period (Lake et al. 2000). Additionally, InterStudy (26 April 2000) found that most of the growth in HMO enrollment since 1998 was driven by the growing number and market shares of plans that use relative-value scale payment systems rather than capitation. In some ways, the world of provider compensation, which once appeared poised to heavily rely on global capitation and thus to differ dramatically from the world that Arrow described, appears to have receded to some middle ground. Why did this happen, and what does it imply for the future? Much of Arrow's original observations are instructive in answering the first question. These answers combined with the lessons learned through our experiences with capitation will likely help us discern what could happen in the future.

EXPLANATIONS FOR THE RETRENCHMENT IN PROVIDER CAPITATION

Why has provider capitation faltered? This is an important question to address given the high hopes that many expressed for capitation as a means for improving efficiency without increasing consumer risk. Arrow's 1963 article provides many insights to answer this question. In particular, I argue that our current problems with capitation largely relate to

— the conflict between capitation and the trust relationship between health providers and patients;

— growing risk exposure of provider intermediary organizations in successive rounds of capitation rate negotiation;

— the nonmarketability of certain types of risk bearing—in this case, the risks borne by health providers and their intermediary organizations—as they take on capitation.

Capitation and Trust Relationships
Capitation by its very nature conflicts with patient expectations of physician behavior as described by Arrow. Namely, Arrow stated that "advice given by physicians to further treatment by himself or others is supposed to be completely di-

vorced from self-interest" (949–950) and that "the very word 'profit' is a signal that denies trust relations" (965). Yet, if capitation amounts to supply-side cost sharing in that health providers absorb the marginal costs of treatment, provider decisions must be affected by financial considerations or there could be dour consequences for them and their intermediary organizations. Further, the newest generation of performance-based, blended payment systems frequently is based on the intermediary's profitability. In essence, capitation generally and performance-based payment systems specifically have turned health providers into "double agents," who on the one hand are expected to act on the patient's behalf but on the other hand are financially accountable to their intermediary organizations. Increasingly, patients have become aware of the conflicted position their health providers are in and have, in some instances, sought state legislative relief to eliminate financial incentives that may promote undertreatment. In addition, patients with specific health needs and their advocacy groups are increasingly concerned about skimping on certain types of service (for example, mental health services), and they too have raised concern and sought relief. Capitation may require the development of new, or the expansion of existing, institutional arrangements to deal with the agency failures that it creates.

Dynamics of Capitation and Provider Risk Exposure

Another reason that capitation faltered was the simple dynamics of this payment mechanism in a competitive HMO marketplace. Specifically, as health providers realize efficiency gains through capitation (for example, by reducing inpatient hospital admissions and lengths of stay), these efficiency gains lead HMOs in a highly competitive insurance market to ratchet down the premiums they charge to compete with other health plans in the market. Namely, a competitive HMO market inevitably requires HMOs to reduce premiums as providers become more efficient, which then in turn leads the HMO to reduce subsequent capitation in successive rounds of contracting. Thomas Bodenheimer (1999) and Joan Trauner and Julie Chestnutt (1996) noted this phenomena when they discussed the pressure HMOs were exerting on large physician organizations in the 1990s to accept lower global capitation rates even when further reductions in inpatient utilization were considered difficult to achieve and potentially harmful to patients. Thus, as capitation plays out year after year, providers have less money to work with and less available financial cushion to cover what could be substantial health needs for certain enrollees. This situation becomes especially complicated by the phenomenon described by Robert Miller (1996) in that initial efficiency gains come easy because health providers take advantage of the "low hanging fruit," but as time progresses, they can only achieve efficiency gains by trying to reach tougher and riskier "higher hanging fruit." These dynamics have led to the perception among some health providers that they have largely squeezed out con-

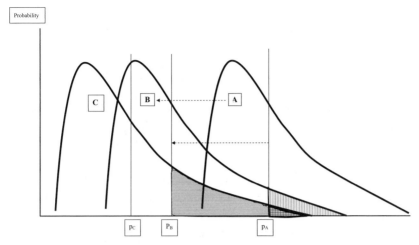

Figure 1   Effects of Declining Capitation on Provider Risk Exposure

trollable medical risks (e.g., unnecessary, expensive variations in health care) and that they are now left with largely uncontrollable risks (e.g., due to adverse selection, uncertainty in the incidence of expensive illness and costs of new and expensive technological advances).

Figure 1 illustrates this process and the resulting implications for health providers. Specifically, the figure depicts three hypothetical distributions of annual health expenditures per enrollee that a particular provider intermediary organization might face. Distribution A represents annual expenditures per person assuming a fee-for-service payment system in which there are no incentives for physicians to economize on care. Distribution C, on the other hand, represents a distribution that embodies some minimum acceptable level of care based on professional norms in a community or based on a style of practice that physicians are unwilling to economize on further because of concerns about losing patients or malpractice.[1] Distribution B represents an interim case in which health providers have taken some action to reduce unnecessary and duplicative treatments. For simplicity, we assume that capitation rates are set equal to the average annual expenditure per person for a given expenditure distribution. Thus, given Distribution A, a capitation rate of pA would be set and would provide expected profit of (pA – pB) if the provider intermediary organization was able to motivate expenditure reductions that would shift the expenditure per person distribution to B. The organization faces financial risk in that its actual expenditures per person may exceed the capitation rate. The probability of such a loss equals the area under Distribution B for expenditure levels greater than pA.

As the expenditure per person distribution moves from A to B, a capitation rate of pA becomes unsustainable in a competitive HMO market. Negotiation between the HMO and the provider intermediary organization will lead to a capitation rate of pB, and health providers will need to reach for the "higher hanging" efficiency actions if they are to move the distribution of expenditures closer to Distribution C and realize an efficiency gain. If they do so, they have an expected profit of approximately pB – pC, but the likelihood that the provider intermediary will experience health expenditures in excess of the capitation rate increases and is measured by the area under Distribution C for expenditure levels greater than pB. Generally, as health providers become more efficient (i.e., move the distribution of expenditures per person from A toward C), their ability to generate profits under capitation declines and their exposure to financial losses increases. Health providers and their intermediary organizations are keenly aware of this phenomenon, typically saying that they are being penalized for the efficiencies that they generate under capitation. Figure 1 adds depth to this provider perception in that the "penalty" they observe involves both a decline in the rewards they previously received for their actions to promote efficiency and greater exposure to downside financial risks.

Of course, theoretically, health providers and their intermediaries could obtain some degree of protection from the vagaries of this process. In principle, capitation could be risk adjusted to reduce the variance in expenditures per person depicted in Figure 1. However, risk adjustments used for capitation rates remain crude in practice, typically relying on simple gender and age adjustments, even though research on risk adjustment methods has advanced substantially. The reasons why HMOs have been slow to adopt more refined methods of risk adjustment are unclear and worthy of careful study. One could also imagine that markets would arise to offer insurance products to health providers that would allow them to purchase protection from excessive losses. In fact, insurance of this type exists in the form of stop-loss coverage. This insurance limits the provider's obligation for absorbing the costs of care for individuals with extraordinary health expenses that exceed some threshold. Typically, this coverage is obtained if the provider intermediary organization assumes both professional and institutional service risk. Cost thresholds for this coverage tend to be very high, on the order of $25,000 to $50,000 per case. Provider intermediary organizations often purchase this coverage from HMOs as a deduction from their negotiated capitation rates. Generally, the intermediary groups feel that the tying of capitation rate negotiation with purchase of stop-loss coverage is to their disadvantage and yields premiums for stop-loss coverage that are higher than otherwise competitive rates.

Further, Randall Ellis and Thomas McGuire (1993) suggest that fairness of provider payments depends on the relationship between expected payments and expected costs for treating a group of patients. Stop-loss coverage, however, seeks to curtail random, extraordinarily high costs for individual patients. As such, this coverage can only reduce the difference between expected payments and expected costs, but without adequate risk adjustment of capitation rates, the balance between expected payments and costs from the perspective of health providers may still not be perceived as fair.

Nonmarketability of Capitated Health Provider Risks

Finally, Arrow commented on the nonmarketability of certain risks, and I argue that provider risks under capitation may be equally nonmarketable for similar reasons. In relation to patients, Arrow (945) argued that insurers are not able to distinguish unavoidable risks that relate to the underlying uncertainty of illness from avoidable risks in which patients can take action to reduce their health needs. Rather than facing unavoidable risks, health providers under capitation face *uncontrollable risks*—namely, due to the underlying uncertainty of illness in their patient populations and uncertainty in the efficacy of treatments. Further, providers face *controllable* risks—namely, they can take action to economize on patient health services that provide little benefit. Insurers may not be capable of distinguishing controllable from uncontrollable provider risks due to information asymmetries or fear of patient or provider backlash.[2] The health insurer surely has good experience and knowledge to estimate the underlying likelihood of different illnesses within given patient populations. However, they are not likely to be able to distinguish what treatments are right and at what levels of intensity, and they likely cannot surmise these answers based on health outcomes after a patient's course of care, given uncertainties in the effects and efficacies of treatments. Considering that the task of distinguishing controllable and uncontrollable risks may be difficult for a health insurer, this may explain why few private insurance companies are entering the stop-loss coverage market.

Facing the problems identified above, health providers and their intermediary organizations can take and have taken action. They can implement a variety of clinical management methods, including case management, disease management, clinical pathways, and physician profiling, to better manage patient care and further wring out inefficiencies in the system. Doing so represents attempts to get at the tougher "higher-hanging" fruit after all the "low-hanging" efficiency gains have been exploited. Michael Chernew et al. (2000) found evidence suggesting that physician groups that took capitation for pharmaceutical risk were initially successful in this regard in managing drug cost growth for their enrolled populations. However, these gains were short lived most likely because they could not affect technology-related changes that were out of the direct control of physicians. Health providers and their intermediaries can also engage more actively in risk selection as suggested by Newhouse (1996). Doing so on an individual patient basis is likely to be problematic because it would reflect poorly on trust relationships, revealing that health providers are indeed putting financial motives ahead of individual patient interests. Instead, actions of provider intermediaries have generally focused on the extensive margins, namely, dropping capitated contracts with certain HMOs altogether. Such actions seem a step removed from individual patients because these actions relate to a contract with an HMO rather than an implicit contract with an individual.

IMPLICATIONS FOR THE FUTURE OF PROVIDER
COMPENSATION ARRANGEMENTS

The evolution of provider compensation arrangements is an interesting phenomenon, which Arrow could not have expected. However, the enduring contribution of his work is that it provides insights almost forty years later that help explain contemporary phenomena in the U.S. health sector. In particular, I have argued in this essay that trust relations and the underlying uncertainty of patient illness coupled with the nonmarketability of provider risks under capitation are major factors in growing disinterest among providers in capitation arrangements.

What have we learned through this process, and what are the implications for the future of provider compensation? First, we have learned just how difficult it is to balance insurer-provider agency costs in relation to developing arrangements that align incentives and behavior and the costs to health providers of bearing medical service risk. Certainly, a balance between these two types of costs must be struck if capitation is to have a solid footing in the U.S. health system.

Second, it may be worthwhile to step "outside the box" and think of the next generation of provider payment methods. Arrow (964) raised the notion of paying health providers based on the health benefits they achieve for patients. He spoke of this idea in terms of "ideal insurance," which, given his frequent discussion of the inherent uncertainty of the outcomes of health treatments, suggests that he realized this ideal could not be easily met. However, efforts to decode the human genome create the ability to tailor courses of treatment to specific individuals and this may bring us closer to this ideal. In the interim, however, we may need to advance ideas expressed in a 2001 Institute of Medicine report, which recommends payment based on actions to improve quality of care (e.g., meet immunization goals, meet age and gender recommended preventive service goals, etc.), for which some good models already exist. Further, economists have discussed the merit of "mixed" payment systems (Ellis and McGuire 1993; Newhouse 1996). Such mixed models have in fact been developed in tiered payment arrangements involving capitated provider intermediary organizations and their affiliated health providers. However, there is a need for similar innovation in the development of blended systems between HMOs and provider intermediaries. Some purchaser coalitions, namely, the Buyers Health Action Group in Minnesota, have in fact moved in this direction and also have implemented advances in risk adjustment technology (Christianson et al. 1999; Knutson 1998). These efforts merit careful study and evaluation to learn lessons that can be applied to other organizations.

Third, there may be a role for the government in the short term and perhaps the long term in dealing with the incomplete market for insuring health providers and their intermediary organizations against the financial risks they face. At a minimum, this role may involve the development and testing of model insurance products that promote general fairness in provider payment and provide incentives for providers to take action to reduce controllable risks. Ultimately, the U.S. health system has produced a rich set of experiences from prior efforts to place health providers at risk for health services. Through future research and evaluation of these experiences, refinements in existing contracting methods hopefully can be developed that place health providers at risk for what they can manage but minimize their exposure to risk they cannot.

NOTES

This essay was supported in part by the Robert Wood Johnson Foundation's Investigator Awards in Health Policy Research program (no. 038649) and by the foundation's Health Care Financing and Organization grant (no. 36348), in which the author is studying organizational and regulatory implications of provider risk bearing in collaboration with Robert H. Miller, Ph.D., of the University of California, San Francisco. The author wishes to thank Richard C. Lindrooth, Ph.D., for very helpful input and comments on earlier drafts of this essay.

1 One could otherwise say that Distribution C represents an efficient level of health care practice in which no unnecessary care was provided to individuals. However, such efficiency is unlikely to be realized given the inherent uncertainties of treatment and their outcomes and variations in medical practice. As such, thinking of Distribution C as a style of practice that physicians will not economize beyond is probably more realistic than thinking of it as efficient practice, although the former is certainly no easier to identify and measure than the latter.

2 While this also could be said of malpractice coverage, namely, that insurers may be unable to distinguish controllable from uncontrollable risks, malpractice has an important difference. Malpractice carries a stigma (the suggestion that the physician provides substandard care) that motivates health providers to control malpractice risks as best they can. Medical service risk under capitation may not pose this kind of problem for health providers, especially if patients are concerned about undue skimping on their care due to financial incentives.

REFERENCES

Advisory Board. 1993. *The Grand Alliance*. Washington, DC: Advisory Board Company.

Arrow, K. J. 1963. Uncertainty and the Welfare Economics of Medical Care. *American Economic Review* 53(5): 941–973.

Bazzoli, G. J., L. Dynan, and L. R. Burns. 1999/2000. Capitated Contracting of Integrated Health Provider Organizations. *Inquiry* (winter 1999/2000): 426–444.

Bazzoli, G. J., R. H. Miller, and L. R. Burns. 2000. Capitated Contracting Relationships in Health Care. *Journal of Healthcare Management* 45(May/June): 170–188.

Bodenheimer, T. 1999. The American Health Care System: Physicians and the Changing Medical Marketplace. *New England Journal of Medicine* 340(7): 584–588.

Burns, L. R., and D. R. Wholey. 2000. Responding to a Consolidating Health Care System: Options for Physician Organizations. In *Advances in Health Care Management*, ed. J. D. Blair, M. D. Fottler, and G. T. Savage. Amsterdam: JAI Press.

Capitation Management Report. 2001. Stick with Capitation? For Many the Answer Is Yes. *Capitation Management Report*, January.

Casalino, L., and J. C. Robinson. 1997. The *Evolution of Medical Groups and Capitation in California*. Oakland: California Healthcare Foundation.

Center for Studying Health System Change. 2000. Insolvency and Challenges of Regulating Providers that Bear Risk. *Issue Brief from HSC*, 26 February.

Chernew, M., M. E. Cowen, D. M. Kirking, D. G. Smith, P. Valenstein, and A. M. Fendrick. 2000. Pharmaceutical Cost Growth under Capitation: A Case Study. *Health Affairs* 19 (November/December): 266–276.

Christianson, J., R. Feldman, J. P. Weiner, and P. Drury. 1999. Early Experience with a New Model of Employer Group Purchasing in Minnesota. *Health Affairs* 18(6): 100–114.

Conrad, D. A., C. Maynard, A. Cheadle. S. Ramsey, M. Marcus-Smith, H. Kirz, C. A. Madden, D. Martin, E. B. Parrin, T. Wickizer, B. Zierler, A. Ross, J. Noren, and S. Y. Liang. 1998. Primary Care Physician Compensation Method in Medical Groups: Does It Influence the Use and Costs of Health Services for Enrollees of Managed Care Organizations? *Journal of the American Medical Association* 279: 853–858.

Ellis, R. P., and T. G. McGuire. 1986. Provider Behavior under Prospective Reimbursement: Cost Sharing and Supply. *Journal of Health Economics* 5 (summer): 129–152.

———. 1990. Optimal Payment Systems for Health Services. *Journal of Health Economics* 9 (December): 375–396.

———. 1993. Supply-Side and Demand-Side Cost Sharing in Health Care. *Journal of Economic Perspectives* 7 (fall): 135–151.

Glied, S. 2000. Managed Care. In *Handbook of Health Economics*, vol. 1A, ed. A. J. Culyer and J. P. Newhouse. Amsterdam: Elsevier.

Hurley, R., J. Grossman, T. Lake, and L. Casalino. 2002. Longitudinal Perspective on Health Plan–Provider Risk Contracting. *Health Affairs* 21 (July–Aug.): 144–153.

Institute of Medicine. 2001. *Crossing the Quality Chasm: A New Health System for the 21st Century*. Washington, DC: National Academy Press.

InterStudy Publications. 2000. HMOs Lose Over 500,000 Enrollees since January 1, 1999. Press release for HMO Industry Report 10.1, 26 April.

Knutson, D. 1998. Case Study: The Minneapolis Buyers Health Care Action Group. *Inquiry* 35 (summer): 171–177.

Kohn, L. T. 2000. Organizing and Managing Care in a Changing Health System. *Health Services Research* 35 (April, pt. 1): 37–52.

Kralewski, J. E., E. C. Rich, R. Feldman, B. E. Dowd, T. Bernhardt, C. Johnson, and W. Gold. 2000. The Effects of Medical Group Practice and Physician Payment Methods on Costs of Care. *Health Services Research* 35 (August): 591–614.

Lake, T., M. Gold, R. Hurley, M. Sinclair, and S. Waltman. 2000. Health Plans' Selection and Payment of Health Care Providers. Final report to the Medicare Payment Advisory Commission, 16 May.

Lesser, C. S., and P. B. Ginsburg. 2000. Update on the Nation's Health Care System: 1997–1999. *Health Affairs* 19(6): 206–216.

Los Angeles Times. 2000. Health Plans Seek to Address Consumer Ire. *Los Angeles Times*, 6 April, A:1.

Miller, R. H. 1996. Health System Integration: A Means to an End. *Health Affairs* 15(2): 91–106.

Newhouse, J. P. 1996. Reimbursing Health Plans and Health Providers: Selection versus Efficiency in Production. *Journal of Economic Literature* 34 (September): 1930–1934.

Reinhardt, U. E. 2000. The Rise and Fall of the Physician Practice Management Industry. *Health Affairs* 19(1): 42–55.

Robinson, J. C. 1999. Blended Payment Methods in Physician Organizations under Managed Care. *Journal of the American Medical Association* 282: 1258–1263.

Robinson, J. C. and L. P. Casalino. 1995. The Growth of Medical Groups Paid through Capitation in California. *New England Journal of Medicine* 333: 1684–1687.

Shortell, S. M. 1988. The Evolution of Hospital Systems: Unfulfilled Promises and Self-Fulfilling Prophesies. *Medical Care Research and Review* 45: 177–214.

Trauner, J. B., and J. S. Chestnutt. 1996. Medical Groups in California: Managing Care under Capitation. *Health Affairs* 15 (spring): 159–170.

J. B. SILVERS

■ The Role of the Capital Markets in Restructuring Health Care

Who would have predicted at the time of the Arrow article in 1963 the growth in assets invested in health care that we have seen[1] fueled by an unprecedented use of tax-exempt debt, retained earnings, and new stock? Enfranchisement of the formerly uninsured through Medicaid and Medicare plus the continued growth of private health insurance have given marginal providers the cash flow that allowed this dynamic growth in capital investment while substantial subsidies lowered their financing cost.

Yet it is not clear whether access to new sources of funds precipitated the restructuring of health care or the demand for capital[2] was simply the result of fundamental need. Irresponsible investments by managers certainly have occurred.[3] Yet once the industry embraced capitalism's largess, it found that the accompanying market discipline was a demanding counterforce to its excesses. The capital markets have been a major factor in both expansion and contraction, allowing excesses and demanding fiscal responsibility.

How much of this was anticipated in the classic Arrow article? More important for our day are (1) how and why the capital market provides the funds it does to the health sector and what it expects in return; (2) how the resulting market discipline extends to both for-profit firms and nonprofit organizations; (3) what this means for the structure of ownership and control of the industry; and (4) what the implications are for access, quality, and cost.

WHAT DID ARROW SAY ABOUT THE CAPITAL MARKETS, AND WHAT HAS CHANGED?

Professor Arrow implicitly assumed that capital was an integral part of the production of health services, but he did not particularly distinguish it from other factors. He discussed the "ownership of assets and skills that command a price on the market" in passing but did not consider it explicitly as a critical element (Arrow 1963). The overall manner in which health care providers presented themselves to potential buyers was his concern in achieving a Pareto optimal distribution. This lack of explicit attention may reflect the relatively smaller reliance on capital investments in the production of health services at that time. Furthermore, Arrow's world was physician-centric with little attention to the hospital except as a "physician workshop," a concept popular during the subsequent period (Pauly and Redisch 1973). Hospitals and other institutional providers were not viewed as separate economic actors.

However, the massive private investment and financing of capital assets in the years since Medicare have changed all of this. Community fund-raising and the Hill-Burton program (grants and loan guarantees) of Arrow's time had provided most of the capital in the previous decade, and profits were largely nonexistent. Since then funding has come largely from retained profits, tax-exempt bonds, and stock issues. These later sources depend completely on payment systems, which did not exist in 1963. Medicare and Medicaid, in particular, converted formerly unprofitable segments (the poor and elderly) into paying customers. Furthermore, the original cost-based payment systems used by the government in 1965 included interest and depreciation as reimbursable expenses thus assuring the cash flow needed for debt interest and principal payments. As a result, the credit ratings of formerly weak organizations improved to the levels of those who promised to reimburse them — namely, the government and private insurers. With better ratings came full access often aided by tax-exempt bond authorities established in many states to further lower the cost of borrowing (Gershberg, Grossman, and Goldman 1999). By any stretch of the imagination, this form of payment and subsidy dramatically reduced the required return on investment to justify expansion or replacement. With such reduced cost, investment was sure to boom, and it did. As long as patients with insurance showed up, almost any expenditure could be justified and financed whether clinically or financially responsible. It is little surprise that certificate of need regulations were imposed to slow down this growth.

The advent of fixed price payment in 1983 for each case or service (i.e., the Medicare Prospective Payment System based on diagnosis rather than treatment) gave hospitals the ability to retain substantial profits if service cost were carefully managed. The obvious increase in financial risk under this system was more than offset by a growth in profit margins. The possibility for entrepreneurial gain expanded the profit-making potential of all hospitals regardless of their tax status. Since 1965, only investor-owned hospitals had been paid a return on investment as an allowable cost under the prior Medicare system. But now the playing field was leveled, and the margins and thus the financing abilities of most hospitals soared. Average total profit margins rose from 2.6 percent in 1980 to 6.7 percent in 1997 (Gutterman 2000). Average Medicare inpatient margins peaked at 17 percent in 1997 and have fallen some under recent cutbacks. Academic medical centers did much better with Medicare profits, reaching 28.6 percent of payment for inpatients offset partially by a 10.4 percent loss on outpatients and much more on uncompensated care (MedPAC 2000). These high margins certainly influenced Congress in limiting payment to hospitals under the Balanced Budget Act (BBA) of 1997. Although the BBA has hurt, subsequent legislation[4] has restored a significant amount to the industry.

The prospective payment system has been very generous overall, although the results varied widely, largely based on policy-based additions to base payments for teaching, care to the poor, and location. In most years one quarter to one half of all hospitals had negative Medicare inpatient margins. The risk imposed on these hospitals was very real, sometimes cutting them off from capital financing. However, the rewards were substantial, especially for the winners, and far exceeded what was required to justify the increased risk they were asked to bear.

The resulting unprecedented increase in free cash flow unencumbered by prior commitments drove growth. Agency theory suggests that this prosperity would tempt management to spend the money just because it was there (Jensen 1986). Having historically high profits opened access to greater debt financing also subsidized by tax deductibility and guarantees. While some were cut off from financing due to their individual risk, the average hospital had easy access to the capital markets for most of this period. The debris of disintegrating integrated health systems is testimony to the fact that many agents (i.e., management) made poor use of their low-cost funds as predicted by agency theory.

On the other hand, the use of outside financing should have had two positive implications. The fixed cost of debt magnifies the bottom-line impact of variations in operating income under prospective payment, thus increasing the pressure to avoid losses. Economic theory also suggests that the "bonding" of future cash flows to repay debt has an ameliorating effect on the free cash flow problem by reducing management flexibility to make poor investments. Both of these should serve to strengthen the fiscal responsibility of institutions. However, payment subsidies and differentials often covered poor investments. Bad investments often were justified as socially necessary, strategically critical, or required for quality and access. But the fact was that payment and financing subsidies allowed excesses that would not have occurred in other industries. As long as sufficient cash was available, the discipline of the capital markets was blunted, and such investments continued as high margins covered up mistakes.

Another interesting melding occurred as the capital market increased pressure to maintain and enhance profitability. Management of nonprofit providers began to behave more like their investor-owned counterparts in the rest of the economy. In fact, in the long run, the greatest impact of the recent decades of capital financing may be a narrowing of the fundamental differences between for-profit and not-for-profit institutions.

THE DISCIPLINE OF THE CAPITAL MARKETS

The capital market is dominated by an economic perspective, which leaves little room for broader measures of welfare. Those who lend money want it paid back. The fact that they are just intermediaries entrusted with other people's money makes actions to this end a legal imperative. In this role, they must be focused on a health provider's ability to pay interest and principal, and retain earnings as a cushion or as a return on investment. This is the source of market discipline.

Both the excess cash flow under improved payment and this market discipline are the engines of industry restructuring, first, in straightforward ways, by funding expansion, and, later, in ways often both unexpected and unintended by those who originally responded to the siren song of marginal investment and easy financing. The fact is that when profits falter and investments fail, the investors who provided funds can force management changes, mergers, or even liquidation as they attempt to meet their fiduciary duty. This discipline can be harsh indeed and certainly can restructure the landscape.

In contrast to this, Arrow's "value judgments," which dominated decision making in his world, were made in a sociopolitical marketplace, not one dominated by purely mercantile exchange (Arrow 1963). The desire is that government action would make the market reflect the appropriate values of society. However, in his extensive discussions of social welfare Arrow clearly recognized that perfection was impossible (Arrow 1970).

Government subsidies have an impact on capital by providing either (1) increased assurance of stable revenue or (2) direct loan guarantees or grants. If such interventions had been applied perfectly, then we would have the exact amount of technology, bricks and mortar, and working capital needed to provide the proper amount of care to all who need it. Instead, we have maldistribution of resources, unequal access, and excess capital investment. Social welfare tools are hard pressed to achieve broad equilibrium when the dominant sources of capital only care about getting an economic return, the government is not all-wise in administering subsidies, and the voters are not in agreement over who deserves them. In other words, health care is a perfect example of the Arrow Impossibility Theorem posited seven years after the base article for this series (ibid.).

In spite of imperfections in design, it is clear that health care providers do respond to incentives and subsidies although the consequences of their actions may differ from the original policy intent. The problem is often exhibited as a boom-bust-boom cycle found in many areas of health care. Skilled nursing facilities are a good example. Medicare originally included a fairly generous payment for nursing home care on the grounds that it is a substitute for low-level hospital care. Furthermore, there were few such facilities in existence at the time of this landmark legislation. However, in the two years following the start of Medicare in 1965, entrepreneurs built thousands of new beds. The new for-profit nursing home chains, such as Humana and Four Seasons, became the darlings of Wall Street with unlimited horizons for making money. Of course, when Congress tightened the rules to pay for only a limited time after discharge from an acute care hospital, the bubble burst. Bankruptcy followed for some (e.g., Four Seasons) while others exited the sector (e.g., Humana). Growth resumed only when state Medicaid programs were convinced to be more generous in their payment levels for the medically indigent. The same payment-induced capital capacity cycles have happened in hospitals, dialysis centers, mental health facilities, rehabilitation, and other service providers.

Capacity clearly follows payment. Often the cycle overshoots prudent bounds of rationality as profit-seeking entrepreneurs interact with myopic subsidizers. Government subsidies clearly have not resulted in market clearing prices that balance supply and demand consistent with social objectives.

MARKET IMPERFECTIONS

Arrow did suggest market imperfections based on information asymmetry and uncertainty regarding the incidence of disease and the efficacy of treatment. These provided the conceptual basis for the existence of insurance (Arrow 1963).

In addition to these two, further imperfections not recognized in the Arrow article may exist if the capital market does not respond properly. Entry barriers that make it difficult for competitors to enter a market and exit barriers that limit the liquidation of unneeded investments may lead to suboptimal levels of investment as investors see either more or less risk respectively in the two cases than in a fully competitive market. Entry barriers are well-discussed phenomena coming from technology, experience, or other competitive advantages (Thompson and Formby 1993).

Exit barriers, on the other hand, can be created by the presence of ongoing debt obligations coupled with the fact that specialized investments in health facilities often have limited alternative use and relatively low liquidation value, most often ending up as inefficient nursing homes. In the presence of debt and specialized assets, ending a marginal activity may not release enough funds to make it a rational short-term decision even though the long-term need is past.

On the other hand, when ending an activity would release net funds after debt repayment that are not needed in the enterprise, the not-for-profit form of organization typical among delivery institutions truncates their ability to return excess equity capital and retained earnings to those who invested it or to the capital markets to be recycled to a better use. Only debt repayment, not share repurchase or cash dividends, is an allowable means of distributing excess cash. This immobility of capital may also be a serious barrier to exit, as institutions tend to take on a life of their own independent of how much value they create for the community. Thus hospitals tend to close only when no patients show up rather than when their prospective return on investment is too low to justify continuation. It is not surprising that the exit rate of hospitals is still relatively low given the number of unoccupied beds (Bellandi 2000).

Also, under pressure for profitability, there clearly exists a potential for suboptimal decision making arising from a primary focus by providers on the paying segment rather than the whole population. Competition for insured business, although very spirited, will lead away from a global optimum unless subsidies are very precise. In effect, rather than the single market implicit in Arrow, we have multiple segments with greatly varying levels of imperfection.

THE MARKET FOR CORPORATE CONTROL

The large role of capital also has encouraged the growth of a new "market for corporate control" of health care enterprises (Jensen and Ruback 1983). It is not surprising that creditors and large stockholders of publicly held firms would force mergers and acquisitions, bankruptcies[5] and reorganizations, and changes in management. However, the very idea that not-for-profit organizations as well would experience similar fates was hard to imagine in 1963. Most of this restructuring activity was instigated and fueled by access to new sources of capital that did not exist when local fund drives and government grants were the financing of choice for most new health ventures. With the use of other people's money came the responsibility to meet more stringent financial requirements. The loss of managerial control was the consequence of not doing so.

In any event, every not-for-profit that accepted financing from outside investors put itself "in play" in the market for corporate control whether it understood it or not. Of course, those who voluntarily converted from not-for-profit corporations to investor-owned entities clearly were put at risk of radical change at the hands of unhappy or insurgent stockholders. Yet the threat of bankruptcy is the ultimate lever of control and may be even stronger than the votes of share-

holders. In 1963 such challenges to control simply were not possible in the conge-
nial club that constituted most nonprofit health care boards. However, in recent
years, competitive or financial threats have compelled a very large portion of all
providers to merge with larger entities with resulting loss of local managerial
control.

Merger and acquisition activity also is a barometer of the optimism of the
capital market for health ventures. In most areas of health care, these have followed a long-term growth pattern until 1997 when the BBA turned down the cash
spigot. This dampened the belief that the next management group could do a
better job than the last. However, the ride has been wild.

The finance literature posits the existence of market efficiency where all available information is instantly incorporated in prices and no excess profit is available beyond a market-based, risk-adjusted return on investment (Ross, Westerfield, and Jaffe 1999: 319). However, *in retrospect*, the information incorporated
in valuation decisions may be incomplete or just plain wrong. Perfect markets
do not eliminate uncertainty; they only value it as well as is possible. The price
of beds, patients, enrollees, residents, or other units of worth reflects speculation and uncertainty about the future. For instance, acquisition prices of HMOs
peaked at about $1,000 per enrollee in 1997 but dropped by 25 percent in the next
two years as profits stalled. Hospital acquisition values fell from a median price
of about $250,000 per bed in 1997 to about $170,000 by 1999. Not coincidentally,
in 1997 the BBA reduced payment for Medicare. On the other hand, the price per
assisted and independent senior living unit continues to rise from about $55,000
in 1995 to $75,000 in 1999 due to the fact that they depend on a growing cash
stream from more affluent individuals (Monroe 2000).

While valuation of health care assets is an imprecise art at best, it clearly is
driven by expectations of what others will pay and what can be done to improve
the cash flow to enhance this valuation. Furthermore, if there are enough assets
of a similar nature trading hands, one can report a meaningful market price for
the asset stated in terms of a standard unit of capacity or volume. In some situations, it may be possible to "securitize" that unit (i.e., bed, patient, enrollee) and
view it as an undifferentiated commodity. Uwe Reinhardt has provided a good
example of this process for physician practices (Reinhardt 1997). The resulting
market allows those with less knowledge of specific situations to invest in the
underlying asset (hospitals, nursing homes, etc.) more freely. But it also permits
them to speculate and chase opportunities to an extreme. The defensive actions
of nonprofits intent on independence and survival may further feed the merger
frenzy as they try to block encroachment of outsiders by their own acquisitions.
The end is predictable. When disappointing results are first reported, a pall is
cast over all similar assets, and the merger game stops.

The resulting boom-and-bust pattern has happened twice in the last thirty years in hospitals. After a speculative run-up in stock prices and a chase of acquisitions to maintain accounting growth (and thus justify high price-earnings ratios), the inevitable crash resulted in massive sell-off of hospitals and repurchase of stock by virtually every for-profit chain in the 1980s and again in the 1990s. After going private and paring down operations, a new initial public offering in a few years sets off a new speculative round. The latest cycle is just ending with the spectacular failure of Columbia HCA and its subsequent sale of assets. Investor speculation has resulted in the building, expansion, and renovation of many redundant facilities and organizations. It also has driven "roll ups" of existing providers into physician practice management firms, dialysis centers, laboratory corporations, and the like (Robinson 1999).

The fact now is that changes in Medicare payment under the BBA have radically cut merger and acquisition activity because the excess cash that made these attractive is less available. Thus, nursing homes, home health agencies, HMOs, and almost every other health care organization are at the bottom of the speculative trough that drove their growth in assets in prior years (Monroe 2001).

CONCLUSIONS

By any measure the capital market has had a major role in restructuring the health care sector in the four ways listed at the outset of this essay:

The capital market provides the funds it does to the health sector and expects a return just the same as in any other area of enterprise. Reliance on private investment sources in the United States has fundamentally shaped the focus of the industry in a manner dramatically different from the systems found in other countries where governments supply capital. For all of the disclaimers about the importance of patients, service, and community, the fact is that all institutions with outstanding debt must meet their financial obligations first if they are to continue. As the level of outside financing has grown, other differences blur, and traditional concern for the public or even attending physicians may come second after profitability.

The resulting market discipline extends to both for-profit firms and nonprofit organizations in several ways. Both are competing for the same population pool, lenders expect debt service from both, and payment systems do not discriminate on ownership. Medicare does subsidize teaching and care to the poor in its formula, perhaps giving large medical centers an advantage. However, with most forces in their environment indifferent to ownership and significant economic challenges to each, the impact of market discipline is large for all.

As a result, *the structure of ownership and control of the industry in future years probably is not of as great concern as it was in the great debates of the 1980s* (Gray 1986). This is not to minimize disruptions in care and loss of wealth and jobs in the boom-and-bust cycles of investor-owned providers. The more important question will be whether the requirements of private capital can be made compatible with larger needs of society to provide service to marginal populations. Stated in another way, the concern is the ability of government to set payment levels and subsidies so as to allow privately financed providers to meet these needs while staying solvent and avoiding suboptimal decisions in the pursuit of paying customers. At the same time, society must be prepared for occasional windfall profits when one private entity gains at the expense of less agile or poorly positioned competitors who suffer losses or close.

However, given the inability of government to broker reductions in excess capacity, allowing private failure may be the most efficient or perhaps the only way to reconfigure our capacity to fit our need without years of pain and loss. Interestingly, the last acquisition cycle in hospitals had the effect of preserving massive amounts of community capital that otherwise might have disappeared through the losses of the marginal not-for-profit facilities acquired by for-profits. In fact, many were ultimately closed as their underlying weakness became apparent to the new owners. Fortunately, the cash paid was safe in the conversion foundations formed to accept the payment from for-profit chains that acquired them in their drive for growth in earnings. This culling of poor performers and the preservation of invested capital for other social uses are somewhat surprising benefits from the speculative role of private equity capital in this sector. Whether this will happen again and whether it is an appropriate way to reconfigure such an important sector is a fruitful area for policy discussion.

The implications for access, quality, and cost coming from the role of private capital in the health sector are very uneven depending on location, health status, and insurance coverage. The mere fact that the implications are mixed probably is enough to raise concern over this manner of financing our investment in health providers. Few would argue that a social good like health care should be so tied to market forces that many are denied access. Furthermore, the variation in outcomes shown in many studies (Wennberg and Gittlesohn 1982) demonstrates that even for those who have access, the private capital markets have not assured high quality. Finally, the impact of private capital on cost is debatable. Some would argue that the flexibility and responsiveness provided by this form of financing have forced competitors to innovate to provide value (Robinson 1999). However, international comparisons of outcomes and costs suggest our privately financed system is lacking on both dimensions (Millenson 1998).

On the other hand, it is not clear that a governmentally financed system would be superior. The performance of government-financed schools, transit, and communications has not been noticeably better than either private or public organizations who receive capital from the market as in health care. The advantage of having an external financial monitor is not to be taken lightly.

The fact is that the United States cannot change the role of the capital markets at this point in time due to the massive existing investment. The issue before us is how to make it work better.

NOTES

This essay was supported by Grant No. 28665 from the Robert Wood Johnson Foundation's Investigator Awards in Health Policy Research Program. The opinions and conclusions expressed in this article are solely those of the author and do not necessarily reflect those of the foundation.

1 The Bureau of Economic Analysis, U.S. Department of Commerce (www.bea.doc.gov), reports that net fixed assets have grown to a level five times higher proportionally than the parallel quantity index for all health services over the 1960–1999 period.

2 Note that *capital* can mean both *capital investment* in plant and equipment and other long-lived assets as well as *capital financing*, meaning the sources of funding for assets. This essay distinguishes between the two in this way but generally uses the term *capital markets* to describe the institutions and investors who provide capital financing.

3 Perhaps the most outstanding recent example of poor investment of corporate assets in health care is the case of the AHERF (holding company for a Pennsylvania hospital and medical school complex built with endowment and borrowed funds), which was forced into bankruptcy in 1998 (Burns et al. 2000).

4 The Balanced Budget Refinement Act (BBRA) of 1999 and the Medicare, Medicaid Benefits Improvement and Protection Act (BIPA) of 2000 have restored a significant fraction of the amount lost under the BBA.

5 Although corporate law precludes a creditor forcing a not-for-profit into involuntary bankruptcy, the ability to withhold further funds to maintain operations generally would be sufficient leverage to allow them to exert control or induce voluntary bankruptcy.

REFERENCES

Arrow, K. J. 1963. Uncertainty and the Welfare Economics of Medical Care. *American Economic Review* 53(5): 941–973.

———. 1970. *Social Choice and Individual Values*. New Haven, CT: Yale University Press.

Bellandi, D. 2000. More Hospitals Close. *Modern Healthcare*, 7 August, 22.

Burns, L., J. Cacciamani, J. Clement, and W. Aquino. 2000. The Fall of the House of AHERF: The Allegheny Bankruptcy. *Health Affairs* 19(1): 6–40.

Gershberg, A. I., M. Grossman, and F. Goldman. 1999. *Health Care Capital Financing Agencies: The Intergovernmental Roles of Quasi-Government Authorities and the Impact on the Cost of Capital*. National Bureau of Economic Research Working Paper no. W7221 (July). Cambridge, MA: National Bureau of Economic Research.

Gray, B. 1986. *For-Profit Enterprise in Health Care*. Washington, DC: National Academy Press.

Gutterman, S. 2000. *Putting Medicare in Context: How Does the Balanced Budget Act Affect Hospitals?* Urban Institute Working Paper (July). Washington, DC: Urban Institute.

Jensen, M. 1986. Agency Costs of Free Cash Flow, Corporate Finance Takeovers. *American Economic Review* 76: 323–339.

Jensen, M., and R. Ruback. 1983. The Market for Corporate Control: The Scientific Evidence. *Journal of Financial Economics* 11(1): 5–50.

Medicare Payment Advisory Commission (medpac). 2000. Report to the Congress: Selected Medicare Issues. Washington, DC: Medicare Payment Advisory Commission.

Millenson, M. L. 1998. *Demanding Medical Excellence: Doctors and Accountability in the Information Age.* Chicago: University of Chicago Press.

Monroe, S. 2000. Down, Not Out: Mergers & Acquisitions. *Modern Healthcare*, 30 May, 20.

———. 2001. *The Health Care M & A Report, Fourth Quarter, 2000.* New Canaan, CT: Irving Levin Associates.

Pauly, M. V., and M. Redisch. 1973. The Not-for-Profit Hospital as a Physicians' Cooperative. *American Economic Review* 63(1): 87–99.

Reinhardt, U. E. 1997. Hippocrates and the "Securitization" of Patients. *Journal of the American Medical Association* 277(23): 1850–1851.

Robinson, J. C. 1999. *The Corporate Practice of Medicine.* Berkeley: University of California Press.

Ross, S. A., S. Westerfield, and J. Jaffe. 1999. *Corporate Finance.* Boston: Irwin/McGraw-Hill.

Thompson, A., and J. Formby. 1993. *Economics of the Firm: Theory and Practice.* Englewood Cliffs, NJ: Prentice Hall.

Wennberg, J. E., and A. Gittlesohn. 1982. Variations in Medical Care among Small Areas. *Scientific American* 246(4): 120–134.

PART III

Information, Knowledge,

and Medical Markets

DEBORAH HAAS-WILSON

■ *Arrow and the Information Market Failure in Health Care: The Changing Content and Sources of Health Care Information*

Kenneth Arrow's "Uncertainty and the Welfare Economics of Medical Care," published in the *American Economic Review* in 1963, makes profound contributions in the areas of health economics and, more generally, in the economics of information.

At the time Arrow was writing this article, unlike today, there was almost no scholarship on the economics of information. The only article on this topic published at that time in the economics literature was "The Economics of Information" by George Stigler (1961), and its focus was on consumers' information about price rather than quality. In *Public Health Reports*, however, Selma Mushkin had published "Toward a Definition of Health Economics" in which she discussed how consumers' lack of information about quality could result in market failure in medical markets. She wrote, ". . . they [consumers] reveal considerable absence of accurate knowledge about the quantity and quality of health services required. The nature of the medical service itself and its intangible character reinforce the consumer's lack of knowledge about his purchases, and impede a rational choice that could guide the allocation of resources" (Mushkin 1958: 787).

This essay is organized into three parts. First is a description of Arrow's contributions with respect to information problems leading to market failures in medical care markets. Second, it is shown that theoretical work by economists since 1963 is consistent with Mushkin's and Arrow's thinking—specifically, information imperfections result in market failure. Third, it includes a discussion of the changing nature of the informational asymmetry between physicians and patients since 1963.

ARROW'S UNDERSTANDING OF THE NATURE
OF INFORMATION IN MEDICAL MARKETS

Arrow recognized that medical care markets are characterized by extremely high levels of uncertainty and, in particular, patients' uncertainty about the consequences of purchasing medical treatments. Patients' inherent uncertainty about the effectiveness of medical treatments — uncertainty about which treatments can best cure their illnesses or relieve their pain — makes it extremely difficult for patients to learn about and evaluate the quality of medical care services. *"Uncertainty as to the quality of the product is perhaps more intense here than in any other important commodity. Recovery from disease is as unpredictable as is its incidence. . . . Further, the amount of uncertainty, measured in terms of utility variability, is certainly much greater for medical care in severe cases than for, say, houses or automobiles, even though these are also expenditures sufficiently infrequent so that there may be considerable residual uncertainty"* (951).

Second, Arrow recognized that under conditions of uncertainty, accurate information becomes a very valuable commodity and that, in many ways, medical markets are really markets for information. *"When there is uncertainty, information or knowledge becomes a commodity. . . . but, information, in the form of skilled care, is precisely what is being bought from most physicians"* (946).

Third, Arrow recognized that information's "elusive character" limits its marketability on both the demand and supply sides of the market. In his analysis there are limits on consumers' abilities to acquire information and limits on consumers' abilities to process information. Specifically, for cases of severe illness the limits on acquiring information are *"the uncertainty due to inexperience"* (inadequate number of trials to learn from) and *"the intrinsic difficulty of prediction"* (951).

With respect to limits on consumers' abilities to process information, he described consumers as not knowing the value of the information being bought from physicians. *". . . if, indeed,* [the consumer] *knew enough to measure the value of the information, he would know the information itself"* (946). Further, Arrow understood illness and *". . . demand for medical services is associated, with a considerable probability, with an assault on personal integrity. There is some risk of death and a more considerable risk of impairment of full functioning"* (949). Compared to periods of good health, in periods of poor health (especially those associated with an impairment of cognitive functioning, pain, and anxiety about death), consumers may not be able to fully process information. Further, individuals confronted with new illnesses often have limited time to collect information since the effectiveness of many medical treatments depends on minimizing the time between the onset of the illness and the start of the treatment.

Fourth, Arrow recognized that some market participants will be better informed than others. *"Like other commodities, it* [information] *has a cost of production and a cost of transmission, and so it is naturally not spread out over the entire population but concentrated among those who can profit most from it"* (946). The quantity of information acquired by each consumer depends on that individual's expected costs and benefits of acquiring information. Consumers will vary in these costs and benefits due to differences in income (or opportunity costs of time), analytical abilities, and other factors.

Fifth, Arrow recognized the special asymmetric nature of the information in medical markets. Arrow focused his attention on informational asymmetries between physicians and their patients (rather than informational asymmetries between insurers and their enrollees). *"Because medical knowledge is so complicated, the information possessed by the physician as to the consequences and possibilities of treatment is necessarily very much greater than that of the patient, or at least so it is believed by both parties. Further, both parties are aware of this informational inequality, and their relation is colored by this knowledge"* (951).

Sixth, despite the lack of economic scholarship on information about quality, Arrow understood that the nature of information in medical markets — patients' uncertainty about the effectiveness of medical treatments, the *"informational inequality"* between patients and physicians, and the imperfect marketability of information provided by physicians — would result in market failure, specifically *"a failure to reach an optimal state in the sense of Pareto"* (947).

ECONOMIC THEORY ON INFORMATION MARKET
FAILURE SINCE ARROW

Economists have spent a great deal of time and energy in pursuit of a better understanding of the efficiency properties of markets for information and markets characterized by imperfectly informed consumers.[1] It is now recognized that markets for information are characterized by peculiarities that frequently lead to market failure and inefficiencies. One peculiarity is that sellers of information often have difficulty capturing the returns on the information they provide. This will be the case when sellers of information are unable to prevent buyers from reselling the information to others. The inability of information sellers to prevent resale of their information potentially leads to the market failure of too little information being traded. In markets for physician services, however, this market failure is averted through the tie-in between information and physician services and the patient-specific nature of the information traded. A second peculiarity (and one discussed by Arrow) is that buyers of information rarely know the value of the information until after it is purchased and sometimes never at all.

Another widely recognized market peculiarity is that buyers of a product often have less information about the product's value (price and/or quality) than do its sellers.[2] That the quality of the product is not apparent on inspection by prospective buyers is especially true in the market for physician services and was recognized by Arrow: *"the social obligation for best practice is part of the commodity the physician sells, even though it is a part that is not subject to thorough inspection by the buyer"* (965).

When no information on quality is available prior to purchase, quality deteriorates to the lowest level in the market — a serious market failure since mutually advantageous trades involving higher quality products do not take place. George Akerlof (1970), in his classic article on lemons in the market for used cars, showed that when sellers of used cars know their quality, but potential buyers do not, only lemons will be traded. Since buyers cannot tell the difference between good used cars and lemons, all used cars sell for the same price. In this situation owners of good used cars have no financial incentive to sell their cars, and thus only lemons will be traded. Similarly, Hayne E. Leland (1979) showed that quality deteriorates to the lowest level in markets where price can be observed costlessly, quality cannot be observed at all, and price is not a signal of quality. Richard Schmalensee (1978) and Dennis Smallwood and John Conlisk (1979) also showed equilibria exist in which the lowest quality brands have the largest shares in markets where consumers follow an adoptive strategy while searching among sellers and that buyers can learn price but not quality before purchase.

Clearly there is an asymmetry in information about quality in markets for physician services, yet this sort of lemons' equilibrium, with only low-quality physicians selling their services, does not occur. The difference can be explained by two assumptions of the Akerlof model. First, in the Akerlof model, quality is determined exogenously, and in the market for physician services, quality is at least partially determined by the physician. Unlike the sellers of used cars in the Akerlof model, physicians have some control over the quality of care they sell. Second, in the Akerlof model, buyers of used cars are totally ignorant about quality prior to purchase, while in markets for physician services, patients can obtain at least partial information on physician quality prior to purchase. Medical care consumers almost always have some indication of physician quality, either from past experience, discussions with friends, relatives, or co-workers about their past experiences, physician signaling, or other sources.

Arrow recognized that while a medical care consumer cannot directly observe whether *"the physician is using his knowledge to the best advantage,"* the medical care consumer can obtain partial information about physician quality prior to purchase. Arrow recognized that consumers may use a physician's avoidance of *"the obvious stigmata of profit-maximizing"* as *"a signal to the buyer of his intentions to act as thoroughly in the buyer's behalf as possible"* (965).

Since Arrow, economists have studied markets characterized by signaling: when consumers use seller-specific attributes, screening devices, or signals (other than avoidance of profit-maximizing behavior) as substitutes for direct information about quality (see Akerlof 1976 and Spence 1973). For example, if consumers infer that physicians who work the longest hours provide the highest quality care (possibly because those physicians are the most competent and thus have the most patients), consumers may use hours of work as a signal of quality and select their physicians accordingly.

Unfortunately, over time both competent and less competent physicians will start to work longer hours to exploit consumers' screening device—a dynamic called the *rat race*. It is unclear whether hours worked will continue to convey information about quality. If all physicians increase their hours proportionally, then there will be no change in relative hours, and the signal continues to convey information about quality. If, on the other hand, the less competent physicians increase their hours, then the positive correlation between quality and hours disappears and the signal conveys no information about quality.

Economists have shown that even when consumers obtain partial information on quality, quality deterioration is still a possible market outcome. When uninformed consumers use high price as a signal of high quality, as shown by Russell Cooper and Thomas W. Ross (1984), "dishonest firms" may sell low-quality goods at high-quality prices. Charles Stuart (1981) showed that equilibria exist with only low-quality goods in markets where consumers maximize expected utility and can purchase partial information on product quality. Likewise, Yuk-Shee Chen and Hayne Leland (1982) showed that in the presence of asymmetric information, even when consumers can obtain price and quality information about individual sellers, consumers may still pay high-quality prices for low-quality products.

Thankfully for individuals in need of health care services, when consumers can obtain information on physicians' reputations for high- or low-quality care, the problem of quality deterioration may be ameliorated. When firms' reputations become public information, Benjamin Klein and Keith B. Leffler 1981 showed wealth-maximizing firms would not cheat on promises to sell high-quality products, if prices are sufficiently above costs. In other words, firms will sell high-quality products at high prices rather than try to sell low-quality products at high prices. Likewise, assuming all consumers prefer higher to lower quality, but differ in their willingness to pay for quality, and some provider-specific information about quality reaches potential consumers, Asher Wolinsky (1983) showed that higher quality products will sell at higher prices and lower quality products will sell at lower prices.

The hope is that more informed health care consumers will be able to select the physicians (or health plans) offering the lowest quality-adjusted prices. In turn, more informed health care consumers may result in physicians (or health plans) decreasing their quality-adjusted prices by decreasing price and or increasing quality.

This is easier said than done in health care markets because consumers may be better able to learn about some aspects of quality than others. Health care quality is a multidimensional construct with at least two components: technical quality (including how well medical knowledge is applied to the diagnosis and treatment of the medical problem) and interpersonal quality (including the responsiveness, friendliness, and attentiveness of the physician or health plan).[3]

Consistent with this, empirical evidence suggests that patient satisfaction is positively related to interpersonal quality but independent of technical quality (Haas-Wilson 1994; Chernew and Scanlon 1998). Further, consistent with economic theory, empirical evidence suggests that market-determined prices are positively correlated with the easier to learn aspects of quality, such as interpersonal quality, but not related to the more difficult to learn aspects of quality, such as technical quality (Haas-Wilson 1994).

OUR UNDERSTANDING ABOUT INFORMATION IN MEDICAL MARKETS SINCE ARROW

To address the nature of informational asymmetries between physicians and patients now, relative to 1963, one must examine at least two related questions.

First, has there been a change in physicians' abilities to learn about the relative effectiveness of alternative treatments, and thus their abilities, to recommend the most effective treatments for their patients? Second, has there been a change in medical care consumers' abilities to learn about and evaluate, independent from the physician, the quality of the diagnostic and treatment information and medical treatments provided by their physicians?

To really answer these questions one needs to be able to measure information in the hands of both medical care consumers and physicians. Unfortunately, we cannot because information is an extremely difficult concept to quantify. However, there have been attempts to develop "proxies" that are at least correlated with the extent of health care information.

Economists have used at least two proxies to show the extent of information on physician-specific quality—one, a marketwide measure, is the number of physicians in an area (Satterthwaite 1979; Pauly and Satterthwaite 1981); and the other, a physician-specific measure, is the prevalence of a physician's referrals from informed sources (such as other physicians) rather than less-informed sources (such as self-referrals) (Haas-Wilson 1990). The argument behind the first proxy is that since physician services are a reputation plus, and since individuals learn about physician-specific quality by talking to their friends, relatives, and co-workers about their experiences with their physicians, as the number of physicians in an area increases, the probability that one's friends, relatives, and co-workers will have experience with any particular physician decreases. Thus, as the number of physicians increases, the availability of information about any individual physician deceases. The argument behind the second proxy is that physicians make referral recommendations based on their perceptions of other physicians' expertise and professional competence. Accordingly, referral patterns among physicians may reflect perceptions (information) of physician-specific quality of care.

Both of these information proxies are of limited value for measuring the availability of information in markets today because both were developed prior to the growth of managed care. Under managed care the total number of physicians is less relevant because individuals in managed care plans have insured access to only those physicians included in their plan's provider network. Likewise under managed care, referral patterns are increasingly influenced by financial considerations and network membership.

Accordingly, there are no particularly good measures of the availability of information about quality, and quantitative answers to the two questions just mentioned are not possible. Rather, what follows are broad-brush observations.

At least three types of information are of value to patients — information about what is causing patients' illnesses and symptoms (diagnostic information), and, given their diagnoses, information about the effectiveness of alternative treatments to restore their health (treatment information), and information about which physicians provide the most accurate, useful information or the highest quality care (physician-specific quality) — were the focus of Arrow's analysis. Diagnostic and treatment information are extremely valuable to patients faced with decisions about what health care services to consume. Patients experiencing chest pains first need to know whether they are suffering from a heart attack or indigestion, and second, if it is a heart attack, what is the best (most effective) treatment option — cardiac catheterization followed by an angioplasty (a procedure that involves a balloon at the end of a catheter to eliminate blockages), cardiac catheterization followed by bypass surgery (an open-heart surgical procedure to bypass the blockages), drug treatments using aspirin, thrombolytics (which inhibit clotting), beta-blockers, or ACE inhibitors, or some combination of these treatments.

Diagnostic and treatment information are at least as relevant to health care consumers today. In fact, the number of available treatments has expanded greatly, making this sort of information even more valuable. Further, there is little reason to argue that today's patients are better able to diagnose their own health problems.

What has changed since 1963 is patients' abilities to identify possible treatments, given their diagnoses, and patients' abilities to learn about the likely consequences of those treatments. Patients have access to new sources of information on alternative treatments and their consequences, independent from their physicians.

In 1989 the federal government, through its Agency for Healthcare Research and Quality,[4] started to fund research on the effectiveness of alternative clinical interventions — the linkages between clinical practices and clinical outcomes. The goal of this research is to provide evidence for or against the effectiveness of alternative clinical interventions. Research of this sort can demonstrate whether, on average, a treatment is effective for a given illness.[5] Funded projects have included treatment effectiveness for acute myocardial infarction (heart attack), prostate disease, cataracts, arthritis of the knee, coronary artery disease, diabetes, gallbladder disease, pneumonia, hip fracture and osteoarthritis of the hip, and other clinical conditions.

Simultaneously, there has been explosive growth in the amount of health care information available online. As of March 2001 there were approximately 26,000 health-related Web sites (Firstman 2001). The National Guideline Clearinghouse (www.guideline.gov) publishes evidence-based clinical practice guidelines on multiple topics, including acute pain management, urinary incontinence, cataracts, sickle cell disease, unstable angina, heart failure, and smoking cessation. Similarly, CBS Health Watch, WEBMD (www.webmd.com), and the National Library of Medicine (www.nlm.nih.gov) have become popular sources of information on treatment effectiveness, on-going clinical trials, and new drugs. Patients can also use the Internet to communicate with and learn from others with similar diagnoses. Jeff Goldsmith (2000: 152), a health care forecaster, wrote, "The patient who types 'lupus' into the search box of an Internet portal is within minutes of discovering an online community of fellow lupus sufferers, which brings a framework for collective learning about how to cope with the disease independent of one's physician."

Another change since 1963 is that we now have a better understanding of the importance of information about *where* to obtain health care services (as opposed to information about *what* health care services to buy, such as diagnostic and treatment information). We now have a better understanding of the importance of patients' uncertainty about which physicians (or hospitals) provide the highest quality care. Patients' uncertainty concerning where to buy is at least as important as patients' uncertainty about what to buy. For example, since 1991 the New York State Department of Health has published a report[6] showing significant variation in surgeon-specific coronary artery bypass graft surgery outcomes (Hannan et al. 1997).

In general, there is tremendous variation across physicians in terms of the quality of care (the treatments recommended and the health outcomes realized). Physicians' styles of practice or their propensity to use medical resources vary greatly even within a geographic region. This implies that some patients are getting too much treatment and some too little treatment — a situation that can only exist in markets characterized by imperfect consumer information about physician quality (Phelps 2000). In fact, it is well documented that many Americans do not receive care that is based on the best scientific knowledge (Institute of Medicine 2001).

Accordingly, the most important decision a patient makes is from whom to get treatment recommendations and treatment. Patients would like to select the physicians or hospitals with the best record for improving health outcomes among patients with their particular medical problems. Unfortunately, at this point in time, information technologies provide patients with new, but very limited, opportunities to learn about the health outcomes achieved by particular physicians and hospitals.[7] Currently available measures of physician-specific quality are more apt to measure other dimensions of quality. For example, the Association of State Medical Board Executive Directors publishes information on physicians' education, malpractice judgments, and disciplinary histories.[8] The Pacific Business Group on Health, a group of thirty-three employers, publishes a study of patient satisfaction with medical groups and physician networks in California and the Pacific Northwest.[9] This report ranks groups and networks on patient satisfaction, ease of getting referrals, and their records of keeping blood pressure and cholesterol under control and counseling patients on preventive care.

Another change since 1963 is that it has become increasingly clear that physicians' uncertainty in health care markets is more profound than Arrow's analysis suggested. While Arrow never claimed that physicians are all-knowing, he also did not address the limitations in physicians' abilities to collect, process, and use all relevant information. Since 1963, however, we have gained a better understanding of physicians' incomplete knowledge about treatment effectiveness. Despite many years in medical school and residency training programs, physicians, like their patients, have incomplete information about the relationships between the thousands of possible diseases and the effectiveness of all alternative treatments and are forced to make medical decisions under conditions of uncertainty.[10]

Further, we have a better understanding of the two-sided nature of the asymmetry in medical information. In some aspects the physician knows more, and in other aspects the patient knows more. Patients may know more about their own medical histories (including health care services received in other settings and medications prescribed by other clinicians), their willingness to comply with medical treatments, and their individual preferences between the consequences of their illnesses and the side effects of the treatment than their physicians. Accordingly, physicians (like their patients) are forced to make treatment decisions without the benefit of complete information.

CONCLUDING THOUGHTS

New sources of information provide the potential for a metamorphosis of physician-dependent patients (patients dependent on their physicians for information on treatment effectiveness) into better-informed consumers (patients with multiple sources of information on treatment effectiveness).

This is not to say, however, that the Internet will replace physicians as patients' primary source of information on the effectiveness of various medical treatments. Even if patients have access to all the relevant medical information, there are limits to patients' abilities to process it and to make choices between treatments independently from their physicians. Patients tend to rely on guidance from their physicians to understand medical factors in the context of their particular medical problems and to give these medical factors their proper weight in treatment decisions.

Even well-informed patients will most likely continue to follow their physicians' recommendations concerning choice of treatment. All the technological innovations in the world cannot make the informational asymmetry between physicians and patients go away. "No Internet site will ever replace the intangibles of the doctor-patient relationship. Data crunching will never eliminate the vast gray areas where technology, medical judgment, and patient preference intersect" (Millenson 2000: 273).

Accordingly, for potential patients no choice is more important than their choice of physician. Hopefully, patients in the future will have access to reliable and precise physician-specific information about quality, such as measures of physician-specific health outcomes. There are reasons to be hopeful. Advances in information technology and research methods make this a possibility (McClellan and Staiger 1999).

NOTES

The author would like to thank Barbara Krimgold and Al Tarlov for their support, trust, and vision for this project.

1 Due to space constraints this is a very brief review of the literature. For a more thorough review, see Stiglitz 1989.

2 Many economists, including Stigler (1961), Rothschild (1973), and Salop and Stiglitz (1977), examined the nature of market equilibrium when consumers are uncertain

about sellers' prices. Since the problem of price uncertainty seems less important than the problem of uncertainty about quality in medical care markets, these articles will not be discussed in this brief review.

3 Donabedian 1980. Another aspect of health care quality is the amenities of care (including the appeal and comfort of the health care facilities).

4 Formerly the Agency for Health Care Policy and Research.

5 However, clinical research cannot demonstrate whether a treatment will be effective for a particular patient with that illness.

6 The New York reports contain information on the number of cases, the number of deaths, observed mortality rates, expected mortality rates, and risk-adjusted mortality rates.

7 The development of high-speed computer systems and standardized, computerized medical records has made the collection and analysis of clinical and administrative data feasible. This, in turn, has made measurement and comparison of some aspects of quality within and across physician organizations feasible.

8 Web site visited on 11 December 2000. The on-line address is www.docboard.org.

9 *American Medical News* 1 December 1997, 5; and *Wall Street Journal* 17 September 1997, B6.

10 Physicians' uncertainty is due, at least in part, to the increasing availability of more and increasingly complex treatment options.

REFERENCES

Akerlof, George. 1970. The Market for "Lemons": Quality Uncertainty and the Market Mechanism. *Quarterly Journal of Economics* 84(3): 488–500.

———. 1976. The Economics of Caste and of the Rat Race and Other Woeful Tales. *Quarterly Journal of Economics* 90: 599–617.

Arrow, Kenneth J. 1963. Uncertainty and the Welfare Economics of Medical Care. *American Economic Review* 53(5): 941–973.

Chen, Yuk-Shee, and Hayne Leland. 1982. Prices and Qualities in Markets with Costly Information. *Review of Economic Studies* 49: 499–516.

Chernew, Michael, and Dennis P. Scanlon. 1998. Health Plan Report Cards and Insurance Choice. *Inquiry* 35: 9–22.

Cooper, Russell, and Thomas W. Ross. 1984. Prices, Product Qualities and Asymmetric Information: The Competitive Case. *Review of Economic Studies* 51: 197–207.

Donabedian, A. 1980. *Explorations in Quality Assessment and Monitoring: The Definition of Quality and Approaches to Assessment.* Ann Arbor, MI: Health Administration Press.

Firstman, Richard. 2001. Heal Thyself. *Time.* Special Issue, 5 March.

Goldsmith, Jeff. 2000. How Will the Internet Change Our Health System? *Health Affairs* 19(1): 148–156.

Haas-Wilson, Deborah. 1990. Consumer Information and Providers' Reputations: An Empirical Test in the Market for Psychotherapy. *Journal of Health Economics* 9: 321–333.

———. 1994. The Relationships between the Dimensions of Health Care Quality and Price: The Case of Eye Care. *Medical Care* 32(2): 175–182.

Hannan, Edward L., Cathy C. Stone, Theodore L. Biddle, and Barbara A. DeBuono. 1997. Public Release of Cardiac Surgery Outcomes Data in New York: What Do New York State Cardiologists Think of It? *American Heart Journal* 134(6): 1120–1128.

Institute of Medicine. 2001. *Crossing the Quality Chasm: A New Health System for the 21st Century*. Washington, DC: National Academy Press.

Klein, Benjamin, and Keith B. Leffler. 1981. The Role of Market Forces in Assuring Contractual Performance. *Journal of Political Economy* 89(4): 615–641.

Leland, Hayne E. 1979. Quacks, Lemons, and Licensing: A Theory of Minimum Quality Standards. *Journal of Political Economy* 87(6): 1328–1346.

McClellan, Mark, and Douglas Staiger. 1999. *The Quality of Health Care Providers*. National Bureau of Economic Research Working Paper no. 7327. Cambridge, MA: National Bureau of Economic Research.

Millenson, Michael L. 2000. Opinion: Medicine's Next Big Opportunity. *The Industry Standard*, 10 April.

Mushkin, Selma J. 1958. Toward a Definition of Health Economics. *Public Health Reports* 73(9): 785–793.

Pauly, Mark V., and Mark A. Satterthwaite. 1981. The Pricing of Primary Care Physicians' Services: A Test of the Role of Consumer Information. *Bell Journal of Economics* 12(2): 488–506.

Phelps, Charles E. 2000. Information Diffusion and Best Practice Adoption. In *Handbook of Health Economics*, vol. 1A, ed. Joseph P. Newhouse and Anthony J. Culyer. Amsterdam: Elsevier.

Rothschild, Michael. 1973. Models of Market Organization with Imperfect Information: A Survey. *Journal of Political Economy* 81: 1282–1308.

Salop, Steven C., and Joseph E. Stiglitz. 1977. Bargains and Ripoffs: A Model of Monopolistically Competitive Price Dispersion. *Review of Economic Studies* 44: 493–510.

Satterthwaite, Mark A. 1979. Consumer Information, Equilibrium Industry Price, and the Number of Sellers. *Bell Journal of Economics* 10: 483–502.

Schmalensee, Richard. 1978. A Model of Advertising and Product Quality. *Journal of Political Economy* 86(3): 485–503.

Smallwood, Dennis E., and John Conlisk. 1979. Product Quality in Markets Where Consumers Are Imperfectly Informed. *Quarterly Journal of Economics* 93(1): 1–23.

Spence, A. M. 1973. *Market Signaling*. Cambridge: Harvard University Press.

Stigler, George. 1961. The Economics of Information. *Journal of Political Economy* 69: 213–225.

Stiglitz, Joseph E. 1989. Imperfect Information in the Product Market. In *Handbook of Industrial Organization*, vol. 1, ed. Richard Schmalensee and Robert D. Willig. Amsterdam: North-Holland.

Stuart, Charles. 1981. Consumer Protection in Markets with Informationally Weak Buyers. *Bell Journal of Economics* 12(2): 562–573.

Wolinsky, Asher. 1983. Prices as Signals of Product Quality. *Review of Economic Studies* 50: 647–658.

JAMES C. ROBINSON

■ *The End of Asymmetric Information*

The most pernicious doctrine in health services research, the greatest impediment to clear thought and successful action, is that health care is *different*. Of
course the medical sector has features not found elsewhere in the economy
and polity, but then there is a uniqueness to every other industry. Each of the
salient characteristics of health care, including professionalism, licensure, nonprofit organization, third-party payment, and heavy government regulation, can
be found in other sectors, albeit not bundled in quite the same distinct and dysfunctional manner. The uniqueness doctrine hence proves too much. More importantly, the principle serves as a two-way barrier to entry between the health
and nonhealth sectors. In one direction it discourages mainstream economists
from importing the principles of industrial organization, game theory, and transactions costs to health care issues by raising a wall of acronyms and institutional trivia that impedes dialogue. In the other direction it fosters a compla-
cency among the virtuosi of health policy analysis, allowing us to achieve fame
and fortune in our small pond without fear of competition from denizens of the
scholarly shark tank.

To some within the health care community, the uniqueness doctrine is self-
evident and needs no justification. After all, health care is essential to health.
That food and shelter are even more vital and seem to be produced without professional licensure, nonprofit organization, compulsory insurance, class action
lawsuits, and 133,000 pages of regulatory prescription in the *Federal Register* does
not shake the faith of the orthodox. For the sophisticates, however, the uniqueness doctrine does demand a foundation or least a pedigree. It is here that the
theory of asymmetric information enters, gets comfortable, and decides to reside
permanently in the intellectual edifice of health economics, medical sociology,

health politics, and the other subspecialties of this faction-ridden but homologous research community. Which brings me to "Uncertainty and the Welfare Economics of Medical Care" (Arrow 1963).

This is a good article by a great economist, a creative application of the theory of risk and uncertainty to the thorny problems of the health sector, exactly the sort of boundary-crossing, barrier-penetrating work that opens the possibility of progress in thought and action. Would we have more of the same. But its effects on the field of health services research, for which the author cannot be held responsible, must be judged more ambivalently. The central proposition of his article, that health care information is imperfect and asymmetrically distributed, has been seized upon to justify every inefficiency, idiosyncrasy, and interest-serving institution in the health care industry. The article makes the protean claim that unusual contractual, organizational, and normative features of the health care sector derive from efficiency-enhancing responses to underlying informational limitations. This is a fecund alternative to the intellectual status quo of the time, which interpreted unusual institutional features largely as efforts at monopoly power. Yet it has served to lend the author's unparalleled reputation to subsequent claims that advertising, optometry, and midwifery are threats to consumer well-being, that nonprofit ownership is natural for hospitals though not for physician practices, that price competition undermines product quality, that antitrust exemptions reduce costs, that consumers cannot compare insurance plans and must yield this function to politicians, that price regulation is effective for pharmaceutical products despite having failed in other applications, that cost-conscious choice is unethical while cost-unconscious choice is a basic human right, that what consumers want is not what they need, and, more generally, that the real is reasonable, the facts are functional, and the health care sector is constrained Pareto-efficient.

METHODOLOGY

The heart of Arrow's analysis, the methodological prolegomenon from which all substantive claims derive, is the juxtaposition of the conceptual model of general competitive equilibrium with the organizational, legal, and normative characteristics of medical care. It is noted that a social system conforming to the competitive model would exhibit no waste (Pareto optimality) and could be made to produce any technologically feasible allocation of services by pure income redistribution (e.g., tax policy) without the need for ethical norms, professional licensure, nonprofit organization, and other features so salient to the health sector. It is clear that the real world, and in particular the health sector, do not conform to the postulates of the model, especially in terms of the lack of information. A causal relationship is then postulated linking the two sets of gaps:

the gap between the real world and the competitive model in terms of information asymmetry and the gap between health care and other economic sectors in terms of organizations, laws, and norms. In short, it is argued that the unusual features of health care are due to unusual (or unusually virulent) information imperfections.

The methodological approach used by Arrow has much to commend it, including most obviously its commingling of theoretical and empirical bodies of work that often remain in blissful ignorance of each other. Yet the dangers of this approach, once in the hands of less-able and more-interested partisans and pleaders, are evident. Imperfect and asymmetric information is at most a necessary, not a sufficient, condition for the observed facts about health care (Arrow never claims otherwise). Informational deficiencies could produce organizational and normative features quite different from those actually observed in the United States of 1963, and in fact they did. The health care systems of Great Britain, the Soviet Union, and the Republic of South Africa in 1963 each lay atop missing markets for information and risk bearing, but nevertheless differed markedly among themselves. It strains the imagination to attribute cross-sectional variation in health system characteristics to cross-sectional variation in information asymmetries. Longitudinal variations are no more easily interpretable in this context. The evolution of the medical profession, the hospital industry, the insurance and managed care sector, and the other components of the system are not immediately and obviously due to contemporaneous changes in the underlying information structure (though more on this below). Arrow's article thus tends to receive less acclaim among historians than among those for whom history is bunk (Starr 1982).

If imperfect information is not sufficient for explaining the organizational and normative features of health care, neither is it necessary. While a world of perfect information undoubtedly would look quite different from the status quo, it is easy to find explanations for the special features of health care without primary appeal to information asymmetry. The most obvious alternative category of explanations, of course, derives from the vast literature on bureaucratic and legislative capture, contrived monopoly and barriers to entry, mythology and mystification, fraud and abuse, and sleaze in all its manifestations. Arrow does a great service, in my opinion, in promoting an alternative to this class of explanations, which was (and remains) a major explicative contender in some quarters. Arrow cites, and we read updates of, arguments that licensure is a limit on physician supply, sliding-fee scales are evidence of discriminating monopoly, nonprofit hospitals are shells for physician revenue maximization, and so on. But the unfortunate fact that the inhospitality tradition in law and economics (which ascribes every unusual organizational arrangement to monopolization) often spreads beyond its legitimate bounds does not justify an equally unfortunate ascription of efficiency-enhancing attributes to every unusual arrangement. Capture is real. Agency failure is real. People of the same trade seldom meet together, even for merriment and diversion, but the conversation ends in a conspiracy against the public or in some contrivance to raise prices (Smith 1776).

While the greatest abuse of Arrow's suggestion that asymmetric information can explain health care norms and organizations has been perpetuated by noneconomists, economists have contributed their fair share to the conceptual muddle. There is indeed no institutional feature that cannot be formally modeled as a response to asymmetric information, once the author imputes the asymmetries in an appropriate manner (*post hoc ergo propter hoc*). The creativity of the formal models of asymmetric information echo an earlier generation of equally creative (and misleading) models based on asymmetric risk aversion, in which everything from sharecropping to business cycles was ascribed to a trade-off between moral hazard and the (asymmetric) aversion to risk between principals and agents. The once-universal ascription of unusual organizational and institutional structures to asymmetric risk aversion has in recent years been discredited, due both to econometric refutation of its key empirical implications and to a more general feeling that the postulate of unmeasured perceptual factors stultified the pursuit of more plausible and empirically supportable explanations (Goldberg 1990; Allen and Lueck 1999). Transactions cost economics and contemporary agency theory are more likely to ascribe risk neutrality (or, more generally, symmetric risk aversion) to contracting partners and move on to multiple agency, two-sided moral hazard, sunk investments, or other explanations for the matters under consideration. By analogy, models of health care contracting (organization, norm, and so forth) should hesitate before blithely relying on information asymmetry (especially when unmeasured and simply imputed) as the causal explanation without rigorous comparison of informational with noninformational candidates.

RESEARCH AGENDAS

In reflecting on the fate of his article on the nature of firms after thirty years, Ronald Coase described it as "oft cited and little used" (1972: 63). At least until the advent of transactions cost economics in the 1970s, the mainstream of economic theory did not inquire in any sustained fashion why the allocation of goods and services happens so often within firms rather than across markets. I believe that similarly weary words can be ascribed to "Uncertainty and the Welfare Economics of Medical Care." Certainly this article is oft cited. Is it really used? One might, without stretch, interpret the article as a research agenda, a call for the refinement of explanations for organizational, legal, and normative phenomena. Imperfect and asymmetric information would be one, but no more than one, of these potential explanations. Cognitive factors, including bounded rationality; perceptual factors, including risk aversion; and motivational factors, including opportunism (the conjunction of self-interest with guile), would figure prominently in the list, as would others. This research agenda would seek a middle ground between the inhospitality tradition that Arrow targeted and what I might refer to as the laziness tradition, which uses Arrow's article as the end rather than the beginning of the quest for understanding. For example, such an agenda would seek a more satisfying understanding of the physician-patient relationship than the fuzzy notion of "trust," plumbing game theory (credible threats), transactions cost economics (credible commitments), and legal scholarship (relational contracting) in search of sanctions that permit handshake agreements and apparently one-sided contracts to be self-enforcing.

I would claim that "Uncertainty and the Welfare Economics of Medical Care" indeed has been little used as a model for the analysis of health care organizational and normative structures despite the ritualistic citations. Asymmetric information and its consequences, moral hazard and adverse selection, have proved to be among the most fertile economic ideas in recent decades, opening up new conceptual possibilities and empirical studies in labor, financial, product, and other markets. Within health economics, these ideas have been used to shed light on the incentive distortions created by tax subsidies, insurance, and rate regulation. But they have not been used extensively to analyze the manner in which the unusual organizational, legal, and normative characteristics of health care serve as efficiency-enhancing societal responses to underlying informational, cognitive, and motivational deficiencies. Forty years ago Arrow proposed the view that "when the market fails to achieve an optimal state, society will, to some extent at least, recognize the gap, and nonmarket social institutions will arise attempting to bridge it" (947). Most economic analyses of licensure, nonprofit organization, sliding-fee schedules, professional control over accreditation and quality standards, and so forth, do not begin from Arrow's foundation, however, but either pursue the inhospitality tradition (e.g., the nonprofit hospital as the physician's cooperative) or fall back into naive public interest theories (e.g., the nonprofit hospital as an institution of the good, by the good, and for the good).

Economists are socialized to overestimate the capabilities of the price mechanism for allocating goods and services, and for them Arrow's primary message should be to more fully incorporate other allocation mechanisms into their field of vision. Markets are important. But institutions, organizations, associations, and norms are important as well. Noneconomists, on the other hand, are socialized to underestimate the capabilities of the price mechanism (and to overestimate the capabilities of formal organization, social norms, professional associations, and legal rules) and thus are at risk of interpreting Arrow as a preeminent economist who agrees with their prejudices. For the noneconomist, Arrow's primary message should be that most sectors of the economy work reasonably well (at least compared to medicine) without many of the organizational curiosa of this sector and hence that the price mechanism should be accorded greater respect and its potential applicability to the health sector be pushed higher on the list of research priorities.

Allusion was made earlier to the difficulty of applying informational explanations to changes in organizational arrangements because we typically have no a priori reason to expect commensurate changes in informational imperfections. This statement requires partial retraction, but in a manner that sharpens my skepticism as to the acceptability of common explanations of health care facts. It is obvious that the four decades that separate us from the publication of Arrow's article have witnessed a considerable convergence between the organizational features of health care and those of the economic mainstream. For-profit ownership, price competition, vertical and horizontal integration, prepayment, advertising, and other conventional market features are ever more prevalent in health care. To ascribe this convergence primarily to an underlying convergence of information structures fails the laugh test. Changes in the availability of health care information, including hospital outcome statistics, patient satisfaction surveys, health plan accreditation criteria, and physician practice profiles, can best be interpreted as consequences rather than causes of the changes in markets, organizations, and norms.

Forty years ago Arrow held that "virtually all the special features of this industry, in fact, stem from the prevalence of uncertainty" (946). Today, this broad ascription of organization to asymmetric information is untenable. In seeking to understand the contemporary institutions, organizations, and norms of health care and in particular when seeking to understand the remarkable manner in which they have changed since Arrow's article was published, we should look first at theories based on antitrust enforcement, purchasing alliances, federal budgetary deficits, failed experiments at rate regulation, and other events that are not primarily informational in nature. But as a secondary explanation for what has occurred and perhaps as a primary explanation for what is about to occur in health care organization, changes in information and the attenuation of asymmetries are attractive. Patients, consumers, and citizens are ever more educated with respect to their own health and health care, and this fundamental fact cannot fail to have revolutionary implications for the organizational, legal, and normative structures of medicine (coming full circle to Arrow's article). In particular, the Internet, the greatest revolution in communications technology ever compressed into so short a period, threatens to turn much of the system on its head. Patients with serious chronic disease — those responsible for most health care utilization and in Arrow's framework those most reliant on trust and professionalism — now increasingly have more, not less, information concerning their specific clinical condition than do their treating physicians. Some arrive in the office with a stack of articles downloaded from the clinical journals that the doctor has no time to read, with performance statistics on the services provided by particular providers and facilities, and with support from cybernetworks of fellow sufferers who trade experiences, anecdotes, and Web site references. Obviously, the typical physician will always understand clinical medicine better than the typical patient; that is why we send young people to medical school. But we stand at the beginning of a new era, or perhaps the continuation of an era that began with the doctrine of informed consent, in which the patient and the physician become partners, with the physician being the junior partner, in the quest to understand the disease process, intervene where possible, and find the wisdom to accept those declines in health status that are the fate of the mortal.

CONCLUSION

The irony of "Uncertainty and the Welfare Economics of Medical Care" is that it brought to articulation a view of professionalism and the physician-patient relationship on the very eve of a massive and largely successful assault on that view and the social relationships it embodied. The decade of Arrow's article produced a generation of now-classic critiques of the principle that patients must rely on trust in the benevolence of physicians for understanding, treatment, and personal coping with their diseases. Medical sociology turned its back on Talcott Parsons (1962) and savaged professional dominance through the writings of Elliot Freidson and his followers. The Boston Women's Health Book Collective denounced the paternalism and status inequalities inherent in the conventional clinical relationship, founding what became known as the women's health movement. Thomas Szasz's denunciation of psychiatry as pseudoscience and a threat to personal freedom launched the mental patients' rights movement, building on exposés of coercive institutions that embodied the ultimate in asymmetric information between physician and patient. Ivan Illich carried the Szasz framework to the whole of medicine, characterizing medical professionalism as the expropriation of health from the people, the deliberate creation of unequal access to information.

"Uncertainty and the Welfare Economics of Medical Care" was and remains an important article, a spur to thinking and an identifiable starting point for the modern moment in health economics. Its influence pales, however, in comparison to the rich and radical debates spurred by Professional Dominance (Freidson 1970), *Our Bodies Ourselves* (BWHBC 1969), *The Myth of Mental Illness* (Szasz 1961), *Medical Nemesis* (Illich 1976), and the other calls for a new social and clinical contract, a relationship of equals between patients and physicians, the people and the profession. Arrow's article experienced the fate of many seminal writings, to describe as the present a world that already was past. In the words of the greatest historian of the western intellect, "When philosophy paints its grey in grey, then has the shape of life grown old. By philosophy's grey in grey it cannot be rejuvenated but only understood. The owl of Minerva spreads its wings only with the falling of the dusk" (Hegel [1807] 1967: 63).

REFERENCES

Allen, D. W., and D. Lueck. 1999. The Role of Risk in Contract Choice. *Journal of Law, Economics, and Organization* 15(3): 704–736

Arrow, K. J. 1963. Uncertainty and the Welfare Economics of Medical Care. *American Economic Review* 53(5): 941–973.

Boston Women's Health Book Collective (BWHBC). 1969. *Our Bodies, Ourselves.* Boston: BWHBC.

Coase, R. H. 1972. Industrial Organization: A Proposal for Research. In *Policy Issues and Research Opportunities in Industrial Organization,* ed. V. Fuchs. New York: National Bureau of Economic Research.

Freidson, E. 1970. *Professional Dominance: The Social Structure of Medical Care.* New York: Atherton.

Goldberg, V. P. 1990. Aversion to Risk Aversion in the New Institutional Economics. *Journal of Institutional and Theoretical Economics* 146: 216–222.

Hegel, G. W. F. 1967 [1807]. *The Philosophy of Right.* Oxford: Oxford University Press.

Illich, I. 1976. *Medical Nemesis.* New York: Bantam.

Parsons, T. 1962. *The Social System.* London: Tavistock.

Starr, P. 1982. *The Social Transformation of American Medicine.* New York: Basic Books.

Szasz, T. 1961. *The Myth of Mental Illness.* New York: Harper & Row.

LAWRENCE CASALINO

■ Managing Uncertainty: Intermediate

Organizations as Triple Agents

In "Uncertainty and the Welfare Economics of Medical Care" (1963), Kenneth Arrow focused on the physician-patient relationship, which was by far the most important relationship in U.S. medical care at that time. With the development of managed care, "intermediate organizations" began to impinge on this formerly sacrosanct dyad, interacting in a complex web of relationships with patients, physicians, and one another (Figure 1). These organizations—including Health Maintenance Organizations (HMOS), Preferred Provider Organizations (PPOS), large medical groups such as Independent Practice Associations (IPAS), Physician-Hospital Organizations (PHOS), accreditation organizations such as the National Committee for Quality Assurance (NCQA), and large public and private purchasers of health insurance—function as double agents or, more often, as triple agents (at a minimum).

A health plan, for example, is an agent not only of patients, but also of purchasers, regulatory agencies, and accrediting organizations in addition to having its own interests. While all these organizations are supposed to represent patient interests, it is by no means certain that they will do so (Rodwin 1995). Whose interests does an intermediate organization that is a triple agent serve?

In this essay, I suggest that managed care has significantly *increased* uncertainty for patients and physicians while *decreasing* uncertainty for purchasers and payers (Table 1). These differential effects help explain both why managed care is unpopular (Blendon et al. 1998) and why it has continued to grow despite its unpopularity. I also suggest that intermediate organizations have the potential to decrease uncertainty—even for patients and physicians—more effectively than was possible in the traditional, fee-for-service–based system about which Arrow wrote.

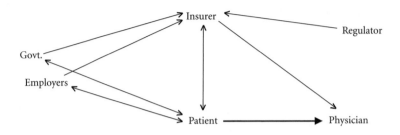

CONTEMPORARY PRINCIPAL-AGENT RELATIONSHIPS

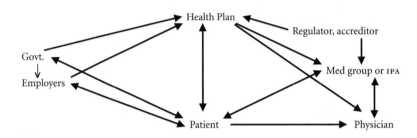

Figure 1   Traditional Principal-Agent Relationships in U.S. Medical Care (circa 1963).
Note: Darker lines indicate more active relationships.

For patients and physicians, uncertainty creates fear and dissatisfaction. For economists, uncertainty is a source of market failure, especially when combined with information asymmetries between buyers and sellers.[1] At the extreme, uncertainty can prevent the very existence of a market (Akerlof 1970);[2] more commonly it interferes with exchange and with productive efficiency. But "uncertainty in medical care" is too broad a concept. What kind of uncertainty is meant, and for whom? It is useful, I suggest, to distinguish three types: patient uncertainty about the ability to afford care; patient, purchaser, and payer uncertainty about the quality of care; and purchaser and payer uncertainty about the cost of care.

Part 1 of this article briefly discusses uncertainty in medical care during the indemnity fee-for-service era about which Arrow wrote. Part 2 discusses ways in which intermediate organizations decrease purchaser and payer and increase patient and physician uncertainty in the contemporary U.S. managed care system. Part 3 discusses the potential of intermediate organizations to reduce uncertainty for patients in addition to purchasers and payers and briefly indicates market and nonmarket measures, which might help them do so.

Table 1   Key Perceived Changes in Uncertainty in the Managed Care Era Compared to
the Indemnity Fee-for-Service Era

	Ability to Pay	Quality of Care	Overall Costs of Care
Patients	↑	↑	
Physicians		↑	
Payers, purchasers			↓

PHYSICIAN PROFESSIONALISM AS A REMEDY FOR
MARKET FAILURE CAUSED BY UNCERTAINTY

Arrow translated Talcott Parsons's functionalist analysis of physician professionalism (Parsons 1954) into the economic language of market failure. In Arrow's
view, the "nonmarket social institution" (947) of physician professionalism was
a means of compensating for uncertainty in the context of the severe information
asymmetry that existed between physicians and patients and between physicians
and corporate purchasers of and payers for medical care (health insurance companies). Though neither patients nor purchasers or payers had sufficient information to evaluate physicians' actions, physician professionalism was supposed
to enable patients to trust that they would receive only appropriate services and
that the quality of these services would be high, and purchasers and payers to
trust that these services not only would be appropriate and of high quality, but
that they also would be provided at a reasonable cost. Arrow argued, in other
words, that physician professionalism could reduce two of the three forms of
uncertainty: patient and payer uncertainty about the quality of care and payer
uncertainty about the overall costs of care.

During this pre-Medicare and pre-Medicaid era, many patients, particularly
the elderly and the poor, experienced a great deal of uncertainty about their
ability to pay for care. The creation of Medicare and Medicaid reduced this uncertainty for many patients but increased purchaser uncertainty about the costs of
care, which rose sharply in response to the influx of new resources into the medical system. The increasingly rapid introduction of new, often expensive medical
technologies also increased purchaser uncertainty about the costs and quality of
care, as did the publication of new data describing large variations among U.S.
communities in the types of care provided for common diseases (Chassin et al.
1987; Wennberg, Freeman, and Culp 1987).

INTERMEDIATE ORGANIZATIONS AS INSUFFICIENT REMEDIES FOR
MARKET FAILURE CAUSED BY UNCERTAINTY

By 1970 both government and large corporate purchasers of medical care, increasingly uncertain that they could rely on physician professionalism to produce consistently high quality at a reasonable cost, began to look for ways to reduce this uncertainty. A 1970 editorial in *Fortune* magazine, for example, argued that "much of U.S. medical care . . . is inferior in quality, wastefully dispensed, and inequitably financed. . . . The management of medical care has become too important to leave to doctors . . ." (cited in Bergthold 1990). Their search led to the federal HMO Act of 1973 and the numerous state HMO laws which soon followed, as well as laws permitting PPOs, which began to emerge in the early 1980s.

Managed care can be understood as an attempt by previously passive purchaser and payer intermediate organizations — Medicare, Medicaid, large corporate employers, and private health insurance plans — to use market mechanisms to reduce all three forms of uncertainty in medical care. Rather than continue to rely completely on physician professionalism, purchasers began to use newly created intermediate organizations to "manage care." New types of payer (HMOs and PPOs) developed new types of relationships (involving selective contracting, capitation, and utilization management) with new types of provider organization (IPAs, large capitated medical groups, and PHOs). Proponents of managed care argue that competition among intermediate organizations will increase efficiency, reduce costs, and improve quality (Enthoven 1993).

Reducing Purchaser Uncertainty
During the 1990s, medical care cost inflation slowed considerably as capitation, selective contracting using discounted fee schedules, and utilization management became prevalent. Recently, costs have risen more sharply, but even so purchasers' uncertainty over costs is reduced[3] — they no longer feel that they are signing blank checks for any amount of care at any price. Their uncertainty about the quality of care has also begun — though only begun — to be reduced by the growth of intermediate organizations. For decades purchasers accepted physicians' argument that only professionals, that is, physicians themselves, could evaluate quality. Now intermediate organizations, including purchaser coalitions such as the Pacific Business Group on Health (Schauffler, Brown, and Milstein 1999) and the Buyers Healthcare Action Group (Christianson 1999; Knutson 1998), accrediting organizations such as the NCQA (Iglehart 1996; Thompson et al. 1998), and HMOs themselves are developing expertise and data systems with the potential to evaluate the quality of care from outside the formerly closed professional world. Because both statistical analysis and adjustment for the health status of a group

of patients can be done more accurately for intermediate organizations—medical groups, IPAs, and HMOs themselves—than for individual physicians, these organizations provide units of analysis at which quality can be more accurately evaluated and (potentially) rewarded.

The much more active role played at present by the federal and state governments and by large corporate purchasers of health insurance is illustrated schematically in Figure 1. The darker arrows depict purchasers' more active relationships with intermediate organizations. Their increased influence over physicians is mediated through health plans and physician groups (medical groups and IPAs).

Increasing Patient and Physician Uncertainty
Patients' perception of managed care is quite different. Managed care appears to have increased patients' uncertainty both about their ability to pay for care and about the quality of care they will receive. Though HMO patients typically have zero deductibles, low copayments, and good coverage for preventive care and for medications, all of which reduce uncertainty over ability to pay for care compared to the indemnity fee-for-service era, patients fear that needed services may be denied by the utilization managers of the HMO and/or physician group with which they are enrolled. If this happens, they must either do without the service or pay the entire cost themselves. The media contribute to this perceived uncertainty by repeatedly describing cases in which families have been unable to obtain (or have paid for out of pocket) what they believed to be potentially life-saving services which had been denied by an HMO, medical group, or IPA (Rochefort 1998).

Patients' increased uncertainty over quality stems from multiple sources. In the indemnity fee-for-service era, they trusted to a considerable extent in the reputation and professional ethics of their physician. Now their HMO, their physician, and their physician's medical group or IPA typically have financial incentives (incentives about which patients know little) to withhold services. Patients are uncertain that their physician will recommend important services, uncertain that the physician's group or the health plan will approve the services if recommended, and uncertain that the services, when recommended and approved, will be provided by a high-quality specialist and/or hospital (Grumbach et al. 1999). They fear that the provider network with which their health plan contracts will not include the specialists and hospitals they will need should they develop a serious and unusual illness and that they will not be permitted to go outside the network.

Patients' uncertainty about quality is reduced when they develop a long-term relationship with a physician (Schmittdiel et al. 1997), but selective contracting by health plans with physicians and hospitals causes them to fear that they will lose these relationships due to changes in the health plan offered by their employer—nearly 50 percent of employees have only one health plan offered to them (Etheredge, Jones, and Lewin 1996[4]—or to the failure of their health plan and their physician or physician group to continue contracting with each other. As purchasers ratchet payment rates lower, contracting disputes between health plans, physician groups, and hospitals have become more frequent and intense. Last-minute, high-stakes games of brinkmanship, affecting tens of thousands of patients, are regularly played out through full-page newspaper ads advising patients that because of the greed of the opposing organization, they will have to switch hospitals and/or physicians. These hard-nosed business tactics, the overt emphasis on profit as the organizing principle of the new medical market—Arrow argues that "the very word, 'profit,' is a signal that denies trust relations" (965)—and the many direct and indirect messages given by purchasers, health plans, and the utilization management process itself that the professionalism of physicians cannot be trusted all increase patient uncertainty about the quality of the care they will receive.

The complex pattern of principal-agent relationships depicted in Figure 1 has somewhat increased physician uncertainty over quality because selective contracting and utilization management sometimes prevent physicians from choosing the specialists, hospitals, services, and drugs they believe best for their patients. Managed care has also increased physicians' uncertainty over their incomes and over their professional autonomy (Burdi and Baker 1999; Luft 1999; Sulmasy et al. 2000). Neither of these forms of uncertainty makes a market inefficient, but they do increase physician dissatisfaction (Feldman, Novack, and Gracely 1998). This dissatisfaction is communicated to patients in innumerable daily physician-patient interactions throughout the United States, which increases patient uncertainty over costs and quality, which does make the market work less efficiently.

Intermediate Organizations as Triple Agents

The proliferation of new types of organization and relationship is yet another source of patient uncertainty. If the web of relationships depicted in Figure 1 looks complex to knowledgeable readers of this book, how are patients to understand it?

A branch of economics called *agency theory* or *principal-agent theory* provides a useful approach to Figure 1 (Eisenhardt 1989; Sappington 1991; Sharma 1997). Agency theory seeks the most effective ways in which a principal—a patient, for example—can contract with an agent—a physician, for example—to act as the principal would desire, even when the agent has more information than the principal and when the principal cannot observe all of the agent's actions. As Figure 1 shows, during the indemnity fee-for-service era there was only one important principal-agent relationship: that between patient and physician. Other agency relationships did exist (light arrows), but they were relatively inactive.

Managed care has created multiple highly active principal-agent relationships. The patient no longer feels like the principal: there are many principals and many agents, and each principal is an agent in at least one relationship. Health plans, physician groups, and physicians are triple agents. Patients as principals would like purchasers and health plans as their agents to help reduce their uncertainty about ability to pay and quality, but purchasers have other interests (e.g., those of their managers and/or stockholders), and health plans respond to purchasers, regulators, and accreditors as principals in addition to patients. Patients themselves are treated as agents by purchasers and health plans—agents who must be discouraged from spending health care dollars unnecessarily. Patients are particularly concerned that physicians, whom they would like to be their agents, now answer to multiple principals (at least three, as shown in Figure 1), and therefore may have incentives other than those which the patient gives them. During the indemnity fee-for-service era, patients understood that physicians had their own interests (that they would earn more if they provided more services), but they believed that physician professionalism would minimize this behavior, and in any case patients appear to prefer to believe that too much care will be recommended to them, rather than that care which they may want or need will be denied (Hillman 1998; Kao et al. 1998).

CAN THE REMEDY BE REMEDIED? MARKET AND GOVERNMENT RESPONSES

Can intermediate organizations as triple agents reduce uncertainty in medical care? The short answer is that they could *if* the medical care market is structured so that they compete through increasing quality and reducing unnecessary costs, rather than through skimming, skimping, and wielding market power— that is, through avoiding sick patients, denying appropriate care, and striving to become so big that they can dictate contract terms to other intermediate organizations. It is probably impossible to create a market where individual physicians compete on costs and quality (because of severe difficulties with risk adjustment and statistical power at the individual physician level), but intermediate organizations can potentially be evaluated as to their cost and quality and therefore potentially can serve as the basic units of a competitive market. And the fact that intermediate organizations are organizations means that they can create organized processes for preventive care and for care for patients with chronic disease—in short, for population-based health care—which are not even imaginable for individual physicians (Shortell et al. 1996). The fact that intermediate organizations are triple agents can be understood as negative, but can also mean that these organizations can be supervised by sophisticated principals, such as large purchasers, regulators, and accreditors, with an ability to monitor their performance that far exceeds that of individual patients and certainly exceeds the virtually nonexistent supervision of individual physicians during the indemnity fee-for-service era. Certain intermediate organizations may also develop reputations for quality—essentially brand names that convey information, which may reduce uncertainty.

Current policy controversies in managed care can and should be evaluated in terms of their effects on patient uncertainty. Easy-to-use appeals, external review and arbitration processes, and reasonable disclosure of information on financial incentives would go a long way toward reassuring patients that they will receive the right care from the right person at the right time. Health plans and physician groups have, belatedly, begun to offer such processes. Insofar as they do not do so voluntarily, federal and state governments will (Landers 2000) and should do it for them.

At first glance, patient protection laws that mandate access to certain types of specialists or dictate care for a specific medical condition (e.g., length of stay after delivery) appear to be another means for reducing patient uncertainty. But such "body parts" mandates can reduce efficiency (Noble and Brennan 1999), can be harmful to patients, and would not be necessary if utilization review and appeals were handled as described above. These laws are likely to represent the interests of well-organized patient and/or provider advocacy groups rather than of patients as a whole. They prevent intermediate organizations from allocating resources rationally, promote further distrust and uncertainty among patients ("I need the government to force the health plan to provide decent care for me"), and may result in patients receiving care of both lower quality and higher cost than they otherwise would. This is probable, for example, when laws mandate that obstetricians—who are not trained to provide primary care—must be permitted to serve as primary care physicians.

Patients' uncertainty is increased by the possibility that they may be forced to switch physicians. When this occurs, all the value of the patient's and physician's mutual knowledge and trust built up over time vanishes—a deadweight loss for the patient, the physician, and the economy (Raddish, Horn, and Sharkey 1999). Physician group bankruptcies are one important cause of such involuntary switching. These typically occur in groups accepting large amounts of financial risk from health plans and would be fewer if plans exercised due diligence in selecting groups, negotiating contract terms with them, limiting the amount of financial risk borne by the groups, and overseeing groups' financial status during the contract period. If health plans fail to do these things—as they have frequently failed, most notably in California (Bodenheimer 2000)—then government will set standards.

A patient may also be forced to switch physicians when his or her employer switches health plans or when his or her physician group terminates or loses a contract with the patient's health plan. Very large employers, Medicare, and Medicaid can minimize the chance of this occurring and increase patient choice by offering multiple health plans, but it is prohibitively costly for smaller employers to do so. Very large employers, Medicare, and Medicaid, but again, not most employers, could also reduce patient uncertainty by developing quality measures, rewarding health plans, hospitals, and physician groups for improving quality and providing comparative quality information to patients (Lo Sasso et al. 1999). Health insurance purchasing coalitions could also offer multiple health plans, reward quality performance, and disseminate quality information (Long and Marquis 1999; Yegian et al. 2000), but the medical market has not supplied many of these, at least in part because of collective action problems. The transactions costs of organizing small employers into a purchasing coalition are very high, and no individual or organization stands to be adequately compensated for making the effort. Large employers can more easily organize, but some will free ride on the organizing efforts of others, and employers with a relatively healthy workforce will be reluctant to join a pool with employers with less healthy workers. Because of these collective action problems, it appears likely that government action will be required if adequate numbers of purchasing coalitions are to be created (though the coalitions themselves need not be government organizations).

CONCLUSION

It sounds very bad for intermediate organizations to be triple agents, but it need not be so. Triple agents balance their own interests against those of the patient and those of a third principal. This third principal, for example, a health plan or physician group overseeing a physician or an employer and an accreditor overseeing a health plan, can make it more likely that the physician and the health plan will act in the patient's interest. In fact, if intermediate organizations were not triple agents, the patient would be left alone dealing with double agents — the physician as agent for him- or herself as well as for the patient (Shortell et al. 1998) and/or the health plan as agent for itself as well as for the patient. Furthermore, third agents, with their concern for the cost as well as the quality of medical care, can also do something which neither the patient nor the physician is well placed to do, that is, serve as a principal for society as a whole by trying to balance the interests of all patients with that of the individual patient — an unpleasant but necessary function (Bloche and Jacobson 2000; Mechanic 1997).

Decreasing patient uncertainty would both reduce the managed care backlash and increase the efficiency of the managed care market. Regulation and self-regulation are not cost free, but they will be cost effective if they reduce uncertainty sufficiently for the managed care market to function more efficiently. Arrow believed that physician professionalism arose as a nonmarket response to patient and purchaser uncertainty. Physician professionalism alone was not enough, but the intermediate organizations created to replace the physician-dominated system about which Arrow wrote have created new uncertainties. Nonmarket and market responses are needed now to reduce these uncertainties, but their emergence is by no means inevitable. They may fail to appear because they are blocked by powerful interests, or because the technology to implement them does not exist, or simply because of organizational inertia and lack of innovation.

The intermediate organizations that have been created during the managed care era can be thought of as new tools. Like any new tool, they provide new opportunities, but their actual effects will depend on how they are used, and how they are used will depend on the incentives created both by market forces and by government as both purchaser and regulator. Market and government responses to the new uncertainties created by intermediate organizations have been late in coming; it remains questionable whether they can overcome both the highly developed public distrust of these organizations and the uncertainty caused by the sheer complexity of their interrelationships.

NOTES

Written with support from the Robert Wood Johnson Investigator Awards in Health Policy Research program.

1 Economists contrast uncertainty with risk. Situations that involve risk can be defined as those in which probabilities are available to guide choice, which makes it possible, for example, to develop an insurance market, whereas in uncertain situations, information is too imprecise to be summarized by probabilities (Epstein and Wang 1994).

2 Uncertainty alone does not prevent market exchange. For example, I may be uncertain about what will happen to the price of a stock that I am considering buying, yet still buy the stock. However, I will be less likely to do so if my uncertainty is worsened by suspicion that the stockbroker I use and/or the information provided by the company whose stock I am considering and/or the information provided by rating agencies about that company are deliberately misleading, and if there are no safeguards to prevent them from deceptions.

3 Purchasers and payers have always had the ability to convert uncertainty over the likely cost of care for an individual patient to risk—that is, to a narrower range of probable costs for a large group of patients. By decreasing both payment rates and inappropriate variation in the care provided to individual patients, managed care could reduce risk by reducing both the mean and the standard deviation of the cost of a group of patients.

4 Patients who have a choice of health plans report higher satisfaction with their plan (Davis et al. 1995).

REFERENCES

Akerlof, G. A. 1970. The Market for "Lemons": Quality Uncertainty and the Market Mechanism. *Quarterly Journal of Economics* 84(3): 488–500.

Arrow, K. J. 1963. Uncertainty and the Welfare Economics of Medical Care. *American Economic Review* 53(5): 941–973.

Bergthold, L. 1990. *Purchasing Power in Health: Business, the State, and Health Care Politics.* New Brunswick, NJ: Rutgers University Press.

Blendon, R., M. Brodie, J. Benson, D. Altman, L. Levitt, T. Hoff, and L. Hugick. 1998. Understanding the Managed Care Backlash. *Health Affairs* 17(4): 80–94.

Bloche, M. G., and P. D. Jacobson. 2000. The Supreme Court and Bedside Rationing. *Journal of the American Medical Association* 284(21): 2776–2779.

Bodenheimer, T. 2000. California's Beleaguered Physician Groups: Will They Survive? *New England Journal of Medicine* 342(14): 1064–1068.

Burdi, M. D., and L. C. Baker. 1999. Physicians' Perceptions of Autonomy and Satisfaction in California. *Health Affairs* 18(4): 134–145.

Chassin, M., J. Kosecoff, R. Park, C. Winslow, K. L. Kahn, M. J. Merick, J. Keesey, A. Fink, D. H. Solomon, and R. H. Brook. 1987. Does Inappropriate Use Explain Geographic Variations in the Use of Health Care Services? *Journal of the American Medical Association* 258(18): 2533–2537.

Christianson, J., R. Feldman, J. P. Weiner, and P. Drury. 1999. Early Experience with a New Model of Employer Group Purchasing in Minnesota. *Health Affairs* 18(6): 100–114.

Davis, K., K. Collins, C. Schoen, and C. Morris. 1995. Choice Matters: Enrollees' Views of Their Health Care Plans. *Health Affairs* 14(2): 99–112.

Eisenhardt, K. 1989. Agency Theory: An Assessment and Review. *Academy of Management Review* 14(1): 57–74.

Enthoven, A. C. 1993. The History and Principles of Managed Competition. *Health Affairs* 12(suppl.): 24–48.

Epstein, L., and T. Wang. 1994. Intertemporal Asset Pricing under Knightian Uncertainty. *Econometrica* 62(2): 283–322.

Etheredge, L., S. B. Jones, and L. Lewin. 1996. What Is Driving Health System Change? *Health Affairs* 15: 93–101.

Feldman, D. S., D. H. Novack, and E. Gracely. 1998. Effects of Managed Care on Physician-Patient Relationships, Quality of Care, and the Ethical Practice of Medicine: A Physician Survey. *Archives of Internal Medicine* 158(15): 1626–1632.

Grumbach, K., J. V. Selby, C. Damberg, A. B. Bindman, C. Quesenberry, A. Truman, and C. Uratsu. 1999. Resolving the Gatekeeper Conundrum: What Patients Value in Primary Care and Referrals to Specialists. *Journal of the American Medical Association* 282(3): 261–266.

Hillman, A. L. 1998. Mediators of Patient Trust. *Journal of the American Medical Association* 280(19): 1703–1705.

Kao, A. C., D. C. Green, A. M. Zaslavsky, J. P. Koplan, and P. D. Cleary. 1998. The Relationship between Method of Physician Payment and Patient Trust. *Journal of the American Medical Association* 280(19): 1708–1714.

Knutson, D. 1998. Case Study: The Minneapolis Buyers Health Care Action Group. *Inquiry* 35(1): 71–177.

Iglehart, J. K. 1996. The National Committee for Quality Assurance. *New England Journal of Medicine* 335(13): 995–998.

Landers, S. J. 2000. New Rules Call for Faster HMO Appeals. *American Medical News* 43(46): 1–2.

Long, S. H., and M. S. Marquis. 1999. Pooled Purchasing: Who Are the Players? *Health Affairs* 18(4): 105–111.

Lo Sasso, A. T., L. Perloff, J. Schield, J. J. Murphy, J. D. Mortimer, and P. D. Budetti. 1999. Beyond Cost: "Responsible Purchasing" of Managed Care by Employers. *Health Affairs* 18(6): 212–223.

Luft, H. S. 1999. Why Are Physicians So Upset about Managed Care? *Journal of Health Politics, Policy and Law* 24(5): 957–966.

Mechanic, D. 1997. Managed Care as a Target of Distrust. *Journal of the American Medical Association* 277(22): 1810–1811.

Noble, A. A., and T. A. Brennan. 1999. The Stages of Managed Care Regulation: Developing Better Rules. *Journal of Health Politics, Policy and Law* 24(6): 1275–1306.

Parsons, T. 1954. The Professions and Social Structure. In *Essays on Sociological Theory*. ed. T. Parsons. Glencoe, IL: Free Press.

Raddish, M., S. D. Horn, and P. D. Sharkey. 1999. Continuity of Care: Is It Cost Effective? *American Journal of Managed Care* 5(6): 727–734.

Rochefort, D. A. 1998. The Role of Anecdotes in Regulating Managed Care. *Health Affairs* 17(6): 142–149.

Rodwin, M. 1995. Conflicts in Managed Care. *New England Journal of Medicine* 33(2): 604–607.

Sappington, D. E. 1991. Incentives in Principal-Agent Relationships. *Journal of Economic Perspectives* 5(2): 545–566.

Schauffler, H. H., C. Brown, and A. Milstein. 1999. Raising the Bar: The Use of Performance Guarantees by the Pacific Business Group on Health. *Health Affairs* 18(2): 134–142.

Schmittdiel, J., J. Selby, K. Grumbach, and C. P. Quesenberry. 1997. Choice of a Personal Physician and Patient Satisfaction in a Health Maintenance Organization. *Journal of the American Medical Association* 278(19): 1596–1599.

Sharma, A. 1997. Professional as Agent: Knowledge and Asymmetry in Agency Exchange. *Academy of Management Review* 22(3): 758–799.

Shortell, S. M., R. R. Gillies, D. A. Anderson, K. M. Erickson, and J. B. Mitchell. 1996. *Remaking Health Care in America: Building Organized Delivery Systems.* San Francisco: Jossey-Bass.

Shortell, S. M., T. M. Waters, K. W. Clarke, and P. P. Budetti. 1998. Physicians as Double Agents: Maintaining Trust in an Era of Multiple Accountabilities. *Journal of the American Medical Association* 280(12): 1102–1108.

Sulmasy, D., M. G. Bloche, J. Mitchell, and J. Hadley. 2000. Physicians' Ethical Beliefs about Cost-Control Arrangements. *Archives of Internal Medicine* 160(5): 649–657.

Thompson, J. W., J. Bost, F. Ahmed, C. E. Ingalls, and C. Sennett. 1998. The NCQA's Quality Compass: Evaluating Managed Care in the United States. *Health Affairs* 17(1): 152–158.

Wennberg, J. E., J. Freeman, and W. Culp. 1987. Are Hospital Services Rationed in New Haven or Over-Utilized in Boston? *Lancet* (1): 1185–1189.

Yegian, J. M., T. C. Buchmueller, M. D. Smith, and A. Monroe. 2000. The Health Insurance Plan of California: The First Five Years. *Health Affairs* 19(5): 158–165.

MICHAEL L. MILLENSON

MERVIN SHALOWITZ, M.D.

■ *Moral Hazard vs. Real Hazard:*

Quality of Care Post-Arrow

The doctor is essentially a small businessman. He is selling his services, so is as much in business as is anyone else who sells a commodity.
—American Medical Association official to the *Wall Street Journal*, 1956

It is clear from everyday observation that the behavior expected of sellers of medical care is different from that of business men in general. . . . The ethically understood restrictions on the activities of a physician are much more severe than on those of, say, a barber.
—Kenneth J. Arrow

Was Kenneth Arrow naïve? Did the ivory tower inure him to manifestations of medical mendacity? Probably not. In "Uncertainty and the Welfare Economics of Medical Care" (1963) Arrow carefully chooses his qualifiers:

> Advice . . . is *supposed to be* completely divorced from self-interest. . . . It is *at least claimed* that treatment is dictated by the objective needs of the case [although] . . . *the ethical compulsion is surely not as absolute in fact* as it is in theory. (949–950)

> The physician avoids the *obvious stigmata* of profit-maximizing. (965; emphasis added)

And yet for all his caution, Arrow was at the same sort of disadvantage writing about medical care in 1963 as a political scientist analyzing presidential accountability would have been on the cusp of the Vietnam War and Watergate. Just as no analyst could have foreseen the dramatic legal and social changes related to governance that emerged from those events, so, too, was it impossible to foresee the manner in which post-1963 legal and social changes would transform health care.

Arrow did not, and could not, anticipate the passage of Medicare and Medicaid. Nor did he foresee how the profession's subsequent behavior would undermine trust in medicine as surely as the unexplained eighteen-and-a-half-minute gap in a crucial Watergate tape shredded the credibility of the Nixon administration. The resulting end of untrammeled clinical autonomy would also give rise to a form of managed care much different from the "prepaid group practices" of Arrow's day and, in the process, lead to further redefinition of the trust relationship.

Moreover, when Arrow wrote about information asymmetry, he could not foresee how information technology, most notably the Internet, and the consumer empowerment movement would combine to redefine information asymmetry in a manner similar to the way trust had been. (See James C. Robinson's article in this book.)

The balance between clinical autonomy and clinical accountability—to patients, to payers, and to society—has changed enormously since Arrow's day. As nineteenth-century British parliamentarian put it: "A reform is a correction of abuses; a revolution is a transfer of power" (Edward George Bulwer-Lytton in an 1866 speech to the House of Commons on the Reform Bill). The product-formerly-known-as-insurance has taken on the revolutionary role of not just providing access to care, but of shaping the content of that care through financial incentives to providers and to patients. At the same time, public interest groups and the news media now address the information asymmetry problem regularly and in unprecedented detail, while the Internet has opened up sources of information once available only to physicians. Taken together, the information from "old" and "new" media can shame the physician community as a whole into action. This article briefly examines how developments since Arrow that relate to trust and information asymmetry have affected quality of care.

DOLLARS VERSUS DUTY

In Arrow's conception, the patient's trust in the physician substitutes for hard information: "Medical knowledge is so complicated, the information possessed by the physician as to the consequences and possibilities of treatment is necessarily very much greater than that of the patient, or at least so it is believed by both parties" (951). Arrow wrote at a time when the spectacular achievements of post–World War II medicine made the public willing to overlook hints of hypocrisy that hovered around the Hippocratic oath. The tone of a 1954 article in *Fortune* was typical: "The physician, after all, is organized into a guild whose rules require mutual back scratching and forbid face clawing. The physician cannot say aloud that a hospital has weak departments or that a medical school has inadequate equipment" (Maurer 1954: 179).

Arrow thought the paucity of for-profit hospitals signaled patients that providers understood the corrosive effect profit-seeking behavior could have on trust. The physician "cannot act, or at least appear to act, as if he is maximizing his income at every moment of time," Arrow wrote (965). In retrospect, the paucity of for-profit hospitals and obviously profit-seeking physicians may have been linked to lack of opportunity. Medicare and Medicaid took effect on 1 July 1966. The rate of increase in physician fees promptly doubled, causing even the American Medical Association (AMA) to urge restraint (*American Medical News* 1969). The cost of a day in the hospital, which had increased by an average 7 percent annually between 1963 and 1966, climbed 13 percent per year from 1966 to 1969. Between 1965 and 1969, the net income of nonprofit hospitals shot up 76 percent (Stevens 1989: 291).

The problem was not just price, but utilization. Arrow believed professional norms would guarantee appropriate use of services: "By certifying the necessity of a given treatment or the lack thereof, the physician acts as a controlling agent on behalf of the insurance companies." It was "a far from perfect check," he acknowledged, leaving physicians open to overusing "marginal" care for well-insured patients who, for instance, pressed for "more expensive medication." (It was, as we now know, a prescient fear.) Still, Arrow argued that the "moral hazard" (961) danger of overuse would be less on big-ticket items such as hospitalization and surgery, which were "more under the casual inspection of others" than care in the doctor's office (962).

FLIMSY SUPPORT FOR FAITH

Alas, Arrow did not appreciate just how flimsy a barrier that "casual inspection" was. As late as 1960, patient price sensitivity was still a major factor in treatment decisions; half of all care was paid for out of patients' own pockets, and polls showed most patients thought physicians charged too much. That price sensitivity limited physicians' incomes. Then came Medicare and Medicaid. Millions of patients were suddenly granted an insurance card backed by a federal promise to pay whatever fees physicians decided were "usual, customary and reasonable." Price sensitivity was replaced by the "income effect," particularly in regard to big-ticket items, since Medicare and Medicaid coverage was the most comprehensive with regard to inpatient care.

Arrow also underestimated the degree to which the physicians of his time felt economically deprived. Postwar physicians continually fretted "about the cost of running their offices . . . about what plumbers make for house calls and what a liquor dealer's net is compared to their own" (Carter 1958: 74). The spread of insurance offered physicians the opportunity to raise their standard of living, and the culture of medicine strongly discouraged second-guessing of colleagues. As medical sociologist Eliot Freidson (1970: 347) wrote: "When doctors were asked what they would do about a colleague whose behavior violated technical norms of conduct, the most common response was 'nothing.' " Less than one year after Medicare took effect, Congress had to increase the Social Security tax by 25 percent. Within three years, Congress was holding hearings on physician profiteering and fraud. Within five years, a book entitled *How to Avoid Unnecessary Surgery* was a best-seller—even though its physician-author hid behind a pseudonym to protect his surgical career.

Six years after Medicare took effect, Congress made it clear that "just trust me" medicine was unacceptable. The 1972 amendments to the Social Security Act gave Medicare the right to disallow "any costs unnecessary to the *efficient* provision of care" (emphasis added). The same authority was extended automatically to Medicaid (Davis, Anderson, and Rowland 1990). Although some physicians characterized this as "a major government intrusion on medical practice," the legislation was actually a response to the failure of what has been called "professionally dominated pseudo-regulation" (Brennan and Berwick 1996: 72). The private sector responded in a similar manner. By 1988, 95 percent of large corporations had some sort of utilization review in place for their health plans. In effect, insurance company–contracted physicians were now overseeing patient-care physicians.

How could Arrow have foreseen that a profession in which so many individuals were talented and caring could be so corrupt as a group? It would have been like imagining a U.S. president feeling constrained to publicly declare, as Richard Nixon did in 1973, "I am not a crook."

THE KNOWLEDGE PROBLEM

Arrow also did not anticipate the way in which the physician's information advantage would be directly challenged by those paying the bills. He wrote: "The social obligation for best practice is part of the commodity the physician sells, even though it is a part that is not subject to thorough inspection by the buyer" (965). But what if the physician, even unwittingly, does not know what best practice is? The radical answer was for the insurer to help determine the treatment.

The seeds of change in the role of insurance from "check-payer" to "checking-up payer" were planted by decades of revelations about overuse, starting with work on unnecessary hysterectomies in the 1940s. The change reached fruition with the widespread adoption of utilization review noted earlier. Helping speed that change was the publicity given to John E. Wennberg's work on small-area practice variation. In the early 1980s, Wennberg's cataloging of variation more related to physician preference than to patient differences was the subject of attention in publications ranging from *Health Affairs* to the *New York Review of Books*. His findings became a kind of catechism: Appendectomy rates varied threefold. So did the rates of prostate surgery. Hernia surgery rates were about a third higher in the high-rate areas than in the low-rate ones. In town after town, there were large variations in the frequency of hysterectomies, mastectomies, the removal of hemorrhoids, and surgery for other common conditions (Wennberg 1984).

If the physician's decisions were not based on hard scientific fact, what effect does that have on trust? As Wennberg noted, "Inevitably, once you start down the variation path and ask which rate is right, you come up against who's making the decision and whose preferences are being reflected" (Millenson 1997: 163).

Whose preferences should be reflected? The worry by physicians that those who paid the piper would try to call the tune came true — but it came true because the fragility of professional knowledge was exposed by researchers who themselves were often physicians.

Nonetheless, how much influence third-party payers should have over care, and whether their intervention protects or harms patients, have consistently injected issues regarding trust and information asymmetry into public policy debates over issues such as the role of Medicare peer review organizations, the managed care patients' bill of rights, and minimum-stay maternity laws. When are third-party payers protecting patients by trying to influence the decision of the treating physician, and when are they just trying to protect their own and/or the patient's pocketbook? As Arrow noted, "Compromise in quality, even for the purpose of saving the patient money, is to risk an imputation of failure to live up to the social bond" (966). There are credible examples of each type of action. Policy makers, wrote David Mechanic (1994: 219), must confront "the uncertainty of medicine, the extraordinary range of practice variations, and the frequent absence of an objective standard to sustain a specific practice decision. Under such circumstances errors occur in providing both 'too much' and 'too little' care, and each type of error may be exaggerated depending on . . . [what] incentives are operative."

The failure of professional norms as adequate in and of themselves is nowhere more evident than in the area of patient safety. The Harvard Medical Practice study's review of New York State hospital records found an error rate that translated to 180,000 deaths and 1.3 million injuries each year (Brennan et al. 1991). One of the study's authors, Lucian Leape, later estimated that 120,000 of those deaths were due to preventable errors. Yet this study and others in the literature were essentially ignored for years. It took a 1995 *Boston Globe* exposé, reporting the death of *Globe* columnist Betsy Lehman from a medication error at the renowned Dana Farber Cancer Institute, to jump-start accountability for mistakes.

THE VIRTUES OF SHAME

Indeed, public shaming, a phenomenon not touched upon by Arrow, has regularly proved a successful motivator. In the 1970s, congressional hearings on unnecessary tonsillectomies finally helped curb a practice that the medical literature had been urgently denouncing since a study by the American Child Health Association in 1934 (*Cost and Quality of Health Care* 1976). Congressional hearings and news articles on practice variation in the 1980s prompted the first serious professional efforts to address the problem. Similarly, the profession assiduously downplayed the importance of medical errors before the Lehman incident. In late 1994, a *Journal of the American Medical Association* commentary bemoaned: "Concerning medical error and its prevention, the profession has, with rare exceptions, adopted an ostrichlike attitude. . . . Mistakes have been treated as uncommon and atypical, requiring no remedy beyond the traditional incident reports and morbidity and mortality conferences" (Blumenthal 1994: 1867). Within two years, the AMA was trumpeting its sponsorship of the National Patient Safety Foundation. In the same vein, continued media attention to errors helped prompt the 1999 Institute of Medicine report, *To Err Is Human*, and also helped prompt attention to the report by policy makers. That attention, too, led to renewed vows by the profession to accelerate change.

This is not surprising. In *Diffusion of Innovations*, Everett Rogers (1983) writes that the perception of competitive advantage is critical to an innovation's adoption. Public trust, even if eroded, remains the bedrock of the physician's special status; physicians "cannot act, or at least appear to act" as if he or she is indifferent to patient concerns about quality of care. As former *New England Journal of Medicine* editor Jerome Kassirer (2001: 587) acknowledged, acceptance of accountability is now the price of professionalism: "To preserve our remaining autonomy, we must show that we are serious about protecting the public." The critical difference between now and Arrow's time is that the public, through the media, public interest groups, and other mechanisms, is much more willing to make sure that noble professional promises are actually put into practice.

Without public pressure, only small steps take place. Consider the conflict over evidence-based medicine. In Arrow's time, the failure of physicians to keep up with the medical literature was known but not fully appreciated. Today, it is arguably even more difficult to keep up (see the chapter on technological change in this book by Annetine C. Gelijns, Joshua G. Zivin, and Richard R. Nelson), and the failure to do so is well documented.

A RAND metanalysis found that more that 60 percent of patients with chronic disease receive the care indicated by the medical literature, while 20 percent get care that is contraindicated. In acute care, 70 percent get the indicated treatment, but a full 30 percent get contraindicated care (Schuster, McGlynn, and Brook

1998)! Yet despite a series of reports since 1998 by a presidential commission and the Institute of Medicine, public opinion has not been mobilized over the issue of evidence-based medicine. Health insurers, on the other hand, have taken a number of actions.

While, as Arrow wrote, "information, in the form of skilled care, is precisely what is being bought [by the patient] from most physicians" (946), insurers have begun buying something slightly different. One might call it operationalization by the treating physician of the information the insurer has determined to be relevant, be it the correct surgery or the formulary-approved drug regimen. This, of course, brings us back to the above-mentioned discussion over whose interests—clinical or financial—are really being protected. While those arguments still rage, there are intimations that we may be able to move away from this familiar battleground.

PATIENT (AND PAYER) EMPOWERMENT

Regina E. Herzlinger (1996) notes that marketplace accountability depends on what she terms DADS: disclosure, analysis, and dissemination of performance information. That correlates with Arrow's description of "ideal insurance," in which "the patient would actually have no concern with the informational inequality between himself and the physician, since he would only be paying by results anyway, and his utility position would in fact be thoroughly guaranteed" (965).

Insurance company bureaucrats may yet help achieve Arrow's dream. "Bureaucratic administration," wrote famed sociologist Max Weber (1947: 339), "means fundamentally the exercise of control on the basis of knowledge." Insurers have begun using their financial influence to gain control of clinical knowledge that can be used to improve results. Some of these efforts are long-standing: in Arrow's day, few hospitals were accredited. Post-Medicare, almost all are, either by the Joint Commission or a state agency. Other initiatives are newer. Managed care oversight has come to include site visits, examination of clinical records, and evidence about attention to specific clinical processes ranging from bypass surgery to disease management. In addition, health plans are increasingly giving consumers financial incentives to intensify their use of quality-related information when making decisions about care.

What Arnold S. Relman (1988: 1221) called "the Revolt of the Payers" is spawning a generation of accountability activists. While their numbers may yet be modest, their influence is often outsized. For example, the Pacific Business Group on Health has begun to wield payment incentives linked to both service-related and clinical indicators. Meanwhile, a coalition of Fortune 500 companies called the Leapfrog Group is pressing hospitals to install computerized physician order entry systems to prevent drug errors. (At present, only 5 percent of hospitals have such systems.) The group's members, who cover more than 20 million Americans, cite IOM estimates that lost income, lost household production, disability, and health care costs from medical errors that result in harm to patients cost between $17 billion and $29 billion. It is, of course, their money that is being unnecessarily spent.

Individual health plan and provider "report cards" remain in their infancy — an exception is the coronary artery bypass surgery data in New York State and Pennsylvania — but organizations ranging from the academic to the entrepreneurial are working to refine them. For patients, the availability of even rudimentary "scores" offers the beginning of an alternative to relying on "long run . . . experience with the quality of product of a given seller," as Arrow puts it (949 n. 14). For providers, meanwhile, the public availability of negative information that can be seen by peers — even if not used by patients — has proved a surprisingly motivating form of public shaming.

DOING WELL BY DOING GOOD

The more sophisticated providers are actually embracing accountability. In Arrow's time, the lack of information on quality allowed high price to be marketed as a signal of high quality, as Deborah Haas-Wilson notes elsewhere in this book. As the balance of power shifts to purchasers, however, firm-specific information about quality is seen by some providers as protection against undifferentiated price competition.

To give just one example, thirteen of the largest and most prestigious U.S. cancer treatment centers formed a National Comprehensive Cancer Network with the admitted goal of competing for patients by diminishing variations that negatively impact quality of care and health care costs. The impetus, organizers acknowledged, was competition for patients. That, of course, is very similar to Arrow's suggestion about "paying for results." Indeed, one group of cardiac specialists has proposed a "fee-for-benefit" strategy, under which payment would be directly proportional to the expected benefit to the patient of the service provided (Diamond, Denton, and Matloff 1993).

There is a further twist that Arrow did not anticipate: for providers to truly obtain the best results, they must be willing to break down some of the information asymmetry. In Arrow's day, most physicians believed that patients needed only "caring custody," with the physician acting as "rational agent" on the patient's behalf. Sharing information was "inimical to good patient care" (Katz 1984: 207). This model actually has severe drawbacks. Albert Schweitzer once wrote that "we are at our best when we give the doctor who resides within each patient a chance to go to work." A metanalysis by Michael Von Korff and colleagues (1997) supports that belief:

> There is now strong evidence that self-management can improve the process and outcomes of care for chronic illness. . . . Across a wide variety of chronic conditions, co-management has repeatedly led to improvements in: daily functioning; adherence to medical treatments; control of pain and other symptoms; disease severity; [patients'] confidence in ability to manage illness; sense of control over illness; emotional well-being; and health care utilization and costs. . . .

Arrow's "convergent expectations" of physician and patient (966 n. 37) are likely to involve a very different mix of trust and information sharing in the future. Timothy E. Quill and Howard Brody (1996: 763) have proposed "an intense collaboration between patient and physician . . . [that is] informed by both the medical facts and the physician's experience."

None of this will be easy. After all, being sick is, as Mark A. Hall notes in this volume, fundamentally an emotional experience, not an economic one. "Uncertainty in the face of disease and death fosters a compelling need for patients to trust someone and a reciprocal authority among doctors," an editorial in Lancet (1995: 1451) pointed out. "A leap of faith will always be needed. Information does not, and cannot, provide all the answers."

Arrow would very probably concur.

NOTE

This work was supported in part by an Investigator Award for Health Services Research from the Robert Wood Johnson Foundation and by William M. Mercer, Inc.

REFERENCES

Arrow, Kenneth J. 1963. Uncertainty and the Welfare Economics of Medical Care. *American Economic Review* 53(5): 941–973.

Blumenthal, David. 1994. Making Medical Errors into "Medical Treasures." *Journal of the American Medical Association* 272 (23): 1867–1868.

Brennan, Troyen A., Lucian L. Leape, Nan M. Laird, Lee Hebert, A. Russell Localio, Ann G. Lawthers, Joseph P. Newhouse, Paul C. Weiler, and Howard H. Hiatt. 1991. The Incidence of Adverse Events and Negligence in Hospitalized Patients: Results of the Harvard Medical Practice Study I. *New England Journal of Medicine* 324(6): 370–376.

Brennan, Troyen A., and Donald M. Berwick. 1996. *New Rules: Regulation, Markets and the Quality of American Health Care.* San Francisco: Jossey-Bass.

Carter, Richard. 1958. *The Doctor Business*. New York: Doubleday.

Cost and Quality of Health Care: Unnecessary Surgery. 1976. Report by the Subcommittee on Oversight and Investigations of the Committee on Interstate and Foreign Commerce, 94th Cong., 2nd sess. Washington, DC: U.S. Government Printing Office.

Davis, Karen, Gerard F. Anderson, and Diane Rowland, eds. 1990. *Health Care Cost Containment. Johns Hopkins Studies in Health Care Finance and Administration*, Vol. 3. Baltimore, MD: Johns Hopkins University Press.

Diamond, George A., Timothy A. Denton, and Jack M. Matloff. 1993. Fee-for-Benefit: A Strategy to Improve the Quality of Health Care and Control Costs through Reimbursement Incentives. *Journal of the American College of Cardiology* 22(2): 343–352.

Finch Sees No End to Health Cost Rise. 1969. *American Medical News*, 4 August, 11.

Freidson, Eliot. 1970. *Profession of Medicine: A Study of the Sociology of Applied Knowledge*. New York: Dodd, Mead.

Herzlinger, Regina E. 1996. Can Public Trust in Nonprofits and Governments Be Restored? *Harvard Business Review* 74 (March–April): 97–107.

Kassirer, Jerome P. 2001. Pseudoaccountability. *Annals of Internal Medicine* 134(7): 587–590.

Katz, Jay. 1984. *The Silent World of Doctor and Patient*. New York: Free Press.

Leap of Faith over the Data Tap. 1995. *Lancet* 345(8963): 1449–1451.

Maurer, Herrymon. 1954. The M.D.'s Are off Their Pedestal. *Fortune*, February: 139–186.

Mechanic, David. 1994. Trust and Informed Consent to Rationing. *Milbank Quarterly* 72(2): 217–223.

Millenson, Michael L. 1997. *Demanding Medical Excellence: Doctors and Accountability in the Information Age*. Chicago: University of Chicago Press.

Quill, Timothy E., and Howard Brody. 1996. Physician Recommendations and Patient Autonomy: Finding a Balance between Physician Power and Patient Choice. *Annals of Internal Medicine* 125(9): 763–769.

Relman, Arnold S. 1988. Assessment and Accountability: The Third Revolution in Medical Care. *New England Journal of Medicine* 319(18): 1220–1222.

Rogers, Everett M. 1983. *Diffusion of Innovations*. 3d ed. Detroit: Free Press.

Schuster, Mark A., Elizabeth A. McGlynn, and Robert H. Brook. 1998. How Good Is the Quality of Health Care in the United States? *Milbank Quarterly* 76(4): 517–563.

Stevens, Rosemary. 1989. *In Sickness and in Wealth: American Hospitals in the Twentieth Century*. New York: Basic Books.

Von Korff, Michael, Jessie C. Gruman, Judith Schaefer, Susan J. Curry, and Edward H. Wagner. 1997. Collaborative Management of Chronic Illness. *Annals of Internal Medicine* 127(12): 1097–1102.

Weber, Max. 1947. *The Theory of Social and Economic Organizations*. Glencoe, IL: Free Press.

Wennberg, John E. 1984. Dealing with Medical Practice Variations: A Proposal for Action. *Health Affairs* 3(2): 6–32.

PART IV

Social Norms and

Professionalization

PETER J. HAMMER

Arrow's Analysis of Social Institutions:

Entering the Marketplace with Giving Hands?

Frame 10. "Entering the Marketplace with Giving Hands"
You go to the marketplace barefoot, unadorned
Smeared with mud, covered with dust, smiling.
Using no supernatural power
You bring the withered trees to bloom.
— *The Ox-Herding Pictures* (trans. in Levering and Stryk 2000)

The apparent inconsistency between the altruistic intention of "giving hands" and the self-interested behavior normally expected in the marketplace is suggestive of the tensions underlying Arrow's effort to establish an economic role for social institutions. At times, Arrow's (1963: 947) analysis appears to be equal parts economics and mysticism: "I propose here the view that, when the market fails to achieve an optimum state, society will, to some extent at least, recognize the gap, and nonmarket social institutions will arise attempting to bridge it." "I am arguing here that in some circumstances other social institutions will step into the optimality gap, and that the medical-care industry, with its variety of special institutions, some ancient, some modern, exemplifies this tendency." In *The Ox-Herding Pictures*, the seeker is able to enter the marketplace with giving hands in the tenth and final frame of the story only after a long and arduous journey.[1] The seeker must first search for, capture, tame, and train the ox, where the ox and ox-herding are Buddhist metaphors for gaining control over one's own mind. One should expect unvarnished social institutions to be at least as stubborn as the untrained ox. Social institutions may well be able to serve Arrow's ultimate economic role, but such giving hands cannot be taken for granted. Such an outcome is more likely to be the *result of a process* of careful planning and constant struggle. Moreover, in taming the ox, the ox-herder is also changed, raising questions about the effects that Arrow's efforts to rationalize a role for social institutions may have on our understanding of economics itself.

This essay examines Arrow's treatment of social institutions and its implications for policy making. The first section looks at what his 1963 article has to say about social institutions and its specific treatment of the nonmarket roles of licensing, subsidies for medical education, and professional norms. The second section examines the policy-making implications of Arrow's optimality-gap-filling conjecture. From such a perspective, Arrow's thesis is evocative, but substantially underdeveloped. This section explores the difficulties of trying to herd social institutions, both within the domain of welfare economics and in a realm where the composition of "markets" and the metric of welfare economics are themselves contestable. The final section argues why setting workable boundaries between market and nonmarket institutions matters and tentatively explores implications that Arrow's insights may have for some contemporary health policy problems.

ARROW'S ANALYSIS OF SOCIAL INSTITUTIONS

Institutions as Economic Data

One can discern two important insights about social institutions in Arrow's 1963 article: an admonition to economists to take social institutions more seriously and an ambitious conjecture about the possible optimality-gap-filling role of certain nonmarket institutions. In wrestling with the complexities of the second and more controversial proposition, the inherent wisdom of the first should not be overlooked. At a basic level, Arrow issued a wake-up call to economists that social institutions matter and that nonmarket institutions may have important economic content. In his introductory discussion of economic methodology, Arrow contends that "institutional organization and the observable mores of the medical profession" should be included as "data to be used in assessing the competitiveness of the medical care market" (944). This is an important insight that, outside the realm of new institutional economics, has been substantially overlooked by the profession (Williamson 2000).

The Role of Institutions in Arrow's Economic Theory

The call to consider social institutions as economic data highlights the fact that Arrow's analysis of nonmarket institutions is ultimately grounded within his framework of welfare economics and general equilibrium theory. The challenge for Arrow is to reconcile the apparently idiosyncratic features of health care markets (and markets plagued with market failures more generally) with the often seamless world reflected in theoretical economic models. The result is his intriguing if not somewhat heroic conjecture that in the presence of market failures, society "will, to some extent at least, recognize the gap, and nonmarket institutions will arise attempting to bridge it" (947). A few observations are appropriate at the outset. This is predominantly a negative thesis, constructed by Arrow to compensate for the limitations of economic theory. It is not an affirmative story about the role or function of social institutions more generally. Institutions are justifiable, in this account, only to the extent that they are responses to "gaps" and "failures" in markets. As such, social institutions represent a sub-theme within the dominant narrative of welfare economics. For Arrow, this is still an economic story.

Arrow's attempt to establish an economic role for nonmarket institutions might best be understood as an effort to salvage the relevance of the general equilibrium framework in the face of a real world plagued with market failures. The challenge, of course, is whether one can successfully maintain the boundaries of a tight economic analysis once the limitations of markets and the economic theories underlying them have been acknowledged and nonmarket institutions have been called upon to fill the breach. The concern here is the opposite of the one at the heart of the Richard Titmuss–Kenneth Arrow debate over commercialization of blood banks (Titmuss 1971; Arrow 1972; Singer 1973). The issue there was whether markets (commodification of blood) would drive out voluntary, non-market systems of blood supply (altruism). The issue here is whether efforts to integrate social institutions into economic models will somehow corrupt or drive out traditional forms of economic analyses. Arrow might view social institutions as operating like a discrete plug designed to fix a leaking dike, but other possible comparisons come to mind. Introducing social institutions into the framework of general equilibrium analysis might be like introducing an exotic new species into an ecosystem with unpredictable consequences, mixing oil and water or combining matter and antimatter. Even if one stays with the image of the dike, given that market and nonmarket institutions are forged in distinctly different fires and engineered with different gauges, there is no reason to believe that the plug will fit perfectly. There will likely be new leaks around the seal and the need for a commitment to a continual process of patching and fixing or perhaps the invitation for the creation of a new science of engineering altogether.

These are complicated questions, both as a matter of theory and as a matter of practical policy implementation. The questions are complicated if one seeks to take Arrow's conjecture seriously while continuing to operate in the domain of welfare economics. The questions are even more complicated, perhaps hopelessly so, if one goes outside the frame of welfare economics and tries to understand Arrow's contention about nonmarket institutions within a framework that appreciates that "markets" themselves are social institutions, often competing in the political realm with and against the very optimality-gap-filling institutions they seek to absorb. Arrow is not naïve about the difficulties of trying to integrate a role for social institutions within economic theory. He acknowledges that the "process is not necessarily conscious; nor is it uniformly successful in approaching more closely to optimality when the entire range of consequences is considered" (947). Moreover, he appreciates the possibility that nonmarket institutions can interfere with as well as facilitate the functioning of markets, foreseeing the propensity of the "social adjustment towards optimality" to put "obstacles in its own path." (947). Before examining these complicating factors further in the next section of this essay, it is useful to examine the 1963 article's treatment of particular nonmarket interventions to gain a more textured insight into the types of problems and trade-offs that Arrow envisioned as well as ones that he might have failed to perceive.

Arrow's Analysis of Health Care Institutions

■ IN THE BEGINNING, THERE WAS PERFECT COMPETITION As the benchmark for his analysis, Arrow uses the results of a general competitive equilibrium in a world without market failures. In this world, there is no need for social institutions, and there is a range of private organizational forms where particular economic structures do not have a substantial affect on market outcomes. For example, in this ideal world there would be no meaningful difference between fee-for-service forms of provider compensation and systems of provider prepayment (962). There would be no need for government regulation or medical licensing because buyers would be able to accurately assess health care quality for themselves (956). Moreover, in this competitive equilibrium with complete information, the market would likely provide a wide range of quality offerings corresponding to heterogeneous consumer preferences (953).

In a world with market failures, however, one can envision various nonmarket institutions serving plausible economic objectives. The 1963 article addresses government licensing for health care professionals, subsidies for medical education, and a variety of social norms layered over the physician-patient relationship. The economic bases for these "interventions" stem primarily from imperfect and asymmetric information—patients cannot assess the quality of medical services prior to consumption and cannot obtain adequate insurance against the risk of incomplete medical recovery (947). In light of these market failures, the competitive equilibrium will no longer be efficient, and competition will likely produce less than the socially optimum level of medical quality.

■ LICENSING OF HEALTH CARE PROVIDERS Licensing is a standard form of nonmarket intervention in the face of quality uncertainty. The direct effects of licensing are straightforward. Licensing restricts entry, which theoretically decreases the total number of providers but increases the average quality of providers. Arrow highlights the types of trade-offs and distortions that nonmarket intervention can introduce (952–953). Licensing increases the unit costs of production to the extent that higher quality providers can demand higher rates of compensation. Licensing (and other forms of quality standards) tends to produce uniformity in the market. In addition, professional licensing prevents the supply-side substitution of nonlicensed alternatives. For example, under a system of licensing there are tasks that only a physician can perform and others that only a nurse can perform. These restrictions introduce rigidities into the production of medical services. In contrast, an unregulated market would be freer to experiment with the use of physician assistants or the desirability of expanding the role of nurses relative to physicians.

■ SUBSIDIES FOR MEDICAL EDUCATION Arrow is struck by the degree to which nonmarket institutions (medical schools) control both the supply and quality of medical services (953). Educational subsidies will attract higher quality providers who might otherwise go into nonmedical fields. This will increase quality in medical markets but will be associated with a distinct social loss from a general equilibrium perspective (956). The subsidy attracts high-quality individuals whose talents may be socially more valuable in nonmedical pursuits. In addition, subsidies can produce an oversupply of physicians, although this possibility is checked by limitations imposed on the number of medical students accepted (rationing). Significantly, the combination of subsidies and restricted admissions affords medical schools substantial discretion in defining the composition of medical services. "Quality" in this sector of the economy, in terms of *who* practices medicine and the substance of their training, is established largely outside the domain of market control (953).

Wearing the hat of the welfare economist, Arrow's instincts are to make medical education more responsive to market incentives — calling for an end to educational subsidies and a move to a system of insured loans where government action would be limited to ensuring the proper functioning of credit markets (955–956). Arrow reacts negatively to the discretion that resides in professional education and seeks to reestablish forms of market control and market incentives. Those trained in disciplines other than economics might look at the social role of this discretion quite differently (Starr 1982). Even Arrow, who elsewhere envisions a legitimate institutional role for professional norms, may underappreciate the need for potentially elaborate social mechanisms (such as professionally dominated systems of professional education) to help shape and police those social practices.

Arrow's treatment of educational subsidies illustrates an interesting phenomenon. When the analytic frame is tightly defined around traditional economic concerns, the policy prescription is often straightforward: end educational subsidies and rely on market incentives. The wider the social frame is defined and the more textured the stories explaining the role and function of nonmarket institutions become, the more divorced the rhetoric and analysis becomes from standard welfare economics. The proper policy prescription is also less clear. In addition, one must begin to struggle with questions that go beyond traditional economics, such as nonmarket forms of accountability. How will the economic power (discretion) residing in medical schools as a result of subsidies and rationing be exercised? Who will make these decisions? How will the decision makers be held accountable? Market actors are held accountable to dollar-backed consumer preferences, but what forces will influence or control medical school administrators?

■ PROFESSIONALISM Arrow's assessment of physician norms is less precise and more deferential than his economic analysis of any other aspect of medical markets. Arrow views professional norms, particularly those facilitating trust, as a response to a novel form of market failure—the inability to craft and sell an insurance policy that will cover the risk that a patient will suffer a delayed or incomplete recovery once medically treated (965). This risk is compounded by the profound informational asymmetries that define the parties' general relationship. In response, he postulates that trust in the context of the physician-patient relationship becomes a surrogate form of "guarantee" (a promise to use best efforts) and that "trust" itself becomes an integral part of the commodity being bought and sold (965).

How one markets "trust" in a competitive economy is a difficult question. Arrow is of two minds on this subject. Part of his analysis focuses on information, reputation, and signaling devices in a manner that anticipates subsequent developments in the game theory literature.[2] Other parts of his analysis, however, tend largely to defer, without substantial explanation, to the mere existence of professional institutions that would functionally appear to facilitate or enforce behavior consistent with the existence of trust. In some areas these approaches can overlap. Professional standards, peer review, and professional sanctioning (to the extent that it takes place) can facilitate reputational mechanisms. These professional actions convey valuable information to the market. In most areas, however, physician norms do not fit easily into an economic analysis. Some of these norms may serve second-order economic ends. For example, aspects of the physician's professional persona may have the effect of reinforcing the public perception that doctors are trustworthy. Arrow suggests that the popular belief that physicians were engaged in price discrimination to subsidize charity care is consistent with this purpose (949–950). Ironically, this same concern over public image may lead physicians to fail to economize on treatment, even when it is in the patient's best interest, for fear of undermining their credibility in the patient's eyes (963). Unfortunately, once one moves beyond simple reputational stories, it is difficult for economists to tell when professional norms are consistent with optimality-gap-filling objectives or when such norms serve other objectives. Arrow makes little effort to parse economically desirable from potentially undesirable or even expressly anticompetitive forms of professional restraints.

Summary

Arrow's analysis of specific nonmarket institutions in health care illustrates some interesting and quite diverse tendencies. The analysis of licensing provides a careful treatment of the distortions that nonmarket institutions can have and highlights the types of trade-offs that policy makers must make in choosing between market and nonmarket institutions. The analysis of medical education illustrates the tendency of traditional welfare economics to marginalize social institutions (calling for an end of subsidies and a return to market incentives), and suggests the complexities involved with broadening the policy frame. (How should we view subsidies if we view the discretion created by combinations of subsidies and rationing as important to instilling social norms?) Significantly though, Arrow's treatment of professional norms illustrates the dangers of too much deference to social institutions. Once an "economic" rationale for professional norms is provided, little attention is given to further questions such as the proper scope of professional deference or the possibility of professional autonomy being abused and manipulated for the private benefit of the professional group.

POLICY MAKING: THE DIFFICULTIES OF HERDING SOCIAL INSTITUTIONS

How should one approach policy making if one takes Arrow's optimality-gap-filling conjecture seriously? The challenge is to identify plausible nonmarket institutions, consider the idiosyncratic problems associated with the interaction between market and nonmarket institutions, and determine how to monitor and mediate the contested boundary between markets and nonmarket institutions over time. This section first explores how this might be approached within the frame of welfare economics; it then discusses how such analyses might proceed within a broader context.

Herding within the Domain of Welfare Economics

■ MARKET FAILURES AND MULTIPLE EQUILIBRIA Market failures substantially complicate economic analysis. Given the satisfaction of appropriate conditions, Arrow and Gerhard Debreu's early work demonstrated both that a general competitive equilibrium will be efficient and that such an equilibrium will be unique (Arrow and Debreu 1954). Market failures undermine not only the efficiency attributes of competition, but also the resulting equilibrum's claim to uniqueness. As a result, policy makers will most likely face multiple sets of competing equilibria, none of which will be efficient in the strict Pareto sense. Market failures also introduce complicated second-best concerns (Lipsey and Lancaster 1956–1957). From this perspective, Arrow's appeal to nonmarket institutions can be seen as an innovative attempt to circumvent second-best problems through nonmarket means. But how can nonmarket institutions accomplish this task?

It is difficult to envision just how market and nonmarket institutions are supposed to interact with each other. Prices in the general equilibrium context govern the interaction between markets. There is no analogous mechanism governing the internal conduct of nonmarket institutions or the interaction between markets and nonmarket institutions. Moreover, there is no necessary reason to expect that the incentives of nonmarket actors will be properly aligned with social incentives or that the interaction between market and nonmarket institutions will be seamless in important respects. Recalling our earlier analogy, the plug in the dike is likely to leak around the edges. The possible misalignments between market and nonmarket institutions are complicated further once a temporal dimension is layered over the relationship. Markets will change over time, as will the underlying nature of market failures and their economic consequences. As markets and market failures change, so will the nature of Arrow's "optimality gaps" and the composition of desired nonmarket institutions.

Unfortunately, market and nonmarket institutions are likely to possess very different aptitudes for being able to recognize and adapt to changes. This is compounded by the fact that changes come in the form of inertial evolutionary developments as well as responses to exogenous shocks. Nonmarket institutions are likely to evolve in a relatively more rigid and path-dependent manner than private markets. Nonmarket institutions are also likely to respond in ways that will tend to further their own self-preservation and continued survival. To the extent that nonmarket institutions enjoy relatively autonomous sources of political and economic power, these tendencies will be exacerbated.

■ MENUS OF DISCONTINUOUS CHOICES   The combination of market failures and the possible rigidities of nonmarket institutions produces numerous challenges for policy makers. To illustrate, it is useful to emphasize one aspect of this puzzle that is often overlooked or underappreciated. In the absence of a unique, Pareto-efficient equilibrium, policy makers will face a menu of choices, each choice corresponding to a distinct set of market-nonmarket institutions, each choice representing a distinct set of advantages and disadvantages, and each choice reflecting a different possible equilibrium. These are lumpy choices. In this setting, fairly stark trade-offs between mutually desired goals are almost unavoidable. Some of these trade-offs are directly apparent, others are necessary by implication. Economic models that make sufficiently strong assumptions provide policy makers with ranges of continuous choices—the ability to get a little more of this by sacrificing a little more of that on the margin. When these models break down, policy makers are often faced with discontinuous choices — they can have all of this or all of that, but not some adjustable mix of the two.

Some examples from Arrow's article and from health policy help illustrate this point. First, price discrimination, as discussed by Arrow, might be a socially desirable means of cross-subsidizing services for the poor through higher charges to the wealthy. Price discrimination, however, cannot take place in the presence of active price competition. It requires the types of restraints traditionally found in medical markets, such as prohibitions on professional advertising. One can have the benefits of price competition or informal cross-subsidies, but not both. A choice must be made. Second, the objectives of quality standards via licensing and consumer choice come into conflict. Licensing tends toward uniformity with all individuals consuming comparable types of products or services. Well-functioning markets, on the other hand, tend to provide a range of differentiated options in the face of diverse consumer preferences. Standardization to ensure product quality must be "purchased" at the expense of differentiation and consumer choice. Finally, the objectives of price competition and nonprice competition can come into conflict. Most managed competition proposals were predicated upon a commonly defined benefits package (Enthoven 1993; Glied 1997: 170–175). Uniform benefits facilitate cross-plan comparisons and simplify the information that consumers must process in making decisions. Competition between plans is consciously channeled along price instead of nonprice dimensions. Enhanced price competition, however, is obtained only by sacrificing forms of nonprice competition and policy differentiation.

■ POLICY-MAKING HEURISTICS How does one make policy in this type of environment? What types of nonmarket institutions should be embraced? How should they be defined? In the end, one collapses back to a version of Charles E. Lindblom's (1959) "muddling through" as extrapolated to an Arrowinian world of market and nonmarket institutions. Policy makers must ask and re-ask the following types of questions: Is a particular nonmarket institution still welfare enhancing? Is one set of nonmarket institutions better than another set? Are various midcourse corrections necessary given changes in the underlying economic environment? At what point is it necessary to fundamentally change the public-private nature of the regime governing a sector such as health care? What are the appropriate policy heuristics for determining whether market or nonmarket forces should prevail in instances of policy conflict?

Elsewhere, I have explored how courts and legislatures working within a framework of welfare economics might proceed to determine when market failures justify forms of nonmarket intervention (Hammer 2000a, 2000b). The factors identified there are equally useful in assessing the balance between market and nonmarket institutions as envisioned by Arrow. First, the existence of identifiable market failures establishes a domain where such nonmarket institutions are economically plausible, although some might rightfully point out how concepts such as market failures and externalities are themselves highly manipulable (Herzog 2000). Second, one must be sensitive to the possibility of special interest co-option. The policy maker needs to be able to sort the public from the purely private interest. Proof that a particular set of market-nonmarket institutions resulted in an increase in social welfare in comparison to markets working alone (static efficiency) helps address this concern. Third, one must be concerned with the effects of nonmarket institutions from an evolutionary perspective (dynamic efficiency). This is a difficult question to answer, but an important one to ask. The policy maker should be reasonably satisfied that a particular constellation of market and nonmarket institutions will be able to efficiently adapt over time and respond to changes in the environment. Finally, inquiry should be made into whether there are less restrictive alternatives to the proposed role for the nonmarket institution and whether the nonmarket intervention is appropriately narrow in scope. These considerations are not self-defining, nor do they necessarily lead to clear and unambiguous answers, but they help frame discussion and start to channel the welfare analysis in a constructive direction.

Herding beyond the Domain of Welfare Economics

■ METAINSTITUTIONAL COMPLEXITIES The above analysis has operated within Arrow's framework of welfare economics, where it is natural to distinguish between markets and social institutions. If one acknowledges, however, that in various ways markets are also social institutions, yet another level of complexity must be layered onto the discussion. Economists may respond that of course markets are institutions and of course such institutions are embedded in a deeper social context, but that such embeddedness is sufficiently entrenched to treat the existence of markets and their boundaries as exogenous for purposes of economic analysis. In many settings, like certain commodities markets, this may be a sufficient reply. In health care, however, the role and scope of markets as a means of resource allocation is contestable. The role of markets as opposed to forms of nonmarket planning has varied substantially over time, and the current backlash against managed care illustrates the continued contestability of markets in health care.

Conceding the social dimensions of markets does not make all aspects of markets or nonmarket institutions equally contestable. Oliver E. Williamson (2000) presents a useful schematic suggesting different levels of embeddedness of markets and institutions. Norms, traditions, and informal institutions are the most embedded, proceeding next to the formal rules governing the institutional environment (property law, government bureaucracies), to governance issues determining the play of the game (rules of contract and cooperation), and finally to practices controlling the specific allocation of resources. Within this framework, not all aspects of market and nonmarket institutions pass directly through the political process. Indeed, the political process itself operates against the backdrop of informal institutions, norms, and customs. Accordingly, analysis of issues such as the role and function of trust in the physician-patient relationship might well proceed quite differently from an analysis of issues such as licensing laws.

■ IMPLICATIONS FOR POLICY ANALYSIS Appreciating the fact that markets are themselves contingent social institutions leads to a number of related insights. Rather than being taken as immutable units, the composition of markets is subject to negotiation and change. Moreover, the lines separating market and nonmarket institutions are often endogenously determined. Appreciating this endogeneity leads to concerns over possible forms of strategic behavior. Actors meet one another both in the marketplace and in the political arena. Consequently, sources of political power and economic power are interrelated. This provides an alternative explanation for the perceived rigidity of certain institutions. Rigidity may not simply be an artifact of the transactions costs of change and the misalignment of incentives; it may also be in the political and economic self-interest of constituents who are benefited by such rigidity because it forestalls developments they view as disadvantageous.

Adding a political dimension to the economic analysis provides interesting possibilities as well as complications. Markets are not the only means of aggregating individual preferences and making allocative decisions. Arrow himself acknowledges a legitimate role for government in the face of market failures (947). Some health care problems may be more amenable to political rather than economic decision making. At a minimum, the option of utilizing the political process in lieu of markets provides an additional point of reference for conducting comparative institutional analyses.[3] The decision-making heuristics identified in the discussion of welfare economics are largely applicable to policy making in this realm as well. One should still be concerned about defining the domain of legitimate justifications for displacing markets with nonmarket institutions, constructing a functional screen for identifying conduct that is in the public interest, maintaining a sensitivity to notions of dynamic efficiency and the adaptability of nonmarket institutions, and, finally, hedging against the possible overbreadth of nonmarket interventions. The primary differences are that in this setting the underlying metric of welfare economics is itself contestable and up for grabs, and an appreciation of the endogeneity of the line between markets and nonmarket institutions heightens the need to be concerned about strategic behavior. Social institutions can be used not only as a means of filling the optimality gap, they can also serve as fortresses from which even the socially productive evolution of markets can be forestalled, if such evolution is contrary to the interests of those controlling prevailing institutional structures.

CONTEMPORARY POLICY RELEVANCE OF MARKET AND NONMARKET INSTITUTIONS

Striking the wrong balance between market and nonmarket institutions can be costly. Few people would defend the totality of health care institutions that existed in 1963 as being consistent with Arrow's optimality-gap-filling conjecture. In antitrust parlance, even if some of the nonmarket institutions served legitimate economic purposes, many aspects of the professional domination of medical services were not necessary to such ends, nor would many traditional nonmarket restraints constitute the least restrictive means of pursuing such objectives. Developments since 1963 illustrate some of the dangers of misalignments between markets and nonmarket institutions interacting over time.

Painting with admittedly broad strokes, the argument is as follows: In the four decades since Arrow's article was written, we have been confronted with studies documenting widespread variations in clinical practices (substantially unrelated to quality of care concerns) and a surprising lack of scientific evidence to justify many routine clinical procedures (Wennberg and Gittelsohn 1982). The rate of technological innovation, dissemination, and obsolescence in health care proceeds at tremendously high levels (Newhouse 1992). Some estimates suggest that technology-driven inflation accounts for a substantial percentage of historic health care costs (Peden and Freeland 1995). Studies comparing heath care expenditures and health care outcomes among nations raise serious questions about whether the United States is getting its money's worth for the health care dollar. The United States spends far more than most other countries on health care, yet U.S. health outcomes lag behind other countries in terms of a number of important health indicators (Anderson et al. 2000). Each of these factors should give us reason to pause and seriously consider what forces have brought us to this point.

Discussion needs to move beyond a simple market versus nonmarket distinction, which is often overly simplistic and ordinarily misleading. Comparative analysis of health care systems provides concrete insight into the notion of multiple possible equilibria and competing sets of market-nonmarket institutions. Highly defensible systems can be constructed using combinations of building blocks from each domain. What is more important (and what arguably has been missing from U.S. health policy) is a commitment to intrasystem rationality. A fruitful research agenda would be to explore the ways in which a lack of policy consistency, coupled with misalignments between market and nonmarket institutions (compounded over time), have contributed to many of the health care problems we face today. Some of the most important challenges facing health care policy makers involve the need to impose greater rationality on patterns of clinical practice and processes of technological innovation.

Within Arrow's framework, social institutions and professional norms are instrumentally employed to serve specific economic/policy objectives. They are second-best responses to identifiable market failures. A little reflection on the part of policy makers will often reveal that there are other conceivable market-nonmarket substitutes that could further similar objectives. We are not necessarily stuck with the nonmarket institutions that we inherit, nor can we take for granted the fact that social institutions that once served appropriate optimality-gap-filling roles will necessarily evolve over time in ways that continue to serve such functions. From the standpoint of policy making, there is a need for more vigilance in monitoring the role of nonmarket institutions and for reassessing the boundaries separating market from nonmarket institutions over time. Social institutions can provide the market giving hands, but without active oversight there is no guarantee that the efficiency-enhancing role of such institutions will be realized. The ox must still be tamed and trained, and the process of herding never really ends.

NOTES

1   *The Ox-Herding Pictures* is a series of ten images and poems dating back to twelfth-century China illustrating the Buddhist path to enlightenment. The ten frames consist of searching for the ox; seeing the tracks; glimpsing the ox; catching the ox; taming the ox; returning home on the back of the ox; the ox is forgotten, the ox-herder is still present; herder and ox both forgotten; reverting to the origin and returning to the source; and entering the marketplace with giving hands (Sheng-Yen 2001: 205–222). The tenth frame has been translated in different ways, described as entering the marketplace with open hands, "helping hands," and "bliss-bestowing hands" as well as giving hands. The image of "giving hands" stands in sharpest contrast with the self-interested conduct ordinarily associated with markets and was hence chosen for this essay.

2   Arrow discusses the experience nature of medical services and the role that consumer learning over time can play to influence provider behavior (949 n. 14). Similarly, Arrow examines the role of professional norms and nonprofit status as signaling devices to buyers (965). These devices may also be seen as attempts by providers to precommit to forms of nonopportunistic behavior. Finally, Arrow discusses the role that clear behavioral norms can play in facilitating trade by establishing the necessary focal points for the convergence of provider/patient expectations (966 n. 37). Each of these mechanisms suggests ways of generating trust through self-enforcing market or contractual mechanisms. In discussions involved with the presentation of the articles in this volume, Professor Arrow suggested that he finds many game-theoretic explana-

tions for trust incomplete, arguing that the type of trust necessary for trade goes deeper than these models imply. One also gets a sense of a belief in a deeper source of these norms when reading Arrow's reply to Pauly on the topic of moral hazard (Arrow 1968; Pauly 1968).

3   The example of a uniform benefits package under managed competition is again illustrative. These proposals relegated the definition of the contents of such a package to a political rather than a market process. The wisdom of such proposals depends upon one's views of the relative merits of markets versus politics in determining the type of health care benefits individuals should be entitled to. These types of institutional choices, however, have implications that go beyond the present moment. Not only are market and political processes likely to converge on different initial packages, markets and political processes are also likely to make different types of choices about whether and when to adopt new medical treatments and technologies in the future (as well as to send different types of signals to the research and development sector regarding the profitability of particular types of R&D). The evolution of the health care sector is also likely to differ, perhaps substantially, under the two competing regimes. An appreciation of such prospective differences should feed back in some fashion to inform the initial determination.

REFERENCES

Anderson, G. F., J. Hurst, P. S. Hussey, and M. Jee-Hughes. 2000. Health Spending and Outcomes: Trends in OECD Countries, 1960–1998. *Health Affairs* 19(3): 150–157.

Arrow, K. J. 1963. Uncertainty and the Welfare Economics of Medical Care. *American Economic Review* 53(3): 941–973.

———. 1968. The Economics of Moral Hazard: Further Comment. *American Economic Review* 58(3): 537–538.

———. 1972. Gifts and Exchanges. *Philosophy and Public Affairs* 1(4): 343–362.

Arrow, K. J., and G. Debreu. 1954. Existence of an Equilibrium for a Competitive Economy. *Economica* 22(3): 265–290.

Enthoven, A. C. 1993. The History and Principles of Managed Competition. *Health Affairs* 12(suppl.): 24–48.

Glied, S. A. 1997. *Chronic Conditions: Why Health Reform Fails.* Cambridge: Harvard University Press.

Hammer, P. J. 2000a. Antitrust beyond Competition: Market Failures, Total Welfare, and the Challenge of Intramarket Second-Best Tradeoffs. *Michigan Law Review* 98(4): 849–925.

———. 2000b. Medical Antitrust Reform: Arrow, Coase and the Changing Structure of the Firm. University of Michigan Law and Economics Working Paper no. 00–012.

Herzog, D. 2000. Externalities and Other Parasites. *University of Chicago Law Review* 67(3): 895–923.

Levering, M., and L. Stryk. 2000. *Zen: Images, Texts, and Teachings.* New York: Artisan.

Lindblom, C. E. 1959. The Science of "Muddling Through." *Public Administration Review* 19(2): 79–88.

Lipsey, R. G., and R. K. Lancaster. 1956–1957. The General Theory of Second Best. *Review of Economic Studies* 24(1): 11–32.

Newhouse, J. P. 1992. Medical Care Costs: How Much Welfare Loss? *Journal of Economic Perspectives* 6(3): 3–21.

Pauly, M. V. 1968. The Economics of Moral Hazard: Comment. *American Economic Review* 58(3): 531–537.

Peden, E. A., and M. S. Freeland. 1995. A Historical Analysis of Medical Spending Growth, 1960–1993. *Health Affairs* 14 (summer): 235–247.

Sheng-Yen, C. 2001. *Hoofprint of the Ox.* New York: Oxford University Press.

Singer, P. 1973. Altruism and Commerce: A Defense of Titmuss against Arrow. *Philosophy & Public Affairs* 2(3): 312–320.

Starr, P. 1982. *The Social Transformation of American Medicine.* New York: Basic Books.

Titmuss, R. M. 1971. *The Gift Relationship: From Human Blood to Social Policy.* New York: Pantheon.

Wennberg, J. E., and A. Gittelsohn. 1982. Variations in Medical Care among Small Areas. *Scientific American* 246(4): 120–133.

Williamson, O. E. 2000. The New Institutional Economics: Taking Stock, Looking Ahead. *Journal of Economic Literature* 38 (September): 595–613.

M. GREGG BLOCHE

■ *The Market for Medical Ethics*

At the core of Kenneth Arrow's classic 1963 essay on medical uncertainty is a claim that has failed to carry the day among economists. This claim—that physician adherence to an anti-competitive ethic of fidelity to patients and suppression of pecuniary influences on clinical judgment pushes medical markets toward social optimality—has won Arrow near-iconic status among medical ethicists (and many physicians). Yet conventional wisdom among health economists, including several participants in this symposium, holds that this claim is either naïve or outdated. Health economists admire Arrow's article for its path-breaking analysis of market failures resulting from information asymmetry, uncertainty, and moral hazard. But his suggestion that anticompetitive professional norms can compensate for these market failures is at odds with economists' more typical treatment of professional norms as monopolistic constraints on contractual possibility.

Arrow acknowledged that all indusrywide norms of conduct limit the options for economic exchange (Arrow 1972). For some commentators, the fact of such limits is proof enough of the perniciousness of professional norms from an efficiency perspective. Richard Posner (1993) treats the common "ideology" of guild members concerning matters of quality and craftsmanship as a tool for cartelizing production in order to serve the self-interest of members.[1] Guild *ideology*, in this view, deceives both its own adherents and the public concerning members' furtherance of their own interests at society's expense, and guild norms that express this ideology do not deserve the law's deference. To the contrary, suppression of competition through guild norms ought to be the object of legal attack.

Nowhere did Arrow deny that physician adherence to the ethic of fidelity to patients and suppression of pecuniary influences at the bedside serves the medical profession's self-interest. Indeed, implicit in Arrow's account is a short-term/long-term tradeoff: physicians resist bedside financial temptation case-by-case[2] in order to reap reputational (and financial) rewards from the profession's perceived adherence to this ethic. The norm of fidelity to patients is, by this account, a product of the marketplace. Arrow and critics who view this and other professional norms as pernicious from a social welfare perspective differ not over whether these norms reflect professional self-interest, but over whether they yield welfare gains or welfare losses by comparison with a hypothetical absence of such self-constraint.

This difference of opinion is not merely academic. The question of how health care policy and law should treat professional ethics is key to a variety of ongoing legal controversies. To the extent that health policy and law strive toward optimality in resource allocation, the social welfare impact of professional norms, including the ethic of fidelity to patients and suppression of pecuniary influences at the bedside, is an important public policy matter.

The effect of professional ethics norms on social welfare is most visibly an issue in antitrust law. Over the past twenty-five years, antitrust doctrine has come to treat professional norms with skepticism, as so-called naked restraints on trade (see Havighurst in this book). Yet ethics norms have survived antitrust scrutiny through a variety of doctrines that enables defenders of these norms to argue that they advance consumer welfare or other public purposes,[3] and the U.S. Supreme Court recently signaled an increased willingness to entertain such arguments.[4]

The implications of professional ethics norms for social welfare are at issue in other areas of law marked by tension between these norms and the market paradigm. Conflicts over the lawfulness of financial rewards to physicians for frugal practice, the authority of treating physicians versus health plan managers to determine medical need, and the supervisory powers of plan managers over clinical practitioners pit professional norms against immediate market pressures.

If the goal of health care policy and law is to maximize the social welfare yield from medical spending, consideration of the place of professional ethics norms in health policy requires that we pose three questions. First, how can we distinguish between professional norms that enhance social welfare (even if "anticompetitive" in some sense[5]) and therefore merit our deference (and perhaps even some legal protection) and norms that reduce welfare? Second, when we conclude that a professional norm is socially undesirable, how should we go about choosing among regulatory and legal strategies and deference to markets as means for dissolving the norm? Third, when we conclude that a professional norm is socially desirable, how should we go about preserving it? Should we defer to market outcomes — and perhaps shield select forms of professional collusion from antitrust intervention? Or should we defend this norm actively, through legal and regulatory intervention?

This essay focuses on the first of these three questions, since it is the subject of Arrow's article. From a public policy perspective, however, the second and third are just as important. It is hardly obvious that a socially undesirable norm should be targeted by judges or regulators rather than left to wither in the marketplace; nor is it clear that a socially desirable norm needs legal or regulatory support to survive.

ARROW AND THE MARKET FOR MEDICAL ETHICS

The idea that actors' unrestrained pursuit of self-interest sometimes reduces social welfare was well accepted among economists in 1963, as Arrow noted in his article. But economists were disinclined to acknowledge that ungoverned self-interest, without negative externalities or monopoly power, could yield socially suboptimal results. The notion that, absent externalities, competing producers without market power might sometimes better advance social welfare by suppressing their self-interest boldy challenged conventional wisdom.

Arrow's explanation for the ethic of suppression of self-interest in medicine put information problems front and center. Indeed, from the perspective of academic economists, Arrow's principal contribution in this article was his path-breaking analysis of information asymmetry and uncertainty as causes of market failure — and thus as reason for restraints on economic actors' pursuit of self-interest. Arrow argued, in brief, that patients' uncertainty about the effectiveness of medical care is a barrier to the marketability of medical services. The classic market response to uncertainty and risk, he noted, is the offering of *insurance* against undesired outcomes, but for an array of technical reasons, a market for insurance *for the outcomes of medical treatment* has not developed and is unlikely to emerge soon.

Without such insurance, Arrow contended, consumers who might benefit from medical care but are disinclined to bear the risk of poor results will demand medical services at socially suboptimal levels. Here is where the professional ethic of fidelity to patients and suppression of self-interest comes in. By making medical advice more trustworthy, Arrow suggested, this ethic compensates to some degree for consumers' uncertainty about clinical outcomes and for their inability to purchase insurance against disappointing results. It thereby moves clinical demand toward socially optimal levels.

The means by which this professional ethic is forged and sustained were nebulous in Arrow's account. Arrow proposed that "when the market fails to achieve an optimal state, society will . . . recognize the gap, and nonmarket social institutions will arise attempting to bridge it" (947). He pointed to government as the classic example of such an institution[6] but held that "in some circumstances other social institutions will step into the optimality gap" (947) and that medicine's anticompetitive norms and organizational forms are illustrative. Arrow, however, offered no theory to explain how *nonmarket* bridging occurs—to explain who identifies optimality gaps (based on what incentives) and how, consciously or unconsciously, these gaps are closed without the intervention of market forces.

Later in his article, however, Arrow offered a different account, along more classic economic lines. Having presented the ethic of fidelity to patients and suppression of self-interest as a nonmarket response to consumer ignorance and uncertainty, he recharacterized professional commitment to this ethic as, in essence, a long-term marketing strategy. Physicians make this commitment in order to win their patients' confidence: thus this ethic is "part of the commodity the physician *sells*" (965; emphasis added).

Arrow's parallel, market-based explanation presents physicians' commitments to professional standards of care, suppression of self-interest, and avoidance of "the obvious stigmata of profit-maximizing" as signals of their "intentions to act as thoroughly in the buyer's behalf as possible" (965). Because prospective buyers respond to these signals by purchasing medical care at increased levels, professional norms that reinforce such conduct and commitment are in physicians' *long-term*, collective self-interest. These professional norms, in other words, reflect and reinforce a rational trade-off strategy that forgoes short-term opportunities for exploitation of consumer ignorance in order to win consumer trust and to thereby increase consumer demand over the long term. And because consumer reliance on medical advice yields net benefits (something Arrow was inclined to presume but that current commentators tend to question), physicians' anticompetitive professional norms also enhance social welfare, Arrow held.

This hard-nosed account of physicians' anti-competitive norms has fared better over time with health policy commentators than has Arrow's almost-mystical story of inexorable optimality-seeking by "nonmarket social institutions." The rise of public choice theory—and of cynicism about the public-regarding potential of government in particular and other social institutions more generally—created an unfavorable intellectual climate for the proposition that nonmarket institutions can do other than function as venues for pursuit of private self-interest. Public choice theory denies that anything about the operation of these institutions tends toward social optimality, except by coincidence. Arrow's failure to propose a mechanism in support of his contrary claim that such institutions detect and bridge optimality gaps may have made this claim more difficult to sustain in the face of public choice theory's prevailing wind. On the other hand, Arrow's market-based account of trust-inducing professional norms as "part of the commodity the physician sells" has taken root among scholars of health care law and policy. Not only did this interpretation fit the fundamental economics premise of pursuit of self-interest by rational actors; it squared with historical accounts of the medical profession's success, during the first half of the twentieth century, at suppressing practitioners' commercial behavior, committing them to higher standards of care, and thereby winning greater consumer confidence (Starr 1982).[7]

ARROW'S DOUBTS

Although Arrow's account of physicians' anticompetitive norms stressed their social welfare–enhancing effects, he cautioned that noncompetitive physician behavior ensuing from adherence to these norms could interfere with the pursuit of optimality. "The social adjustment towards optimality," he wrote, "puts obstacles in its own path" (947). With this caveat, Arrow acknowledged a thing often discounted in economics commentary: that institutions and mores understandable in functionalist terms, as adjustments tending toward efficiency, can exhibit adaptive inflexibilities, or structural constraints,[8] that reduce social welfare. Such constraints can arise from human cognitive shortcomings, institutional rigidities, and the coherence of systems of social and moral belief (Bloche 2002).

Arrow said nothing in his article about the ways by which the medical market's anticompetitive features, including the professional ethic of suppression of self-interest and the institutions that reflect and reinforce this ethic, might interfere with progress toward optimality. Such interference was, for Arrow, a footnote to his story about the overall social welfare gains from this professional ethic. Yet during the generation or so that followed publication of Arrow's essay, this footnote became one of the principal storylines in health care economics and law, eclipsing in influence Arrow's case for the social welfare benefits of anticompetitive professional norms.

THE RISING TIDE OF SKEPTICISM

Since the 1970s, a growing number of commentators from across the ideological spectrum has cast the ethics of the medical profession as a program for self-interested restraint of trade. Arrow himself, as I noted earlier, acknowledged that all industrywide behavioral norms restrain trade by putting some contractual alternatives off limits (Arrow 1972). Whether a given restraint on commerce reduces (or enhances) social welfare is, as Arrow realized, a separate question. But some commentators seem to presume that mere "discovery" that an ethical norm limits buyers' and sellers' options (and benefits sellers) is enough to establish the norm's social undesirability.

More sophisticated critics of professional ethics offer powerful arguments for the inefficiency of particular anticompetitive norms, including prohibitions against advertising, price competition, and contractual lowering of clinical standards of care (Blumstein 1994; Havighurst 1995). These critics tie the norms they target to lost opportunities for consumers to learn more about the quality and prices of alternative providers, to obtain equivalent services more cheaply, and to act on their own cost-benefit trade-off preferences by choosing lower levels of care at lower cost. These arguments have had large real world impact. Invoking antitrust law, courts have rejected collaborative price-setting and ethical proscriptions against professional advertising as impermissible restraints on trade. A variety of legal protections for professional self-governance, including the rule against the "corporate practice of medicine," have fallen by the wayside, and use of financial incentives to both promote and deter physician utilization of clinical services has become widespread.

Consideration of the social welfare implications of professional norms can now draw upon a new body of research and scholarship that aspires to explain the origins and persistence of informal, nonlegal norms in myriad settings. Robert Ellickson's (1991) theory of welfare-maximizing norms—his hypothesis that "members of a close-knit group develop and maintain norms whose content serves to maximize the aggregate welfare that members obtain in their workaday affairs with one another"—is arguably consistent with portrayals of physicians' ethical norms as self-serving restraints on trade. Ellickson and his followers have studied a variety of close-knit groups, from Shasta County cattlemen in California to diamond traders in New York, identifying governing, nonlegal norms and offering persuasive arguments for these norms' efficiency within these communities. The medical profession to some degree resembles these close-knit groups, which sustain their nonlegal norms through peer feedback, gossip, and reputational sanctions. But divisions among physicians arising from specialization, geography, status, and institutional arrangements make sustenance of self-serving norms through informal feedback, gossip, and sanctions more problematic. These informal behavior control mechanisms are crucial to close-knit groups' ability to maintain norms that maximize members' aggregate welfare, in Ellickson's account. Groups insufficiently cohesive for these mechanisms to work thus fall outside the ambit of Ellickson's model.

There is good reason to suspect that the medical profession has become less cohesive since publication of Arrow's article. Physicians practice today within much more diverse institutional and financial contexts. Multispecialty group practices, myriad arrangements with health plans and provider networks, and highly variable economic incentives exist alongside the solo and small group fee-for-service model that was the norm in 1963. A more tangible sign of the profession's diminished cohesiveness is the increased willingness of physicians to testify against their peers, on plaintiffs' behalf, in medical malpractice suits, which were rare before the 1960s in large part because of physicians' distaste for testifying against each other. If Ellickson is right about the crucial role of group cohesion in the creation and maintenance of norms that maximize a group's aggregate welfare, then the medical profession may no longer be capable of sustaining ethical norms that maximize its welfare.

The medical profession's internal cleavages also cast doubt on the notion that any one set of norms can maximize the welfare of all or most physicians. The profession has become a complex mix of overlapping subgroups with both shared and competing interests. Norms that might maximize one subgroup's common interests might yield less desirable results for another subgroup or for the profession as a whole. Conversely, norms that maximize interests shared by most of the profession might yield unwanted results for particular subgroups.

It is thus hardly clear that traditional physician ethics — including the norm of fidelity to patients and suppression of financial self-interest — maximize the medical profession's aggregate welfare, let alone society's. Recent efforts to explain the persistence of nonlegal norms in terms of their expressive function cast further doubt on the thesis that physician norms maximize the profession's (or society's) welfare. It has been suggested that people often abide by social norms to signal their cooperative nature, and thus their desirability as potential partners in collaborative effort, irrespective of whether the norms being followed and thereby sustained yield benefits that outweigh their costs (Posner 1998). Once a norm is fixed in place, by common understanding, as such a signal, it is difficult to dislodge even if it is wasteful in the aggregate to the group that abides by it as a signal — and even if adherence to an alternative norm could, in theory, perform this signaling function at lower cost. To the extent that physician norms perform this signaling function, their persistence cannot be taken as evidence that they maximize the profession's welfare; it may merely reflect the difficulty of shifting to an alternative, agreed-upon symbol.

The upshot is that recent thinking about the social welfare impact of physicians' anticompetitive norms is deeply skeptical of Arrow's assertion that these norms have desirable welfare effects. Indeed, contemporary law-and-economics models for the creation and sustenance of social norms invite doubt about whether physicians' anticompetitive norms further *the medical profession's* aggregate welfare. On the other hand, these models do not support the sweeping conclusion that physicians' anticompetitive norms, including the ethic of fidelity to patients, are socially wasteful *per se*. I turn next to some ideas about how we might sort out this confusing picture for some of the anticompetitive medical ethics norms most at issue today.

A DYNAMIC MODEL OF THE MARKET FOR MEDICAL ETHICS

I start with a premise favorable toward economic analysis: that it makes no sense to speak, without explanation, of a tendency for nonmarket means, including ethical norms, to emerge and to fill optimality gaps that ensue from market imperfections. Arrow's contribution toward our understanding of professional ethics was not his almost-mystical invocation of "nonmarket" forces tending toward optimality; it was his bold but down-to-earth proposition that an ethical commitment to fidelity to patients and suppression of pecuniary self-interest is "part of the commodity the physician sells." Whether or not one accepts Arrow's further claim that "sale" of this commitment moves society toward optimality, his account of a market for ethical commitment as a response to consumer uncertainty about medical outcomes is intuitively appealing and compatible with the premise of self-interested actors. It is also consistent with the medical profession's success, during the late nineteenth and early twentieth centuries, at increasing its prestige, credibility, and income as it restrained practitioners' commercial excesses.

Indeed, Arrow arguably underestimated consumer demand for professional commitment to an ethic of devotion to patients and suppression of self-interest. In looking exclusively to consumer uncertainty about medicine's biological efficacy as the source of consumer demand for professional trustworthiness, Arrow neglected the affective dimension of patients' experience of illness—their yearnings for support and comfort, reassurance, and credible explanation of frightening developments. To the extent that sick patients value trusting relationships with their doctors as a way to cope with these emotional needs, Arrow's exclusive focus on consumer information deficits undervalues consumer desire for the ethical commitment he seeks to explain.

Arrow's characterization of this ethical commitment in static terms, as part of a market equilibrium, missed dynamic features of the market for medical ethics that play a large role in ongoing health systems change. Over the past hundred or so years, physician commitment to the ethic of suppression of self-interest for the sake of patients has fluctuated considerably, almost certainly in response to changing demand-side pressures. At the dawn of the twentieth century, competing clinicians were hardly reserved about their entrepreneurial pursuits and claims for remedies. The raucous commercialism parodied in George Bernard Shaw's *The Doctor's Dilemma* undermined consumers' belief in the value of what the healing professions had to offer. But by the second decade of the twentieth century the medical profession was responding aggressively to its image problem by closing proprietary medical schools, cracking down on clinical commercialism, and presenting its ethical commitments as evidence of superiority over other kinds of clinical practitioners (Starr 1982). By the time Arrow published his article, patient confidence in the medical profession had risen from an abysmal low to a historic high. Physicians, in short, identified and met a previously unfulfilled consumer "demand" for trustworthiness.

Yet having won consumers' confidence, American physicians were, by 1963, under less market pressure to "prove" their trustworthiness. Many took opportunistic advantage by acquiring ownership interests in hospitals, clinical laboratories, and other health care businesses. Anticommercial norms that Arrow treated as part of a lasting equilibrium fell by the wayside as physicians advertised aggressively and stopped providing free and discounted care to the poor. The profession, in short, began to drift back toward the commercialism of the late nineteenth and early twentieth centuries.

I have suggested elsewhere that growing consumer awareness of this drift (and consumer skepticism about claims that physicians are little motivated by money) opened the way for managed health plans to be explicit, in the 1980s and 1990s, about financial rewards to physicians for limiting care (Bloche 1998). The managed care revolution has transformed the market for medical ethics. The involvement of health care payers in clinical decision making introduced a cost-sensitive buyers' perspective that differs from the vantage point of sick patients. From the payers' perspective, physician responsiveness to financial incentives is not problematic, either ethically or clinically, and division of physician loyalties between health plans and patients is acceptable, even desirable (Berenson 1991). On the other hand, the managed care "backlash" of the last few years suggests growing consumer unhappiness over economic arrangements that are at odds with the ideal of undivided physician loyalty to patients. Whether the medical profession will respond to market pressure for a return to more robust professional commitment to this ideal remains uncertain. What is clear, though, is that the constellation of ethical norms that Arrow's article treated as a market equilibrium arose, in fact, through a dynamic process in which both physician willingness to suppress self-interest and consumer concerns about doctors' trustworthiness changed over time.

This dynamism remodels medical ethics in response to changing market pressures and market actors' shifting perceptions. The landscape of ethical obligation has changed dramatically since 1963. Physicians now routinely advertise, accept discounted fees from managed health plans, take ownership interests in facilities financially affected by clinical utilization patterns, and sign contracts that reward them financially for withholding care. Yet many physicians at least say they remain committed to the ethic of undivided loyalty to patients (Sulmasy et al. 2000). A difficult but pertinent question is whether the constellation of anticompetitive norms Arrow identified should be treated as indivisible — as tied together by deep cognitive, cultural, or other structures that make the preservation of some of these norms impossible if others are allowed (or even encouraged) to erode. For example, is the ethic of suppression of self-interest when making clinical recommendations undermined by robust price competition, elimination of prohibitions against advertising, or frank manipulation of financial incentives to influence utilization of services? Arrow treated ethical proscriptions against advertising and price competition as critical signals of the profession's commitment to suppression of self-interest in matters of clinical judgment. But the meaning of signifiers is often in flux, and we lack an empirical basis for distinguishing systems of norms that are cognitively, culturally, or otherwise indivisible.

CONCLUSION: THE EFFICIENCY OF SUPPRESSION OF SELF-INTEREST

The market pressures that continually remodel medical ethics are not acknowledged in law-and-economics treatments of professional ethics that portray these norms as self-serving restraints on trade. There is surely failure, to some degree, in the market for medical ethics: third-party payment and consumer ignorance about the efficacy of clinical services are spawning grounds for opportunism. But market pressures from both consumers and health care purchasers constrain this opportunism, and the growing availability, to consumers and purchasers, of information about treatment efficacy and financial arrangements is boosting these actors' countervailing power.

Acknowledgment of a market for medical ethics, and of the power of purchasers in this market, should push debate over the social implications of the ethic of undivided loyalty to patients and suppression of pecuniary self-interest away from the presumption that this ethic produces a welfare loss. The survival of this ethic under current market conditions, after the breaking of professional price cartels and the proliferation of information about medical prices and quality, suggests this ethic's desirability to consumers.

With almost forty years of hindsight, we are able to tell a more nuanced story than Arrow offered about the social welfare effects of physician commitment to this ethic. One might argue, for example, that this ethic ascends in importance for patients as their health deteriorates and their clinical choices and prospects become more complicated and frightening. Essentially healthy people who face simple, low-stakes therapeutic choices for minor ailments tend to have more emotional and cognitive resources (and time) for information-gathering than do sicker people, and their information needs are comparably modest. Information asymmetries between relatively healthy patients and their doctors may therefore also be modest, even trivial, and the social welfare gains, if any, from physician trustworthiness may be minimal. At the affective level as well, the welfare advantages of physician trustworthiness may be small for such patients, since they are typically not in much psychic distress and therefore not in great need of emotional support and reassurance.

For the seriously ill, however, clinical alternatives are typically much more complicated and frightening. Their information needs are large, if they are to make informed, reflective choices. Meanwhile, these patients' cognitive and emotional resources are under extraordinary strain. Information asymmetries between these patients and their physicians therefore tend to be enormous, and the social welfare gains from physician trustworthiness are likely to be large. These patients' emotional needs, for support, comfort, and credible explanation for their frightening life circumstances, also are likely to be high, yielding further welfare gains from trustworthiness at the bedside.

From a legal and policy perspective, therefore, it might make sense to distinguish between situations that place very different emotional and cognitive demands upon doctors and patients. Anticompetitive ethical norms that call upon physicians to suppress their short-term self-interest when exercising clinical judgment may yield net welfare gains, and net losses, in different clinical and institutional circumstances. That Arrow did not tease out the ramifications of his reasoning for diverse clinical and institutional circumstances is hardly a criticism of his work. His seminal contribution, from a medical ethics perspective, was his account of ethical commitment as a market-driven phenomenon. This basic idea has stood the test of time.

NOTES

1 Guild *ideology*, so interpreted, discourages would-be defectors and free riders by persuading them that guild cooperation serves the public good and by shaming deviant guild members as self seeking.

2 As other participants in this symposium have noted, Arrow was also a realist about the extent of professional adherence to this ethic, which he acknowledged was sometimes honored in the breach. But it surely has some influence on clinical judgment, he insisted, and to the extent that it does it moves medical resource allocation in different directions than would physician decisions driven purely by short-term financial incentives.

3 These doctrines include the *worthy purpose* exception, which permits open-ended arguments for the public policy value of a restraint; the *rule of reason*, which nominally calls for analysis of a restraint's effects *on competition* but in practice entails assessment of a restraint's effects upon consumer welfare; and the *market failure* defense, which allows restraints to stand if they represent welfare-enhancing responses to informational or other malfunctions in competitive markets. (See Havighurst in this book.)

4 In *California Dental Association v. Federal Trade Commission*, 119 S. Ct. 1604 (1999), the Court overturned an FTC ruling against a professional association's ethical rules governing members' claims to the public about low fees and discounts. The justices

offered a "market failure" rationale, arguing that consumers are at high risk for misunderstanding professionals' advertising claims and that ethical restraints that make
such claims easier for consumers to grasp can therefore be "procompetitive."

5 I employ the word anticompetitive here not in its antitrust law sense, as a term of art
to convey a mix of judgments about a practice's effects upon both competition and
consumer welfare (Hammer 2000), but in a more literal sense, to convey proscription
of alternative competitive strategies inconsistent with professional norms.

6 In so doing, Arrow aligned himself against what later came to be known as *public choice
theory*, which treats government as an alternative market venue and public policy as
the outcome of bidding and negotiation among competing private interests, not as
the product of a disinterested quest to identify and compensate for market failures.

7 Law-and-economics scholars broadened Arrow's story about the marketing of indicia
of trustworthiness as a response to consumer inability to assess results. Henry Hansmann (1980) interpreted the nonprofit form as an answer to what he termed "contract
failure" — the diverse inabilities of patrons (whether charitable donors or paying customers) to knowledgeably monitor a firm's performance to assess its compliance with
patrons' expectations. For Hansmann, the nonprofit form's essential feature was its
bar against distributing money (aside from compensation at market rates) to stakeholders — a prohibition analogous to the professional ethic of suppression of financial
self-interest. Along similar lines, Robert Cooter treated the law of fiduciary obligation
as a tool for reinforcing principals' confidence in agents' reliability when principals
cannot closely monitor agents' exercise of discretion (Cooter and Freedman 1991).

8 Neoclassical economists pursue functionalist explanations of social phenomena — that
is, they seek to interpret behavior and institutions as adaptive responses to the environment — just as classical evolutionary theorists sought to explain the anatomy and
physiology of organisms entirely in terms of adaptive purposes served. In economics,
as in biology, there is a growing realization that adaptation to environmental pressures is often incomplete, due to limits (i.e., structural constraints) on the social and
biological possibilities for change.

REFERENCES

Arrow, Kenneth J. 1963. Uncertainty and the Welfare Economics of Medical Care. *American Economics Review* 53(5): 941–973.

———. 1972. Social Responsibility and Economic Efficiency. *Public Policy* 21: 303–317.

Berenson, Robert. 1991. A Physician's View of Managed Care. *Health Affairs* 10: 106–119.

Bloche, M. Gregg. 1998. Cutting Waste and Keeping Faith. *Annals of Internal Medicine* 128:
688–898.

———. 2002. Trust and Betrayal in the Medical Marketplace. *Stanford law Review* 55(3):
919–954.

Blumstein, James. 1994. Health Care Reform and Competing Visions of Medical Care:
Antitrust and State Provider Cooperation Legislation. *Cornell Law Review* 79(6):1459–
1506.

Cooter, Robert, and Bradley J. Freedman. 1991. The Fiduciary Relationship: Its Economic Character and Legal Consequences. *New York University Law Review* 66: 1045–1075.

Ellickson, Robert. 1991. *Order without Law: How Neighbors Settle Disputes*. Cambridge, MA: Harvard University Press.

Hammer, Peter. 2000. Antitrust beyond Competition: Market Failures, Total Welfare, and the Challenge of Intramarket Second-Best Tradeoffs. *Michigan Law Review* 98: 849.

Hansmann, Henry B. 1980. The Role of Non-Profit Enterprise. *Yale Law Journal* 91: 835–901.

Havighurst, Clark C. 1995. *Health Care Choices: Private Contracts as Instruments of Health Reform*. Washington, DC: American Enterprise Institute Press.

Posner, Eric A. 1998. Symbols, Signs, and Social Norms in Politics and the Law. *Journal of Legal Studies* 27: 765–798.

Posner, Richard A. 1993. The Material Basis of Jurisprudence. *Indiana Law Journal* 69(1): 35–37.

Shaw, George Bernard. 1996. *The Doctor's Dilemma*. Studio City, CA: Players' Press.

Starr, Paul. 1982. *The Social Transformation of American Medicine*. New York: Basic Books.

Sulmasy, Daniel P., M. Gregg Bloche, Jean M. Mitchell, and Jack Hadley. 2000. Physicians' Ethical Beliefs about Cost-Control Arrangements. *Archives of Internal Medicine* 160: 649–657.

JACK NEEDLEMAN

■ *The Role of Nonprofits in Health Care*

The very word, "profit," is a signal that denies the trust relationship.
—Kenneth J. Arrow

In his essay "Uncertainty and the Welfare Economics of *Medical Care*," Kenneth Arrow (1963) focuses on asymmetric information as a key feature of the relationship between health care providers and patients, on the need for trust to supplement arm's length market relationships, and on the limits of standard market analysis to describe and explain these relationships. Agency is a central theme of the essay. While the word is not used explicitly in his essay, it is about the potential for exploitation in these relationships.

Arrow's discussion of nonprofit organizations is largely (although not exclusively) focused on the issue of trust and agency. Other aspects of nonprofits — the role of donations in creating and sustaining them, their role in providing community services or public goods — are less developed. The role of community-based nonprofit insurers such as Blue Cross for pooling insurance across risks, for example, and the threat of competition to this arrangement is (presciently) noted, but the market power or institutional structures that created or sustained these arrangements are not discussed.

While Arrow's comments on nonprofit organizations are almost throwaway lines, his insights have become central to an analysis of nonprofits. They form part of the basis of the New Industrial Economics, with its emphasis on information and transaction costs and agency relationships. That framework, adopted and expanded by Henry B. Hansmann especially but also others, has become the standard approach to discussing the economics of nonprofit institutions. Even certain aspects of nonprofits not closely analyzed by Arrow, such as donations, have been recast in these later works into a framework structured by issues of trust and asymmetric information.

In the literature on nonprofits spawned in part from Arrow's initial insights, two related questions are repeatedly raised: (1) Why are nonprofits created and supported? and (2) How do nonprofits behave, and how different is their behavior from profit maximizing for-profits? Implicit in these analyses are questions about whether nonprofit institutions can and should continue to play their historic role in the health care system, and whether public policies on such issues as nonprofit tax exemption, nonprofit to for-profit conversion, and nonprofit antitrust immunity should be geared to preserving and promoting nonprofit health care institutions.

Addressing the question whether, in the absence of changes in public policy, nonprofits can survive without becoming indistinguishable from for-profits requires looking at the changing markets in which nonprofits operate. Answering the question whether policy "should" tilt toward nonprofits must be based on three considerations: (1) whether the conditions calling forth nonprofits continue to exist, (2) whether the costs associated with the benefits of nonprofit ownership have come to outweigh the benefits, and (3) whether the actual behavior of nonprofits sufficiently distinguishes them from for-profits to sustain support for them.

This essay reviews the theory and evidence on the origins and behavior of nonprofits and, at the end, turns to the implications of this analysis for the "should" and "can" questions. It draws principally on the literature and history of nonprofit hospitals, with a limited discussion of nonprofit health plans and insurers. Other health care agents, such as nursing homes and long-term care in which there is a substantial nonprofit presence, are not discussed.

WHY ARE NONPROFIT ORGANIZATIONS IN HEALTH CARE CREATED AND SUPPORTED? FOSTERING TRUST, AVOIDING EXPLOITATION

In his 1963 essay, Arrow puts forward a succinct statement of the problem of agency in the medical sphere: "As a signal to the buyer of his intentions to act as thoroughly in the buyer's behalf as possible, the physician avoids the obvious stigmata of profit-maximizing. Purely arms-length bargaining behavior would be incompatible, not logically, but surely psychologically, with the trust relations. From these special relations come the various forms of ethical behavior discussed above, and so also, I suggest, the relative unimportance of profit-making in hospitals" (965).

Following Arrow, efforts to explain the creation and support of nonprofits have focused on the problem of asymmetric information and agency. The central article in this regard is Hansmann's 1980 article on contract failure. Hansmann, building on Arrow and Richard Nelson and Michael Krashinsky (1973), argues that nonprofits have a comparative advantage in offering goods or services when consumers are not well positioned to evaluate the service offered. He argued that under these circumstances, ownership by anyone other than the customers would create incentives and opportunities for exploitation. Yet, as Hansmann described it in his 1996 book *The Ownership of Enterprise*, when "customers are so situated that the costs to them of exercising effective control over the firm are unacceptably large . . . the solution is to create a firm without owners — or, more accurately, to create a firm whose managers hold it in trust for its customers," that is, a nonprofit firm (Hansmann 1996: 228). The dynamic driving these models is that, once created in this market, nonprofits would be preferred by consumers over for-profit providers.

Others building on Arrow (e.g., Ben-Ner 1986) identify additional reasons for consumers to prefer nonprofits, including cases of monopoly where consumers wish to retain consumer surplus or assure production above the monopoly levels and where fund-raising by a nonprofit provider can be viewed by consumers as voluntary price discrimination to expand access to the service. (Arrow, in discussing physician pricing, introduces a distinction between profit maximizing monopoly discrimination and charitable price discrimination that foreshadows these issues. He also posits an alternative model to his direct consumer choice model in which donors prefer nonprofits and their donations lower prices leading further to consumer preferences for these institutions.) The dynamic driving these models is that nonprofits would offer lower prices to significant groups of consumers and this would result in a consumer preference for nonprofits at the time of purchase.

Donative Nonprofits and Private Provision of Public Goods

The second argument put forward for nonprofits is to funnel donations to non-commercial activities — the private provision of public goods, such as charity or merit goods — at levels above that the government would provide (Weisbrod 1975; James 1989). This donative dimension of nonprofits has also been placed in the context of asymmetric information, agency theory, and fear of exploitation, using models built on an assumption that contributors cannot efficiently monitor whether the funds they provide are being fully utilized for the intended purpose. In these models, the creation and sustaining of nonprofits is driven largely by their access to contributions for operations and capital.

Subsidy and Regulation

An alternative explanation of the growth and survival of the nonprofit form is that it is due to preferential public policies such as tax exemption and subsidized capital financing (Hill-Burton subsidies for hospital construction, federal subsidies for nonprofit community health centers, state and federal regulations favoring nonprofit health plans such as Blue Cross or Kaiser, for example). A recent extension of this argument by Darius Lakdawalla and Tomas Philipson (1998) argues that firms with objectives other than strict profit maximization need not be nonprofit, but that nonprofit status may be chosen by such firms if the cost/subsidy/regulatory advantages offered by such status outweigh potential profits, given how the market is structured.

Why would public policies favoring nonprofits in a particular industry be adopted in the first place? The standard argument put forward is that the presence of subsidies represents consumer preference for nonprofits for the reasons advanced by Arrow, Burton Weisbrod, and others, preferences expressed in the political system rather than the market. Hansmann (1985) argues that subsidies to nonprofits are provided to protect nonprofits against competition in places where nonprofits already have a large presence, and finds some evidence for this. The two perspectives can be blended, with consumer preferences providing an initial impetus for such policies, and subsequent policy influenced both by consumer preferences and the political power of the institutions created by the subsidies.

The Coexistence of Nonprofits and For-Profits

Related to the issue of why nonprofits are created and sustained is the question of why there are mixed markets in which nonprofits and for-profits coexist. Several answers have been put forward for this, including: timing: that at any given time, the nature of the market will favor either for-profit or nonprofit institutions and that a mix is simply a reflection of being in transition from dominance by one form to that of another; firm heterogeneity: that many firms are not strict profit maximizers but have mixed objective functions, and choose nonprofit or for-profit status based on the advantage of nonprofit status and profit opportunities in their markets (Lakdawalla and Philipson 1998); *consumer heterogeneity*: since some consumers cannot detect agency failure while others can, those who cannot will prefer nonprofit firms while those who can detect agency failure may prefer for-profits for other reasons; *isomorphism and mimicry*: because of regulatory pressures, learning from others and adoption of successful models, or consumer or community norms and expectations, organizations that compete or carry out similar functions tend to mirror one another, thus reducing the likelihood of the market pushing one or the other out (DiMaggio and Powell 1983); and *asymmetric advantages of each form*: coexistence is due to asymmetric advantages (e.g., access to capital through donations versus equity markets) that adapt each form to different market niches or provide offsetting advantages in competition in the same niche.

Economic models that explore these explanations often lead to different predictions of the behavior of nonprofit and for-profit institutions. Depending on the assumptions in the model, for example, models of consumer heterogeneity can result in predictions of either higher or lower prices in for-profits. The role of norms and expectations in explaining coexistence may lead to a different set of analyses than that for other factors. Normative isomorphism may be particularly important if trust is critical. If one form (such as the nonprofit) dominates an environment, it may establish norms that other forms must meet to be successful as they enter that market. If this is the case, differences between nonprofits and for-profits may not appear in within-market comparisons, but only in cross-market comparisons, and only if the comparisons are structured to differentiate between nonprofit- and for-profit–dominated markets.

HOW WELL DOES HISTORY SUPPORT AGENCY FAILURE AND TRUST
AS EXPLANATIONS FOR NONPROFIT DOMINANCE?

One way to test all these theories and their applicability to health care is to examine the history of the creation and evolution of nonprofit hospitals and health plans. Presentations of this history can be found in Stevens 1989; Starr 1982; and Brown 1997. Needleman 1999 and Patel, Needleman, and Zeckhauser 1994 present shorter versions that synthesize these and other sources.

One potential mechanism by which preference for nonprofits might be exercised to sustain them in the market is through consumer preference in response to fear of exploitation. This is the model posited by Arrow and Hansmann. History suggests that the direct role of consumer preference for nonprofit hospitals or health plans is not a major element sustaining nonprofits. It did not inhibit the growth of for-profits in the late nineteenth and early twentieth centuries. By 1910, the number of for-profit hospitals outstripped the number of nonprofits (Steinwald and Newhauser, cited in Bays 1983). It did not inhibit the growth of for-profit chains in the post-Medicare period. It does not appear to have constrained the growth of for-profit insurers or health plans over the past two decades.

Public opinion surveys reinforce the sense that trust and agency issues do not dominate individual patient or consumer decision making. Steven E. Permut (1981) reports that people are often unaware of whether organizations they deal with are for-profit or nonprofit. More recent surveys suggest that the public has conflicting views of the quality of nonprofit versus for-profit hospitals. A 1995 survey found "Americans generally believe for-profit hospitals, HMOs and health insurance plans are more efficient and provide better quality care than not-for-profits" (Pallarito 1995: 3), while a 1998 survey found preferences for nonprofit institutions, but respondents often unaware of the ownership status of the institutions with which they deal (*Trustee* 1998). The Blues, in justifying nonprofit to for-profit conversion, cited research showing "that the vast majority of consumers either did not know the difference between for-profit and non-profit insurers, or did not care. The vast majority of business decision makers who bought health insurance had decidedly negative impressions of the non-profit form" (Orloff 1997: 290).

The donative and subsidy models offer better explanations for the growth and role of nonprofits in these sectors. Contract failure, that is, consumer fear of exploitation, might explain the willingness of the public to make donations or create public subsidies, but not consumer choice in markets per se. Differential access to capital over time has played a strong role in nonprofit and for-profit hospital and health plan growth and decline. The ability of many nonprofits to survive the depression, when many for-profits closed, was due to access to operating and capital subsidies from their communities (Stevens 1989). Post–World War II growth of nonprofit hospitals was in part attributable to the Hill-Burton program. The growth of nonprofit HMOs was likewise assisted by the Federal HMO Act of 1973 (Schlesinger, Gray, and Bradley 1996).

By contrast, the growth of for-profit hospitals in the late nineteenth century and post-Medicare era and for-profit health plans in the past two decades is explained in part by the access of these institutions to equity capital. Indeed, one of the rationales cited by the Blue Cross and Blue Shield Association in allowing its members to organize as for-profits was to expand their access to capital markets (Silas et al. 1997). This experience suggests that asymmetric advantage also plays a role in sustaining both forms in the market and explaining changes in market share. Whether markets have changed to the point that nonprofit hospitals or health plans are no longer viable competitors to for-profit firms is an issue I return to after reviewing the evidence on the differences in market behavior of nonprofit and for-profits.

HOW DO NONPROFITS BEHAVE, AND HOW DO THEY DIFFER FROM PROFIT MAXIMIZING FOR-PROFITS?

Even if consumer preferences do not explain the growth or market role of non-profits, evidence of behavioral differences between nonprofits and for-profits, consistent with theories of contract failure, can serve as a basis for preferring one form over the other in public policy making. Thus, the second question addressed with respect to nonprofits in health care is how they behave and how that behavior may differ from that of profit maximizing firms.

Theory is not clear on this point. Typically, theorists present a two-argument objective function for nonprofits, with profits or breakeven status as one argument and "something else" as the second. The "something else" varies from paper to paper. In Joseph P. Newhouse's seminal model (1970), prestige is the hospital's goal, and it is achieved through size (quantity of services) and quality. Newhouse's model implies that nonprofit hospitals will be larger and of higher quality than is socially efficient.

Nonprofits may strive for goals other than prestige, quantity, and quality. Among the goals which have been put forward are: reducing unmet need in the community (Frank and Salkever 1991); cost recovery and cash flow maximization (Davis 1972); meeting donor expectations (Rose-Ackerman 1987); meeting the needs of the medical staff (Lee 1971; Pauly and Redisch 1973); and offering lower prices (Ben-Ner 1986).

There are many nonprofits, and the lack of agreement on the objective function of these organizations may reflect the reality that these objectives will vary widely from one nonprofit to another.

Based on the theoretical models of nonprofit behavior, including those emerging from extension of Arrow's analysis of contract failure and trust, among the key predictions of nonprofit behavior are: (1) *quality* should be higher in nonprofits or, alternatively, if norm setting operates, in nonprofit-dominated markets; (2) nonprofits should engage in more *"trustworthy" behavior*; (3) where hospitals or health plans have market power, how they use this power should differ. For-profits are expected to maximize profits. Nonprofits will be more likely to maintain lower *prices*, or expand *charity care* or other *unprofitable services*, raising prices enough to cover the additional costs of these services (cost shift), or *implement voluntary price discrimination*, such as community rating, so that the healthy subsidize the sick and large groups subsidize small groups and individuals. Also, (4) nonprofits should have a stronger *commitment to place*, to maintaining themselves in the communities in which they are established. This can cut both ways, depending on the strength of market signals. In a market where the signals for entry and exit are complete reflections of social goals, nonprofit ownership will result in less efficient deployment of capital. Where market signals are incomplete, nonprofit ownership may compensate for this market failure. And (5) community-based nonprofits should be less interested in *expansion* outside these communities. The financial structure of nonprofits also should make expansion hard because of limited access to capital.

I turn to the evidence of behavioral differences between nonprofit hospitals and health plans. The behaviors that affect the patient-provider interaction and thus relate to the issues of contract failure and agency raised by Arrow and developed by Hansmann — quality, trustworthiness, and efficiency — are discussed first. Those that relate to community service — pricing, charity and subsidized services, commitment to place, and involvement in the community — follow.

Quality
Evidence on quality differences between nonprofit and for-profit hospitals is skimpy and mixed. Studies provide contradictory evidence on quality at each.

Arthur J. Hartz et al. 1989 found adjusted mortality at for-profit hospitals higher, but other studies have found no difference in either mortality or other measures between for-profit and nonprofit hospitals (Shortell and Hughes 1988; Sloan et al. 2001; Ettner and Hermann 2001), or found differences between nonprofit teaching hospitals and for-profits but not nonteaching nonprofits (Kuhn et al. 1991; Kuhn et al. 1994; McClellan and Staiger 1999; Taylor, Whellan, and Sloan 1999; Yuan et al. 2000). One study, using adverse events as a measure but limited to New York, found higher for-profit quality (Brennan et al. 1991).

There are stronger indications from studies of dialysis and nursing home care that quality is higher among nonprofit firms (Aaronson, Zinn, and Rosko 1994; Garg et al. 1999; Irvin 2000), but at least one other study found no differences (Bell and Krivich 1990).

Available studies of health plans, while limited, suggest that quality or patient satisfaction is lower in for-profit plans. These studies use a variety of outcome measures — surveys of members (Greene 1998; Landon et al. 2001), disenrollment and appeals (PROPAC 1994), and HEDIS quality measures (Himmelstein et al. 1999). The differences in satisfaction with care and observed quality across plans may reflect differences that result from ownership. They may also reflect differences in health care quality across regions, the age of the plans, or length of enrollment in the plan. Further study is warranted.

Trustworthiness

There is fear that in a health system dominated by for-profit institutions, the nonprofit norms would be replaced by standards that are less protective of patients and that physicians would be under great pressure to skimp on their patients. One potential test is whether for-profit hospitals or health plans exploit their customers when able and whether they are able to influence physicians to participate in this. Studies have found that for-profits' charges are higher (Gray 1991; Hall and McGuire 1987; Sloan et al. 2001), that for-profit hospitals are more likely to upcode Medicare claims, and that nonprofits in heavily for-profit markets are nearly as likely to do so (Silverman and Skinner 2001). There is some evidence of differences in services under the direct control of their physicians for patients treated in for-profit institutions, including: cesarean sections (Tanio 1989; Stafford 1991), length of stay (Kuttner 1996), and referral for transplantation (Garg et al. 1999). While not conclusive, this evidence provides some support for the concern about the ability and willingness of for-profit institutions to directly and indirectly influence billings and services received by patients.

Costs and Efficiency

Virtually all the well-designed studies that have looked at the cost and efficiency of nonprofit hospitals compared to for-profits have found no differences among the forms (e.g., Pattison and Katz 1983; Becker and Sloan 1985; Watt et al. 1986; Zuckerman, Hadley, and Iezzoni 1994; Menke 1997).

Community Benefits

There is now an extensive literature that attempts to define the elements of non-profit community benefit, including: Clement, Smith, and Wheeler 1994; Butler 1996; Kertesz 1996; Schlesinger, Gray, and Bradley 1996; Buchmueller and Feldstein 1996; Trocchio 1996; Chollet, Lamphere, and Needleman 1996; Gray 1997; and Claxton et al. 1997. This section reviews the evidence for the principal benefits claimed for nonprofit organizations in health care.

■ CHARITY CARE AND CARE FOR THOSE WHO CANNOT PAY   The community benefit most frequently cited in literature is charity care (or a proxy for charity care, uncompensated care). In some states, there are wide differences in the levels of uncompensated care between nonprofit and for-profit hospitals, while in others, the differences are small (Lewin and Eckels 1988). Some of the differences are due to the location of the hospitals and thus the demand for uncompensated care (Norton and Staiger 1994).

Conversions offer a window into nonprofit/for-profit differences. Studies of hospital conversions in California, Florida, and Texas (Young, Desai, and Lukas 1997; Needleman, Lamphere, and Chollet 1999; Desai, Young, and Lukas 1998) found converting nonprofit hospitals had levels of uncompensated care comparable to for-profits prior to conversion, and these similarities did not decline following conversion. Tami L. Mark and colleagues (1997), based on a limited sample of conversion, likewise concluded that uncompensated care did not decline post-conversion. One study found a decline in uncompensated care at converting nonprofit hospitals (Thorpe, Florence, and Seiber 2000).

■ UNPROFITABLE SERVICES   There is a wide range of services provided by hospitals that are valued by their community but generally considered unprofitable, including emergency rooms and trauma services, AIDS education, and others that target low-income populations. Studies have found for-profit hospitals less likely than nonprofit hospitals to offer such services (e.g., Gray 1986) but wide variability in nonprofit provision of such services. Examining conversions, Mark et al. 1997: 131 concluded: "Preliminary evidence suggests conversion has little effect on . . . the provision of typically unprofitable services."

■ LOWER PRICES AND VOLUNTARY PRICE DISCRIMINATION   Studies of hospital pricing in the 1980s generally found that for-profit hospitals priced their services higher than nonprofits (which appear to price to achieve a fixed margin over costs). There are indications that price differences between for-profit and nonprofit hospitals have narrowed in the 1990s, but it is unclear whether this is due to market pressures squeezing prices or more aggressive pricing by nonprofit hospitals.

Two of the early features of nonprofit insurers and health plans were community rating and open enrollment. Arrow mentions such policies in his 1963 essay and notes that "the equalization [of community rating], of course, could not in fact be carried through if the market were genuinely competitive" (964). In fact, efforts to maintain access to insurance through community rating has been virtually eliminated by market pressures.

■ TEACHING Prior to the recent conversions of a small number of nonprofit and public teaching hospitals, virtually no for-profit hospitals had medical school affiliations or substantial commitments to medical education. Among converting nonprofit hospitals, however, 9 percent have been teaching hospitals. The for-profit chains appear to have maintained the teaching mission. Nonprofit health plans have been more active in teaching and research than for-profits.

■ COMMITMENT TO PLACE AND CONTINUITY OF OWNERSHIP Local nonprofit ownership has been associated with commitment to the local community and continuity of ownership. These, in turn, have often led these institutions and their leaders to view themselves as serving the community, not just their customers, and to play a substantial role in health care issues in their communities.

For-profits have played less of a leadership role in their communities and viewed their relationship to their communities as commercial. Over the past twenty-five years, for-profit hospital chains have formed and reformed, and the companies have demonstrated a willingness to sell hospitals that no longer fit their corporate plans (Patel, Needleman, and Zeckhauser 1994; Clement and McCue 1996). Nonprofit hospitals have increasingly become affiliated with regional or national chains, however, and no studies have been done to show how these affiliations have influenced sale or closure or other dimensions of community involvement.

Lawrence D. Brown (1997) has described Blue Cross and Blue Shield plans as resting on three core values: voluntarism, community, and a cooperative ethos, a description easily extended to other nonprofit health plans. Historically, these values have been reflected in the role nonprofit insurers and health plans have played in expanding access to care through innovative products, in health services research and education, and by restructuring the health system through leadership and negotiation. Reviewing the retreat of Blue Cross/Blue Shield plans and other nonprofit health plans from their historic community roles, one might reasonably conclude that market pressures have fundamentally eroded the ability of these plans to offer such community benefits. To some extent this has been acknowledged by the Blue Cross and Blue Shield Association description of the evolution of its members from "social service" models to "mutual company models" with their primary commitment to their subscribers (Silas et al. 1997). Other nonprofit HMO leaders, however, cite their continuing community roles as their reason for preserving their nonprofit form (Lawrence, Mattingly, and Ludden 1997).

THE FUTURE OF NONPROFITS IN A MARKET-DRIVEN HEALTH SYSTEM

Arrow's 1963 essay led to the focused attention on issues of asymmetric information, agency, and trust in health care and other aspects of the economy. This in turn contributed to the development of a theory of nonprofits driven by consumer preferences. The data on the history of U.S. nonprofit hospitals and health plans does not support the conclusion that consumers prefer to purchase health services and insurance from nonprofits, but does leave open a role for preferences expressed through private donations and public policy that tilts toward nonprofit organizations.

While consumers may not actively prefer nonprofits, there is evidence that suggests that some of the arguments put forward for consumers to prefer nonprofits — lower prices, higher quality, increased trustworthiness, and provision of community services — are valid. The evidence is mixed, however, and there has been and will continue to be debate and further study.

While nonprofits and for-profits in health care have differed in the past, there is also evidence of convergence in nonprofit and for-profit behavior. This is most apparent in the shift in nonprofit health plans from "social service" models to "mutual" models and in the convergence of pricing between nonprofit and for-profit hospitals. It is also apparent in the conversion of nonprofit health plans and hospitals to for-profit status, which often creates a legacy foundation to pursue the historic mission of the converting entity. The conversion process has been generally one-way with respect to health plans, but two-way with respect to hospitals (Needleman, Chollet, and Lamphere 1997).

For public policy, the issue is whether to conclude that market changes have made the nonprofit–for-profit distinction irrelevant, accept convergence and conversion, and, through conversion foundations, free nonprofit assets to be employed where those managing have more discretion and the assets will have more impact. Or, alternatively, whether to conclude that the differences between nonprofit and for-profit behavior are such that the public policy should strengthen nonprofits and allow them to continue to serve their historic role.

I have reviewed the evidence on how well the historic role has been played. The decision must also turn on whether there are alternative approaches to meeting the public policy goals that nonprofit institutions have served.

With respect to access and community service roles, the historic ability of nonprofit health plans to address these goals has already been seriously eroded and partly replaced by Medicaid expansions, state high-risk pools, and other state mechanisms. Likewise, the public has already responded in part to the pressures on hospitals to cut back charity and unprofitable services by replacing private cost shifting with public subsidy either through expanded insurance or direct payments to hospitals and institutionalizing cost shifting through state free-care pools. These mechanisms reduce the need for ownership-based commitments to these services. Universal insurance would virtually eliminate the need for private provision of these services. Is this the direction we should be moving in? Will we move in it fast enough that nonprofit commitment to these services will become irrelevant?

With respect to quality, trustworthiness, and fair dealing, in the face of increased market pressures, are there alternatives to agency that would make ownership status irrelevant? One market response to concerns about quality has been to encourage the collection and dissemination of data on outcomes, processes of care, and patient satisfaction. A second response has been to establish explicit standards of care, making more use of evidence-based medicine. With clearer standards and better ability to monitor care against standards it is argued that ownership as a guarantor of quality would become less important. How accurate is this argument?

Perhaps the most difficult aspect of the historic nonprofit mission to preserve in a market-driven health system is the role nonprofits have played in community leadership and innovation, a role which grew out of a commitment to their communities, not just their customers. The debate on the future of nonprofit providers in health care must consider how vital these benefits are, how threatened they are in the current health care system, and whether and how their loss might be reversed. We might conclude that preservation of these institutions for these reasons is critical and public policy should tilt more heavily toward promoting nonprofits. Alternatively, we might conclude that, in the new market environment, the benefits of nonprofits can be better achieved through the operation of legacy foundations from for-profit conversions, and conversion to create such foundations should be encouraged. The work that grew from Kenneth Arrow's 1963 essay has provided us with the language and context to debate these issues.

REFERENCES

Aaronson, W. E., J. S. Zinn, and M. D. Rosko. 1994. Do For-Profit and Not-for-Profit Nursing Homes Behave Differently? *Gerontologist* 34(6): 775–786.

Arrow, K. J. 1963. Uncertainty and the Welfare Economics of *Medical Care. American Economic Review* 53(5): 941–973.

Bays, C. W. 1983. Why Most Private Hospitals Are Nonprofit. *Journal of Policy Analysis and Management* 2(3): 366–385.

Becker, E. R., and F. A. Sloan. 1985. Hospital Ownership and Performance. *Economic Inquiry* 23(1): 21–36.

Bell, R., and M. Krivich. 1990. Effects of Type of Ownership of Skilled Nursing Facilities on Residents' Mortality Rates in Illinois. *Public Health Reports* 105(5): 515–518.

Ben-Ner, A. 1986. Nonprofit Organizations: Why Do They Exist in Market Economies? In *The Economics of Nonprofit Institutions: Studies in Structure and Policy*, ed. S. Rose-Ackerman. New York: Oxford University Press.

Brennan, T. A., L. E. Hebert, N. M. Laird, A. Lawthers, K. E. Thorpe, L. L. Leape, A. R. Localio, S. R. Lipsitz, J. P. Newhouse, P. C. Weiler, and H. H. Hiatt. 1991. Hospital Characteristics Associated with Adverse Events and Substandard Care. *Journal of the American Medical Association* 265(24): 3265–3269.

Brown, L. D. 1997. The Metamorphosis: Conversion in Historical Context. *Bulletin of the New York Academy of Medicine* 74(2): 238–247.

Buchmueller, T. C., and P. J. Feldstein. 1996. Hospital Community Benefits Other Than Charity Care: Implications for Tax Exemption and Public Policy. *Hospital & Health Services Administration* 41(4): 461–471.

Butler, P. A. 1996. *Profit and the Public Interest: A State Policymaker's Guide to Non-Profit Hospital and Health Plan Conversion.* Portland, ME: National Academy for State Health Policy.

Chollet, D. J., J. Lamphere, and J. Needleman. 1996. Conversion of Hospitals and Health Plans to For-Profit Status: A Preliminary Investigation of Community Issues. Washington, DC: Alpha Center.

Claxton, G., J. Feder, D. Shactman, and S. Altman. 1997. Public Policy Issues in Nonprofit Conversions: An Overview. *Health Affairs* 16(2): 9–28.

Clement, J. P., and M. J. McCue. 1996. The Performance of Hospital Corporation of America and Healthtrust Hospitals after Leveraged Buyouts. *Medical Care* 34(7): 672–685.

Clement, J. P., D. G. Smith, and J. R. Wheeler. 1994. What Do We Want and What Do We Get from Not-For-Profit Hospitals? *Hospital & Health Services Administration* 39(2): 159–178.

Consumers Give Edge to Not-For-Profits. 1998. *Trustee* 51(2): 7.

Davis, K. 1972. Economic Theories of Behavior in Nonprofit, Private Hospitals. *Economic and Business Bulletin* 24(2): 1–13.

Desai, K. R., G. J. Young, and C. V. Lukas. 1998. Hospital Conversions from For-Profit to Nonprofit Status: The Other Side of the Story. *Medical Care Research & Review* 55(3): 298–308.

DiMaggio, P., and W. W. Powell. 1983. The Iron Cage Revisted: Institutional Isomorphism and Collective Rationality in Organizational Fields. *American Sociological Review* 82: 147–160.

Ettner, S. L., and R. C. Hermann. 2001. The Role of Profit Status under Imperfect Information: Evidence from the Treatment Patterns of Elderly Medicare Beneficiaries Hospitalized for Psychiatric Diagnoses. *Journal of Health Economics* 20(1): 23–49.

Frank, R. G., and D. S. Salkever. 1991. The Supply of Charity Services by Nonprofit Hospitals: Motives and Market Structure. *RAND Journal of Economics* 22(3): 430–445.

Garg, P. P., K. D. Frick, M. Diener-West, and N. R. Powe. 1999. Effect of the Ownership of

Dialysis Facilities on Patients' Survival and Referral for Transplantation. *New England Journal of Medicine* 341(22): 1653–1660.

Gray, B. H. 1991. *The Profit Motive and Patient Care: The Changing Accountability of Doctors and Hospitals*. Cambridge: Harvard University Press.

———. 1997. Conversion of HMOs and Hospitals: What's at Stake? Health Affairs 16(2): 29–47.

Gray, B. H., ed. 1986. *For-Profit Enterprise in Health Care*. Washington, DC: National Academy Press.

Greene, J. 1998. Blue Skies or Black Eyes? HEDIS Puts Not-for-Profit Plans on Top. *Hospitals & Health Networks* 72(8): 26–30.

Hall, S., and T. G. McGuire. 1987. Ownership and Performance: The Case of Outpatient Mental Health Clinics. *Medical Care* 25 (12): 1179–1183.

Hansmann, H. B. 1980. The Role of the Nonprofit Enterprise. *Yale Law Review Journal* 39(April): 835–901.

———. 1985. The Effect of Tax Exemption and Other Factors on Competition between Nonprofit and For-Profit Enterprises. New Haven, CT: Yale University Program on Nonprofit Organizations.

———. 1996. *The Ownership of Enterprise*. Cambridge: The Belknap Press of Harvard University Press.

Hartz, A. J., H. Krakauer, E. M. Kuhn, M. Young, S. J. Jacobsen, G. Gay, L. Muenz, M. Katzoff, R. C. Bailey, and A. A. Rimm. 1989. Hospital Characteristics and Mortality Rates. *New England Journal of Medicine* 321(25): 1720–1725.

Himmelstein, D. U., S. Woolhandler, I. Hellander, and S. M. Wolfe. 1999. Quality of Care in Investor-Owned vs. Not-for-Profit HMOs. *Journal of the American Medical Association* 282(2): 159–163.

Irvin, R. A. 2000. Quality of Care Differences by Ownership in United States Renal Dialysis Facilities. *ASAIO Journal* 46 (6): 775–778.

James, E., ed. 1989. *The Nonprofit Sector in International Perspective*. New York: Oxford University Press.

Kertesz, L. 1996. California Group Adopts Policy on For-Profit Conversion. *Modern Healthcare* 26 (4): 22.

Kuhn, E. M., A. J. Hartz, M. S. Gottlieb, and A. A. Rimm. 1991. The Relationship of Hospital Characteristics and the Results of Peer Review in Six Large States. *Medical Care* 29 (10): 1028–1038.

Kuhn, E. M., A. J. Hartz, H. Krakauer, R. C. Bailey, and A. A. Rimm. 1994. The Relationship of Hospital Ownership and Teaching Status to 30- and 180-Day Adjusted Mortality Rates. *Medical Care* 32(11): 1098–1108.

Kuttner, R. 1996. Columbia/HCA and the Resurgence of the For-Profit Hospital Business. *New England Journal of Medicine* 335(5): 362–367.

Lakdawalla, D., and T. Philipson. 1998. Nonprofit Production and Competition: National Bureau of Economic Research Working Paper no. 6377. Cambridge, MA: NBER.

Landon, B. E., A. M. Zaslavsky, N. D. Beaulieu, J. A. Shaul, and P. D. Cleary. 2001. Health Plan Characteristics and Consumers' Assessments of Quality. *Health Affairs* 20(2): 274–286.

Lawrence, D. M., P. H. Mattingly, and J. M. Ludden. 1997. Trusting in the Future: The Distinct Advantage of Nonprofit HMOs. *Milbank Quarterly* 75(1): 5–10.

Lee, M. L. 1971. A Conspicuous Production Theory of Hospital Behavior. *Southern Economic Review* 38: 48–58.

Lewin, L. S., and T. J. Eckels. 1988. Setting the Record Straight. *New England Journal of Medicine* 318(18): 1212–1215.

Mark, T. L., C. L. Schur, C. Paramore, E. Rodriguez, P. Neumann, E. Schwalenstocker, and C. Good. 1997. The Motivation for and Effect of Nonprofit to For-Profit Hospital Conversions: Results from Ten Case Studies. *Abstract Book/Association for Health Services Research* 14: 131–132.

McClellan, M., and D. Staiger. 1999. Comparing Hospital Quality at For-Profit and Not-for-Profit Hospitals. Cambridge: National Bureau of Economic Research.

Menke, T. J. 1997. The Effect of Chain Membership on Hospital Costs. *Health Services Research* 32 (2): 177–196.

Needleman, J. 1999. Nonprofit to For-Profit Conversions by Hospitals, Health Insurers, and Health Plans. *Public Health Reports* 114(2): 108–119.

Needleman, J., D. J. Chollet, and J. Lamphere. 1997. Hospital Conversion Trends. *Health Affairs* 16(2): 187–195.

Needleman, J., J. Lamphere, and D. Chollet. 1999. Uncompensated Care and Hospital Conversions in Florida. *Health Affairs* 18(4): 125–133.

Nelson, R., and M. Krashinsky. 1973. Two Major Issues of Public Policy: Public Subsidy and Organization of Supply. In *Public Policy for Day Care for Young Children*, ed. D. Young and R. Nelson. Lexington, MA: Lexington Books.

Newhouse, J. P. 1970. Toward a Theory of Nonprofit Institutions: An Economic Model of a Hospital. *American Economic Review* 60: 64–74.

Norton, E. C., and D. O. Staiger. 1994. How Hospital Ownership Affects Access to Care for the Uninsured. *RAND Journal of Economics* 25(1): 171–185.

Orloff, M. A. 1997. A Perspective from the National Blue Cross and Blue Shield Organizations. *Bulletin of the New York Academy of Medicine* 74(2): 286–291.

Pallarito, K. 1995. Poll: For-Profits, Not-for-Profits Both Have Advantages. *Modern Healthcare* 25(51): 3.

Patel, J., J. Needleman, and R. Zeckhauser. 1994. *Changing Fortunes, Hospital Behaviors and Ownership Forms*. Cambridge: Kennedy School of Government, Harvard University.

Pattison, R. V., and H. M. Katz. 1983. Investor-Owned and Not-for-Profit Hospitals. A Comparison Based on California Data. *New England Journal of Medicine* 309(6): 347–353.

Pauly, M. V., and M. Redisch. 1973. The Not-for-Profit Hospital as a Physicians' Cooperative. *American Economic Review* 63: 87–99.

Permut, S. 1981. Consumer Perceptions of Nonprofit Enterprise: A Comment on Hansmann. *Yale Law Journal* 90: 1623–1632.

Prospective Payment Assessment Commission (ProPAC). 1994. Enrollment and Disenrollment Experience in the Medicare Risk Program. Washington, DC:ProPAC.

Rose-Ackerman, S. 1987. Ideal versus Dollars: Donors, Charity Managers, and Government Grants. *Journal of Political Economy* 95(August): 810–823.

Schlesinger, M., B. Gray, and E. Bradley. 1996. Charity and Community: The Role of Nonprofit Ownership in a Managed Health Care System. *Journal of Health Politics, Policy and Law* 21(4): 697–751.

Shortell, S. M., and E. F. Hughes. 1988. The Effects of Regulation, Competition, and Ownership on Mortality Rates among Hospital Inpatients. *New England Journal of Medicine* 318(17): 1100–1107.

Silas, J., E. Hamburger, C. W. F. Bell, and M. Hunter. 1997. Blue Cross Conversion: Consumer Efforts to Protect Public's Interest. *Bulletin of the New York Academy of Medicine* 74(2): 256–285.

Silverman, E., and J. Skinner. 2001. Are For-Profit Hospitals Really Different? Medicare Upcoding and Market Structure. Cambridge, MA: National Bureau of Economic Research.

Sloan, F. A., G. A. Picone, D. H. Taylor, and S. Y. Chou. 2001. Hospital Ownership and Cost and Quality of Care: Is There a Dime's Worth of Difference? *Journal of Health Economics* 20(1): 1–21.

Stafford, R. S. 1991. The Impact of Nonclinical Factors on Repeat Cesarean Section. *Journal of the American Medical Association* 265(1): 59–63.

Starr, P. 1982. *The Social Transformation of American Medicine.* New York: Basic Books.

Stevens, R. 1989. *In Sickness and in Wealth: American Hospitals in the Twentieth Century.* New York: Basic Books.

Tanio, C. 1989. *Unnecessary Cesarean Sections, a Rapidly Growing National Epidemic.* Washington, DC: Public Citizen Health Research Group.

Taylor, D. H. Jr., D. J. Whellan, and F. A. Sloan. 1999. Effects of Admission to a Teaching Hospital on the Cost and Quality of Care for Medicare Beneficiaries. *New England Journal of Medicine* 340 (4): 293–299.

Thorpe, K. E., C. S. Florence, and E. E. Seiber. 2000. Hospital Conversions, Margins, and the Provision of Uncompensated Care. *Health Affairs* 19(6): 187–194.

Trocchio, J. 1996. What Are True Community Benefits? *Health Progress* 77(5): 34–37.

Watt, J. M., R. A. Derzon, S. C. Renn, C. J. Schramm, J. S. Hahn, and G. D. Pillari. 1986. The Comparative Economic Performance of Investor-Owned Chain and Not-for-Profit Hospitals. *New England Journal of Medicine* 314(2): 89–96.

Weisbrod, B. A. 1975. Toward a Theory of the Voluntary Non-Profit Sector in a Three-Sector Economy. In *Altruism, Morality and Economic Theory*, ed. E. Phelps. New York: Russell Sage Foundation.

Young, G. J., K. R. Desai, and C. V. Lukas. 1997. Does the Sale of Nonprofit Hospitals Threaten Health Care for the Poor? *Health Affairs* 16(1): 137–141.

Yuan, Z., G. S. Cooper, D. Einstadter, R. D. Cebul, and A. A. Rimm. 2000. The Association between Hospital Type and Mortality and Length of Stay: A Study of 16.9 Million Hospitalized Medicare Beneficiaries. *Medical Care* 38(2): 231–245.

Zuckerman, S., J. Hadley, and L. Iezzoni. 1994. Measuring Hospital Efficiency with Frontier Cost Functions. *Journal of Health Economics* 13(3): 255–280.

MARK A. HALL

■ *Arrow on Trust*

THE IMPORTANCE OF TRUST TO ARROW'S THESIS

Trust and other special attributes of the physician-patient relationship have a prominent position in Kenneth Arrow's 1963 seminal article, something that I failed to appreciate until now. During prior readings of Arrow's tour de force, I focused, as most readers have, on the structural and institutional aspects of health care delivery (information asymmetries, licensure and medical education, nonprofit hospitals, etc.) and on the interplay between health insurance and different forms of market failure. As Arrow's title and primary exposition directed, I thought about the connection these special market and institutional features have with the phenomena of risk and uncertainty. However, I failed previously to appreciate the central role that trust plays in making the connection between uncertainty and these special features. Indeed, I am now tempted to think that the word *trust* could easily be substituted for *uncertainty* in the article's title and in many of its most important passages. Thus Arrow's principal claim could easily be restated to say that "*virtually all the special features of this industry, in fact, stem from the prevalence of* [trust]" (946). Because trust arises from vulnerability, and uncertainty is one major form of vulnerability,[1] the psychological phenomenon of trust is just as important an adaptive response to the problematic aspects of health care delivery as is insurance. Most of the unique features of the medical marketplace, therefore, can be understood as enhancing or justifying the high level of trust that is needed in order to cope with the intense anxiety that results from uncertainty in the face of illness.

I came to this appreciation of trust only recently, as an outgrowth of my own interest in articulating a more empirically and psychologically grounded basis for thinking about issues of health care law and public policy, a perspective known as therapeutic jurisprudence (Hall 2002). This phenomenological viewpoint contrasts with the formalism of a more theoretically oriented perspective of the sort often taken by economists. It was exciting to rediscover that a foundational work in health economics can be informed by both perspectives.

The psychological and emotional realities of trust and illness bookend Arrow's more institutionally focused and theoretically informed economic analysis. Following his highly formal statement of the nature of the optimality gap problem, including various theorems and conceptual definitions from economic theory, Arrow begins the heart of his exposition with the following observation about the brute reality of illness: "The most obvious distinguishing characteristics of an individual's demand for medical services is that . . . [they] afford satisfaction only in the event of illness, a departure from the normal state of affairs" (948). Therefore, "the demand for medical services is associated, with considerable probability, with an assault on personal integrity" (949). Arrow could have made much more of the obvious yet profound impact of illness,[2] but he chose to let this observation stand unadorned, as his fundamental starting point.

Arrow's next observation relates to trust: "The customer cannot test the product before consuming it, and there is an element of trust in the relation" (949). From the predicate of trust, Arrow rattles off a host of unique features, including ethical restrictions on physician behavior, fiduciary devotion to the patient's interest and abnegation of the physician's self-interest, minimization of financial motivation, lack of price competition, a "discriminatory" pricing structure that takes income into account, the nonprofit status of most hospitals, mandatory licensure and barriers to entry in the profession, and uniform adherence to a high professional standard of care (or, unwillingness to bargain for a lower standard of care). Arrow makes some of these connections at the outset of the main exposition and others at the end of the article. In his final words, Arrow reminds us that medical care transactions are more akin to "personal and especially family relationships" than they are to exchanges in "the impersonal price system" (967).

Sandwiched between these discussions of the importance of trust and the special qualities of the physician-patient relationship is an elaboration on the topics (uncertainty, insurance, information asymmetry, and the role of government) for which this work is much more widely remembered. Without detracting from the significance of those themes, I focus on the alpha and omega of the article. In the spirit of his discipline, Arrow regards trust strategically, as an adaptive response to uncertainty that serves as a functional alternative to the costs of heightened monitoring or to market failures in insurance. In lieu of market-based mechanisms to reduce dysfunctional uncertainty, various social and professional conventions emerge to promote and enforce trust. With brief yet bold sketches,

Arrow anticipates the groundbreaking work of social theorists such as Nicholas Luhmann (1973) and the core insights of agency cost theory. As M. Gregg Bloche observes in this volume, Arrow's analysis of trust contains, in nascent form, many of the modern-day analytical tools of rational choice theory and behavioral law and economics, including a game-theoretic view of social norms and signaling behavior.[3]

Equally impressive is Arrow's ability to see beyond the perspective of his discipline and to recognize, if only briefly, the deeply emotional and interpersonal nature of trust in medical settings. Most economists think of trust in rational or calculative terms, as a form of confidence based on incentives, rules, or institutional features that gives one person reason to believe that another person will protect his or her interests (Hardin 2001; Williamson 1993). This somewhat lifeless, purely analytic form of trust neglects the brute reality of seeking care in the debilitating state of illness. Arrow recognizes that the psychology of trust shapes not only the behavior of the parties, expressed as the attributes of supply and demand, but also the fundamental nature of the product itself: "It is a commonplace that the physician-patient relation affects the quality of the medical care product. . . . That purely psychic interactions between physician and patient have effects which are objectively indistinguishable in kind from the effects of medication is evidenced by the use of the placebo as a control in medical experimentation" (951).

Perhaps more than anything else in his farsighted essay, this therapeutic perspective of trust anticipates radically new and astonishingly modern views of what health care delivery is about. In the decade following Arrow's article, discussions of trust fell into disfavor with the ascendancy of patient autonomy as a governing principle and more focus on patients' rights. Trust became associated with old-style medical paternalism, which medical ethicists were devoted to correcting (Sherlock 1986). Ensuing decades saw a resurgence of interest in the economic perspectives that Arrow both espouses and critiques, but this body of work, exemplified by Jaime Robinson's and Frank Sloan's critiques of Arrow in this volume, tends to neglect the psychological limitations of illness in favor of regarding patients as consumers engaged in market transactions.[4]

In recent years, however, there has been an outpouring of renewed interest in trust (Hall et al. 2001; Pearson and Raeke 2000; Mechanic 1998). Also, there is rapidly growing interest in holistic approaches to healing that reject the Cartesian dualism of traditional medicine and instead look to unorthodox schools of practice to understand the psychic and emotional dimensions of the treatment relationship to which Arrow alludes in his mention of the placebo effect. As Arrow suggests, these nonspecific or charismatic dimensions of healing are now seen as pervasive in medicine, and trust is thought to play a crucial role in these as-yet dimly understood, bio-psycho-social mechanisms (Brody 1997; Basmajian

1999). Thus—even regarding trust (as Peter Hammer does in this volume) as a purely instrumental good rather than something to be valued in its own right— preserving the psychology of trust in the core physician-patient relationship is essential to the efficacy of medicine. Interpersonal trust cannot, as Hammer suggests, be entirely diffused or replaced by alternative institutional arrangements because its unique psychology, rather than some contractual or regulatory surrogate, appears necessary to activate the full healing power of medicine.

ASSESSMENT

Arrow is to be congratulated for recognizing the fundamental importance of trust, but are the implications he draws from trust convincing, and are his observations still relevant in view of the growing cynicism that attends managed care? We must assess both whether Arrow's description of trust is accurate and whether the consequences he attributes to trust necessarily follow.

The Existence and Nature of Trust
Despite claims that trust is rapidly diminishing (Peters 2000), trust remains an essential component in patients' relationships with providers. A wave of empirical studies in the past five years documents that interpersonal trust in a specific, known physician remains at remarkably high levels and that most variation in trust is within the moderate-to-high range rather than from low-to-high (Hall et al. 2001, 2002a). It is sometimes observed that many patients have expectations that their godlike physicians can cure any ailment. Moreover, physician trust is highly resilient. Various patient characteristics have little or no effect on the level of trust, including demographics, health status, preferred role in medical decision making, or even patients' general level of cynicism about people or social institutions (Hall et al. 2001).[5] Because trust entails an optimistic view of physicians' benevolent motivation, patients are capable of extraordinary, and perhaps excessive, levels of forgiveness. Trust induces patients to view poor performance in the most positive light, as unintended or unavoidable isolated events that do not undermine their fundamental assumptions about their physician's intentions and abilities (Ben Sira 1980; Murray, Holmes, and Griffin 1996).

Contrary studies, which Mark A. Peterson and others in this volume cite to show lower trust, refer to trust in the medical profession as a whole, to "leaders in medicine," or to physicians' role in social and public policy affairs rather than their role in care delivery. This captures only trust at a social, institutional, or system level, not interpersonal trust,[6] which has a distinctly different psychological basis. In the inner sanctum of the treatment relationship, the concern is that trust may be too high, not too low, creating impossible demands on physicians and institutions to meet such unrealistic expectations. A number of commentators criticize this excessive level of trust as irrational and unjustified, and they argue for a legal or ethical regime that seeks to institutionalize greater wariness or distrust (Buchanan 2000; Veatch 2000). Others maintain that elevated trust is either desirable for therapeutic reasons or is inevitable for psychological reasons, and so it would be either counterproductive or futile to attempt to lower trust (Pellegrino and Thomasma 1993). Overstated confidence may be a necessary defense mechanism that enables patients to cope with the psychological distress of illness and that allows them to submit to highly invasive and risky treatment, and it may activate internal healing mechanisms that enhance the effectiveness of more observable biochemical therapies. Whether or not high trust is desirable or inevitable, however, it unquestionably remains a central feature of medical care. On this point, Arrow hit the target dead center.

Where Arrow's treatment of trust might be critiqued descriptively is in his failure to attribute trust to the inherent vulnerability created by illness and by the process of treatment. He first views the uncertainty of illness as a statistical, not a psychological, phenomenon — one that occurs episodically and unpredictably and can entail large expenditures — but this is also true of the weather, which does not necessarily produce trust. The episodic and catastrophic nature of illness is more relevant as a psychological phenomenon that produces intense levels of anxiety. Arrow focuses on uncertainty over the success of treatment, but he only briefly acknowledges that the very condition of illness alters one's fundamental mental framework and sense of self.[7] Beyond the existential reality of illness, seeking treatment greatly intensifies the sense of vulnerability that gives rise to trust. Treatment entails exposing our bodies and personal histories, and, depending on the particular illness and treatment, tremendous levels of vulnerability are often created by giving physicians unprecedented access to every part of ourselves, down to our very blood and guts, while we remain prostrate or unconscious. The resulting implications for trust are much more profound than are the statistical and monetary aspects of illness and treatment.

Recognizing these intrinsic characteristics of medical care delivery helps respond to the leading criticism of Arrow's thesis. Critics claim that the unique features he identifies are artifacts of the particular institutional arrangements that existed at the time and so are contingent effects rather than fundamental attributes. Focusing on trust, however, points us toward features of medical care that are inherent, universal, and uniquely intensified. These roots are deeper and more profoundly transformative than the contingent social conditions, institutional arrangements, or physician behaviors that may affect trust at the margin.

Implications of Trust for Market Structures
Granted that trust is strong, pervasive, and resilient, what are the consequences for economic and regulatory policy? Arrow is clearly correct that trust funda-

mentally alters the structure of medical transactions and institutions, but each of his particular examples are not equally convincing. The connections he draws are each consistent with trust, but they are not each necessary.

Most convincing are the general claims that high levels of physician trust require strong ethical commitments of professionalism and various methods to assure competence. These protections are needed, either to justify and sustain high levels of trust or to punish violations of trust. The particular methods to achieve these general goals are not cast in stone, however. Arrow recognizes this limitation for medical education and professional licensure, but he overstates his case for the necessity of particular pricing and payment methods and for a uniformly high standard of care.

Medical education and licensure promote trust by creating reasonable assurances that anyone wearing the white coat is skilled and knowledgeable in medicine. These assurances are reinforced by malpractice liability or professional discipline when individual physicians fail to measure up to minimal competence standards. As Arrow explains at some length, these trust-promoting functions could be adequately served without subsidizing medical education and without making medical licensure exclusive. How far licensure might depart from the traditional model without undermining trust is an empirical question, however, for which there still is little hard data.

Arrow claims that trust requires a uniform standard of quality and precludes any compromise in the technologically achievable level of quality in order to save costs. He states: "The safest course [for a physician] to take . . . is to give the socially prescribed 'best' treatment of the day. Compromise in quality, even for the purpose of saving the patient money, is to risk an imputation of failure to live up to the social bond" (966). This is a resounding defense of medicine's traditional embrace of a "one right way" ethic and the rejection of any rationing (cost-benefit trade-offs), at least at the bedside. Under this view, if costs are to be taken into account, as they must be in some fashion, this should occur through external constraints, such as those imposed by government controls.

One is tempted to imagine that Arrow was influenced by an environment in which medicine was much less costly and practiced virtually free of modern-day technology, but this does not appear to account for his strong position against bedside rationing. Medical costs were taken seriously even in 1963, and Arrow clearly recognized the inevitability of resource allocation concerns. Therefore, one can only assume he would maintain the same position today.

I have argued elsewhere that this position cannot be justified in terms of making optimal allocation decisions. Requiring physicians to internalize costs at least to some degree will produce better informed and more nuanced allocation decisions than imposing cost constraints entirely by external, rule-based authority (Hall 1997). A rule-based regime might nevertheless be socially optimal if it is necessary to preserve trust, since making technically accurate decisions would be of little consolation if patients refused to follow their physicians' recommendations, or worse still, refused to even go to physicians. However, subsequent experience and empirical evidence show the contrary—that high trust can be sustained even if physicians consider costs. Trust in managed care physicians is only slightly lower than in physicians paid through indemnity insurance, a difference most likely accounted for by reduced choice of physicians than by concerns over bedside rationing (Safran et al. 1998; Kao et al. 1998). When people are asked whether they prefer government or insurers to set limits rather than their physicians, their resounding response is "no" (Hall 1996). Elsewhere, Bob Berenson and I speculate that the essential ethical requirement for sustaining trust is a pledge of impartiality, that is, for a physician to treat all patients the same, based on their condition, regardless of method of payment (Hall and Berenson 1998). This does not require that each physician pledge to deliver the most expensive conceivable standard of care. Each physician may respond globally, across all patients, according to the particular mix of payment sources. Under this view, a physician paid by capitation for some patients may ethically, and trustworthily, offer less care to patients than a physician paid entirely by fee-for-service, as long as the capitated physician treats all patients the same. This is consistent with how physicians in fact appear to respond to managed care incentives (Glied and Zivin 2000; Balkrishnan et al. under review).

The barriers that trust creates to negotiating for a lower standard of care are greatly reduced today, compared to 1963, by the emergence of managed care organizations. Conditions of trust and vulnerability rightly preclude enforcing care-lowering agreements made ex post, at the time of illness. However, the merger of financing and care-delivery structures now allows these bargains to be struck ex ante, through the purchase of insurance, when patients are not typically ill and are not dealing directly with their personal physicians. Moreover, such decisions are made on behalf of large groups by employers or other representatives with considerable knowledge and bargaining clout. Naturally, various imperfections exist in the insurance and labor markets, which keep these representatives from being perfect purchasing agents, but these flaws are far less serious than if patients were expected to bargain directly with their physicians and hospitals at the time of treatment, in circumstances where vulnerability is much more acute, and maintaining deeply emotional, interpersonal trust much more essential. There may be other strong, psychological reasons not to enforce bargains that constrain future treatment options in circumstances that are impossible to contemplate at the time the contract is made (Ubel 1999). But these reasons are related to concerns other than trust.

Even if physicians respond properly to managed care influences, we still should be concerned about how they are paid, since the presence of conflicting incentives might undermine patients' trust regardless of how upright physicians' behavior might be. Arrow states that trust requires physicians to at least maintain the appearance that money and self-interest are not prime motivators. This position has considerable merit, since the essence of trust is patients' belief that their physician is pursing their best interests. However, Arrow should not be read as overstating the case against financial motivation and financial conflicts of interest. Trust has not been undermined by the agency imperfections entailed in high levels of fee-for-service reimbursement. Cost-*minimizing* incentives come from a different quiver, but, so far, they too appear to be consistent with trust. In one study, trust was not decreased when patients were told that their physicians are paid in a way that rewards cost savings, even among patients who did not realize this. Instead, making this disclosure increased trust a small increment, perhaps as a consequence of demonstrated candor (Hall et al. 2002b).

It is too soon to know whether trust will endure once patients accustomed to physician practice styles and standards of care that developed under fee-for-service medicine experience the full effects of using cost-containment incentives for all medical care. However, there is strong reason to believe that trust will survive. Because its source is the deeply embedded vulnerability of illness and the nature of medical care, trust is not contingent on particular methods of payment. This does not mean that any payment method is acceptable. However, it does indicate that, within reasonable ranges, payment methods can vary without great risk to trust. Therefore, concerns about financial conflicts of interest arising from managed care payment methods (such as those expressed by Gloria Bazzoli in this volume) are addressed more to normative claims regarding trust*worthiness* than they are to empirical claims about sustaining actual levels of trust.

IMPLICATIONS FOR MANAGED CARE REGULATION

So far, this discussion has focused on the descriptive and predictive aspects of Arrow's treatment of trust. Arrow avoided drawing many prescriptive conclusions about how these observations should inform public policy. I will not restrain myself so admirably but will comment briefly on how improved understanding of trust might inform current debates about managed care regulation.

Concerns about the fragility of trust are appropriately directed to institutional trust in contrast with interpersonal physician trust. Trust in medical institutions is not as high, it shows signs of declining, and it appears to be more reactive to social and economic influences (Blendon et al. 1998; Zheng et al. 2002; Balkrishnan, Dugan, and Hall under review). In 1963, institutional trust was not nearly as great a concern in medicine when most physicians practiced solo and insurance was primarily indemnity. Now, medical institutions obviously are much more prominent. Managed care, especially, threatens to permeate the treatment environment with a climate of distrust (Mechanic 1996; Anders 1996). Even if managed care does not undermine the core physician-patient relationship, accessing and paying for care under conditions of distrust surely is not optimal. It is thus both ironic and paradoxical that managed care is the form of insurance that arose to fill several of the optimality gaps that Arrow identified. As Arrow prophesied, "the social adjustment towards optimality [appears to have] put obstacles in its own path" (947). These concerns have recently given rise to patient protection laws intended to restore the public's faith in medical care delivery influenced by managed care institutions.

Managed care undoubtedly has engendered some degree of distrust, but caution is warranted in devising measures to restore trust. Not only may these efforts entail other costs and have no effect, they also can be counterproductive. Efforts to improve trust can, paradoxically, weaken trust. This is so because the law's regulatory functions can compete with its expressive functions, and the expressive effects of law can be complex, unpredictable, and multidimensional (Posner 2000). Efforts to improve the performance of physicians or medical institutions can backfire by confirming the public attitude of distrust and by reducing medical actors' motivations to behave in a trustworthy fashion. A set of elaborate provisions telling patients their rights and regulating the behavior of managed care organizations could easily convey to patients the idea that HMOs and their physicians cannot be trusted. Correlatively, such measures can convey to physicians and insurers that they are not in fact trusted and are not expected to act from intrinsically trustworthy motivation. Economists refer to this as a *crowd-out* phenomenon in which a heavily regulatory legal regime tends to displace intrinsic motivation with extrinsic penalties or rewards (Frey 1997). This can undermine both the perception and the reality of trustworthiness. From the patient's perspective, a perception that the physician or institution does not intrinsically value one's interests undermines the foundation of strong trust because of trust's assumptions about benevolent motivation. From the perspective of the trusted party, explicit regulation tends to produce compliance only with the precise scope of the law and only to the extent of actual enforcement, rather than a more global or inner ethic that reciprocates trust with trustworthy behavior.

This is not meant to be a per se argument against managed care regulation, however. The same points about crowding out intrinsic motivation can also be true for market-oriented incentive reward systems. Both market incentives and regulatory controls are meant to correct for physicians' failure to be perfect agents for their patients' best welfare, yet either strategy has the potential to backfire. But these theoretical possibilities should not forestall all efforts to improve trust or trustworthiness. Instead, realizing the potentially paradoxical nature of trust helps to better craft supportive or corrective measures in a way that is more likely to achieve their trust-related goals. Doing so requires that we distinguish between law's regulatory and its expressive functions and determine whether these effects are likely to be complementary or competing. In the latter event, we must then decide which is likely to dominate and whether it is more important to pursue trust itself or instead to promote trustworthy conditions.

Often this path of reasoning may advise us to adopt broad standards rather than detailed rules, and it may counsel us to have rather weak or nondirective enforcement mechanisms (Sitkin 1995). At certain extremes, it may be possible, or even advisable, to tolerate an environment in which trust-related laws are quietly violated at the same time that the laws' underlying principles are used for rhetorical advantage. Physician assistance in dying is a leading case in point (White 1999). Contradiction between principle and practice is feasible as long as it is not so blatant or severe that cynicism is widespread and the ethos of trust destroyed. Lip-service respect for the law can be attacked as a gross hypocrisy, but it is also possible that heightened tension between principle and practice may, like a stretched rubber band, serve only to strengthen the pull of principle and the motivational force of a trust-based legal regime.

NOTES

1   For a contrasting viewpoint, however, that distinguishes between uncertainty and vulnerability, see Heimer 2001.

2   Edmund Pellegrino (1991) refers to illness as an "ontological assault" on personal identity.

3   For instance, compare the following passage from Arrow with recent (Posner 2000; McAdams 2000) game-theoretic analyses of law and norms:

> Because there is no market in which the risks involved can be insured, coordination of purchase and sales must take place through convergent expectations, but these are greatly assisted by having clear and prominent signals, and these, in turn, force patterns of behavior which are not in themselves logical necessities for optimality. (966)

4   Robinson and Sloan correctly take Arrow and his adherents to task for assuming that uncertainty is a unique difficulty in medicine, viewed as a *statistical* phenomenon, but they fail to appreciate that the *emotional* dimension of uncertainty is uniquely difficult in medicine in ways that profoundly affect a market system, as a consequence of the intense anxiety and greatly diminished capacity that can attend even routine illness. Thus they suppose that health care should be roughly on par with other determinants of *health*, such as food, shelter, and risky behavior, without recognizing the key difference of seeking *care* in a condition of illness.

5 Some of these factors, such as race, age, or education, have been found to have a statistically significant relationship with trust, but these findings have not been consistent across studies and not of a very large magnitude.

6 Even then, some of these studies show that system or institutional trust remains high or at respectable levels (American Medical Association 1997; Zheng et al. 2002; Hall, Camacho, and Dugan 2002).

7 "The demand for medical services is associated . . . with an assault on personal integrity" (949). Arrow trivializes this point by placing illness on par with hunger and by quickly shifting his attention to the "major potential for loss or reduction of earning capacity" (949).

REFERENCES

American Medical Association. 1997. *Public Opinion on Health Care Issues*. Chicago: American Medical Association.

Anders, G. 1996. Health Against Wealth: HMOs and the Breakdown of Medical Trust. Boston: Houghton Mifflin.

Arrow, K. J. 1963. Uncertainty and the Welfare Economics of Medical Care. *American Economic Review* 53(5): 941–973.

Balkrishnan, R., M. A. Hall, D. Mehrabi, G. J. Chen, S. R. Feldman, and A. B. Fleischer. 2002. Capitation Payment, Length of Visit, and Preventative Services: Evidence from a National Sample of Outpatient Physicians. *American Journal of Managed Care* 8(4): 332–340.

Balkrishnan, R., E. Dugan, and M.A. Hall. Under review. A Comprehensive Analysis of Trust and Satisfaction regarding Physicians, Insurers, and the Medical Profession.

Basmajian, J. V. 1999. Debonafide Effects vs. "Placebo Effects." *Proceedings of the Royal College of Physicians, Edinburgh* 29: 243–244.

Ben Sira, Z. 1980. Affective and Instrumental Components in the Physician-Patient Relationship: An Additional Dimension of Interaction Theory. *Journal of Health and Social Behavior* 21: 170–180.

Blendon, R. J., M. Brodie, J. M. Benson, D. E. Altman, L. Levitt, T. Hoff, and L. Hugick. 1998. Understanding the Managed Care Backlash. *Health Affairs* 17(4): 80–94.

Brody, H. 1997. The Doctor as Therapeutic Agent: A Placebo Effect Research Agenda. In *The Placebo Effect: an Interdisciplinary Exploration*, ed. A. Harrington. Cambridge: Harvard University Press.

Buchanan, A. 2000. Trust in Managed Care Organizations. *Kennedy Institute of Ethics Journal* 10(3): 189–212.

Frey, B. S. 1997. *Not Just for the Money: An Economic Theory of Personal Motivation*. Cheltenham, U.K.: Edward Elgar.

Glied, S. A. and J. G. Zivin. 2000. *How Do Doctors Behave When Some (but Not All) of Their Patients Are in Managed Care?* Cambridge, MA: National Bureau of Economic Research.

Hall, M. A. 1996. The Public's Preference for Bedside Rationing. *Archives of Internal Medicine* 156: 1353–1354.

————. 1997. *Making Medical Spending Decisions: The Law, Ethics, and Economics of Rationing Mechanisms.* New York: Oxford University Press.

Hall, M. A. 2002. Trust, Law, and Medicine: Towards a Therapeutic Jurisprudence of Health Care Delivery. *Stanford law Review* 55: 463–527.

Hall, M. A., and R. Berenson. 1998. Managed Care Medical Ethics: A Dose of Realism. *Annals of Internal Medicine* 128: 395–402.

Hall, M. A., E. Dugan, B. Zheng, and A. Mishra. 2001. Trust in Physicians and Medical Institutions: What Is It, Can It Be Measured, and Does It Matter? *Milbank Quarterly* 79(4): 613–639.

Hall, M. A., B. Zheng, E. Dugan, F. Camacho, K. E. Kidd, and R. Balkrishnan. 2002d. Measuring Patients' Trust in Their Primary Care Providers. *Medical Care Research and Review* 59(3): 293–318.

Hall, M. A., E. Dugan, R. Balkrishnan, and D. Bradley. 2002 b. How Disclosing HMO Physician Incentives Affects Trsut. *Health Affairs* 21(2): 197–202.

Hall, M. A., Fabian Camacho. Elizabeth Dugan, and Rajesh Balkrishnan. 2002c. Trust in the Medical Profession: Conceptual and measurement Issues. *Health Services Research* 37: 1419–1439.

Hardin, R. 2001. *Trust and Trustworthiness.* New York: Sage.

Heimer, C. A. 2001. Solving the Problem of Trust. In *Trust in Society,* ed. K. S. Cook. New York: Russell Sage Foundation.

Kao, A., D. C. Green, A. Zaslavski, J. P. Koplan, and P. D. Cleary. 1998. The Relationship between Method of Physician Payment and Patient Trust. *Journal of the American Medical Association* 280: 1708–1714.

Luhmann, N. 1973. *Trust and Power.* Chichester, U.K.: Wiley.

McAdams, R. H. 2000. A Focal Point Theory of Expressive Law. *Virginia Law Review* 86(8): 1649–1730.

Mechanic, D. 1996. Changing Medical Organization and the Erosion of Trust. *Milbank Quarterly* 74: 171–189.

Mechanic, D. 1998. The Functions and Limitations of Trust in the Provision of Medical Care. *Journal of Health Politics, Policy and Law* 23: 661–686.

Murray, S. L., J. G. Holmes, and D. W. Griffin. 1996. The Self-Fulfilling Nature of Positive Illusions in Romantic Relationships: Love Is Not Blind, but Prescient. *Journal of Personality and Social Psychology* 71(6): 1155–1180.

Pearson, S. D., and L. H. Raeke. 2000. Patients' Trust in Physicians: Many Theories, Few Measures, and Little Data. *Journal of General Internal Medicine* 15: 509–513.

Pellegrino, E. D. 1991. Trust and Distrust in Professional Ethics. In *Ethics, Trust, and the Professions: Philosophical and Cultural Aspects,* ed. E. D. Pellegrino, R. M. Veatch, and J. P. Langan. Washington, DC: Georgetown University Press.

Pellegrino, E. D., and D. C. Thomasma. 1993. *The Virtues in Medical Practice.* New York: Oxford University Press.

Peters, P. G. Jr. 2000. The Quiet Demise of Deference to Custom: Malpractice Law at the Millennium. *Washington & Lee Law Review* 57: 163–205.

Posner, E. A. 2000. *Law and Social Norms.* Cambridge: Harvard University Press.

Safran, D. G., D. A. Taira, W. H. Rogers, M. Kosinski, J. E. Ware, and A. R. Tarlov. 1998.

Linking Primary Care Performance to Outcomes of Care. *Journal of Family Practice* 47: 213.

Sherlock, R. 1986. Reasonable Men and Sick Human Beings. *American Journal of Medicine* 80: 2–4.

Sitkin, S. B. 1995. On the Positive Effect of Legalization on Trust. *Research on Negotiation in Organizations* 5: 185–217.

Ubel, P. A. 1999. How Stable Are People's Preferences for Giving Priority to Severely Ill Patients? *Social Science & Medicine* 49: 895–903.

Veatch, R. M. 2000. Doctor Does Not Know Best: Why in the New Century Physicians Must Stop Trying to Benefit Patients. *Journal of Medicine and Philosophy* 25(6): 701–721.

Williamson, O. E. 1993. Calculativeness, Trust, and Economic Organization. *Journal of Law & Economics* 36: 453–486.

Zheng, B., M. A. Hall, E. Dugan, K. E. Kidd, and D. Levine. 2002. Development of a Scale to Measure Patients' Trust in Health Insurers. *Health Services Research* 37: 187–204.

MARK A. PETERSON

■ From Trust to Political Power: Interest Groups,

Public Choice, and Health Care

In 1963 Kenneth Arrow offered a simple empirical observation that suggested a core impediment to the effective functioning of market arrangements in health care. "Because medical knowledge is so complicated," he noted, "the information possessed by the physician as to the consequences and possibilities of treatment is very much greater than that of the patient, or at least it is so believed by both parties" (951). According to Arrow, however, society found a way to manage this information asymmetry that would otherwise leave people vulnerable to suboptimal decision making and exploitation by the suppliers of medical services. "Delegation and trust are the social institutions designed to obviate the problem of informational inequality" (966).

According to this reasoning, we make efficacious choices by permitting our physicians to both define the choice set of the various treatment options and weight their expected values. We feel comfortable delegating a significant chunk of our decision-making sovereignty regarding medical care because of the trust we have in our physicians. But in Arrow's framework, why does this dyadic trust emerge in which we place such faith, given the lack of a formal instrument for insuring against a failure to benefit from medical care? Not primarily because as individuals our physicians are gracious, or benevolent, or even just plain smart, although those characteristics may be relevant. We trust our physicians in this dyadic relationship because of a collective or social attribute we recognize in them, that is, a "generalized belief in the ability of the physician" predicated on his or her formally prescribed, scientifically grounded professional training and license to practice medicine in accordance with the standards of the profession (965). Indeed, should someone fall ill, say, at a public gathering, the general call goes out for "a doctor" and the individuals who may be lending immediate comfort yield without question to the entirely unknown woman or man who appears and establishes this professional link by stating simply "I'm a doctor" and proceeds to treat the patient.

Other essays in this volume explore, and often question, the reliability of individuals granting such inclusive trust to physicians to guide their personal medical care, especially as we know more about what "the doctor" does not know while social and technological change have evened the informational scales at least a bit. I examine a broader consequence of physicians' claims of knowledge and trust that Arrow minimized in his analysis but that have had profound implications for the organization, financing, and delivery of health care services as they are experienced by the nation as a whole. Based on the same claims to science and knowledge that medicine has used to invite our dyadic trust in physicians at the individual level, the medical profession has long sought, and often obtained, broad-based social trust in its leadership of health care policy making by local, state, and federal governments. Organized medicine has sought to dominate the politics and policy of health care by arguing that only it as a profession has the understanding of science and practice necessary to construct optimal social arrangements for providing access to care. Until the legitimacy of this exclusive claim was successfully disputed, starting primarily in the 1970s, and other groups developed the organizational wherewithal and informational capacity to call into question the social trust that physicians had enjoyed, the medical profession, with the rhetoric of commitment to the public good, had employed its trust-based political leverage to extend and protect its economic self-interest. This essay is about the negative social consequences of trust in physicians, which Arrow did not adequately anticipate given his focus on the dyadic form of trust, and how the social role of physicians has changed in the ensuing decades.

TRUST AND DELEGATION AS POLITICAL POWER

Professions gain respect and their members garner both dyadic and social trust because they develop and inculcate among their ranks specialized knowledge that the average person, lacking the profession's formal training, cannot acquire or easily interpret. As captured by the old cliché, however, knowledge is power — not only power evident in the application of a profession's knowledge about particular decisions in its standard workplace, but influence over the entire social structure that defines and regulates the environment in which that work is accomplished.

One of the most preeminent sociologists studying the professions, Eliot Freidson (1986: 185–186), notes that "to gain insight into the full range of professional powers, we must move outside the workplace and into the broader political economy. . . . [and look at] those who are in a position to influence the policies of the state on which the special position of the profession depends." Professions, says Albert Dzur (2002:178), "are political entities, not just when they form interest groups, but because in the intermediary realm of civil society professions possess the power to distract, encourage, limit, and inform public recognition of and deliberation over social problems." In this realm, stated simply by Phillip Elliott (1972: 147), "the profession claims unique responsibility for some aspect of the *public* good. It also claims to know how that good should be achieved" (italics added). That assertion by a profession is always made with calls to the public interest and implied confidence in the objectivity of the profession's stance. Jürgen Habermas (1971) reminds us, however, that these claims may be no more than a politically astute fig leaf covering up efforts to usurp decisions that otherwise would be rightly pursued in the full light of democratic policy making, taking them in a direction contrary to the interests and will of the public. Ultimately an appeal may be made to what Gary Belkin (1998) calls "the technocratic wish," the erroneous notion that issues of real and contentious politics can be answered or managed most effectively by redefining them as scientific, technical, objective — based, of course, on the presumption that the relevant profession can dominate the meaning and historical logic given to these terms (see also Freidson 1970, 1986; Morone and Belkin 1995).

It would be fair to say that medicine is, or more accurately was, the paragon of professional power. Just as Arrow located the individual's need to trust his or her physician in the perspective that "medical knowledge is so complicated" and asymmetrically possessed by the doctor, so too the "profession bases its claim for its position on the possession of a skill so esoteric or complex that nonmembers of the profession cannot perform the work safely or satisfactorily and cannot even evaluate the work properly. . . . They claim that their esoteric expertise is such that only they are able to determine what is wrong with humanity, how it may best be served, and at what price" (Freidson 1970: 45, 368; Starr 1982). "All features of medical service in any method of medical practice," stated a 1934 resolution adopted by the American Medical Association's House of Delegates, "should be under the control of the profession. No other body or individual is legally or educationally equipped to exercise such control" (quoted in Millenson 1997a: 188). In Steven Brint's (1994: 36) terms, medicine "combined civic-minded moral appeals and circumscribed *technical* appeals" to project "social trustee professionalism." What undergirds faith in our individual physicians thus empowers them collectively in issues that are as removed from explicit medical practice as taxation, allocative fairness, public administration, and political accountability — issues on which other legitimate interests and the population as a whole may in fact have quite different positions than those promulgated by medical practitioners themselves.

Just about twenty years after Arrow's seminal analysis, with trust posed as a societal response to fill a crucial gap in the market, Paul Starr won the 1984 Pulitzer Prize for his historical and sociological study of how American medicine waged a long-term battle to gain scientifically grounded legitimacy and establish its professional dominance over clinical practice (physician-patient dyadic engagement), medical organization (the structure and leadership of health care institutions), and health care financing (the sources and arrangements for paying medical costs) (1982). In this struggle physicians were neither predetermined victors nor simply serving, by societal "design" or structural-function adaptability of social institutions, the interests of the larger community (see Elliott 1972: 6). They had to successfully make exclusive claims to science and medical efficacy — liking to view themselves, notes Brint (1994: 59), as "applied scientists" — and do so at the expense of the range of competing practitioners they confronted at the end of the nineteenth century. Establishing its scientific roots (and disparaging those of others), organized medicine gained a legitimacy that allowed it to acquire what Starr (1982: 13) calls "cultural authority, . . . [which] entails the construction of reality through definitions of fact and value." In Freidson's (1970: 205–206) words, "in the course of obtaining a monopoly over its work, medicine has also obtained well-nigh exclusive jurisdiction over determining what illness is and therefore how people must act in order to be treated as ill. . . . by virtue of being the authority on what illness 'really' is, *medicine creates the social possibilities for acting sick*" (italics in original). Through this domination of both its work and the social meaning and consequences of illness, Starr argues that physicians sought to preserve two core domains of autonomy: economic (the size and circumstances of their incomes) and clinical (control over the nature of medical practice and treatment decisions). From those forms of autonomy derives the motive for and resources, material and intellectual, to demand considerable autonomy in setting health policy, nominally the responsibility of federal, state, and local governments that should be responsive to their entire constituencies.

Does, in fact, the professional power of medicine translate into political power for organized medicine? Paul Starr's analysis would seem to make this a question hardly worth asking. Economist Paul Feldstein, in his book, *Health Associations*, states categorically, "In the past, health legislation at both a state and a federal level has been strongly influenced by health interest groups. In many respects, the structure of our health care system is a result of the legislative activity of these groups. . . . The American Medical Association is the most influential of the health professional organizations" (1977: 2, 27).

These declarations, however, are offered devoid of any citations to explicit evidence of this power. As a general proposition, the demonstrated influence of organized interests is far more circumspect. Consider this summary judgment from Frank Baumgartner and Beth Leech (1998), who recently combed the political science literature on interest group efforts to affect the outcomes of policy making:

Early interest-group studies shared the outlook of early subsystem studies. Interest groups were enormously powerful, and insider groups had the advantage. . . . Several important studies published in the 1960s helped challenge this view. Interest-group influence was . . . benign. . . . The popular conclusion drawn from these studies was that interest groups did not exert pressure, indeed were not influential. If it were that simple, we could simply say that interest groups were once seen as all-powerful, but more recent studies have shown this to be wrong. . . . However, interest groups at times probably are weak and ineffectual, and at other times very effective at getting what they want. . . . Unfortunately, the accumulated mass of quantitative and qualitative studies of lobbying behavior has generated a great number of contradictions, with few consistent findings. . . . The studies reviewed . . . . for all their contradictions, have in fact taught us something important: they allow us to stipulate at least occasional interest-group influence and to concentrate instead on the circumstances under which groups are influential. (125, 126, 127, 140, 146)

Briefly stated, having the capacity to shape public policy requires possessing the kinds of attributes that matter to and could influence elected officials, their advisers, and agency officials. A quick survey of the literature reveals a number of group characteristics that would be advantageous in the "political market"[1]:

— *Information*: Government officials who have policy-making authority and are accountable to electoral constituencies need information to overcome two types of uncertainty. The first involves the linkages between proposed policy actions and actual policy outcomes as experienced by the public. The second pertains to how one's own constituency is likely to see and interpret what government does and respond to it politically. Organizations representing knowledge-based, high-status individuals or institutions earn automatic recognition and have particular credibility in helping to resolve both kinds of uncertainty.

— *Recurrent interactions with policy makers*: The credibility of the information provided by organized interests to policy makers is tested through repeated interactions and the establishment of stable relationships. In the competition among groups, active participation in issues that are regularly on the government agenda gives an organization the opportunity to solidify impressions of its value as an information source.

— *Large and dispersed membership*: Because elected officials are so sensitive to the attitudes of the districts or states they represent, organizations have greater access and potential influence when they include a policy maker's constituents (and can make valid claims to actually speak on their behalf). Large and widely distributed memberships or clientele expand the number of elected officials with whom the interest will have a direct relationship. The effects are strengthened if an organization can stimulate grassroots mobilization. However, an interest with a large and dispersed base can also fall victim to the collective action and free-rider problems identified by Mancur Olson (1965) and thus need other attributes, such as an occupational connection and selective benefits, discussed by Olson (1965) and Walker (1991), to overcome this hurdle.

— *Quasi-Unanimity*: Large organizations are also more prone to having disparate interests among their memberships, possibly yielding factionalization, threatening their ability to take expressed positions in issues of public policy. Effective organized interests have to possess enough cohesion and focus on shared core interests to project something representing a unified front on high-priority policy concerns.

— *Organizational resources*: Economic and status resources make it possible for an association to attract one of its most important organizational resources: a large, skilled, experienced, and professional staff. Staffs of this caliber have a better sense of how to frame issues, gather appropriate information and conduct research, mobilize the membership, orchestrate media campaigns, and facilitate communications with policy makers.

— *Electoral Resources*: Policy makers need both political intelligence about their constituencies and campaign funds to launch effective drives for election and reelection. At the national level, since the Federal Election Campaign Act of 1974, campaign contributions by organized interests have been primarily formalized through the establishment of associated political action committees (PACs). In addition to having a large, dispersed, unified membership, PAC money provides signals about an organization's political wherewithal, issue priorities, and constituency influence.

— *Policy niche and coalition leadership*: No group could hope to become a forceful and respected voice on all matters of public policy. Credibility, unity, and impact are enhanced when an organized interest is able to claim a comparative advantage in information and resources over other interests in a particular policy niche or domain, especially if the group's association is recognized and supported by other compatible interests as a coalition leader.

ORGANIZED MEDICINE AS AN ORGANIZED INTEREST, CIRCA 1963

Has organized medicine, as a profession and as formally represented by the American Medical Association (and other physician societies), had the attributes one would associate with being able to influence political agenda setting, debate, and policy making? Most organized interests at the national or state level at any given time do not possess any of these attributes, at least reliably. A relatively small proportion can lay claim to more than a couple, and they may even be in conflict with one another (for example, as noted earlier, a large membership can interfere with developing a unified policy position and establishing niche leadership). It is profoundly striking that at the time Arrow published his article, the American Medical Association—the primary organization representing physician interests—unquestionably possessed *all* of these attributes (see Campion 1984). It may have been the only organized interest in America for which that has ever been true. In addition, among the individual characteristics noted earlier, the AMA quite simply stood out among other interests. When Arrow was surveying the health care marketplace, organized medicine had almost no worthy competitors for providing policy makers with substantive information about medicine and its practice. The trust that individuals felt toward their personal physicians had its social complement in the general trust extended to organized medicine in matters of public policy. Other physician societies and health organizations, too, deferred to the AMA in this collective policy-making role. The entire health services research and health policy research enterprise, and the community of specialists in this domain who eventually challenged positions of the AMA, did not really begin until after 1965 and the passage of Medicare and took years to mature (Brown 1991).

In addition, too, few organizations could compete with the reach of organized medicine, with members in probably close to every single legislative district (state or federal) and certainly every state, responsive to requests for direct grassroots participation and able to expand the effects of their ranks by stimulating favorable reactions among their trusting patients. At the time, more than nine out of ten practicing physicians in the country belonged to the AMA as well as its state associations and county medical societies. The AMA has often spent more money than any other group represented in the nation's capital to influence government policy (Rayak 1967; Feldstein 1977). In AMPAC (the AMA Political Action Committee), the AMA also had the third oldest political action committee in the country (formed just before Arrow began to write his seminal essay); it is far and away the leading campaign contributor among health care organizations (Weissert and Weissert 1996). Certainly in 1963, when the Arrow article was published, the AMA was the undisputed leader of an alliance of physicians, hospitals, insurers, and employers that sought to shape state and federal public policies in accordance with its interests and perspectives (Peterson 1993). It is no wonder, therefore, that Carol Weissert and William Weissert (1996: 97), in their opening summary of health care interests groups, commented that "in 1965 the American Medical Association was the strongest health lobby and probably the most powerful lobby of any kind in the country."

What did organized medicine seek to accomplish with the repeated and sustained application of this political leverage? To use the terminology of Arrow's economist colleagues, a main objective was the acquisition of *rents*. In the public choice framework, physicians, as a rational, self-interested profession, sought to get the state to use its power and resources to their economic benefit. The foundation for this line of analysis, anticipated by Arrow, was laid in 1971 by George Stigler in his article on "The Theory of Economic Regulation." Stigler emphasized industry efforts to secure direct governmental subsidies, control entry, restrict substitutes and promote complements, and engage in price-fixing. These issues were later pursued in much greater detail, with a specific health care application, by Paul Feldstein (1977). He hypothesized that one would find organized medicine promoting "demand increasing policies," "preferred methods of reimbursement," "reductions in the price of complements to the production of physician services," "increases in the price of substitutes for physicians," and "restrictions in the supply of physicians" (chaps. 1 and 2). Like the sociologists Starr and Freidson, Feldstein identified a number of enacted state and federal policies—from constraints on the availability of medical education to required licensure, from public subsidies to expand hospitals to restrictions on the practice of chiropractic, and so forth—that comport with the rent-seeking interests of organized medicine. Cause and effect are not fully drawn by Feldstein, but the health policy parameters of the American state, starting with early in the twentieth century as organized medicine was consolidating its legitimacy, looks a lot like those that physicians as a group desired.

Many of these provisions, such as limiting the number of training slots for new physicians and licensing according to the dictates of the AMA, were sold to the public and policy makers by organized medicine as important means for ensuring quality and preventing the practice of "quack" medicine. But, as Feldstein notes, that justification loses merit when one identifies how few policies have been put forward by organized medicine to ensure the quality of practice once physicians have entered the workforce and how resistant it has been to alternative approaches. In addition, organized medicine purports to endorse a number of public health initiatives in addition to the policies that facilitate the clinical and economic autonomy of physicians. Where, though, does it put its political dollars? AMPAC consistently directs campaign contributions to those members of Congress who vote in favor of physicians' economic and clinical interests, punishes those who do not, and ends up penalizing the very members of the House of

Representatives and Senate who are most in tune with the AMA's publicly stated public health agenda (Gutermuth 1999; Sharfstein and Sharfstein 1994; Wilkerson and Carrell 1999). In the parlance of modern scandal prosecutions, "follow the money."

The rent-seeking activities of organized medicine were matched by its extensive efforts to veto proposed policies that, although perceived by the profession to run counter to physician interests, would have advanced societal objectives. They include expanding insurance coverage and access to medical care, enhancing the efficiency of health care organization and delivery, and constraining inflationary pressures in health care costs. U.S. doctors have not been the only ones in the world pursing this "negative" agenda, but the design of our governing and political institutions, fragmenting government power, have catered to the projection of their will (Maioni 1995; Immergut 1992; Peterson 1993). If one accepts the analyses at face value, President Franklin Delano Roosevelt dropped the study of health insurance coverage as part of Social Security and President Harry Truman could not even get a serious congressional hearing on compulsory health insurance due to the opposition, and widely accepted power, of the American Medical Association (Starr 1982; Poen 1979). The AMA spent most of the twentieth century fighting third-party coverage through private insurance, then public insurance, even retooling for the Medicare debates its rhetoric from the 1940s about socialism and the threat to the very fabric of America's cherished liberties (Starr 1982; Marmor 2000). There was no more stalwart an opponent to wresting control over medical care costs, expanding the range of treatment approaches available to the American public, or ensuring equitable access to even its own definition of medical care. Trust in physicians came with a steep price.

THE POLITICAL FALL OF ORGANIZED MEDICINE

Ironically, a few short years after Arrow had concluded that dyadic trust in physicians mitigated the market deficiencies created by information asymmetries though missed the increasingly clear evidence of the societal costs generated by social trust in physicians, the centrality of organized medicine in U.S. policy making began to wane. Physicians since then, to be sure, have remained a significant force in the United States. Individual "public physicians," if you will, such as Dr. C. Everett Koop, retain considerable authority and stature. Most people continue to report favorable encounters with their own physicians. And some political leverage lingers in specific policy domains. Few other interests, for example, effectively compete with physicians in designing public policies that affect academic medical centers or medical schools to which the public dollars continue to flow. Further, as illustrated by the relatively strong laws that several states have enacted to limit the use of selective contracting by managed care plans, physician organizations may still assert considerable influence in a number of state capitols (Marsteller et al. 1997).

Nonetheless, a number of both exogenous and endogenous factors began to converge in the 1960s that disrupted the old power relationships.[2] An emerging public consensus offered, first, more support for tending to the needs of those lacking health care coverage and other social services, and then later endorsed greater regulatory discipline of medical practice. Myriad groups often opposed to the AMA, including consumer organizations such as Citizen Action, Families USA, and the American Association of Retired Persons (AARP), were spawned or invigorated by the rise of social movements. The availability of supportive "patrons of political action," such as private foundations, government agencies, and wealthy individuals, provided the funding they needed for organizational development and maintenance (Walker 1991). With access to more government and foundation funding, the research community in universities, think tanks, government policy shops, nonprofit firms, and even research arms of traditional interest groups created a new cadre of health services and policy specialists who offered analytical perspectives and results contrary to those of organized medicine (Peterson 1995a). Eventually, employers and insurers (especially small business organizations such as the National Federation of Independent Business and representatives of commercial carriers such as the Health Insurance Association of America) joined together to transform the organizational principles of health care delivery and financing, reinvigorating the market model, and, with the American Association of Health Plans, promoted various versions of managed care leading the way (Peterson 1995b, 1998b). In the meantime, starting with the U.S. Supreme Court's *Goldfarb v. Virginia State Bar* (421 U.S. 773 [1975]) decision in 1975 that opened up "learned professions" to federal antitrust regulation, a series of state and federal judicial actions reduced the economic autonomy and leverage of organized medicine and thus improved the political position of its competitors.

Internally, the physician community began to split politically in response to these pressures, and by the late 1980s the old alliance that the AMA had led in opposition to major government initiatives had weakened considerably. Still invigorated by a number of the attributes that give interest groups perceived strength in the policy-making process, the AMA nonetheless saw its position diminished by erosion in its membership, the loss of "quasi-unanimity" within its ranks, the rise of both competing groups and new sources of information for policy makers, and the loss of its coalition leadership role in the health policy "niche." The concerted and perhaps increasingly explicit efforts of physicians as an organized interest group to protect their own economic interests, especially when other sources of information began to emerge, some far more objective, made it difficult for them to maintain social trust (Gutermuth 1999; Millenson

1997b; Wolinsky and Brune 1994; Sharfstein and Sharfstein 1994; Wilkerson and Carrell 1999).

As with other professions beginning in the 1960s, whose pretensions to serving social purposes came under closer scrutiny, medicine moved more to the image of "expert professionalism," which "emphasized the instrumental effectiveness of specialized, technically grounded knowledge, but included comparatively little concern with collegial organization, ethical standards, or service to the public interest" (Brint 1994: 37). In the process, although people continued to respect and trust their own physicians, albeit now armed with more information and an emerging aura of patient rights, organized medicine lost much of the social trust that had previously been built on those individual relationships and cemented its claims on policy making. Among the public, those expressing "a great deal of confidence in the leaders of medicine" dropped to 44 percent in 2000, down from 73 percent in 1966, and actually plummeted all the way to 22 percent when health care reform dominated the agenda in the early 1990s (Blendon and Benson 2001: 39).

The initial crack came about with the passage of the Medicare program. For the first time, a major government program was enacted over the objections of organized medicine, aided by the force of the extraordinary political circumstances engendered by the 1964 landslide elections (Marmor 2000). Even in "defeat," however, the physicians were influential enough to dictate, in Feldstein's terms, the method of reimbursement and administration under the program, demand enhancing policies and subsidies and constraints on potentially competing providers (Jacobs 1993). The AMA may have opposed Medicare, but with the program's implementation, it compelled the institutionalization—for a time— of "usual, customary, and reasonable" (UCR) retrospective reimbursement that served physicians' economic self-interest well and fueled subsequent medical inflation. Next came a more profound challenge to physician dominance of health care decision making and policy. Under the National Health Planning and Resources Development Act of 1974, not only were competing health care providers and health policy specialists to share the decision-making stage with physicians, but also now even consumers themselves were to have equal status in community-level Health Systems Agencies responsible (unsuccessfully) for effective and coordinated state and federal health policy (Morone 1990).

By the late 1980s, the AMA was just another interest group (Heinz et al. 1993; Weissert and Weissert 1996). A vignette illustrates its decline in clout. In 1991, a young fellow recently hired by the AMA as a lobbyist noticed one of the most influential Democratic members of Congress in the hallway of the Capitol and, knowing that he chaired a crucial subcommittee, thought the occasion provided a good opportunity to introduce himself and begin building a relationship. When he approached the member of Congress, held out his hand, and cheerfully introduced himself and offered the upbeat line "I guess we'll be working together," the member of Congress looked with disdain at the extended hand and uttered simply, "Go f—— yourself."[3] A few years later, the AMA not only did not dominate the health care reform debate, it was hardly even a recognized player (Peterson 1995b). Representatives of small and large businesses, insurance plans, the pharmaceutical industry, consumer groups, and other citizen organizations played a far more significant role (Johnson and Broder 1996; Peterson 1998c; Skocpol 1996).

NEW CLAIMANTS ON SCIENTIFIC LEGITIMACY

In recent years physicians have suffered an additional form of competition with consequences for both Arrow's confidence in dyadic trust and the concomitant social trust nurtured by the profession. As I noted earlier from Starr's account, physicians originally achieved the cultural authority necessary to instill trust based on the profession's perceived direct and unique ties to the progress and application of medical science. Although the advances of medical science itself continue to generate awe among the public, policy specialists, and policy makers, physicians no longer enjoy a monopolist, or even a primary, claim to scientific legitimacy. Organized medicine began to weaken its own authority when the AMA, starting in the 1950s and 1960s, shifted the focus of its meetings and other activities from scientific exploration to more economic and political interests and avoided joining concerted efforts to measure and improve the quality of medical services (Millenson 1997a, 1997b). The discovery by health services research of wide variations in practice patterns (and costs) among physicians unassociated with patient conditions, mixed with physicians responding without collective restraint to the incentives of an unfettered fee-for-service system that produced dramatic increases in the cost of medical care not clearly correlated with improved quality, further eroded the favorable link to science (Dartmouth Medical School 1996; Millenson 1997b, 1998; Wolinsky and Brune 1994).

In response came, first, the development of physician peer review organizations under federal law and later more aggressive accreditation processes that imposed external evaluation of physician decision making. The most significant new claimants on scientific legitimacy, though, are managed care insurance plans, whose sway in the health care system expanded rapidly and dramatically thirty years after Arrow published his article, when Kaiser Permanente was about the only well-known example of what was then referred to as prepaid group practice. Managed care organizations argue, at least implicitly, that they now have the superior link to scientific progress and knowledge, garnered and tested in the application of evidenced-based medicine (Belkin 1998; *JHPPL* 2001). Armed with treatment protocols and guidelines predicated on the results of clinical trials, outcomes research, quality measures, and patient satisfaction surveys, they have moved to supplant physicians as the primary arbiters of what works and does not work in medical practice.

The rise of managed care raises important and perhaps conflicting questions about Arrow's original judgment that trust in physicians serves as a protection against information asymmetry. On the one hand, one can imagine that managed care arrangements help overcome the practice and policy problems generated by placing excessive social trust in physicians. As both a countervailing power politically and a private regulator of medical practice through the use of research and incentives that limit rather than promote intense, often unnecessary utilization, managed care can stymie the rent-seeking behavior of physicians and constrain organized medicine's claims on public resources. In addition, focusing on Arrow's specific argument, health plans well attuned to the latest in biomedical research can help address the adverse consequences of information asymmetry by compelling physicians to treat their patients in accordance with the best practices, even if the patients themselves do not have the information necessary to identify those practices. Ideally, the aggregation of medical decision making in managed care plans erases information asymmetries overall and ensures that individual patients receive the most appropriate care.

On the other hand, there are reasons to question the veracity of this ideal image. First, managed care plans as a group are but one claimant to scientific legitimacy, among others, and their assertions of superiority are potentially as self-serving and politically motivated—including in support of rent-seeking behavior—as that of physicians (Belkin 1998). One has to develop trust in private insurers, much as Arrow identified trust in physicians, to be assured that the best interests of patients are being pursued rather than those of the managed care organization. But such organizations do not even have the professional foundation or personal characteristics that benefited physicians in this regard. Indeed, because most managed care insurance carriers are now for-profit entities and so many decisions by plans are seen by the public as motivated by economic instead of medical considerations, the idea of granting "delegation and trust" to insurance carriers similar to what Arrow suggested for physicians is highly problematic (*JHPPL* 1998, 1999). Following a sustained backlash against managed care, however justified, it comes as no surprise that in 2000 only 29 percent of the public believed that managed care companies were doing "a good job," just one percentage point above the assessment of the tobacco industry, the social nemesis of our era (Blendon and Benson 2001: 40).

Second, because evidence-based medicine with its clinical practice guidelines focuses on what is effective for the average patient presenting a specified set of conditions, it must ignore any idiosyncratic characteristics, histories, and needs of particular patients. Therefore, the physician is once again called to the fore as a mediator between the science of medicine, as encapsulated in managed care protocols and the treatment of specific individuals (Tanenbaum 1994). Which returns us to trust in physicians. Vice President Albert Gore, in his speech accepting the Democratic party's nomination for president in 2000, captured the theme repeated by many: "It's time to take the medical decisions away from the HMOs and insurance companies — and give them back to the physicians, the nurses, and the health care professionals" (*New York Times*, 18 August 2000, A21). But those health care professionals, including physicians, must make their decisions in the managed care context in which they are themselves deeply embedded. A physician has to choose as both a clinician, and perhaps a patient's advocate against the insurer, and as a "businessman" explicitly focused on costs and facing incentives defined by risk sharing and payment mechanisms that directly affect the physician's own bottom line (Stone 1998). If we should have been more circumspect about trust in physicians than Arrow was in 1963, it is difficult to make a case that we should be any less concerned today.

CONCLUSION

If Jamie Robinson in this volume is wrong and we are not about to witness "the end of asymmetrical information" as a result of various market transformations, or if Clark Havighurst is wrong and unfettered contract-based competitive markets cannot work well in health care, then other measures may be required to substitute for the trust on which Arrow relied — and one hopes with fewer pernicious social consequences. Arrow writing today in response to the empirical world he would see might well give more favor to governmental regulation or infusion of explicit protections for patients. Ah, but is that not a prescription for the same costly and distorting rent-seeking behavior associated with organized medicine in the past? Maybe. But today neither physicians nor the managed care industry has the political leverage that the AMA enjoyed in Washington, D.C., and state capitals for so much of this century. Managed care plans, and their American Association of Health Plans (AAHP), have never experienced the trust, status, membership scope, lack of informational and organizational competition, campaign resources, or coalition leadership that marked organized medicine in earlier times and allowed it to wield so much influence. They, too, are just another interest group.

NOTES

1   One could cite an extensive literature, but the main themes that follow can be found in Arnold 1990; Bauer, Pool, and Dexter, 1972; Baumgartner and Leech 1998; Browne 1995; Hansen 1991; Hayes 1981; Hojnacki 1997; Hula 1999; Kollman 1998; Krehbiel 1991;

Olson 1965; Peterson 1993, 1995a, 1998a; Sabao 1984; Walker 1991; and Weissert and Weissert 1996.

2 Heinz et al. 1993; Jacobs 1993; Peterson 1993, 1995b, 1998b, and unpublished; Starr 1982; Walker 1991; and Weissert and Weissert 1996.

3 This story was told to me by a congressional staff member soon after it happened; at the time I was a legislative assistant for health policy in the office of Senator Tom Daschle (D-SD).

REFERENCES

Arnold, R. Douglas. 1990. *The Logic of Congressional Action*. New Haven, CT: Yale University Press.

Arrow, Kenneth J. 1963. Uncertainty and the Welfare Economics of Medical Care. *American Economic Review* 53(5): 941–973.

Bauer, Raymond A., Ithiel de Sola Pool, and Lewis Anthony Dexter. 1972. *American Business & Public Policy: The Politics of Foreign Trade*. Chicago: Aldine-Atherton.

Baumgartner, Frank R., and Beth L. Leech. 1998. *Basic Interests: The Importance of Groups in Politics and Political Science*. Princeton, NJ: Princeton University Press.

Belkin, Gary S. 1998. The Technocratic Wish: Making Sense and Finding Power in the "Managed" Medical Marketplace. In *Healthy Markets? The New Competition in Medicare Care*, ed. Mark A. Peterson. Durham, NC: Duke University Press.

Blendon, Robert J., and John M. Benson. 2001. Americans' Views on Health Policy: A Fifty-Year Perspective. *Health Affairs* 20(2): 33–46.

Brint, Steven. 1994. *In an Age of Experts: The Changing Role of Professionals in Politics and Public Life*. Princeton, NJ: Princeton University Press.

Brown, Lawrence D. 1991. Knowledge and Power: Health Services Research as a Political Resource. In *Health Services Research: Key to Health Policy*, ed. Eli Ginzberg. Cambridge: Harvard University Press.

Browne, William P. 1995. *Cultivating Congress: Constituents, Issues, and Interests in Agricultural Policy Making*. Lawrence: University of Kansas Press.

Campion, Frank D. 1984. *The AMA and U.S. Health Policy Since 1940*. Chicago: Chicago Review Press.

Dartmouth Medical School. 1996. *The Dartmouth Atlas of Health Care*. Chicago: American Hospital Publishing.

Dzur, Albert W. 2002. Democratizing the Hospital: Deliberative Democratic Bioethics. *Journal of Health Politics, Policy and Law* 27(2): 177–211.

Elliott, Philip. 1972. *The Sociology of the Professions*. London: Macmillan.

Feldstein, Paul J. 1977. *Health Associations and the Demand for Legislation: The Political Economy of Health*. Cambridge, MA: Ballinger.

Freidson, Eliot. 1970. *Profession of Medicine: A Study of the Sociology of Applied Knowledge*. New York: Dodd, Mead.

———. 1986. *Professional Powers: A Study of the Institutionalization of Formal Knowledge*. Chicago: University of Chicago Press.

Gutermuth, Karen. 1999. The American Medical Political Action Committee: Which Senators Get the Money and Why? *Journal of Health Politics, Policy and Law* 24(2): 357–382.

Habermas, Jürgen. 1971. *Toward a Rational Society*. Boston: Beacon.

Hansen, John Mark. 1991. *Gaining Access: Congress and the Farm Lobby, 1919–1981*. Chicago: University of Chicago Press.

Hayes, Michael T. 1981. *Lobbyists & Legislators: A Theory of Political Markets*. New Brunswick, NJ: Rutgers University Press.

Heinz, John P., Edward O. Laumann, Robert L. Nelson, and Robert H. Salisbury. 1993. *The Hollow Core: Private Interests in National Policy Making*. Cambridge: Harvard University Press.

Hojnacki, Marie E. 1997. Interest Groups' Decisions to Join Alliances or Work Alone. *American Journal of Political Science* 41(1): 61–87.

Hula, Kevin W. 1999. *Lobbying Together: Interest Group Coalitions in Legislative Politics*. Washington, DC: Georgetown University Press.

Immergut, Ellen M. 1992. *Health Politics: Interests and Institutions in Western Europe*. New York: Cambridge University Press.

Jacobs, Lawrence R. 1993. *The Health of Nations: Public Opinion and the Making of American and British Health Policy*. Ithaca, NY: Cornell University Press.

Johnson, Haynes, and David S. Broder. 1996. *The System: The American Way of Politics at the Breaking Point*. Boston: Little, Brown.

JHPPL. 1998. Special Issue. Managed Care: Ethics, Trust, and Accountability. *Journal of Health Politics, Policy and Law* 23(4).

JHPPL. 1999. Special Issue. The Managed Care Backlash. *Journal of Health Politics, Policy and Law* 24(5).

JHPPL. 2001. Special Issue. Evidence: Its Meaning in Health Care and in Law. *Journal of Health Politics, Policy and Law* 26(2).

Kollman, Ken. 1998. *Outside Lobbying: Public Opinion & Interest Group Strategies*. Princeton, NJ: Princeton University Press.

Krehbiel, Keith. 1991. *Information and Legislative Organization*. Ann Arbor, MI: University of Michigan Press.

Maioni, Antonia. 1995. Nothing Succeeds Like the Right Kind of Failure: Postwar National Health Insurance Initiatives in Canada and the United States. *Journal of Health Politics, Policy and Law* 20(1): 5–30.

Marmor, Theodore R. 2000. *The Politics of Medicare*. 2d ed. New York: Aldine de Gruyter.

Marsteller, Jill A., Randall R. Bovbjerg, Len M. Nichols, and Dianna K. Verrilli. 1997. The Resurgence of Selective Contracting Restrictions. *Journal of Health Politics, Policy and Law* 22(5): 1133–1189.

Millenson, Michael L. 1997a. "Miracle and Wonder": The AMA Embraces Quality Measurement. *Health Affairs* 16(3): 183–194.

———. 1997b. *Demanding Medical Excellence: Physicians and Accountability in the Information Age*. Chicago: University of Chicago Press.

———. 1998. What Physicians Don't Know. *Washington Monthly*, December, 8–12.

Morone, James A. 1990. *The Democratic Wish: Popular Participation and the Limits of American Government*. New York: Basic Books.

Morone, James A., and Gary S. Belkin. 1995. The Science Illusion and the Triumph of Medical Capitalism. Paper presented at the American Political Science Association annual meeting, Chicago, 2 September.

New York Times. 2000. Democrats: In His Own Words: Gore to Delegates and Nation: "My Focus Will Be on Working Families." *New York Times*, 18 August, 21A.

Olson, Mancur. 1965. *The Logic of Collective Action*. Cambridge: Harvard University Press.

Peterson, Mark A. 1993. Political Influence in the 1990s: From Iron Triangles to Policy Networks. *Journal of Health Politics, Policy and Law* 18(2): 395–438.

———. 1995a. How Health Policy Information Is Used in Congress. In *Intensive Care: How Congress Shapes Health Policy*, ed. Thomas E. Mann and Norman J. Ornstein. Washington, DC: American Enterprise Institute and Brookings Institution.

———. 1995b. Interest Groups as Allies and Antagonists: Their Role in the Politics of Health Care Reform. Paper prepared for delivery at the annual meeting of the Association for Health Services Research and Foundation for Health Services Research, Chicago.

———. 1998a. The Limits of Social Learning: Translating Analysis into Action. In *Healthy Markets? The New Competition in Medicare Care*, ed. Mark A. Peterson. Durham, NC: Duke University Press.

———. ed. 1998b. *Healthy Markets? The New Competition in Medicare Care*. Durham, NC: Duke University Press.

———. 1998c. The Politics of Health Care Policy: Overreaching in an Age of Polarization. In *The Social Divide: Political Parties and the Future of Activist Government*, ed. Margaret Weir. New York: Russell Sage Foundation.

———. Unpublished. Stalemate: Opportunities, Gambles, and Miscalculations in Health Policy Innovation. Book manuscript.

Poen, Monte M. 1979. *Harry S. Truman versus the Medical Lobby*. Columbia: University of Missouri Press.

Rayak, Elton. 1967. *Professional Power and American Medicine: The Economics of the American Medical Association*. Cleveland: World Publishing.

Sabato, Larry J. 1984. *PAC Power: Inside the World of Political Action Committees*. New York: Norton.

Sharfstein, Joshua M., and Steven S. Sharfstein. 1994. Campaign Contributions from the American Medical Political Action Committee to Members of Congress—for or against the Public Health? *New England Journal of Medicine* 330(1): 32–37.

Skocpol, Theda. 1996. *Boomerang: Clinton's Health Security Effort and the Turn Against Government in U.S. Politics*. New York: Norton.

Starr, Paul. 1982. *The Social Transformation of American Medicine*. New York: Basic Books.

Stigler, George J. 1971. The Theory of Economic Regulation. *Bell Journal of Economics* 2(1): 3–21.

Stone, Deborah A. 1998. The Doctor as Businessman: The Changing Politics of a Cultural Icon. In *Healthy Markets? The New Competition in Medicare Care*, ed. Mark A. Peterson. Durham, NC: Duke University Press.

Tanenbaum, Sandra J. 1994. "Knowing and Acting in Medical Practice: The Epistemological Politics of Outcomes Research." *Journal of Health Politics, Policy and Law* 19(1): 27–44.

Walker, Jack L. 1991. *Mobilizing Interest Groups in America: Patrons, Professions, and Social Movements*. Ann Arbor, MI: University of Michigan Press.

Weissert, Carol S., and William G. Weissert. 1996. *Governing Health: The Politics of Health Policy*. Baltimore, MD: Johns Hopkins University Press.

Wilkerson, John D., and David Carrell. 1999. Money, Politics, and Medicine: The American Medical PAC's Strategy of Giving in U.S. House Races. *Journal of Health Politics, Policy and Law* 24(2): 335–355.

Wolinsky, Howard, and Tom Brune. 1994. *The Serpent on the Staff: The Unhealthy Politics of the American Medical Association*. New York: Putnam.

PETER D. JACOBSON

■ *Regulating Health Care: From Self-Regulation*

to Self-Regulation?

Debates over the role of government in the private economy date back to the emergence of the U.S. market economy in the early nineteenth century. At that time, the Federalists, led by Alexander Hamilton, argued that a governmental presence was needed to guarantee property rights, enforce contracts, and encourage the nascent entrepreneurial ethos (Sellers 1991). In contrast, the Jeffersonians argued against intrusive government and in favor of self-reliance. That dynamic intersection between economics and political theory continues today regarding the proper regulatory oversight of health care delivery.

ARROW'S THEORY

The health care incarnation of this debate emerged when Kenneth Arrow (1963) identified key market failures in health care, namely "the existence of uncertainty in the incidence of disease and in the efficacy of treatment" (941). Underlying these failures were the "nonmarketability of the bearing of suitable risks and the imperfect marketability of information" (947) (i.e., information asymmetries between patient and physician), making it nearly impossible for patients to verify the quality of medical care. Arrow's analysis presumes that health care markets will not reach a competitive equilibrium without nonmarket intervention but does not specify how the market might self-correct or how nonmarket institutions would correct the optimality gap.

In a subsequent essay, Arrow (1972) depicted government regulation, tax policy, tort liability, and professional ethical codes as the most likely candidates to fill the gap. To the extent that Arrow articulates what might be thought of as a theory of regulation, this revolves around the development of professional ethical codes as essentially a market-based strategy. Arrow postulated that if such codes were widely accepted and established as norms, they would self-correct for information asymmetries and restore general equilibrium.

In 1972, this was a reasonable expectation because physicians still dominated health care delivery and relied heavily on self-regulation through ethical codes. But it soon became apparent that this alone could not redress market failures. In this essay, I will outline the market and nonmarket responses that have arisen since 1963 to fill the optimality gap that Arrow identified. My thesis is that there is an identifiable regulatory trajectory that begins with physician self-regulation and is now dominated by health care system self-regulation through private sector accreditation.

THE SHAPE OF HEALTH CARE REGULATION

Forms of Regulation

I use the term *regulation* to encompass both legislative and regulatory oversight of the health care system. For health care, regulation encompasses two domains: health professionals and the health care system. Historically, physicians have been regulated differently than health care as a system. Physicians have been largely self-regulated, while government has played a more traditional regulatory role in monitoring the health care system. Regulation in general may also be viewed along a continuum from those that facilitate market forces to those that displace the market. Market-facilitating strategies, such as private accreditation or professional ethical codes, are designed to enable the market to function more effectively.[1] Market-displacing approaches, such as health planning or national health insurance, are designed to substitute for market forces. While Arrow does not clearly specify whether professional norms are market-facilitating or market displacing, reliance on self-regulation (including professional norms) to fill the gap is essentially a market facilitating strategy because professional self-regulation operates to obviate market-displacing approaches.

In deciding what type of regulatory system to develop, one might ask three questions. First, what are the specific issues (i.e., market failures) to be regulated? Over the past twenty years, reducing health care costs, improving quality, and increasing access have been the most often cited justifications for regulatory intervention. Second, what is the regulatory structure (i.e., the source of regulatory authority) that should be devised? The possibilities include: government regulation only (state and/or federal), industry or professional self-regulation (a voluntary market-based approach), a mixed-form of public and private sector initiatives; and market self-correction. Third, what is the content (i.e., regulatory detail) of regulation? The possibilities include: general guidance, with process measures to be met (such as NCQA standards); prescriptive detail, where failure to meet the standards can be sanctioned; and compliance agreements, which provide considerable flexibility in how to meet the standards (often used to settle antitrust or fraud and abuse allegations). Market-facilitating and market-displacing theories will, of course, differ on the answers to each of these questions.

Before 1965 — Regulating Professionals

It may seem as though health care has always been a heavily regulated endeavor.[2] In reality, most health care regulation has occurred since the enactment of Medicare and Medicaid in 1965. Before then, health care was largely a private sector enterprise dominated by physicians, and health care regulation (if it existed at all) resided at the state level (Jost 1995; Wing 1999). The predominant regulatory activity was through state licensure laws, which traditionally gave almost complete control over who can practice medicine to the medical profession itself. In effect, the medical profession was self-regulating, which has generally been regarded as a market failure (Jost 1997).

As Arrow recognized, in the prevailing medical ethics of 1963, physicians were expected to place the patient's interests above any other consideration. The physician-patient relationship was at the center of the clinical encounter, not at the periphery. At a time when cost constraints did not impose countervailing social or policy concerns, reliance on these ethical responsibilities to act solely in the patient's best interests may well have been the only effective regulatory strategy, with medical liability available to sanction outright medical errors. The absence of alternative nonmarket social institutions to reduce the information asymmetries and monitor quality of care dictated reliance on physicians' ethical codes.

After 1965

Whatever the merits of a regulatory structure based on ethical codes when physicians totally dominated health care delivery, physician control was already beginning to erode by 1972. The great divide in health care regulation, and probably the reason why Arrow does not discuss regulation in 1963 but pays significant attention to it in 1972, is the 1965 enactment of Medicare and Medicaid. From this point forward, the federal government established a growing presence in health care as provider, insurer, purchaser, and regulator. The structure of regulation shifted from loose monitoring of professional licensure to escalating governmental oversight of health care as a system.[3] More importantly, the market failures identified in 1963 had, if anything, grown worse because the market was increasingly unable to restrain costs and provide access to health care. Arrow's limited theory of which nonmarket institutions could facilitate a more efficient allocation of resources seems inadequate for the task.

Beginning in the early 1970s, the government intervened with a profusion of federal rules and regulations to control health care delivery. A few years later, private accreditation agencies such as the Joint Commission on Accreditation of Healthcare Organizations (JCAHO) and, in the early 1990s, the National Committee for Quality Assurance (NCQA), began to offer a private sector approach to health system oversight, often in conjunction with government agencies. While ostensibly independent and external, in reality the accreditation standards must meet some industry norm to be viable. To the extent that these norms are determined through industry standards, practices, and ethical codes, a regime based on private accrediting agencies would be very consistent with Arrow's regulatory approach.

The question remains, however, whether either government or self-regulation adequately responds to medical market failure. The evidence that either self-regulation or governmental intervention sufficiently addresses market failure is rather thin. This can be illustrated by looking at how Arrow's approach might apply to the problems of access, costs, and quality, the main issues that have occupied regulators subsequent to Arrow's articles.

■ ACCESS The dilemma of access to health care might best be characterized as a distributional concern and not necessarily a market failure. In either case, it seems impervious to both market-facilitating and market-displacing strategies. Absent significant subsidies or national health insurance, access limitations are unlikely to be seriously addressed. Arrow's reliance on professional norms to serve some level of those unable to pay is not realistic now given the large uninsured population.

■ COSTS The debate over cost containment has been over whether the government should act more decisively to control costs or whether that job should be left to the private sector. With the defeat of President Clinton's proposed Health Security Act, the political system answered emphatically that the market (i.e., managed care) should be the primary mechanism for cost containment. Presumably, Arrow would support this approach, though costs are once again rising.

■ QUALITY Growing concerns over the quality of health care and the prevalence of medical errors set the stage for the trends now shaping the regulatory environment: controlling quality of care and shifting regulatory responsibility to the private sector. Not only is quality notoriously difficult to measure and monitor, but also "the quality of care is not heavily regulated" (Brennan 1998: 710). Consistent with Arrow's framework, several nonmarket institutions have emerged to fill the gap, including the major accrediting bodies and employer-sponsored groups devoted to improving quality.

Regulatory Strategies Not Adopted

It is also worth considering how Arrow's gap-filling approach would have applied to regulatory strategies that were on the policy agenda but were not pursued. These include both market-displacing and market-facilitating strategies.

■ NATIONAL HEALTH INSURANCE AND HEALTH PLANNING At least since the Truman administration, national health insurance has been on the policy agenda. At least since then, it has been rejected. Market-displacing theories were prominently debated during the 1970s, especially national health insurance and health planning solutions to redress access deficiencies. The health planning model, on the other hand, was actually implemented in the 1970s but subsequently abandoned (Weissert and Weissert 1996).

What is important about the rejection of these options is what it says about the role of regulation relative to competition. For all the criticism about the intrusiveness of health care regulation, the reality is that serious governmental controls over health care have been consistently rejected. From Arrow's perspective, this seems appropriate. The non-market strategies Arrow designates are specifically designed to avoid the need for such substantial governmental intervention.

■ A PUBLIC UTILITY MODEL Another market-displacing form of regulation would be a public utility model, perhaps along the lines of electricity utility companies or the presplit AT&T. This model posits that because of the health care industry's importance to the general public, the body politic should have power to influence the industry's practices. The suggestion that health care should be regulated like a public utility arose in the 1970s but did not receive serious consideration (Priest 1970). Within Arrow's framework, this would be an inappropriate gap-filling response because it would be market displacing.

■ DUE PROCESS A market-facilitating alternative that is gaining some judicial adherents is a due process model. Under this approach, the private sector retains decision making authority subject to basic due process requirements. Some courts, notably in California and New Hampshire, have required the use of fair procedures ". . . where private organizations are 'tinged with public stature or purpose' or attain a 'quasi-public significance.'"[4] This would seem to apply directly to managed care. Even though it is a very limited regulatory approach, there is no reason why Arrow would not support this as a market-facilitating strategy.

■ MANAGED COMPETITION One might argue that the managed competition model at the heart of the Clinton administration's doomed Health Security Act was a mid-point between market-facilitating and market-displacing strategies. Though popularly derided as a "big government" solution, the concept's reliance on competition to restrain costs and improve quality was closer to a market-facilitating approach.

The Current Structure — Reliance on the Private Sector
The demise of the Clinton health plan coupled with the absence of serious consideration of national health insurance in the 1990s signaled that the primary
source of regulation will be through the private sector, particularly for cost containment and quality of care. What has emerged, less by conscious design than
by happenstance, is a mixed form of regulation that amounts to a public-private
partnership as distinguished from the typical top-down model of governmental
regulation. The public-private partnership (meaning that governmental regulatory oversight is shared with the self-regulatory objectives of the private sector)
operates as the nonmarket gap fillers that Arrow anticipated. This regulatory
partnership has three basic components, with minimal coordination as to the
appropriate regulatory structure and content, which operate largely as market-
facilitating institutions.

The first component, government, continues to focus on access to health care,
but at the margins. Instead of considering universal access, Congress has taken
incremental steps to increase access, such as mandating longer maternity stays.
After largely unsuccessful efforts to expand health insurance to all residents in
the early 1990s, some states have also attempted more incremental measures,
such as mandating direct access to specialists (Brennan 1998).[5] But the regulatory vacuum created by ERISA preemption limits state governmental oversight
of managed care and encourages self-regulation (Jacobson and Pomfret 2000).
To be sure, one would be reluctant to characterize the regulations under fraud
and abuse and HIPAA as marketfacilitating. Yet as onerous as they might be, these
regulations are not marketdisplacing.

The second leg of the triad is the managed care industry itself, exercising
market-based controls. The primary objective is to exercise control over physician behavior, both to contain costs and to ensure quality (Yessian and Greenleaf 1997). Through utilization management and other cost control initiatives
(including bonuses and withholds), MCOs exert pressure to restrain health care
costs and utilization. Through selective contracting, economic credentialing, and
the imposition of continuous quality improvement and similar initiatives, MCOs
exert pressure on physicians to improve quality.

The third leg of the triad, accreditation, most resembles the self-regulatory
structure described earlier for physicians. Self-regulation in this context does
not mean no regulation. Instead, the accrediting bodies exert pressure on health
systems to meet quality of care requirements, including outcome measures and
sentinel event reporting to reduce medical error. These standards are gaining
recognition as a key to the self-regulatory structure. The managed care industry
has successfully argued that the accreditation process can be more effective than
command and control regulations. For MCOs, attaining NCQA's imprimatur is

an important competitive necessity because employers are less likely to contract with MCOs that lack NCQA accreditation.

One might add that employers play an important role in the shift to private sector regulation in dealing with MCOs. I am reluctant to characterize them as a fourth pillar because I remain skeptical as to how much they will use their purchasing power beyond concerns over costs. Nevertheless, large employers are more insistent on demanding that plans provide them with cost and quality data (the latter through the Health Employer Data and Information Set — HEDIS — measurements developed in conjunction with NCQA). At a minimum, employers exert some pressure to restrain costs and improve quality and certainly have the market clout to demand greater quality improvements.

One compelling aspect of the mixed-form arrangement is that the Health Care Financing administration openly embraces certain JCAHO standards in the hospital survey and certification process for Medicare and Medicaid. JCAHO certification is deemed compliance with the Medicare and Medicaid conditions of participation for hospitals. In essence this is public ratification of private standards and a public-private partnership. Another example, though used less frequently in health care regulation than in environmental or occupational and safety regulation, is the government's partnership with the private sector in the growing use of the regulatory negotiation process (dubbed reg-neg). In the reg-neg process, the regulatory agency sits down with the affected industry to develop a regulatory approach that is acceptable to each side to avoid contentious and time-consuming litigation.[6]

The mixed-form result should not be surprising. Most commentators have rejected the one-dimensional notion of regulation versus competition in favor of a more sophisticated approach that tries to balance competition and regulation (Peterson 1997; Health Care Study Group 1994). Indeed, there is a large literature (especially public choice theory) describing governmental failure. Except for libertarians who eschew most governmental intervention in the market, the debate is over the level of regulatory oversight not whether regulations are per se acceptable. In many respects, this pragmatic approach is a typically American response to a problem — an eclectic strategy that borrows and amalgamates ideas from various sources. Whether the amalgam is at all coherent is beside the point — it satisfies enough constituencies to be viable in the short run.

DISCUSSION

Arrow Revisited

In general, neither market-facilitating nor market-displacing theories have adequately filled the optimality gap Arrow (1963) identified. Nonmarket institutions have indeed filled a gap, but not necessarily the gap Arrow had in mind. Not only is there little agreement on what aspects of health care should be regulated, there is no consensus on regulatory content even when agreement exists that regulation is necessary. Nor is it clear whether the roads not taken would have addressed the market failures more effectively. Certainly, national health insurance would reduce (if not eliminate) access disparities and inequalities but would do little to address cost and quality concerns.

In fact, the post-1963 history of health care regulation seems a study in contradictions. The overall regulatory burden has expanded, but the very market failures that presumably justify the regulatory apparatus remain as intractable as ever. Some aspects of health care are heavily regulated, such as fraud and abuse, while other critical aspects, such as quality of care, lie seemingly beyond regulatory scrutiny. Unfortunately, the greater the number and type of regulations, the greater the likelihood that they will be inconsistent. A good example is the concept of gain sharing, where physicians share in costs saved by MCOs. One branch of the government, Congress, encourages such innovations, while another, the Office of the Inspector General (HHS), condemns the concept as violating the fraud and abuse statutes.

Despite these contradictions, there is an identifiable regulatory trajectory that is slowly but inexorably shifting back toward self-regulation and market control that dominated the pre-Medicare health care environment. For example, there is greater reliance on accreditation bodies to regulate quality of care. Even onerous regulatory standards governing health care providers are often tempered by reliance on voluntary compliance programs, such as fraud and abuse compliance agreements, which dramatically reduce potential fines. In addition, ERISA preemption prevents more extensive state judicial and legislative oversight of managed care organizations. Taken together, voluntary compliance programs and ERISA preemption limit effective governmental oversight and shift responsibility to the private self-regulatory mechanisms.

The trend toward private sector solutions has also received considerable support in the courts. In general, courts have not impeded managed care's cost containment programs and have shown considerable deference to emerging market arrangements (Jacobson 1999). Courts are reluctant to interfere with self-regulatory intermediary structures and are likely to support accreditation policies designed to improve quality of care.

Arrow's 1972 argument that ethical norms would be a more feasible alternative than regulation, taxation, or litigation has a certain (if retro) resonance in the current mixed-form structure. The more reliant the system is on self-regulation or accreditation, the more dominant ethical codes and standards are likely to be. As argued above, Arrow's regulatory theory made sense in the context of physician dominance throughout the 1960s, but was probably doomed to be ineffectual in the hyperinflation of the 1980s and early 1990s and the concomitant expansion of health care as an industry. In any event, it is questionable whether the ethic of acting solely in the patient's best interest has survived the pressures of managed care with its emphasis on cost controls and preserving resources for patient populations. Even though the physician's initial loyalty and fiduciary duty is still owed to the individual patient, financial incentives inevitably pose conflicts between individual patients and the patient population.

One might postulate that a properly functioning accreditation process is the health system's equivalent to the role of ethical codes in the fee-for-service era. In that era, Arrow expected ethical codes to reduce information asymmetries between physicians and patients. Accreditation agencies serve a similar function within the more complex health system we now have, along with addressing other market failures, such as quality of care. As with the ethical norms of the early 1960s, the accreditation system may be able to impose its social norms on the entire health care industry. While Arrow would probably not support the remnants of prescriptive regulation (especially the fraud and abuse regime), his regulatory theory appears to allow for a public-private partnership to address market deficiencies, particularly one, as I have argued, that relies largely on market-facilitating strategies.

The movement toward health system self-regulation, while market facilitating, does not necessarily resolve the problems encountered by physicians' professional self-regulation. First, the informational problems experienced by patients in the physician-dominated system seem just as entrenched in the shift to health system preeminence (McLaughlin and Ginsberg 1998). Second, health system self-regulation is not necessarily equivalent to professional self-regulation for physicians. Yet this should not be a barrier to establishing effective industry norms that respond to the optimality gap. Airline safety, for instance, is an analogous public-private model that increasingly relies on industry-sanctioned norms for public safety.

I am generally skeptical that accreditation entities can successfully fulfill this role. Historically, physician self-regulation has not been particularly successful in controlling the behavior of individual physicians. It is doubtful that accreditation will succeed in controlling the behavior of the health care system, in part because there may be considerable tension between accrediting agencies and MCOs. In a recent case, for example, Aetna Inc. argued that ". . . statements concerning [its] commitment to quality health care are 'mere puffery.' "[7] This admission hardly bodes well for agreement on how to ensure quality.

At the same time, there is no substantial evidence of the government's ability to monitor quality or reduce information asymmetries. And despite efforts such as small group insurance pools, neither the market nor the government has solved Arrow's key issue of the nonmarketability of risk. To be sure, the development of evidence-based medicine reduces the uncertainty of medical treatment to some extent. But it is not clear how either the government or the market can do more to address the uncertainty of medical risk. This problem is further exacerbated by the absence of consistent quality measures across health care plans and physicians.

By default, I suppose, the health care industry is entitled to an opportunity to prove that it can learn from past mistakes and effectively regulate itself. Recent action by the managed care industry to impose external grievance panels to review health care denials is certainly a step in the right direction. Accreditation bodies are expanding their quality-of-care efforts through the use of evidence-based medicine, sentinel event reporting, and the use of quality-of-care report cards. An advantage of the accreditation approach is that it can impose social norms on the health system similar to the prevailing ethical norms when physicians dominated health care delivery in 1963.

As Gregg Bloche (2002) notes, however, most of the changes introduced by the managed care industry have come as the result of threatened legislation or regulation. This suggests that it remains premature to abandon a strong governmental regulatory presence in favor of either Arrow's equilibrium theory or accreditation-based self-regulation.

CONCLUSION

Kenneth Arrow's contribution lies in identifying the impediments to a competitive health care market and setting forth a framework to restore equilibrium. Not many defend the current regulatory environment, and the political process has consistently rejected increased governmental control over the health care system. Others remain skeptical that the market can be self-correcting. It may be that an updated formulation of Arrow's regulatory framework as applied to health systems can provide some needed insight into how to restore the proper balance between health care regulation and the market.

NOTES

The author appreciates the financial support provided by a grant from the Robert Wood John Foundation's Investigator Awards in Health Policy Research program. The author also thanks Gail Agrawal for extremely helpful comments on a previous draft.

1   I thank Peter Hammer for suggesting this line of inquiry. One might argue that professional ethical codes have some attributes that are market displacing in the sense that aspects of these codes are designed to empower professionals to resist market pressures (especially financial pressure) (personal communication from Gail Agrawal, 5 March 2001). For a more detailed analysis, see Jacobson (2002).

2 The absence of regulation should not necessarily be construed as favorable to the market. As Peter Hammer points out, the absence of governmental antitrust activity and the government's failure to contest the medical profession's political power frustrate the ability to implement market reforms.

3 This analysis is consistent with Krause's (1996) argument that the physician guild began to decline in power in the mid-1960s when government began to exert greater control over medical care.

4 Potvin v. Metropolitan Life Ins. Co., 997 P.2d 1153 (Cal. 2000).

5 It is not clear whether these state laws will survive ERISA preemption challenges (Jacobson and Pomfret 2000).

6 It would be naïve to think that affected industries were ignored in regulatory policy before reg-neg, but the explicit inclusion of the industry in the regulatory process is substantially different.

7 Maio v. Aetna Inc., 1999 U.S. Dist. LEXIS 15056 (E.D. Pa. 1999), 2000 U.S. App. LEXIS 19172 [3d Cir. 2000]).

REFERENCES

Arrow, K. J. 1963. Uncertainty and the Welfare Economics of Medical Care. *American Economic Review* 53(5): 941–973.

———. 1972. Social Responsibility and Economic Efficiency. *Public Policy* 21(3): 303–317.

Bloche, M. G. 2002. One Step Ahead of the Law: Markets and Medicine in the 1990s. In *The Privatization of Health Care Reform*, ed. M. G. Bloche. New York: Oxford University Press.

Brennan, T. A. 1998. The Role of Regulation in Quality Improvement. *Milbank Quarterly* 76: 709–731.

Health Care Study Group. 1994. Understanding the Choices in Health Care Reform. *Journal of Health Politics, Policy and Law* 19: 499–541.

Jacobson, P. D. 1999. Legal Challenges to Managed Care Cost Containment Programs: An Initial Assessment. *Health Affairs* 18(4): 69–85.

———. 2002. *Strangers in the Night: Law and Medicine in the Managed Care Era*. New York: Oxford University Press.

Jacobson, P. D., and S. D. Pomfret. 2000. ERISA Litigation and Physician Autonomy. *Journal of the American Medical Association* 283: 921–926.

Jost, T. S. 1995. Oversight of the Quality of Medical Care: Regulation, Management, or the Market? *Arizona Law Review* 37: 825–868.

———. 1997. *Introduction to Regulation of the Healthcare Professions*, ed. T. S. Jost. Chicago: Health Administration Press.

Krause, E. A. 1986. *Death of the Guilds: Professions, States, and the Advance of Capitalism, 1930 to the Present*. New Haven, CT: Yale University Press.

McLaughlin, C. G., and P. B. Ginsburg. 1998. Competition, Quality of Care, and the Role of the Consumer. *Milbank Quarterly* 76: 737–743.

Peterson, M. A. 1997. Introduction: Health Care into the Next Century. *Journal of Health Politics, Policy and Law* 22: 291–313.

Priest, A. J. G. 1970. Possible Adaptation of Public Utility Concepts in the Health Care Field. *Law and Contemporary Problems* 35: 839–848.

Sellers, C. 1991. *The Market Revolution: Jacksonian America, 1815–1846.* New York: Oxford University Press.

Weissert, C. S., and W. G. Weissert. 1996. *Governing Health: The Politics of Health Policy.* Baltimore, MD: Johns Hopkins University Press.

Wing, K. R. 1999. *The Law and the Public's Health,* 5th ed. Chicago: Health Administration Press.

Yessian, M. R., and J. M. Greenleaf. 1997. The Ebb and Flow of Federal Initiatives to Regulate Healthcare Professions. In *Regulation of the Healthcare Professions,* ed. T. S. Jost. Chicago: Health Administration Press.

WILLIAM M. SAGE

■ The Lawyerization of Medicine

By my rough estimate, nearly as many Americans possess both medical and law degrees as there are practicing attorneys in Japan. To be sure, this artfully phrased factoid omits important context about the relationship between professional education and professional practice in the two countries. The comparison still reveals more than it conceals. First, there are a lot of lawyers in the United States. Second, a lot of work done elsewhere by nonlawyers is performed here by lawyers. Third, the formal fusion of legal and medical expertise in the United States, while a small percentage of either profession, is in absolute terms quite substantial.

Step back forty years. In 1963, Nobel Prize–winning economist Kenneth Arrow published the first theoretical analysis of health care markets. Arrow concluded that failures of information, which he termed *uncertainty*, render health care and health insurance largely unmarketable. Moreover, Arrow looked to some rather uneconomical constructs, such as physician-patient trust and physicians' professional code of ethics, as substitutes for direct government regulation in response to uncertainty.

What do M.D.-J.D.s have to do with the current relevance of Arrow's thesis? Quite a bit, I believe. When Arrow examined the medical marketplace, physicians had been little exposed to lawyers. Although forensic medicine dates from the early nineteenth century, professional associations for lawyers with practices devoted to the health care industry were not founded until 1968 (the American Academy of Hospital Attorneys) and 1971 (the National Health Lawyers Association). The first legal treatise and law school casebook with "health care law" in the title did not arrive until the mid-1980s (Macdonald, Meyer, and Essig 1985; Furrow 1987).

Today, lawyers are familiar faces in health care. In 1960, there were approximately 285,000 lawyers in America (one for every 627 people); by 1990, there were approximately 775,000 (one for every 320 people) (American Bar Association 1992). There are now over a million lawyers in the United States. A smaller percentage of modern lawyers are solo practitioners serving individual clients; a greater percentage do corporate and government work in law firms. Many lawyers spend significant portions of their time on medical matters: the American Health Lawyers Association currently has 10,000 members.

More surprising than increased contact per se is the degree to which American medicine has embraced the mode of reasoning, style of discourse, and professional role of the lawyer. This phenomenon is distinct from, though clearly related to, the dramatic expansion since 1963 of legal rights and obligations affecting the health care system. Arrow prefaced his article with the disclaimer that he was analyzing medical care rather than health. Echoing Arrow, my subject is health care lawyers not substantive health law. In other words, I intend to discuss the "lawyerization" of medicine rather than its "legalization." My thesis is that health lawyering has changed the nature and extent of uncertainty in medicine and has altered the way in which both market and nonmarket institutions respond to it.

I begin with M.D.-J.D.s not because they serve in practice as the principal mediators between law and medicine — they most assuredly do not — but because the way they perceive themselves and are perceived by others is a useful bellwether for the influence of lawyering on doctoring. In the popular imagination, *physician* and *attorney* traditionally brought to mind very different personalities. Countless anecdotes contrast the two professions ("a doctor, a lawyer, and a _____ were stranded on a desert island . . ."). And though a counterculture comic strip of the 1970s called "Doctor-Lawyer" seems prescient today, its humor lay primarily in the absurdity of its premise: a Harvard student who mistakes law school for medical school ends up completing both and emerges "[able to] destroy human lives in two entirely different ways" (Subitzky 1990). Real people who held both medical and law degrees were seen by and large as either lost souls or disenchanted refugees from one profession to the other. During the years I spent as a medical resident and a law firm associate in the late 1980s and early 1990s, overworked colleagues in each profession regarded my dual expertise primarily with "grass-is-greener" envy, and I confess that the combination of the lawyers' wistfully expressed beliefs that I would make a great physician and the physicians' remarks that I would make a great lawyer took its toll on my self-confidence.

Indeed, physicians and lawyers *are* very different (Fox 1987; Annas 1988). Physicians tend to prefer consensus to conflict, value expertise over impartiality, and think in terms of roles rather than rules. Lawyers generally take the opposite view. Some of these traits are selected; others are socialized. Nonetheless, the

M.D.-J.D. and the interplay of legal and medical values he or she embodies is a much less puzzling figure today than in 1963, or even 1985. Lawyerly thought and conduct have been thoroughly integrated into the health care system. What brought America's two "sovereign professions" into intellectual proximity? In my view, it was the emergence, growth, or transformation of four areas of substantive law: medical malpractice, bioethics, public entitlements, and managed care.

MEDICAL MALPRACTICE

If not for medical malpractice litigation, organized medicine and the bar might have been allies. After all, the two professions shared a successful history. Both had roots in prerevolutionary English practice, both had overcome Jacksonian populism and reconsolidated their authority in the years surrounding the Civil War, and both had fought off challenges from other professions to their license monopolies in the late nineteenth and early twentieth centuries (Starr 1982; Stevens 1983).

It is true that medicine and law had diverged in significant ways by World War II. One difference is the exclusivity of professional training. Arrow noted that strict licensure standards, restrictions on entry into clinical training, and subsidies for medical education increase quality of care but potentially limit its availability because patients must pay higher prices. However, Arrow justified such practices, which resulted in large part from the publication of the Flexner Report in 1910, as countering uncertainty by improving reputation and reinforcing trust, while invoking the charitable traditions of medicine as at least a partial solution to the problem of access. Law did not follow medicine's example. The 1921 Reed Report concluded that the crisis in law was not of quality but of professional diversity and access to legal services among immigrant and minority populations, and therefore declined to restrict legal education to "superior" institutions.

Still one could almost imagine physicians and lawyers working together to preserve professional prerogatives against both market competition and the incursions of the welfare state. This never happened. Rifts between medicine and law became a chasm. Something convinced doctors that lawyers were foes, not friends. That something was medical malpractice, which (along with being cross-examined as an expert witness) exposed physicians to public humiliation, sometimes placing entire careers at risk during a single day's testimony (Mohr 1993). By 1900 the medical profession had abandoned any thought of working with lawyers for the social good and had decided to keep lawyers at a safe distance instead.

Medicine's "strategy" changed from avoidance to confrontation much more recently. Again, medical malpractice was largely responsible. Malpractice grew from an annoyance to physicians in 1960 to an economic and personal affront sufficient by 1975 to be labeled "medicine's most serious crisis" in *Newsweek*. The frequency of malpractice claims nationally rose from 1 per 100 physicians in 1960 to 17.5 per 100 at its peak in the mid-1980s, while average jury verdicts increased in severity from $50,000 in Chicago and $125,000 in San Francisco in the early 1960s to $1.2 million in each city by the early 1980s (Weiler 1991). As more physicians came to know lawyers in connection with malpractice suits, the dislike and distrust between the two professions intensified. These emotions ran deep enough, for example, to lead a department chair at a major public teaching hospital to veto my intended service as a part-time volunteer physician on the grounds that he didn't want a lawyer in his emergency room, notwithstanding the fact that my regular employment practicing securities law at a prominent, "white-shoe" firm was highly unlikely to involve me in personal injury litigation.

Hand-to-hand combat with lawyers inevitably led physicians to adopt new tactics. The plaintiff's malpractice bar, and to some degree even defense counsel, taught the medical profession several unhappy lessons. For one, enemies now had faces. The battle metaphors involving physicians traditionally involved death and disease, not human agency, and even their opposition to government control and other institutional threats to professional autonomy was based largely on abstractions. Not so for malpractice claims, which introduced physicians to professional conflict at the individual level. Worse still, malpractice litigation made physicians, for the first time, regard their own patients as potential adversaries. This affected both existing therapeutic relationships and those that were feared and therefore avoided, ranging from policy-trivial resistance to treating lawyers' families to the more pernicious, albeit infrequent, refusal to care for the poor or severely ill.

A second lesson was that lives could be, and would be, measured in dollars. This lesson was made more vivid by the fact that the dollars at risk were the physician's (or at least his or her insurer's). Postwar advances in medicine's technical capabilities had accelerated in the 1960s and 1970s, accompanied by rising public expectations of medicine. Physicians were already grappling with these expectations and the related temptation to exploit the availability of virtually unlimited insurance reimbursement by providing high-cost, low-benefit services. Although the rhetoric of "defensive medicine" probably outweighs its true importance as a determinant of national health expenditures, medical malpractice litigation gave physicians even greater justification for spending other people's money.

A third lesson was that the best remedy for a nasty lawsuit is a good lobbyist. Organized medicine was no stranger to legislation but had concerned itself primarily with protecting its license monopoly and related self-regulatory privileges. The looming storm of malpractice litigation sent medical societies scurrying to statehouses for shelter, especially after the Supreme Court confirmed that changes to state malpractice law did not offend the Constitution. Tort reform, of course, brought the medical profession into even greater conflict with lawyers. An arms race of political spending ensued, with physicians and attorneys vying for the top position. Considering the bar's experience leveraging natural affinities between practicing lawyers and lawyer-legislators into self-protective regulation, medicine did surprisingly well. Nearly every state placed constraints on medical malpractice litigation in the 1970s, and more than half the states enacted caps on damages.

Most importantly, watching lawyers conduct malpractice litigation reinforced physicians' beliefs that little good could come of subjecting medical practice to outside review. Uncertainty about the benefits of particular therapies was, to Arrow, a factor responsible for the failure of medical markets. Arrow also predicted an eventual need for third-party control of clinical decisions in order to counter insurance moral hazard. On its face, malpractice law had the potential to help both processes by uncovering improper treatment and defining a "standard of care." Moreover, attorneys were very effective at surfacing information that had previously been unavailable to injured patients and the public. It turned out, however, that a courtroom trial and a clinical trial had nothing in common. Physicians quickly concluded that lay juries and judges cared little and understood even less about truth. Claims, settlements, and verdicts seemed arbitrary (an impression that later acquired empirical support [Brennan, Sox, and Burstin 1996]), and even the likelihood of victory in cases brought to a jury did not compensate physicians for the time, anxiety, and loss of self-esteem involved in defending a lawsuit.

Physicians' perceptions of illegitimacy extended as well to the nominal peers brought in by each side to assess the defendant's adherence to the standard of care. Because of the extreme partisanship with which scientific evidence is adduced in U.S. courts, physicians came to view expert testimony as, at best, manipulation of the uninformed and, at worst, outright professional betrayal. This was true even in Arrow's time — an article in the *New England Journal of Medicine* asserted that 50 to 80 percent of malpractice suits could be eliminated if physicians would only stop criticizing each other's unavoidable errors (Regan 1954) — but it has persisted despite mounting evidence of suboptimal practice. For example, the Institute of Medicine's 1999 report on medical error was criticized for fostering socially unproductive litigation (Brennan 2000). One might also speculate that the medical profession's continued rejection of pay-for-performance derives in part from the extreme distaste with which it came to view lawyer's contingent fees. This is the paradox of medical malpractice in the two decades following Arrow's exposition: it led the medical profession to close ranks against public accountability at the same time it mandated accountability as a matter of law.

BIOETHICS

Bioethics exerted a very different influence on the relationship between the medical and legal professions. The bioethical movement that began in the aftermath of World War II gathered speed through the 1950s and took flight after Arrow wrote in 1963. Just one year later, in 1964, the World Medical Association issued its Declaration of Helsinki regarding the rights of human research subjects. Like the Nuremberg trials from which it derived, the declaration—though not legally binding—was an assertion of the rule of law in the face of Nazi atrocities. In part for this reason, law rather than professional obligation became the lingua franca of modern bioethics. Bioethicists today are not only conversant in law but also dependent upon it (Rothman 1991), a fact brought home to me in a recent dinner discussion with the physician-chairman of a bioethics department whose knowledge of and enthusiasm for arcane provisions of federal regulation rivaled any health care lawyer's.

Under the influence of law, medical ethics reoriented itself. Discarding as paternalistic its traditional emphasis on physician beneficence, contemporary bioethics focuses instead on patient autonomy. The change wrought by law is evident in patterns of physician-patient communication. A study published just two years before Arrow's article found that only 12 percent of physicians routinely told patients they had cancer, even though most patients said they would want to know (Oken 1961). The great majority of physicians considered the information countertherapeutic. By 1980, however, a series of court decisions and statutes establishing the law of informed consent made nondisclosure of a patient's diagnosis virtually impossible.

Substituting autonomy for beneficence is not always comfortable for physicians but intuitively appeals to lawyers. Legal ethics has long emphasized the zealous pursuit of the client's goals, a stance made easier by the adversarial design of litigation and the convenient if somewhat facile separation of substantive ends from technical means in legal practice. Bioethicists continue to debate the appropriateness of this model for medicine (Schneider 1998). Basing medical ethics on autonomy may indeed empower patients (Annas 1988), but also allows physicians to detach themselves from the consequences of their actions. Why grapple with moral dilemmas when one can concentrate on achieving a technical result and let the patient decide if it is good or bad? Similarly, professionals serving solely their clients' self-defined interests may neglect important social responsibilities. As a prominent critic of conventional legal ethics writes: "doctors . . . are not expected to engage in the partisan pursuit of individual ends. . . . Only the lawyer seems to insist on making a virtue of both neutrality and partisanship" (Simon 1978: 37).

Another issue implicit in furthering autonomy is ascertaining patient preferences. Even as malpractice litigation confirmed physicians' distaste for adversarial "expertise," bioethics pushed medicine toward a lawyerlike approach to fact-finding through formal deliberative bodies and frank judicial oversight, overcoming the medical profession's traditional preference for empiricism and deference to experience. Decisions to receive care, to have treatment withheld or withdrawn, and to participate in medical research were recast as legal problems of informed consent or surrogacy. Even nominally collegial bodies such as hospital ethics committees and institutional review boards adopted more lawyerly modes of deliberation, presumably because of concern that less formal processes would fail to dislodge paternalistic biases. In particular, ensuring impartiality by insulating decision makers from conflicts of interest took on far greater importance than the profession's history suggested. This trend is evident over a range of issues, including physician self-referral, financial relationships with drug companies, and the ability of treating physicians to attest to patients' advance directives.

Indeed, law offered medicine the archetype of autonomy: a constitutional right (Capron 1999b). Judicial precedents from Arrow's era had emphasized the ethical integrity of the medical profession (along with its potential civil liability) as a counterweight to patient autonomy. In *United States v. George* (1965), the court mandated blood transfusion over a patient's religious objection, stating:

> The doctor's conscience and professional oath must also be respected. In the present case the patient voluntarily submitted himself to and insisted upon medical care. Simultaneously he sought to dictate to treating physicians a course of treatment amounting to medical malpractice. To require these doctors to ignore the mandates of their own conscience, even in the name of free religious exercise, cannot be justified under these circumstances.

This approach was soon obsolete. Under pressure from a new generation of "public interest" lawyers, state and federal courts in a series of decisions between 1970 and 1990 affirmed constitutional rights to bodily integrity and self-determination with respect to end-of-life care, forced treatment, and reproductive health. Even rulings that rejected formal rights, such as the recent physician-assisted suicide cases, emphasize constitutional history and judicial restraint rather than subordination of autonomy. Today, arguments such as those made by the *George* court are not so much rejected as dismissed out of hand.

Physicians again found something to emulate in this legal trend. The first substantive section of the AMA's revised Code of Medical Ethics consists not of routine professional duties and obligations but of "Opinions on Social Policy Issues" dealing with novel situations and radical science, many of them asserting the primacy of patients' rights in language befitting a statute or government regulation (American Medical Association 1997). Of twenty-three such opinions, only four were issued prior to 1977. It is also significant, and perhaps unfortunate, that these lawyerly expressions have come to dominate the ethics of technology. Using the language of rights, bioethics engaged with technology on an individual basis, accepting limits to further individual autonomy but not to promote social solidarity (Jacobs 1995).

More generally, "lawyerizing" the ethics of death may have hastened the death of ethics (Capron 1999a; Schneider 1994). Although the AMA's code observes in passing that "ethical obligations typically exceed legal duties," patients receiving shelter from the law had less need for the house of medicine. Robert Levine (1987: 362) writes: "A focus on rights and rules . . . has a tendency to yield a 'minimalist ethics.' In a minimalist ethics, much of the behavior we value in the caring physician is regarded as supererogatory or optimal—nice but not morally required." David Hyman (1990: 150) states the point succinctly: "A preoccupation with legal remedies is likely to lead to compliance with the cold letter of the law—nothing less, but certainly nothing more." As medical ethics collapsed into law, the belief implicit in Arrow's analysis that professional self-regulation would render direct government intervention unnecessary became less sustainable.

ENTITLEMENTS

Bioethics introduced physicians to lawyers as a general force for social change in the health care system. Litigation involving the Medicare and Medicaid programs went farther by linking public lawyering to two specific issues that physicians hold dear: their independence and their compensation. When America's elderly and indigent received legal entitlements to health care, the physicians and hospitals that provided such care in compliance with program rules gained parallel rights of payment.

Whereas bioethics gave rise to patient rights of constitutional dimension pronounced by "supreme" courts that commanded physicians' respect, provider rights under public entitlement programs were malleable creatures of statute subject to legal and political maneuvering. For example, enterprising lawyers turned the Boren amendment's language regarding "efficiently and economically operated facilities" from a statement of belief in cost containment to a weapon with which to fight state Medicaid agencies for funding. Similarly, small battles in Medicare's early years acclimated organized medicine—which had cut its teeth lobbying at the state level—to the federal legislative process. Unlike the equally state-oriented automobile industry facing the Motor Vehicle Safety Act of 1965 (Mashaw and Harfst 1990), medicine was not blindsided when sentiment in Washington turned against it. On the other hand, the "stakeholder mentality" engendered by Medicare was a sharp departure from medicine's traditional free market rhetoric, and watching physicians jostling competing interests to feed at the government trough may have done irreparable harm to public belief in the altruism of the profession.

Entitlements also drove another nail into the coffin of traditional medical ethics. Before Medicare, Arrow had offered the professional norm of charity care as reassurance that conferring self-regulatory privileges on physicians to address uncertainty would not be turned to economic advantage. With government paying to cover large groups of previously uninsured patients, however, why emphasize the charitable obligations of physicians and potentially let government off the hook? In 1992, for example, the AMA—on the advice of a prominent M.D.-J.D.—narrowly rejected an ethics committee recommendation that physicians devote 10 percent of their time to serving the poor for fear that an ethical mandate would quickly become a binding legal obligation (Millenson 1992).

Simultaneously, physicians learned from the Medicare experience that a public right of access to health care created both opportunity and danger. As Arrow anticipated, third-party payment led to third-party control. With Medicare expenditures rising rapidly, legislators and regulators kept trying to kill (or at least maim) the golden goose, while prosecutors plucked it feather by feather in pursuit of fraud and abuse (Sage 1999b). Arrow expected that a well-compensated medical profession would have greater ability to provide public service. In the context of entitlement spending, however, the more government tried to relieve its budgetary strain, the harder physicians whom Medicare had accustomed to higher earnings fought back.

Physicians also drew a lesson from the fact that government actions were subject to strict due process constraints. Before Medicare, the medical profession often downplayed procedural rights in order to achieve desirable substantive results. After Medicare, physicians increasingly bought into a model of fairness defined instead by law and lawyers, even though that model frequently elevated procedure over substance. This was true whether process was construed as a shield (e.g., passage of the Health Care Quality Improvement Act to protect physicians from antitrust liability for staff privilege decisions) or as a sword (e.g., judicial decisions such as *Potvin v. Metropolitan Life* giving physicians recourse against managed care plans who "de-select" them).

In the process (pun intended), something essential to medicine may have been lost. Feminist scholarship has long distinguished justice-based from care-based reasoning (Gilligan 1982). Lawyerly process is a justice construct; the physician-patient relationship is based on care. Arrow endorsed what he called the "commonplace that the physician-patient relation affects . . . quality," including through "purely psychic interactions" such as the placebo effect. Although legal procedures may have "dignitary" benefits (Mashaw 1981), medical notions of therapeutic trust find only a pale shadow in the law. Justice can substitute for care instrumentally by conferring legitimacy and securing cooperation, but it cannot improve medical outcomes, something that trust in physicians is thought to do.

MANAGED CARE

In the 1990s, managed care seemed poised to improve the marketability of health care in many ways Arrow had predicted. Changes in Medicare payment policy revealed excess capacity in hospitals, which insurers exploited to generate price competition. Led by large employers, purchasers of health insurance began to demand evidence of treatment effectiveness, narrowing the informational asymmetries that vexed Arrow. Physician prepayment mechanisms such as capitation flourished, and compensation based on medical outcomes became a possibility.

Although the jury is still out, few of these efforts came to fruition. Instead, managed care became the battlefield on which physicians applied the accumulated legal experience of prior decades. From a professional perspective, the most noteworthy feature of this period is the unholy alliance formed by physicians and the personal injury bar to pursue litigation, and lobby for legislation, that would hold managed care organizations legally liable for harm to patients. This apparent rapprochement between bitter adversaries raises puzzling questions. Did the medical profession truly abandon its long-standing resistance to tort law as a quality improvement tool? Has organized medicine forgotten that it adamantly opposed managed care malpractice when it was touted by the Clinton administration under the rubric "enterprise liability" (Sage 1997)? Or do physicians feel so stripped of control that they are willing to use any weapon against managed care, no matter the collateral damage?

Another possibility is that gradual intermingling of medical and legal perspectives combined with relative calm on the tort reform front to create more than an uneasy truce. Among other things, the influence of market forces on the health care system had by the mid-1990s greatly diversified physicians' exposure to attorneys, often with managed care on the "other side." Physicians today employ lawyers to form corporations, negotiate contracts, secure intellectual property rights, and perform a host of constructive tasks that do not involve litigation. At the same time, specialization and competition among physicians have broken down solidarity within the medical profession and have reconciled physicians to a view of professionalism — including legal professionalism — focused more on providing technical services to clients (including physician-clients) than on playing a broader social role (which, at least for lawyers, physicians continue to regard skeptically).

Unexpectedly, physicians also discovered they had something in common with personal injury lawyers: a distrust of concentrated corporate power. Organized medicine always had feared that general business interests would eviscerate physicians' clinical and economic authority if not for long-standing legal prohibitions on corporate practice and selective contracting (Robinson 1999). These lines of defense broke down in the 1980s, allowing managed care to expand and prosper. Lawyers offered a rearguard action. It did not take long for the plaintiff's bar to follow the money and target managed care organizations rather than physicians as unsympathetic, deep-pocketed defendants. (This was less of a change than it might appear: physicians regarded medical malpractice claims as personal attacks, but practical-minded lawyers knew they were really suing liability insurers.) As a result, physicians began to consider the possibility that the enemy of their enemy was their friend, a belief reinforced by class action lawyers' remarkable success as "private attorneys general" against the tobacco industry, which medicine had long opposed on public health grounds.

By challenging the medical profession's clinical authority in the name of employers or "populations," managed care also reawakened a largely dormant sense of calling among physicians as patient advocates. Furthermore, because managed care frequently assumed an adversarial posture toward both physicians and patients, those groups in turn tended to conflate medicine's traditionally broad, normative principles of advocacy with the much narrower, purely instrumental form of advocacy familiar to lawyers (Sage 1999a). (The appeal of the lawyerly model when conflict looms is illustrated by the name two nonprofit hospitals in Chicago chose when they merged to form one of the country's largest integrated delivery systems: Advocate Health Care.) The resurgence of physician-patient trust to oppose cost containment is unpredicted by Arrow's 1963 account. Arrow noted the importance of patients' belief that physicians would act in their interests, but mainly in connection with not recommending unnecessary care. As an economist, he of course understood scarcity, but he also recognized the medical profession's deep denial of it. Managed care spotlighted scarcity and made trust both more essential and more fragile than Arrow had observed.

Managed care therefore led physicians and those who regulate them to reevaluate the pledge of patient loyalty contained in medical ethics and to adopt a view closer to that of lawyers (Bloche 1999). In most types of principal-agent relationships, such as corporate executives' obligations to shareholders, the law concentrates on assuring loyalty while allowing considerable leeway for the exercise of independent judgment (Roe 2001). Medicine went in the opposite direction during the years of unconstrained financing, with malpractice lawyers enforcing fiduciary duties of care but taking physician loyalty for granted. This changed only when managed care began to use financial incentives and selective contracting to counter the moral hazard of insurance for patients and providers.

As a result, prohibitions on conflicts of interest or strict requirements of disclosure and informed consent—devices long familiar to legal ethicists and bar disciplinary committees—have also become components of health care regulation and medical ethics (Rodwin 1993; Sage 1999c).

There are hazards in this trend. Although legal constraints on managed care are both inevitable and desirable, medicine's reorientation toward a lawyerly model not only has made it more difficult for third parties to require scientific justification of professional practice, but also has rendered unreachable any meaningful social consensus regarding the allocation of health care resources. To be sure, academic proponents of managed care were naive to think that a bloodless revolution was possible, and managed care has seldom achieved in operation the successes predicted in theory. Still, it is ironic that a form of health care financing and delivery initially conceived as a cooperative, prevention-focused alternative to the excesses of entrepreneurial fee-for-service medicine has been reframed in adversarial terms and virtually halted in its tracks by physicians and their lawyer allies.

LAWYERS, UNCERTAINTY, AND MARKET FAILURE

In 1963, Kenneth Arrow identified uncertainty as the principal cause of market failure in medical care and looked to insurance, professional self-regulation, and, at least implicitly, government regulation as possible remedies for uncertainty. Not once did Arrow mention the role of lawyers. As we have seen, however, involving lawyers and legal reasoning in health care affected both Arrow's problem and his solutions.

Arrow's uncertainty consisted of information asymmetry between physicians and patients, to which a contemporary observer might add lack of evidence supporting much of medical practice. In theory, lawyers could reduce both forms of uncertainty. Lawyers are trained to anticipate and address contingencies, training that manifests itself in part as skill at uncovering information. Indeed, lawyers have helped regularize consumer expectations of health care in a range of circumstances, from entering into contracts for insurance benefits to recognizing the consequences of medical error. On the other hand, focusing as transactional lawyers do on the possibility of failure or as litigators do on the assignment of blame adds to the perception of uncertainty by reducing trust in the health care product and its producers. In addition, as discussed above, many physicians (and their own lawyers) reacted to adversarial investigation by circling the wagons rather than engaging in cooperative practice improvement.

More importantly, the lawyerization of health care influenced the ability of both market and nonmarket institutions to ameliorate the effects of uncertainty. As we have seen, lawyers changed the tone of medical interactions, which are increasingly oriented to legal rights, constrained by due process, and resolved according to rules rather than standards. Medical ethics itself has become more like legal ethics: categorical rather than contextual (Simon 1998). These changes are sometimes enforced directly by law, but more often are the product of law's effect on extralegal norms of conduct (McAdams 1997).

Specifically, the exercise of discretion, once a dominant feature of health care, is now considered deviant. Arrow did not discuss discretion directly, but it is implicit in his invocation of trust and ethics as responses to uncertainty. Legal process, however, is seldom compatible with discretion. Because of law, no longer may physicians ethically withhold information from patients, practice according to habitual rather than objectively reasonable standards, or engage in bedside rationing or Robin Hood redistribution. Furthermore, the lawyerization of health care has created a positive feedback loop (some might say a vicious circle) in which each new legal rule squeezes out an ethical standard and leaves the remaining standards more vulnerable, a process that ultimately favors explicit government intervention over professional self-regulation as a remedy for market failure.

The discrediting of discretion has taken its greatest toll on managed care. Discretion should be regarded critically in insurance relationships because of the need to assure that prior contractual commitments to pay claims are honored. Still, organized systems of care, as managed care organizations were known in more hopeful times, would be better able to assert compassionate or communal rationales for their clinical and administrative decisions if their nascent professionalism were based on traditional, contextual medical ethics rather than its lawyerlike, categorical successor.

CONCLUSION

My purpose in this essay has been to show the epistemic influence of lawyers as well as their direct impact. It would be convenient but misguided to blame the lawyerization of health care for market failure that persists nearly forty years later. As Shakespeare recognized, an insurrectionist kills the lawyers because of their overall social importance, not their occasional misconduct. Similarly, if lawyers have retarded progress in American health care, it is mainly by generating compromises that forestalled radical reform. Law introduced to health care a common language, a medium through which previously incommensurable concepts could be articulated and offered up for balancing. Because law is a language of which few stakeholders in health care are native speakers, however, conclusions mediated by law sometimes achieve legitimacy at the expense of utility.

This brings us back to the M.D.-J.D., at least as metaphor. Arrow's analysis is enduring in part because it is flexible. Correspondingly, the process of lawyerization detailed in this essay is not intended to foreclose future changes to medical ethics and professional self-regulation that may come from very different directions. Medicine, like Silicon Valley, is always looking for the next next thing, and the profession's flirtation with the values of the physician-lawyer may be short lived. Much as the M.D.-J.D. itself partially displaced the physician-scientist (M.D.-Ph.D.) as medicine's future, medicine may eventually relax its embrace of law in favor of the currently attractive image of the physician-businessperson (M.D.-M.B.A.), or something else entirely. What, then, has medicine learned from its liaison with law? For individual physicians, myself included, the influence of lawyers did much to validate "health policy" as a legitimate career path. For the profession as a whole, communing with lawyers is a sign that medicine has lost its innocence and, perhaps also, its guilt.

REFERENCES

American Bar Association, Section of Legal Education and Admissions to the Bar. 1992. *Legal Education and Professional Development—An Educational Continuum*. Chicago: American Bar Association.

American Medical Association. 2002. *Code of Medical Ethics*. Chicago: American Medical Association.

Annas, George J. 1988. *Judging Medicine*. Clifton, NJ: Humana Press.

Arrow, Kenneth J. 1963. *Uncertainty and the Welfare Economics of Medical Care*. American Economic Review 53(5): 941–973.

Bloche, M. Gregg. 1999. Clinical Loyalties and the Social Purposes of Medicine. *Journal of the American Medical Association* 281(3): 268–274.

Brennan, Troyen A. 2000. The Institute of Medicine Report on Medical Errors—Could It Do Harm? *New England Journal of Medicine* 342(15): 1123–1125.

Brennan, Troyen A., Colin M. Sox, and Helen R. Burstin. 1996. Relation Between Negligent Adverse Events and the Outcomes of Medical Malpractice Litigation. *New England Journal of Medicine* 335(26): 1963–1967.

Brint, Steven. 1994. *In an Age of Experts: The Changing Role of Professionals in Politics and Public Life*. Princeton, NJ: Princeton University Press.

Capron, Alexander M. 1999a. Professionalism and Professional Ethics. In *The American Medical Ethics Revolution*, ed. Robert B. Baker, Arthur L. Caplan, Linda L. Emanuel, and Stephen R. Latham, 180–191. Baltimore, MD: Johns Hopkins University Press.

Capron, Alexander M. 1999b. What Contributions Have Social Science and the Law Made to the Development of Policy on Bioethics? *Daedalus* 128: 295–325.

Fox, Daniel M. 1987. Physicians versus Lawyers: A Conflict of Culture. In AIDS *and the Law: A Guide for the Public*, ed. Harlon L. Dalton, Scott Burris, and the Yale AIDS Law Project. New Haven, CT: Yale University Press.

Furrow, Barry R. 1987. *Health Care Law*. St. Paul, MN: West.

Gilligan, Carol. 1982. *In a Different Voice: Psychological Theory and Women's Development*. Cambridge: Harvard University Press.

Hyman, David A. 1990. How Law Killed Ethics. *Perspectives in Biology and Medicine* 34(1): 134–150.

Institute of Medicine. 1999. *To Err Is Human: Building a Safe Health System*, ed. Linda T. Kohn, Janet M. Corrigan, and Molla S. Donaldson. Washington, DC: National Academy Press.

Jacobs, Lawrence R. 1995. Politics of America's Supply State: Health Reform and Technology. *Health Affairs* 14(2): 143–157.

Levine, Robert J. 1987. Medical Ethics and Personal Doctors: Conflicts between What We Teach and What We Want. *American Journal of Law & Medicine* 13: 351–364.

Macdonald, Michael G., Kathryn C. Meyer, and Beth Essig. 1985. *Health Care Law: A Practical Guide*. New York: Matthew-Bender.

Mashaw, Jerry L. 1981. Administrative Due Process: The Quest for a Dignitary Theory. *Boston University Law Review* 61: 885–931.

Mashaw, Jerry L., and David L. Harfst. 1990. *The Struggle for Auto Safety*. Cambridge: Harvard University Press.

McAdams, Richard H. 1997. The Origin, Development, and Regulation of Norms. *Michigan Law Review* 96: 343–433.

Millenson, Michael L. 1992. AMA *Clarifies Position on Free Care for Poor*. Chicago Tribune, 25 June, C3.

Mohr, James C. 1993. *Doctors and the Law: Medical Jurisprudence in Nineteenth-Century America*. New York: Oxford University Press.

Oken, Donald. 1961. What to Tell Cancer Patients: A Study of Medical Attitudes. *Journal of the American Medical Association* 175(13): 1120–1128.

Regan, Louis J. 1954. Medicine and the Law. *New England Journal of Medicine* 250(11): 463.

Robinson, James C. 1999. *The Corporate Practice of Medicine: Competition and Innovation in Health Care*. Berkeley: University of California Press.

Rodwin, Marc A. 1993. *Medicine, Money, and Morals: Physicians' Conflicts of Interest*. New York: Oxford University Press.

Roe, Mark J. 2001. The Quality of Corporate Law Argument and Its Limits. Columbia Law School Document: Available from the SSRN Electronic Paper Collection.

Rothman, David J. 1991. *Strangers at the Bedside: A History of How Law and Bioethics Transformed Medical Decision Making*. New York: Basic Books

Sage, William M. 1997. Enterprise Liability and the Emerging Managed Health Care System. *Law & Contemporary Problems* 60(1&2): 159–210.

———. 1999a. Physicians as Advocates. *Houston Law Review* 73(5): 1529–1630.

———. 1999b. Fraud and Abuse Law. *Journal of the American Medical Association* 282(12): 1179–1181.

———. 1999c. Regulating through Information: Disclosure Laws and American Health Care. *Columbia Law Review* 99(7): 1701–1829.

Schneider, Carl F. 1998. *The Practice of Autonomy: Patients, Doctors, and Medical Decisions*. New York: Oxford University Press.

———. 1994. Bioethics in the Language of the Law. *Hastings Center Report* 24(4): 16–24.

Simon, William H. 1978. The Ideology of Advocacy: Procedural Justice and Professional Ethics. *Wisconsin Law Review* 1978: 29–144.

————. 1998. *The Practice of Justice*. Cambridge: Harvard University Press.

Starr, Paul. 1982. *The Social Transformation of American Medicine*. New York: Basic Books.

Stevens, Robert. 1983. *Law School: Legal Education in America from the 1850s to the 1980s*. Chapel Hill, NC: University of North Carolina Press.

Subitzky, Ed. 1990. Doctor-Lawyer. In *The Big Book of American Humor: The Best of the Past 25 Years*, ed. William Novak and Moshe Waldoks. New York: HarperPerennial.

Weiler, Paul C. 1991. *Medical Malpractice on Trial*. Cambridge: Harvard University Press.

KENNETH J. ARROW

■ *Reflections on the Reflections*

An author cannot help being flattered by the attention paid in this book. Disagreement and criticism are almost as welcome as praise and extension; the important thing to any author is that his or her ideas matter and are important enough to fight about. Further, these essays offered me a very informative history of the last forty years in health care in the United States, from which I have learned much.

A detailed analysis of the writings in this volume would not be possible in any brief compass. Enough new ideas and challenges have been raised here to lead to a short volume in terms of specific agreements, disagreements, and extensions. My response takes the form of five somewhat linked sets of remarks on the economics of medical care and on more general aspects of economics in which similar themes emerge.

As the authors well know, I have not engaged in research on medical care for a long time and so am certainly not up to date on many specific empirical aspects of the subject. I have some impressions, and I will not let my lack of knowledge preclude my raising points, secure in the understanding that I am privileged to ask questions without knowing the answers.

I am stimulated to respond to critical comments about the relevance of my analysis to the present and recent states of the medical care industry. Some of my remarks are hypotheses about the evolution in the medical care system; some, clarifications or extensions of the positions in my first article on medical care.

I will restate my thesis in a few words: The role of moral hazard in medical insurance arises from inequalities of information between the insurer on one hand and the physician and patient on the other. By itself, this phenomenon was well known in other kinds of insurance (where the term *moral hazard* arose) and was met by various devices, such as deductibles and ceilings. Direct controls came later, as I conjectured. I then came to the view that the same degree of asymmetric information also occurred in the relation between patients and providers. I proposed the hypothesis that many of the special features of the medical care market arose in an attempt to meet the inefficiencies created by this generalized moral hazard.

THE INCREASED DEMAND FOR MEDICAL SERVICES

One point made in several of the chapters is the greatly increased scale of expenditures for medical services. There were plenty of concerns about the great expense of medical treatment in 1963, when the costs were about 4 percent of U.S. national income. Today the costs reach 14 percent or so of national income, and the fear is that still further increases will occur. Prices of medical personal services did rise, at least for a while. The consensus, though, seems to be that the increased availability of expensive technologies is a bigger factor now than increased wages.

One obvious factor, of course, is the great extension of government insurance in the form of Medicare and Medicaid. Clearly, the demand for medical care rises sharply and becomes markedly less elastic under these conditions; that is one of the basic implications of moral hazard in medical insurance. The demands for the services of both labor and capital will clearly rise under these conditions.

But the effect on technology is multiplied by innovation. There has been a large development of new technologies, especially in imaging, and these apparently are very costly. These become medically valuable and even expected, especially under conditions of inelastic demand. Why this sudden spate of innovations? Of course, it could be chance. Undoubtedly, also, the very large expenditures on basic research in medicine, through the National Institutes of Health, certainly must have laid the groundwork for the development of new projects.

There is another systematic reason, which may be relevant here. Ever since Adam Smith, it has been repeatedly asserted that increases in scale lead to innovations for economic reasons. The point is that development of an innovation has a cost independent of its use, while the market value (or social value) of an innovation increases with the demand. Hence, the increased demand for medical services due to the extensions of insurance may itself be a cause of new technological developments, which, in turn, lead to increased medical expenditures.

To be clear, technological improvement in general need not and usually does not lead to increased expenditures. If the same product is supplied more cheaply, then expenditures may fall, not rise. Indeed, when I wrote my article, it was widely anticipated that increased medical knowledge would lead to (relatively inexpensive) cures to replace expensive maintenance therapies. What has happened is that there has been an improvement in the quality of care, or at least in the ability to acquire information, so the net effect has been to increase demand for expensive care, where previously there was no supply at all.

THE BUSINESS MODEL OF MEDICINE

Several of these essays hold that the distinctive elements of the medical profession, as I sketched them in my 1963 article, have become far less prominent. Advertising, both of physicians and of prescription drugs, has become common. Most practice is now organized into groups, and many of these are for-profit organizations. Similarly, many hospitals are for-profit. Even nonprofit hospitals finance themselves through bonds. They are then subject to the market both through competition and through responsibility to the capital market.

Clearly, budget constraints were not unknown to solo practitioners and non-profit hospitals in earlier eras, so the difference may be overdone. Nevertheless there probably was a transition not unlike that from small, individually run shops and factories to large, multiplant firms in the second half of the nineteenth century—though the ultimate productive activities are still face-to-face, with more capital equipment and more complementary goods in the form of prescription (and other) drugs.

I would surmise that the root cause of the increasingly businesslike nature of the medical care industry is the special employer-oriented nature of the U.S. medical insurance system. There is no logical relation between the provision of health care and employment status. Indeed, Medicare and Medicaid were obviously stimulated by the fact that a large proportion of health needs was incurred by individuals retired from employment or only loosely connected to the labor market. But given the spread of employer-based plans, encouraged by tax advantages, the employers emerged as a price-elastic source of demand. This pressure was, of course, intensified by the increase in medical expenditures (increase relative to other costs of production). By a natural process of competitive pressures, easy to spell out in a model, economies of scale and managed care emerged, and these undermined the previous professional relations.

ASYMMETRIC INFORMATION, TRUST, AND EFFICIENCY

Clearly, one of the most controversial parts of my thesis is that the special institutions found in the medical care market are responses to asymmetric information and that these institutions actually improved efficiency. They included licensure, the role of the American Medical Association in regulating hospital affiliations, the inhibitions on overtly profit-making signals (advertising, private ownership of hospitals), and the general aura of a dedicated profession. Instead, it is argued, these special institutions are simply a cloak for the exercise of power by the medical profession for its own purposes, usually assumed apparently to be income maximization.

This critique already existed of course when my essay was written. The same "unmasking" view is found in the work of ardent free-market economists and left-wing critics. This confluence is to be found also in the analysis of other professions, especially law (it is one aspect of the "critical legal studies" movement). The view that social norms arise to meet social needs (which an economist would interpret as meeting Pareto gaps) was a staple of the functionalist view in sociology, associated with such names as Talcott Parsons and Edward Shils, a view that was already being undermined by the time I wrote. Indeed, the methodological emphasis of economics on individual decisions was spreading into the other social sciences. A recent critic of functionalism, Jon Elster, has singled out my views as especially egregious.

As an economist, I was far from immune from this individualistic view. I regarded (and regard) Parsons's work as mostly quite empty of serious content. (I was surprised, therefore, to find that his writings on medical care seemed to make a lot more sense than his more general theories.)

Nevertheless, I found myself compelled by my observations to argue that social norms play a major role in understanding the departures of the medical care market from the standards of markets in general. The asymmetry of information is obvious. (I will argue below that the situation has not changed very much, but in any case no one seems to deny the asymmetry between patient and physician in 1963.)

As I understand the critical remarks, the question is not whether social norms alter resource allocation in medical care from what would be obtained under pure individual optimization (Nash equilibrium). I think this will be conceded. Indeed, since the writing of my article, there has been a steady literature in the social sciences, including economics, emphasizing the role of social norms and social connections throughout the economic system (e.g., Glenn Loury, James Coleman, Steven Durlauf, and Robert Putnam).

Instead, the question is whether these social norms in fact lead to improvements in efficiency. The above-cited writers generally argue that the answer is affirmative. I still believe that the evidence is favorable in the medical care market also, but more evidence addressed specifically to this question would be very useful.

Let me instead address the alternative "exploitation" argument. I think there are serious empirical and logical problems. First, what is the evidence that the American Medical Association, say, was primarily interested in income maximization? We find that they strongly opposed group practice and then, later, government medical insurance. Yet in this volume there are repeated statements that

Medicare and Medicaid led to very considerable increases in physician income. Indeed, this outcome must have been highly predictable at the time.

Various medical groups are continually putting out advice as to health-inducing behavior (diet, exercise, and so forth). Individuals who follow this advice will reduce their demand for medical services. An extreme version is the campaign of the American Dental Association for fluoridation of water, a measure designed to reduce cavities and so the demand for dental services.

There is also a logical problem. How does the relatively small group of physicians acquire power? In a democratic system, political power derives from numbers or from wealth. While physicians are certainly relatively well off, they do not have the concentration of wealth of many industries. Their power, it seems to me, is derived from moral authority. It is derived from the same professional respect that we are trying to explain. Indeed, when the American Medical Association came into conflict with either the retired or with the business interests that bought medical plans, the weakness of its power base quickly became apparent.

I am not denying that moral authority may be based on illusions and that these illusions will be carefully fostered. But I want to emphasize that social norms are based on at least perceived mutual gains and that one must be wary of assuming that these perceptions are not based as much on reality as on other perceptions.

THE INFORMATION REVOLUTION

It has been suggested that the great changes in the technology of information handling and transfer have greatly reduced the inequality of information between physician and patient. This is part of a general perception that the new information technology has led to a revolution in the economy.

Many economists find no "new economy." There are differences of opinion, but even the most sanguine see only a mild favorable change. In fact, during the first quarter century of the spread of computers and the great improvements in communications technology, the rate of growth of productivity throughout the economy was very much slower than it had been in the previous quarter century. Further, most of that productivity increase was in the information industry itself. The last five years have shown some more generalized productivity increase but by no means at historically unprecedented levels. Further, some part of that was due to normal cyclical processes; productivity always rises during a boom.

The Internet is a source of information, but unlike refereed journals, there is no guarantee of accuracy. It is a source of information also for the physician or the HMO, and the latter can make better, because more informed, use of it. The ratings of medical groups and hospitals found on the Web will undoubtedly be of some help for prospective patients.

I do believe we will see a transformation of the economy and of the medical care market because of the information revolution. I think it can take many decades to really understand how to use our information powers. It may well be that there will still be asymmetry of information, in the form of a group that certifies the information, even at the end of the process.

THE MEDICAL CARE MARKET AS A COMPLEX SYSTEM

I conclude with a few remarks even more speculative than the preceding. One writer asked whether asymmetric information could really explain medical care systems. The problem is much the same in all countries, yet the actual systems differed, and differ, very much.

It is a reasonable question. However, the same phenomenon is observed in other parts of the economy (and other parts of the social system). Consider the financing of corporations. In the United States (today) and in the United Kingdom, financing is done largely through the market (bonds and stocks). But on the continent of Europe or in Japan, financing through banks is normal. In that system, a bank and a corporation will have an intimate, long-term relationship, very different in consequence and behavior from the U.S. system. Again, the needs of the system are much the same; why is the response different?

One can give many other examples, such as the role of the family. One type of explanation is that history matters. At a formal level, the system is governed by dynamic relations, which have some degree of instability, so that small variations can produce large and long-lasting deviations in outcome after a while. The equations for predicting weather seem to be of this kind. One decision creates enduring structures that are costly to change.

It may be (though it has not really been proven) that purely market structures are less path dependent in this sense. But as soon as social norms and political decisions arise, the system shows marked permanent influence of initially small steps. The exact sequence of the decisions to meet a succession of perceived crises in medical care may have had long-lasting effects. The Medicare and Medicaid systems led to the increase in medical costs, which in turn led to the rise of HMOs, which in turn has led to reactions by both physicians and patients in the form of a "bill of rights," with consequences that have yet to be foreseen. Would the end result be different if these events had occurred in a different order?

I conclude, as I began, by thanking all those who have contributed to this volume, which, it seems to me, will be a very useful survey of the field and a springboard for further research.

■ Contributors

LINDA H. AIKEN is the Claire M. Fagin Professor of Nursing, professor of sociology, and director of the Center for Health Outcomes and Policy Research at the University of Pennsylvania. Her research interests include health care workforce, determinants of variation in hospital patient outcomes, and AIDS health services in the United States, Canada, and Europe. She is a Robert Wood Johnson Foundation Health Policy Investigator.

KENNETH J. ARROW was born in 1921, studied at public schools, and graduated from the City College of New York in 1940. His graduate studies at Columbia were interrupted by military service as weather officer (highest rank, captain). Arrow received his Ph.D. in 1951, with a dissertation on social choice theory. After research at the Cowles Commission for Research in Economics, he has been on the faculties of the University of Chicago, Stanford, and Harvard, retiring from Stanford in 1991. He has been president of a number of academic societies and received several honors, including the 1972 Nobel Prize in economics.

GLORIA J. BAZZOLI is a professor of health administration at Virginia Commonwealth University in Richmond. Previously, she was research professor with the Institute for Health Services Research and Policy Studies, Northwestern University. Bazzoli undertakes research on the restructuring of health care organizations and health markets. She is a lead investigator in studies of physician-hospital integration, the effects of hospital mergers, the management and policy implications of provider financial risk bearing, and examination of the key strategic/structural characteristics of emerging health organizations. Recently, with her colleagues at the Urban Institute, she completed research examining safety net hospitals. Bazzoli received her M.S. and Ph.D. in economics from Cornell University and her B.S. in economics from the University of Illinois, Champaign-Urbana.

M. GREGG BLOCHE, M.D., J.D., is a professor of law; co-director of the Georgetown-Johns Hopkins Joint Program in Law and Public Health; and an adjunct professor in the Department of Health Policy and Management at Johns Hopkins University. His main area of interest is health law and policy, and his recent and current work addresses the pursuit of efficiency and fairness in health care provision, the dual loyalties of physicians in managed health plans, patients' rights, and the role of for-profit institutions in medicine. His writing has appeared in a variety of medical and health policy journals as well as law reviews and books. Bloche received a Robert Wood Johnson Foundation Investigator Award in Health Policy Research for 1997–2000 to support his research (and forthcoming book) on the legal and regulatory governance of managed care organizations. He has been a consultant to the Institute of Medicine (on patients' rights in managed health plans), South Africa's Trust and Reconciliation Commission (on human rights in the health sector), the Federal Judicial Center, the National Institutes of Health, the World Health Organization, and other private and public bodies. Bloche is a member of the Institute of Medicine's Committee on Understanding and Eliminating Racial and Ethnic Disparities in Health Care and (starting in 2002) the Committee on Scientific Freedom and Responsibility of the American Association for the Advancement of Science. He also serves on the boards of Physicians for Human Rights, Mental Disability Rights International, and other nonprofit groups. Bloche received his M.D. and J.D. degrees from Yale University.

LAWRENCE CASALINO recently moved to the University of Chicago after twenty years as a family physician in Half Moon Bay, California. While continuing his practice, he obtained a Ph.D. in health services research and organizational sociology at the University of California, Berkeley. With support from a Robert Wood Johnson Investigator Award, Casalino is studying the effects of public policies and of public and private purchasing decisions on the organization of physician practice and the structure of physician–health plan relations in thirteen metropolitan areas throughout the United States. He has conducted over eight hundred interviews with U.S. leaders in hospital systems, health plans, and physician groups.

MICHAEL CHERNEW is an associate professor at the University of Michigan in the departments of health management and policy, internal medicine, and economics. He received a Ph.D. in economics from Stanford University. In 1998 he was awarded the John D. Thompson Prize for young investigators by the Association of University Programs in Public Health. In 1999 he received the Alice S. Hersh Young Investigator Award from the Association of Health Services Research. Chernew is a faculty research fellow of the National Bureau of Economic Research and is on the editorial boards of Health Services Research, Medical Care Research and Review, and the American Journal of Managed Care.

RICHARD A. COOPER, M.D., is a professor of medicine and health policy and director of the Health Policy Institute at the Medical College of Wisconsin. A hematologist by training, he previously was director of the University of Pennsylvania Cancer Center and subsequently executive vice president and dean of the Medical College of Wisconsin. His interests center on workforce planning. He recently developed the "Trend Model" for projecting the supply and utilization of physicians and nonphysician clinicians based on an analysis of the major long-term trends that affect health care and health care providers.

ANNETINE C. GELIJNS is director of the International Center for Health Outcomes and Innovation Research (INCHOIR) and is an associate professor of surgical sciences in the Department of Surgery, College of Physicians and Surgeons, and the Division of Health Policy and Management of the Mailman School of Public Health, Columbia University. Her current research focuses on the factors driving the development and diffusion of medical technology and the measurement of the long-term clinical outcomes and economic impact of clinical interventions. She has special expertise in cardiovascular disease. Gelijns is the director of the Data Coordinating Center for the NIH-sponsored REMATCH trial and is the co-PI of a trial comparing off-pump to on-pump coronary artery bypass surgery.

VICTOR R. FUCHS is the Henry J. Kaiser Jr. Professor Emeritus at Stanford University and a research associate of the National Bureau of Economic Research. He was president of the American Economic Association in 1995 and is a member of the American Philosophical Society, the American Academy of Arts and Sciences, and the Institute of Medicine. Fuchs has received numerous awards for his work in economics and health. He is the author of *Who Shall Live? Health, Economics, and Social Choice* (1974, 1988), fourteen other books, and over one hundred articles. His research topics include health and medical care, aging, gender, and children.

SHERRY A. GLIED is an associate professor and chair of the Department of Health Policy and Management of Columbia University's Mailman School of Public Health. She holds a Ph.D. in economics from Harvard University. In 1992–1993 she served as a senior economist to the President's Council of Economic Advisers, under both President Bush and President Clinton, and participated in the latter's Health Care Task Force. Her book on health care reform, *Chronic Condition* (Harvard University Press), was published in 1998. She is a recipient of a Robert Wood Johnson Investigator Award through which she has been studying employer-based health insurance.

JOSHUA GRAFF ZIVIN is an assistant professor in health policy and management, Mailman School of Public Health, and an assistant professor in surgical sciences, College of Physicians and Surgeons, at Columbia University. In addition, he is a senior research associate at the Columbia University International Center for Health Outcomes and Innovation Research. He is an economist whose research focuses on the importance of uncertainty and heterogeneity in individual and societal decision making. His particular areas of interest include environmental regulation and public health, the evaluation of medical technologies, and the physician-patient relationship. In the area of environmental regulation, his research to date has focused on pollution control, occupational safety, and the use of targeted policies to achieve environmental health objectives. His research on medical technologies examines the role of uncertainty in investment decisions and trade-offs between quantity and quality of life. His work on the physician-patient relationship examines the role of institutions and contracts for transactions characterized by imperfect information as well as risk communication and perception.

DEBORAH HAAS-WILSON is a professor of economics and director of the public policy program at Smith College. Her research focuses on the economics of health care markets with an emphasis on (1) restructuring of financing and delivery and the implications for antitrust; (2) consumer information in health care markets and implications for pricing, quality, and regulatory policy; and (3) effects of state abortion restrictions on demand for abortion services and availability of providers. Haas-Wilson, a recipient of a Robert Wood Johnson Foundation Investigator Award, is working on a book for Harvard University Press on health care competition and antitrust policy.

MARK A. HALL is a professor of law and public health at Wake Forest University, where he has appointments in the schools of law, medicine, and management. Hall specializes in health care law and public policy, with a focus on economic, regulatory, and organizational issues. For the past several years he has focused on health insurance regulation. More recently, Hall has turned his attention to the physician-patient relationship under managed care. He currently directs a two-year study of patient trust in HMOs and their physicians and how this trust is affected by the disclosure of financial conflicts of interest.

PETER J. HAMMER is an assistant professor at the University of Michigan Law School. He received a J.D. in 1990 and a doctorate in economics in 1993 from the University of Michigan. His research focuses on the study of federal antitrust law and the legal issues surrounding changes in the health care industry. He is the recipient of a Robert Wood Johnson Foundation Health Policy Investigator Award. He also founded and directs the University of Michigan Law School's Program for Cambodian Law and Development.

CLARK C. HAVIGHURST is the William Neal Reynolds Professor of Law at Duke University School of Law. He has written on many aspects of regulation in the health services industry, the role of competition in the financing and delivery of health care, medical malpractice, private contracts as vehicles for reforming U.S. health care, a wide range of antitrust issues arising in the health care field, and antitrust in health care and other fields. Havighurst is the author of the law school casebook *Health Care Law and Policy* (1988; 2d ed. 1998), *Health Care Choices: Private Contracts as Instruments of Health Reform* (1995), and *Deregulating the Health Care Industry* (1982). A member of the Institute of Medicine of the National Academy of Sciences, he served as a member of the Institute's Board of Health Care Services from 1987 to 1997. He is also an adjunct scholar of the American Enterprise Institute. In 1988–1989 he served as the executive director of the Private Adjudication Center, Inc., an affiliate of Duke Law School specializing in alternative dispute resolution, and currently is a member of the PAC's executive committee. Havighurst has served as chair of the executive and management committees of the *Journal of Health Politics, Policy and Law.*

PETER D. JACOBSON is an associate professor in the Department of Health Management and Policy, University of Michigan School of Public Health. He received his law degree from the University of Pittsburgh School of Law and a master's in public health from UCLA. Before coming to the University of Michigan, he was senior behavioral scientist at RAND from 1988 to 1996. His current research interests focus on the relationship between law and health care delivery and policy, tobacco control policy, and violence prevention. In 1995 Jacobson received an investigator award in health policy research from the Robert Wood Johnson Foundation to examine the role of the courts in shaping health care policy. His book, *Strangers in the Night: Law and Medicine in the Managed Care Era*, was published in 2002 by Oxford University Press.

RICHARD KRONICK is an associate professor in the Department of Family and Preventive Medicine at the University of California, San Diego. With Alain Enthoven, he contributed to the development of the theory of managed competition — proposing that "public sponsors" were needed to protect consumers from health plans and to structure a market that rewarded low price and high quality rather than skill at risk selection. In 1993–1994 he was a senior health policy advisor in the Clinton administration, contributing to the health care reform debacle. More recently he has been working with state Medicaid programs on the development and implementation of risk-adjusted payment systems, analyzing the effectiveness of state programs that provide subsidized insurance to low-income workers, and is beginning a project exploring the implications of the "partially managed marketplace." Kronick received his Ph.D. in political science from the University of Rochester.

MICHAEL L. MILLENSON is the Mervin Shalowitz, M.D. Visiting Scholar in the Health Industry Management Program, Kellogg School of Management, Northwestern University.

JACK NEEDLEMAN is an assistant professor of economics and health policy at the Harvard School of Public Health. His current research focuses on the impact of market change and financial pressures on health care institutions, and access and quality of care, and he has studies under way on for-profit conversions, the future of public hospitals, market change and access to psychiatric inpatient services, and hospital nurse staffing and patient outcomes.

RICHARD R. NELSON is George Blumenthal Professor of International and Public Affairs, Business, and Law at Columbia University. His research has concentrated on the processes of long-run economic change, with particular focus on technological change, and the structure of institutions.

MARK V. PAULY is Bendheim Professor and Chair of the Department of Health Care Systems at the Wharton School of the University of Pennsylvania. He is professor of health care systems, insurance, and risk management and public policy and management at the Wharton School and professor of economics in the School of Arts and Sciences at the University of Pennsylvania. Pauly is coeditor-in-chief of the International Journal of Health Care Finance and Economics and an associate editor of the Journal of Risk and Uncertainty. His classic study on the economics of moral hazard was the first to point out how health insurance coverage may affect patients' use of medical services.

MARK A. PETERSON, former editor of the *Journal of Health Politics, Policy and Law*, is a professor of policy studies and political science and chair of the policy studies department at the UCLA School of Public Policy and Social Research. He previously held faculty appointments at Harvard University and the University of Pittsburgh. He has published widely on the presidency, Congress, interest groups, social learning, and national health care policy making, including *Legislating Together: The White House and Capitol Hill from Eisenhower to Reagan* (Harvard University Press, 1990) and the edited volume *Healthy Markets? The New Competition in Medical Care* (Duke University Press, 1998). A recipient of a Robert Wood Johnson Foundation Investigator Award in Health Policy Research, he is completing a book entitled *Stalemate: Opportunities, Gambles, and Miscalculations in Health Policy Innovation.*

UWE E. REINHARDT is the James Madison Professor of Political Economy at Princeton University. He has spent the past three decades trying to understand the "behavior" of the wondrous U.S. health system. In the process he has served on numerous government and private sector boards, among them the Physician Payment Review Commission and the Health Services Board of the Institute of Medicine of the National Academy of Sciences. He also has served on the board and as president of the Association of Health Services Research. Although persuaded that other nations organize their health systems more cost effectively than does the United States, he does not advocate such systems for the United States and instead believes that this country simply has no choice but to make "managed competition with managed care" work better than it has so far.

JAMES C. ROBINSON is a professor of health economics at the University of California, Berkeley. His research focuses on medical groups, health insurance, the health care Internet, and capital finance. Robinson has published over sixty articles in scientific journals, such as the *New England Journal of Medicine, Journal of the American Medical Association*, and *Health Affairs*. His book on physician organization in the era of managed care, *The Corporate Practice of Medicine*, was published recently by the University of California Press.

WILLIAM M. SAGE, M.D., J.D., is a professor of law at Columbia University, where he teaches courses in health law, regulatory policy, and the professions. Sage received an undergraduate degree from Harvard College in 1982 and medical and law degrees from Stanford University in 1988. He completed an internship at Mercy Hospital and Medical Center in San Diego and served as a resident in anesthesiology and critical care medicine at the Johns Hopkins Hospital. Prior to joining the Columbia faculty in 1995, he practiced corporate law at O'Melveny & Myers in Los Angeles and, in 1993, served on the White House Task Force on Health Care Reform.

J. B. SILVERS is the Elizabeth M. and William C. Treuhaft Professor of Management at the Weatherhead School of Management at Case Western Reserve University with a joint appointment in the School of Medicine. He directed the Health Systems Management Center at the two schools until he took a leave from 1997 to 1999 to serve as president and CEO of QualChoice, an award-winning northeast Ohio–area health plan. In addition, Silvers was a commissioner on the Prospective Payment Assessment Commission (PROPAC, the predecessor of MedPAC) for over six years.

FRANK A. SLOAN is the J. Alexander Professor of Health Policy and Management, professor of economics, and director of the Center for Health Policy, Law and Management at Duke University. He has had a long-standing interest in issues related to the health care consumer, having written on consumers and supply-induced demand in the 1970s and 1980s. He recently completed a book with Kerry Smith and Don Taylor entitled *Parsing the Smoking Puzzle: Information, Risk Perception, and Choice.* Some ideas from that book are reflected in his article in this volume.

■ *Index*

PETER J. HAMMER is an assistant professor at the University of Michigan Law School.

DEBORAH HAAS-WILSON is a professor of economics and the director of the public policy program at Smith College.

MARK A. PETERSON is a professor of policy studies and political science and chair of the policy studies department at the UCLA School of Public Policy and Social Research.

WILLIAM M. SAGE, M.D., J.D., is a professor of law at Columbia University.

Library of Congress Cataloging-in-Publication Data
Uncertain times : Kenneth Arrow and the changing
economics of health care / preface by Victor Fuchs ;
edited by Peter J. Hammer ... [et al.].
p. ; cm.
Includes bibliographical references and index.
ISBN 0-8223-3209-4 (cloth : alk. paper)
ISBN 0-8223-3248-5 (pbk. : alk. paper)
1. Medical economics — United States.
[DNLM: 1. Arrow, Kenneth Joseph, 1921–.
2. Economics, Medical — United States.
3. Ethics, Medical — United States.
4. Insurance, Health — economics — United States.
5. Social Welfare — economics — United States.
6. Uncertainty — United States.
W 74 AA1 U54 2003]
I. Hammer, Peter Joseph.
RA410.53.U513   2003
338.4'33621'0973 — dc21   2003012320